BRITAIN AND THE YEMEN CIVIL WAR, 1962–1965

BRITAIN AND THE YEMEN CIVIL WAR, 1962–1965

MINISTERS, MERCENARIES AND MANDARINS: FOREIGN POLICY AND THE LIMITS OF COVERT ACTION

CLIVE JONES

sussex
ACADEMIC
PRESS
Brighton • Chicago • Toronto

The right of Clive Jones to be identified as Author of this work has been asserted in
accordance with the Copyright, Designs and Patents Act 1988.

2 4 6 8 10 9 7 5 3

First published 2004 in hardcover, reprinted 2010 in paperback with
updated material (page 149), in Great Britain by
SUSSEX ACADEMIC PRESS
PO Box 139
Eastbourne BN24 9BP

Distributed in North America by
SUSSEX ACADEMIC PRESS
Independent Publishers Group
814 N Franklin St, Chicago, IL 60610, USA

British Library Cataloguing in Publication Data
A CIP catalogue record for this book is available from the British Library.

Library of Congress Cataloging-in-Publication Data
Jones, Clive, 1965–
Britain and the Yemen civil war, 1962–1965 : ministers, mercenaries and
     mandarins : foreign policy and the limits of covert action / Clive Jones.
     p. cm.
Includes bibliographical references and index.
ISBN 978-1-84519-198-6 (pbk. alk. paper)
   1. Yemen—Foreign relations—Great Britain. 2. Great Britain—Foreign
relations—Yemen. 3. Great Britain—Foreign relations—1945– I. Title.
DS247.Y48J66 2004
327.410533'09'046—dc22

2004001085

Typeset and designed by Sussex Academic Press, Brighton & Eastbourne.
Printed and bound by CPI Group (UK) Ltd, Croydon, CR0 4YY
This book is printed on acid-free paper.

Contents

Acknowledgements

There are many people to whom I owe a great debt which, without indulging in exaggerated platitudes, can never be fully repaid. In the United Kingdom Dr Neil Winn has been a valued colleague and his friendship has been a great source of support throughout. Professor Ritchie Ovendale, a towering figure in the field of British diplomatic history, inspired my first tentative steps toward serious archival research, while Professor James Piscatori and Professor Caroline Kennedy-Pipe have remained bastions of academic support. The advice and counsel of this wonderful triumvirate has proven invaluable throughout the research and writing of this book. I would also like to record my thanks to the Grants Committee of the British Academy (Grant No.SG-29969) for their financial support that allowed otherwise prohibitive research costs to be covered.

Outside the immediate confines of academia Stephen Walton of the Imperial War Museum (IWM) deserves special mention for making available the papers of the late Colonel Neil McLean DSO, while I was privileged to benefit from the guidance of Mark Seaman, a leading authority on the history of British intelligence and special operations. Mark not only gave sound advice regarding earlier drafts, but provided introductions to individuals closely associated with the Yemen operation, most notably Michael Morgan. Mike kindly provided me with invaluable insights into the conditions experienced by British operatives. His support and encouragement have been greatly valued, while special mention must be made of Mr Bernard Mills who gave generously of his time to answer points of clarification.

In the spring of 2002 I was fortunate enough to spend time as Senior Visiting Research Fellow in the Department of Politics, University of Haifa, Israel. Here, free from the more prosaic demands of academic life in the United Kingdom, the genesis of this book began to take shape among the most convivial of settings. Guy Abrahams, Dr Yoav Alon, Badi Hassisi, Dr Zach Levey, Professor Joseph Nevo, and Dr Ami

Acknowledgements

Pedahzur made my stay both memorable and productive. To all my sense of gratitude remains profound. Shelley Deane and Fiona Butler deserve special thanks for their valued support and friendship throughout the whole project.

My interest in the Yemen Civil War was stirred over a decade ago by reading *Arabian Assignment* by Colonel David Smiley. To him I remain particularly indebted. One of the most remarkable men that I have had the good fortune to meet, he proved a most convivial host, answering what must have appeared at times rather obtuse questions with good grace and patience, while allowing me unfettered access to his private papers and diaries relating to his time in the Yemen. I was deeply honoured by the trust implicit in this act and I hope the account that follows, while remaining objective, does no disservice to his considerable achievements. Colonel Smiley also pointed me in the direction of the papers of Colonel Neil McLean and thus, without his help, this book would have been far more limited in its scope and ambition. I also gratefully acknowledge the kind permission of Daska McLean to reproduce the photograph, borrowed from her late husbands' archive and which graces the cover of this book.

My mother, father and sisters have been unstinting in their support of my academic career and I hope this book goes some way to convincing them that my time away from the lecture hall and seminar room was not entirely misspent. Finally, to Sally, Sam and Alex. Quite simply, it could not have been written without you.

Key Terms, Acronyms and Abbreviations

BMO	British Mercenary Organisation. Also referred to as the European Advisory Group.
Broadway	Former headquarters of SIS and used here as a descriptive synonym.
CIA	Central Intelligence Agency (United States)
CinC	Commander in Chief
DIS	Defence Intelligence Staff (UK)
DSP	David Smiley Papers
EEF	Egyptian Expeditionary Force in Yemen
EIS	Egyptian Intelligence Service
FG	Federal Guard
FIO	Federal Intelligence Officer
FLOSY	Front for the Liberation of South Yemen
FRA	Federal Regular Army
FSA	Federation of South Arabia
GCHQ	Government Communications Headquarters [UK]
Great Smith Street	Address of the Colonial Office and used here as a descriptive synonym.
HMG	Her Majesty's Government [UK]
HUMINT	Human Intelligence
IDF	Israel Defence Forces
IWM-NMP	Imperial War Museum – Neil McLean Papers
JAC	Joint Action Committee [UK]. Established to co-ordinate activity, mainly of a clandestine nature at Cabinet level.
JIC	Joint Intelligence Committee
King Charles Street	Address of the Foreign Office and used as a descriptive synonym
MANGO	Code name given to the clandestine air supply drops to the BMO and Royalist forces in Yemen.

MIDCOM	Middle East Command [UK]
MI5	Security and Counter Intelligence Service [UK]
MI6	British Foreign Intelligence Service, also know as SIS [UK]
MoD	Ministry of Defence [UK]
NLF	National Liberation Front [Aden/Yemen]
POMEC	Political Officer, Middle East Command [UK/FSA]
PR	Photographic Reconnaissance
RAF	Royal Air Force
RANCOUR I and II	Code names given to British clandestine operations designed to ferment unrest among tribes inside the Yemen but close to the Federal border.
SAS	Special Air Service [UK]
SIASI	Intelligence network comprising locally recruited Royalist tribesmen formed by the British Mercenary Organisation.
SIGINT	Signals Intelligence
SIS	Secret Intelligence Service, also known as MI6 [UK]
SOE	Special Operations Executive [UK]
UAR	United Arab Republic
UN	United Nations
UNYOM	United Nations Yemen Observer Mission
W/T	Wireless Telegraphy
YAR	Yemen Arab Republic

The Federation of South Arabia and Yemen, 1964–1965

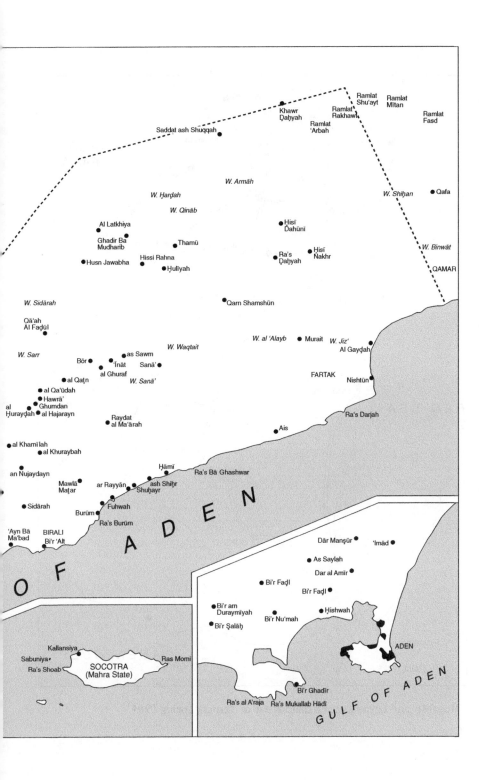

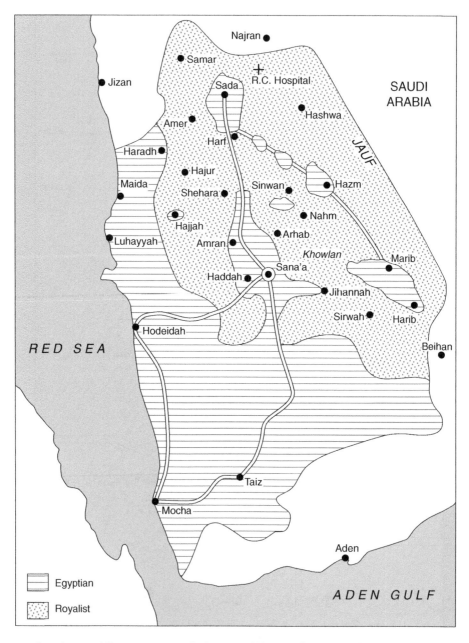

Royalist- and Egyptian-controlled areas of Yemen, Spring 1964

Introduction

Themes and Issues

Civil war has been an enduring theme in human history. With the end of the Cold War however, and with it the attendant demise of its dominant characteristic – the bipolar system – internecine struggle emerged as the dominant mode of conflict in world politics. In Central Asia, the Balkans, the Middle East, throughout Africa and South America, a volatile mix of ethnicity, nationalism and religion – for so long held in check by superpower competition that had allowed indigenous leaders to manipulate these self-same strategic rivalries in the pursuit of parochial gain – proved dynamic enough to overthrow old orders. At the same time, they often proved insufficient to establish new dominant hegemonies over competing claims to land, people and resources.

Civil wars have always been noted for their bloody, if not savage character. Unrestrained by any normative adherence to the rules of war that at least served to moderate the worst excesses of conflict between states, local rivalries are played out and old scores settled in the recrudescence of a Hobbesian world view where life truly can be 'nasty brutish and short'. The bloody civil war that ripped Lebanon apart between 1975 and 1991 remains a most apposite, but far from unique, example.[1] But while exhibiting facets associated with civil wars of the past, the "New" Civil Wars of the post-Cold War world or, as the American academic Donald Snow preferred to call them, 'Uncivil' wars, appeared qualitatively different, driven less by ideology or immediate political concerns and more by a distinctly criminal dynamic.[2]

Others have used the term 'neo-medieval' to characterise this new wave of internecine violence, a term that captures the overlapping loyalties and competing claims that can no longer be contained or controlled by state authorities. Often ethnic in character, such loyalties can also be driven by criminal concerns centred around warlords or, as the case of Afghanistan so visibly demonstrates, transnational terrorist groups.[3] Its 'medieval' character is derived from the analogy of the 'city states' of Italy during this eponymous period where the prime root of conflict was often the desire to exercise hegemony over a given resource or trade. In this regard, much of the violence within so-called 'failed states' fits this definition. The bitter conflict over unfettered access to diamond deposits in Sierra Leone and the Congo are two key examples. Central government control was abandoned to more parochial or localised interests that found expression in loosely formed, invariably ill-disciplined, and often leaderless militias. Material greed, rather than any discernible ideological or political agenda provided the rationale behind the most barbaric forms of violence.[4]

The recidivist nature of civil war, with its attendant collapse of anything resembling a civil society and accompanied more often than not by humanitarian crises have been met with a degree of political circumvention by the international community. Caught between the need to be 'seen to be doing something' but without incurring costs, usually to their own forces, that could otherwise be justified by the threat to national security associated with inter-state conflicts, world leaders have often, to paraphrase Dr Samuel Johnson, used the United Nations as the last refuge of the scoundrel, a mechanism through which collective momentum towards timely and effective intervention is more apparent than real.[5]

Even where altruism has driven intervention in the affairs of a failed state – or what some academics have referred to as a complex emergency – casualties incurred by Western, and in particular American troops, saw such high moral values sacrificed with indecent alacrity on the alter of domestic political expediency. Washington's bitter experience in Somalia in 1993 remains the most salient case in point with the result that American willingness to intervene directly in the wars of the Former Yugoslavia was limited to air power while the fighting was still ongoing.[6] Although the quantity and quality of its troop presence in and around the borders of Afghanistan is overwhelming there remains an apparent reluctance among Western states to commit large numbers of ground troops to prise Osama bin Laden and his cohorts from their coenobite existence in the caves and mountains of Afghanistan. A capability-versus-will deficit has emerged: Western militaries in particular may have the capability to intervene in civil conflict, but often they lack the political will.

There is clearly much that is new in the underlying dynamics of civil war. Equally however, the dilemmas faced by governments over how, where, when and with what means they should involve themselves in civil conflict provide a continuum between the past and present. This not only determined the scope and scale of intervention of the great civil wars of the past century, in Russia, Spain and China for example, but also in lesser known internecine struggles. It is one such struggle that this study is devoted to: British involvement in the Yemen Civil War from 1962 to the end of 1965. In many ways, the issues and debates thrown up by Britain's policy towards and involvement in this war proved to be the direct antecedents of future conflicts: Washington's clandestine involvement with the Afghan *mujahidin* in the 1980s, with all the vagaries of tribal politics this involved, and latterly the role played by mercenary organisations in, for example, Sierra Leone in the latter half of the 1990s. In Afghanistan, the difficulties the Soviets had in dealing with a foe entrenched in the mountains, reliant on strong tribal networks, enthused with a religious nationalist zeal and enjoying the support of outside actors finds more than an echo two decades earlier in the fate that met the Egyptian Expeditionary Force in the mountains and deserts of Yemen. In the case of mercenaries, the spate of civil wars in the post-Cold War era witnessed the arrival of an apparently new breed of mercenary organisation: the Private Military/Organisation Company (PMO/C).[7] However, these modern acronyms should not disguise the fact that the emergence of such 'corporate warriors' have their antecedent in the establishment of the British Mercenary Organisation, formed specifically to train and support the Royalist forces in the Yemen Civil War some three decades previously. Few variables in the study of contemporary civil war can claim to be wholly unique.

A causal link clearly exists between the present scale of civil wars, in whatever guise they manifest themselves and the growing prominence of the PMO/C. Whatever label one applies, the debates surrounding their emergence are usually partisan regarding their function. The case of the British-based PMO/C, *Sandline*, or the now defunct *Executive Outcomes* of South Africa, highlight the polarity of such feeling. For some, they remain the epitome of the 'Dogs of War', exploiting the new wave of civil conflicts to plunder the natural resources of failed states for personal profit. For others, however, they represent the new vanguard of international security, able and willing to impose order and security where state actors now fear to tread.[8]

That PMO/Cs have come to such prominence over the past decade is, as the American commentator P. W. Singer notes, a function of three main factors: the end of the Cold War and the subsequent downsizing of Western militaries; transformation in the nature of war itself; and what he terms the normative rise or ascendancy of economic privatisation.[9] When, in June 1997, UN Secretary-General Kofi Anan was asked about the efficacy of employing PMO/Cs as part of broader UN strategy to end the vicious civil war in Sierra Leone, he rejected the idea outright, arguing that there was no distinction to be made between PMO/Cs and mercenary organisations.[10] This 'one size fits all' approach, was more a reflection of the negative reactions the term 'mercenary' invokes, than a wider appreciation of the types of activity that PMO/Cs actually engage in. PMO/Cs, at first glance, would seem to match the negative stereotype of the mercenary in the sense that, as David Shearer describes, 'They are foreign to a conflict, they are motivated chiefly by financial gain, and in some cases, have participated directly in combat'.[11] When set against the recent involvement of mercenaries in the Congo and Biafra in the 1960s and Angola in the 1970s, Anan's reaction is perhaps understandable. Singer argues, nonetheless, that mercenaries are 'understood to be individual-based in unit and thus ad hoc in organisation'. He continues:

> They work for one client and, focused as they are on combat, provide only one service: guns for hire. Although their trade is technically banned by international law, mercenaries remain active in nearly every ongoing conflict. But because of their ad hoc nature, they lack cohesion and discipline, and thus their strategic impact is limited.[12]

Whether mercenaries *per se* do indeed lack cohesion and discipline remains a moot point. One historical analysis of the role mercenaries have played in warfare throughout the ages argues that, contrary to popular perception, mercenaries have fought bravely and observed the laws and norms of war on the battlefield more often than is realised.[13] The perception, however, that mercenaries remain a warrior caste apart, operating beyond the realm of the laws of war, persists to this day.[14] But as mentioned previously with other characteristics associated with contemporary internecine conflict the embryo of what we know today as a PMO/C has its origins in the Yemen Civil War. To be sure, the more corporate image associated with such an acronym had yet to be realised, but in deference (albeit unconscious) to the language of the free market, Fred Halliday referred to the British mercenaries in the Yemen as 'supposedly private entrepreneurs'.[15] Bernard Mills, a former officer with British special forces and who himself was recruited into the mercenary organisation that supported Royalist forces in Yemen noted:

> At this particular time – we're talking about the 1960s – British governments had lost the will in some ways to engage in this sort of operation [clandestine operations] and we could do something the British government no longer had the will to do, helping to get rid of a foreign power in the Yemen. So it was logical for private enterprise to pick up this particular bill, particularly as we felt it was important for the British national interest.[16]

While reference to 'private enterprise' provides the link with the corporate image associated with the PMO/C of today, this statement also reveals an idealism involved in the formation of what became the British Mercenary Organisation. Though funded by Saudi Arabia, it developed ties with a range of state actors and their agencies, all united in their determination to counter Nasser's hegemonic designs. Whatever the immediate personal gain, the fundamental belief that their involvement in the Yemen Civil War was in defence of British interests imbued those recruited with a moral certitude that went beyond mere avarice. Colonel

David Smiley, a man of exceptional experience in irregular warfare and who was to become field commander of the mercenary force in the Yemen wrote:

> Although mercenary excesses in the Congo brought discredit on our calling, I maintain that it can be an honourable one – with the important provisos that the mercenary's own conduct is honourable, and that what he is doing is in the interest of his own country, or in the defence of his own ideals. Speaking for myself, I was – and am – certain that what we were trying to do in the Yemen was in the interests of Britain.[17]

The more normative debates surrounding the use of mercenaries in civil wars remains beyond the scope of this study. For the record however, the British and French (and some Belgians) who were recruited to train the Royalist forces in the Yemen were never involved in, or were party to, atrocities. Indeed, for the most part, their role was a purely advisory one and proportionally, very few of the mercenaries ever engaged in actual combat operations. It is also worth noting that those recruited, at least where the British were concerned, had a special forces background, some with Britain's premier special forces unit, the Special Air Service Regiment, while others, such as Smiley, had been in the Special Operations Executive during the Second World War. While the suitability of some of those recruited to the operation was suspect with regard to the hardships that service in the Yemen entailed, most, and certainly among the Britons involved, conducted themselves with a moral rectitude, that set them apart from the gratuitous malevolence associated with, for example, mercenary activity in Angola a decade later.

Why direct British involvement in the Yemen Civil War was restricted largely to the activities of a mercenary organisation, paid for by a rich, yet militarily vulnerable dynastic regime, is an important dimension of this study. In this regard, the omission of the word 'foreign' in the title is deliberate. British engagement with and in the Yemen conflagration was more multifaceted than pure diplomatic discourse as practised by Foreign Office officials in King Charles Street, or indeed their Colonial Office counterparts in Great Smith Street. While foreign policy has come to denote the pursuit of state interests in international affairs based upon defined goals and objectives, it is perhaps more accurate to talk of British foreign *policies* towards the Yemen Civil War, given that individuals associated with influential pressure groups, both inside and outside government, were, at crucial stages, able to usurp the recommendations of the mandarins in King Charles Street. Until the end of 1965 all could agree on the interest to be secured – the British presence in Aden and with it, realisation of British oil assets in the Middle East – but the means by which this was to be achieved involved bitter argument and acrimony across Whitehall and in the Cabinet, with coherent decision-making concerning events in the Yemen conspicuous by its absence.

This study details these debates. It does not claim to be an exhaustive study of the Yemen Civil War *per se* though it does highlight important themes in how the war itself unfolded, not least of which was the ever uncertain dynamic of tribal politics that made the capture and retention of land and loyalties – both in the Yemen and South Arabia – an often capricious endeavour. The broader focus is upon how the objective of British policy – retention of the Aden base through a sovereign yet pliable Federation of South Arabia – came to impact upon Britain's relationship with Washington, the United Nations, Saudi Arabia, the rulers and potentates of the Federation itself as well as with the Yemen Arab Republic, Egypt, and of course the Royalist cause. Moreover it examines, for the first time, the extent and range of British clandestine or covert activity inside the Yemen as well as the often vexed relationship officials in London maintained with individuals in the British Mercenary Organisation. Inevitably, such ties involved the exchange of intelligence and this book details for the first time, the extent of those contacts, as well the wider political considerations that determined to what use such intelligence should be put. As will become evident, this was to have wider ramifications for Britain's ability to sustain its position in South Arabia at a time when the Egyptian presence in Yemen was particularly vulnerable.

For the purposes of this study, the terms 'clandestine' and 'covert' are regarded as synonymous, and taken to mean simply 'activity performed to influence foreign states in unattributable ways'.[18] This may rankle with some purists of intelligence studies, but in considering the type of special operations that were either sanctioned by the British government or carried out by the British Mercenary Organisation, it is a particularly apt nomenclature. Indeed, as the case of Israel's involvement in the conflict, detailed here to an extent previously unknown, demonstrates, the British Mercenary Organisation was capable of conducting its own covert operations independent of London and away from the view of their main sponsor, Saudi Arabia.

The book is divided into eight main chapters. Chapter 1 deals briefly with the history of South Arabia and Yemen. Although claiming to be no more than a review of the existing literature, it provides the reader with the all-important context in which British policy towards the Yemen Civil War between 1962 and 1965 can be judged. Chapter 2 details the debates over recognition of the new Yemen Republic, why the British government hesitated to follow Foreign Office advice to extend to it *de jure* recognition, as well the part played by members of the 'Aden Group' in helping to stall moves towards this end. Chapter 3 examines the tension that the issue of recognition caused in London's relationships with Washington and the United Nations, while also highlighting the emerging role that 'para-diplomacy' came to have on the course of British policy towards the Yemen conflict. Chapter 4 details Britain's covert action in the Yemen Civil War and why, faced with an ever growing insurgency in Aden and the Federation, London refused to link these operations to wider support for the Royalist cause. Chapters 5 and 6 provide extensive details for the first time regarding the origins of the mercenary operation in the Yemen, its structure, and the extent to which, with varying degrees of success, it tried to harness support for its activities inside the Yemen from several interested parties. Chapter 7 examines the impact that the election of a Labour government to power in October 1964 had on the course of the Yemen Civil War and concludes that important opportunities were missed that should have allowed London to benefit from Cairo's growing military misfortunes. Lastly, chapter 8 examines why, on the cusp of its greatest triumph, the British Mercenary Organisation suffered an irreversible decline in its fortunes. To conclude, one final note. The methodology employed in this book is strictly historical and based on primary source documentation – including extensive use of the diaries and private papers of Lieutenant Colonel Neil 'Billy' McLean and Colonel David Smiley. Even so, the following, broader themes should be born in mind by the reader: what is meant by a national interest, who or what defines its essence, and the efficacy of the particular means by which it is to be pursued. As British policy towards the Yemen Civil War demonstrates, the answers to these questions were seldom parsimonious.

1
Britain and the Yemen Civil War

Prelude to Intervention

On 30 June 1964, the Chiefs of Staff Committee, the most senior decision-making body of the British armed forces, met in London to discuss
the progress of ongoing military operations in the mountainous area of
Radfan in the Federation of South Arabia (FSA). Faced with growing
unrest throughout the Federation, the meeting presented an opportune
moment to reaffirm the importance of the Aden base in securing British
interests east of the Suez, the most important of which was continued
access to the oil-producing states of the Gulf region. While conceding that
no serious overt military threat to the British position in South Arabia
existed, the minutes clearly identified clandestine activity from the Yemen
Arab Republic (YAR), supported by President Gamel Abdul Nasser of
Egypt, as the main threat to the stability of the Federation. Quoting a
report by the Joint Intelligence Committee (JIC), the main collation and
assessment body of Britain's intelligence community, the Chiefs of Staff
defined Nasser's overall aims in Southern Arabia as: (a) The survival of
the UAR-supported Republican government in the Yemen; (b) The elimination of the British presence from the Protectorate and from the Aden
base and (c) The establishment in Aden state of a Cairo-orientated Arab
nationalist regime. The minutes of their meeting concluded that:

> [M]ore Egyptian trained tribesman could be infiltrated as potential trouble
> makers [into the Federation]; more weapons and money could be provided; a
> policy of assassination could be encouraged. There have been several reports
> that the number of Egyptian intelligence officers in the Yemen has increased and
> that the Egyptians are providing increasing material aid not only for dissidents
> but also for terrorism by extremists in the Federation, including Aden State. As
> activity in the Radfan has recently shown, dissident forces are likely to be increas-
> ingly sophisticated in their equipment, training, and discipline.[1]

Just over three years later, the Labour government under Prime
Minister Harold Wilson effected a total withdrawal from the Federation,

a withdrawal likened by some scholars to a scuttle.[2] Whatever the epithet applied, such action on the part of Britain was regarded as the inevitable outcome of the contradictions inherent in London's policy towards South Arabia from the outset. With their loyalty to London so often a transitory commodity, attempts to cohere the disparate tribal groupings of the Protectorates into a collective whole with the foundation of the FSA in January 1963 were, it was argued, doomed. In practice, local politicians in what had been Aden Colony resisted the idea that their monopoly of power, prestige and influence should be diluted by tribal Shaykhs, Emirs or Sharifs considered to be the very antithesis of progression and modernity. Moreover, the styptic nature of the electoral franchise in Aden Colony served to alienate the burgeoning community of immigrant workers of the Federal hinterland and Yemen, from the very structures the British hoped would secure the future stability of the FSA. When allied to the growing influence of Arab nationalism throughout the Middle East in the late 1950s and early 1960s, the scene was set for a sustained programme of subversion and revolt against British rule, supported both materially and ideologically by President Nasser. Within a decade of the 1957 Defence White Paper which identified Aden as the lynchpin of British power projection east of Suez, Britain had abandoned the Aden colony, bringing to a close a presence in the region that had lasted for 134 years. Comparing the British experience in South Arabia with some notional colonial template that would have dictated French policy in similar circumstances, the former British diplomat, Christopher Gandy, remarked:

> [T]he city state of Aden would doubtless have become a heavily guarded showcase of le rayonnment culturel Francais, with French money lavishly poured out and the hinterland remaining the romantic, undisturbed domain of quarrelsome and unregenerate tribesman. British policy was nobler, demanded greater physical courage, persistence, local knowledge, devotion – all the best qualities of the British colonial tradition – and failed, where France might well have succeeded.[3]

Numerous studies have been written of this period. Books by Karl Pieragostini, Glen Balfour-Paul and Joseph Kostiner have examined the malaise in policy-making in Whitehall amid competing tribal and religious affinities in explaining the demise of the Federation and of British influence. A more recent work by Robert McNamara explores in scrupulous detail the evolution of Anglo-Egyptian relations in this period and the animus generated by shared suspicions of malevolence over events in South Arabia.[4] They remain definitive works in their own right. By contrast, little scholarly attention has been paid to the manner in which policy in South Arabia, both in planning and execution, was influenced by Britain's perception of, and eventual involvement in, the Yemen Civil War.

The Yemen revolution of 26 September 1962 that overthrew the Yemen Royal Family – the *Hamid'Ud'Din* – marked the beginning of eight years of bitter internecine conflict. At its height, some 60,000 Egyptian troops were present in the Yemen to support and sustain a Republican government against forces loyal to the deposed Imam, Mohammed al-Badr. Known collectively as Royalists – a term that often failed to capture the often transient allegiance of the tribal actors recruited to their cause – they soon came to rely upon the largesse of Riyadh, and of Crown Prince Faisal in particular, to sustain their struggle. Saudi Arabia viewed Nasser's involvement as crude opportunism on the part of the Egyptian president and an attempt to undermine the monarchies throughout the Arabian peninsula. Seen as the most open manifestation of an Arab Cold War that pitted dynastic regimes against their Republican counterparts, Riyadh tried throughout the early years of the conflict to court wider international support for its position by playing upon fears that Egypt's role in the Yemen merely opened the door for Soviet penetration of the region.[5]

Britain, for so long faced with the irritant of Yemeni irredentism in pursuit of their claims to South Arabia, now faced a threat of an altogether different magnitude. Aden was seen as the strategic jewel in the East of Suez crown, but for all the investment in and build up of its military potential, the legacy of Suez placed political limits on the extent to which strategic muscle could be flexed openly in defence of British interests. Faced with a regional *zeitgeist* that denied the legitimacy of counterfeit boundaries and regarded the FSA as little more than a fraudulent edifice for British imperialism, London it seemed, lacked the political will, let alone the military ability to defend its interests. As J. B. Kelly remarked of this period, 'Britain betrayed her trust and ran away from her responsibilities in South Arabia. Faced with a terrorist movement which was determined, ruthless and implacable, the British government displayed none of these qualities in return. In the contests of wills it proved spineless.'[6]

Such political ennui has become the accepted narrative of Britain's denouement in South Arabia, a narrative that, to paraphrase the old Marxist dictum, sees British policymakers engage in reactive choices and never amid the most propitious of circumstances. The dirty laundry of acrimony this produced, most notably between the mandarins of the Foreign Office and their counterparts in the Colonial Office and indeed, between the occupants of Great Smith Street and their subordinates in Government House in Aden has been well aired, not least among some of the participants themselves.[7] These bureaucratic battles are however, only part of the story. The extent to which policy-makers were willing to countenance clandestine activity to secure the Federation and the extent to which this should be tied to Royalist fortunes, has remained, for the most part, the untold story of the Yemen Civil War. Accordingly, it is this aspect of the conflict that constitutes the essence of this book.

Britain and South Arabia

In his account of Britain's decision to abandon Aden, historian Jacob Abadi identified five main factors: the failure of the Colonial authorities in Aden to create a new collaborative local elite upon which to consolidate the Federation; the intervention of outside powers that fuelled indigenous unrest; the impact of new technological developments on British defence policy; emergent financial exigencies that cast doubt on the continued sagacity of maintaining British bases east of Suez; and finally 'the change in Britain's perception of her own image as a great power'.[8] Of these, the first two occasioned Britain's departure, while the other three certainly caused it. Technological development and the sterling crisis of 1966 camouflaged the loss of political will on the part of the Labour government of Harold Wilson, despite assurances given to the Federal potentates that Britain would honour its commitments to safeguard the transition to independence and beyond. For those rulers and their followers who had thrown in their lot with the British, their sense of betrayal was profound. As the old Arab adage had it, 'it is better to be the enemy of the British than their friend: if you are their friend, they will sell you whereas if at least you are their enemy they'll attempt to buy you'. The paradox is, as Abadi concedes, that whereas Britain was for the most part happy to divest itself of other colonial possessions, the importance of Aden and the Federation 'increased, rather than decreased in the eyes of British policy-makers during the last decade of its occupation.'[9]

The origins of the British presence in Aden was a direct result of the conquest and occupation of India. The main line of communication with the jewel in the crown of the British Empire ran through the Mediterranean and the Red Sea and as such, British control of at least part of the coastline of the Arabian peninsula carried distinct strategic benefits. Taking advantage of the looting by local inhabitants of a British cargo ship – the *Durya Dawlat* – that had run aground near Aden, the British Indian government in Bombay decided to despatch an expeditionary force under one Captain S. B. Haines to exact recompense for this act of plunder. On 19 January 1839, Aden fell to the British, ushering in over a century of colonial rule.

Demanding satisfaction for the fate of the hapless *Durya Dawlat* was the excuse rather than the actual reason for London casting a covetous gaze on Aden. Not for the first time, a threat from Egypt in the person of its charismatic governor, Pasha Mohammed Ali, with his military campaigning along the parallel coasts of the Red Sea, appeared to threaten British lines of communications to its imperial possessions. As early as 1802, Aden's unique geographical features – a deepwater harbour surrounded by mountains that created a natural fortress – had been brought to the attention of the British Foreign Secretary, George Canning. Now strategic threat coupled with commercial avarice determined Aden's future. Not only was the Egyptian potentate regarded as a threat, but possession of Aden had the distinct advantage of providing a base from where the British East India Company could challenge the monopoly exercised by Cairo over the coffee trade along the Red Sea littoral.

With the opening of the Suez canal in 1869, the strategic importance of Aden increased still further, its location being ideal for establishing a coal bunkering station for steam powered ships making voyages to and from the outposts of empire. This importance increased with the advent of oil, though by the end of the nineteenth century, with Egypt ingested into the British Empire in all but name, the strategic threat to Aden had been reduced significantly. This had wider ramifications for longer-term British policy towards Aden and its immediate hinterland. While successive Imams from the Yemen laid claim to the region, few, if any, of the tribal Shaykhs, Emirs or Princes were willing to sacrifice their feudal bailiwicks in common cause with a *Zeidi* potentate whose religious authority – let alone venal style of government – remained anathema to their *Shaffei* roots. As Jacob Abadi notes:

> [M]ost preferred to conclude protection treaties with Britain. Thus Britain provided protection for the different tribes and in turn took control of their foreign policies. The Sultans, Amirs, and Sheikhs in the area were often hostile to each other, a fact which allowed the British the opportunity to appear as an arbiter and honest broker and thus maintain control.[10]

The actual area of Aden Colony was small, but beyond its boundaries, the Protectorates – named precisely because of the veneer of protection offered by the British in Aden – extended over 112,000 square miles. Because the strategic threat to Aden was deemed insufficient to warrant anything more the perfunctory visit of the occasional Colonial Officer from Aden, the Protectorate rulers were left, by and large, to their own devices, exacting tribute from caravans that passed through their fiefdoms, while investing little in return by way of infrastructure for the betterment of their subjects. While responsibility for Aden as a Crown colony was ceded from the India Office to the Colonial Office in 1937, this bureaucratic exchange did little to cure the political scotomata which afflicted the view of officials in London concerning development of the Protectorates. Indeed, British involvement in the hinterlands was, for the most part, confined to the suppression of tribal revolts that threatened the hegemony of particular rulers. This was achieved for the most part by the expedient use of air power. Under the 1927 Air Control Scheme, the Royal Air Force (RAF) established a series of aerodromes from Aden to Iraq to protect Britain's growing oil interests throughout the Middle East. The construction of an airfield at Khormaksar, within the boundaries of Aden colony, afforded the British an effective method of maintaining, and occasionally enforcing tribal obedience without the costs incurred by expensive garrisons and the expense of maintaining their accompanying infrastructure. As Thomas Mockaitis points out in his treatment of insurgency in South Arabia, 'A century of British occupation had not produced a single yard of tarmac road in the Protectorates' by the time Britain once more found itself at war with Nazi Germany and Fascist Italy.[11]

This archaic arrangement survived the vicissitudes of the Second World War, the only real threat from Italian occupied Somaliland being dealt with in the early stages of the conflict. As such, Aden and the surrounding Protectorates had a quiet war, remaining for the most part untouched by the process of modernisation imposed upon other Colonies or Mandates by dint of their integration into the Allied war effort. A notable example in this regard was the rapid economic development of Palestine. British investment in the local infrastructure, most notably the oil refineries in Haifa, helped to foster an already strong sense of national identity, Zionism, among the Jewish population.[12] It was only in the post-war period that economic developments, coupled with the impact of migrant labour patterns on the political and social cohesion of Aden Colony, finally spurred officials in London to tackle the chronic state of economic underdevelopment beyond the boundaries of the Colony.

In 1954, the Anglo-Iranian Oil Company, the forerunner of British Petroleum, completed construction of a refinery in Little Aden, transforming the Colony from a humid backwater into one of the world's busiest ports in terms of commercial shipping. Aden now assumed a geopolitical significance as great as anything experienced during the heady days of Empire, as the need to realise Britain's energy assets in Iraq, Kuwait and the Trucial States of the Gulf, linked the Colony directly to the health of the British economy. Thus the 1957 Defence White Paper declared that 'Britain must at all times be ready to defend Aden Colony and the Protectorates and the territories on the Persian Gulf for whose defence she is responsible'.[13] Britain had no overt desire to exercise direct control over the Protectorates, but the economic expansion of Aden port with its concomitant demands for an increased labour force and resources meant that, however reluctantly, the development of Aden came directly to be linked to the fate of the hinterland. This was recognised by the Chiefs of Staff who, in 1964 noted the interdependent relationship that marked ties between Aden and the Federal states. Aden, they noted, 'is not and cannot become self-contained or self-sufficient. Not only does the water supply come from wells in the Federation, but the economy of the [Aden] State and the viability of the base depend upon a large labour force derived partly from Aden state labour and partly from Protectorate and Yemeni immigrant workers.'[14]

Herein lay the kernel of dissent that was to sap the British will to retain its military presence in South Arabia. By the mid-1950s, the Colonial Office began to propose the idea of a Federal structure that would unite the Protectorates with Aden Colony. While conceived ostensibly to protect British interests, it was pitched to the Protectorate rulers, not noted for their progressive political ideals, as a means to safeguard their suzerainty from Yemeni irredentism. Even so, many of these potentates proved reluctant participants, concerned that closer association with the British would fan the flames of rebellion already being stoked by a combination of the Imam's intrigues and a vibrant Arab nationalism centred on the persona of Egyptian President Gamel Abdul Nasser. The former problem was at it most intense between 1955 and 1958, with London authorising a series of 'tit for tat' raids, for the most part clandestine, in response to Imam Ahmed's meddling with tribes in the Protectorate. As Spencer Mawby notes, these actions had the great advantage of circumventing Foreign Office objections but they also presaged the more extensive debates over clandestine action that dominated British policy towards the Yemen from the spring of 1964 onwards.[15] Countering the territorial avarice of the Imam proved, in retrospect, far easier than diluting the impact of Arab nationalism upon a fast developing political consciousness among Adenis themselves.[16]

Until the construction of the oil refinery the British had co-opted a local elite, comprising a mixed group of Arab, Asian and European businessmen and merchants, to run the affairs of Aden Colony under the guiding hand of Colonial Office officials. Broad suffrage was unknown and members of the Legislative Council – in effect the government of the Colony – were appointed by the British. These positions of privilege were undermined by the decision of the Colonial Office to forge ahead with the creation of the Federation of the Arab Emirates of the South in January 1959. In time it came to encompass all but one of the states of the Western Protectorate – Beihan, Upper Aulaqi, Lower Aulaqi, Fadhli, Lahej, Dhala, Audhali, Dathinah, Akrabi, Haushabi and Upper and Lower Yafa. Anxious to legitimise its presence and strategic position in South Arabia, London ignored the concerns of the Governor of Aden, Sir William Luce, who argued that establishment of a Federal structure would merely stir up nationalist sentiment. As he saw it, 'the emergence of an independent hinterland could not be squared with a dependant Aden.'[17] Luce concluded that only when Britain was seen to abide by the treaties of

Protection with the hinterland potentates and engage in a determined effort to extend development beyond the confines of Aden, could the hybrid that was the Federation have any chance of sustaining itself beyond the imaginations of officials in Great Smith Street. Aden remained a Crown Colony and outside the immediate purview of the new structure but it was clear that the next step planned in London would be for Aden to divest itself of its Crown Colony status to become a state like any other as part of an expanded Federation that would also include the Eastern Protectorates. To this end, London began push through reforms of the local franchise that widened the base of popular participation for elections to the Legislative Council, in the hope that it would have an elected majority of members by the beginning of 1960.

In this process of controlled liberalisation however, London alienated the old elite that had hitherto supported British hegemony in Aden but without ever overseeing the emergence of a new coterie of likeminded individuals willing to play the part of political entrepreneurs in this state building enterprise. It was hoped that extension of the franchise would foster acceptance of the planned political order. To echo the sentiment of Gandy, it was a noble endeavour, and in more propitious circumstances, there was every chance that the net result of this process of constitutional de-colonisation – one that drew on the experience of Cyprus for inspiration – would have been an independent state of South Arabia, willing to confer sovereign base rights to the British. But the triumvirate of time, timing and location proved effective conspirators in undermining such hopes.

The success of the oil refinery had led to a vast increase in the population of Aden by the beginning of the 1960 as migration followed prosperity. This influx was resented by native Adenis, not least because they represented a challenge to the political and social hegemony that this group had hitherto enjoyed. These new arrivals to the Colony, comprising Somalis, inhabitants of the Protectorates and perhaps most crucially, migrants from the Yemen itself, become the platform upon which some of their number now sought to radically change the prevailing social and political order. While helping the port to prosper, this new indentured labour lived and worked, for the most part, in appalling conditions. Not surprisingly, a number of labour organisations began to emerge. By 1956, these had coalesced into the Aden Trades Union Confederation (ATUC) led by its charismatic Secretary-General, Abdullah al-Asnaj.

The pretensions of al-Asnaj went beyond mere labour reform, however. Many members of the ATUC shared duel membership with the United National Front (UNF) whose activists made no secret of their grandiose nationalist aspirations: to achieve the unification of Aden and the Protectorates with Yemen. Sir Kennedy Trevaskis, the Political Agent for the Western Protectorate who later inherited the mantle of High Commissioner for the FSA, recalled the outspoken comments of al-Asnaj in favour of unification. At a public meeting in Aden on 10 February 1960 the Secretary-General of the ATUC was reported to have declared that, 'A nationalist programme will be carried out to strengthen your belief in a United Yemen. One nation, one Yemen and one struggle only. No north, no south, but one Yemen. No Legislative council, no Federation . . . There is only one Yemen, the occupied part of which must be liberated.'[18] In terms of territorial sovereignty, the demands of the fiery trade unionist were of the age-old irredentism espoused by the dynastic order in Sana'a. But the ATUC was no cover for the claims of the Yemen Royal Family, the *Hamid'Ud'Din*. Its ideals were based on Nasser's view of a new social order in the Middle East which increasingly came to regard the dynastic regimes of the Middle East as degenerate, counterfeit creations designed to serve imperial interests.

The ATUC drew its strength from a relatively small pool of educated Adenis who distrusted the power and influence of the Protectorate rulers. They believed progress towards national self-determination should be settled on their terms and not according to those set by the Federal rulers whose total dependence on London – militarily, politically and financially – made them, in their eyes at least, little more than puppets of Government House in Aden. Most of the Federal rulers now occupied government portfolios under the emergent Federation of Arab Emirates which elevated them to positions of power resented by al-Asnaj and his cohorts in the ATUC. Unlike some members of the British labour movement who saw the ATUC as an indigenous embodiment of the British Trade Union move-ment, Tresvaskis was more sanguine, regarding its itinerant membership as little more than an alternative tribal grouping which gave their lives direction, if not meaning. As he saw it, 'They [the migrant labour force] saw them [the leadership of the ATUC/UNF] as counterparts of the tribal leaders upon whose favour they had depended at home: following them unquestioningly, not as industrial leaders but as guardians of their social and political security.'[19] By the summer of 1962, the ATUC had spawned a political wing, the People's Socialist Party (PSP), designed to impede moves towards integration with the Protectorates as much as anything else. It was quick to show its true nationalist colours. Within days of the coup d'état that brought Colonel Abduallah as-Sallal to power in Sana'a, several leaders of the PSP made their way to the Yemeni capital to proclaim their fidelity to the new Republic and their concomitant grati-tude to Nasser. In a matter of weeks, four of them had been made ministers in the first Republican government headed by Sallal.

For Britain, much that was to now unfold in Aden and the Yemen relates directly to the persona of Nasser and the legacy that the Suez crisis cast over London's ability to safeguard its remaining interests. Undoubtedly the symbols of British power, if not the actual ability to project that power, were badly tarnished in the aftermath of the Suez debacle. Collusion with Israel had undermined relations with the wider Arab world. Saudi Arabia, already in dispute with London over rival claims to the Buraimi oasis, used the international furore in the wake of the ill-fated invasion as the trigger to break diplomatic ties. More broadly, the Suez crisis marked the eclipse of British hegemony in the region. Exploiting Britain's Achilles heel – the febrile state of the national economy – Washington issued veiled warnings that in the absence of a British withdrawal from the canal zone, it would veto a British request for substantial loans from the International Monetary Fund. When news leaked of Washington's proposed coercive measures, more than $300 million was wiped from the treasury reserve in an effort to defend sterling. This more than anything else disabused policy-makers in Whitehall of Britain's ability to act both unilaterally and overtly to secure its interests in the region without support from the United States. In the aftermath of Suez, the Foreign Office took it upon itself to manage Britain's decline in the Middle East in such a way that Washington, while clearly the dominant partner and shouldering the greater defence burden, would remain for the foreseeable future reliant on Britain's greater experience to guide regional policy.[20]

Still, the view that Britain no longer had the political will to deploy military force to protect its regional interests remains conditional. Within two years of Suez, British and American forces acting in concert intervened to secure the Hashemite dynasty in Jordan from elements inspired by, if not beholden to, Nasser. The same year saw the United Kingdom created the Middle East Command (MIDCOM) in Aden and with it the exponential growth in its military facilities. In the neighbouring Sultanate of Muscat and Oman, British troops were instrumental in suppressing a tribal revolt led by the Imam of Oman and backed by Saudi Arabia against the reigning Sultan. The success of this campaign – conducted for the most part away from the glare of publicity – reached its apogee in January 1959 with the taking of the rebel redoubt on Jebel Akhdar by elements of the 22nd Special Air Service Regiment. Finally, the importance of the Aden base was demonstrated in June 1961 following its extensive use by British forces during 'Operation Vantage', the British intervention in Kuwait. The new Iraqi regime of Brigadier Qassem that had come to power in 1958 following the overthrow of the Hashemite order now threatened to press its long-held territorial claims over Kuwait. At the time, Kuwait was the largest producer of oil in the Gulf region. Britain depended upon the Emirate for 40 percent of its oil needs, while expenditure by the ruling al-Sabah family on British goods and services was such that Kuwait was deemed to be the United Kingdom's 'single most important overseas investment.'[21] Such actions demonstrated that while its imprint was less visible, Britain continued to value solid footholds in the mountains and deserts of the Arabian peninsula.

Even though Iraqi irredentism had little to do with Egypt – indeed, the relationship between Baghdad and Cairo was matched by mutual loathing during this period – the belief remained strong among many in Whitehall and especially among the more vociferous elements of the Conservative and Unionist Party that Nasser, ever the populist, not only inspired such anti-British sentiment but actively involved himself in attempts by surrogate movements to undermine British regional interests. This antipathy towards the Egyptian President had found collective expression both before and during the crisis of October 1956 in the activities of the 'Suez Group'. Anthony Nutting, the former Minister of State at the Foreign Office who resigned over the Suez affair referred to them as '[A] hotchpotch collection of embittered ex-ministers and young newly elected back-benchers anxious to cut a figure in Parliament by attacking the Government for selling out imperial British interests'.[22] Nutting had in mind Julian Amery and Lieutenant Colonel Neil 'Billy' McLean. Amery, scion of Sir Leopold Amery, had allowed his house in Eaton Square, London to become the unofficial headquarters of the group during the crisis. It has often been claimed that the Suez Group, smarting under what they saw as Britain's humiliation over Suez, regarded the Aden issue as a means to exact revenge. Certainly, statements made by Amery and McLean in Parliament leave little doubt as to the personal animus with which they regarded Nasser.[23] Equally however, both believed that the future prosperity of Britain as a trading nation was threatened by Nasser's hegemonic ambitions throughout the Middle East, ambitions they believed that served only to strengthen Moscow's hand. Both as Undersecretary of State for War and later as Minister for Aviation, a relatively junior Cabinet position afforded to him by his father-in-law Prime Minister Harold Macmillan, Amery maintained his vilification of the Egyptian President:

> The prosperity of Britain rests on the oil of the Persian Gulf, the rubber and tin of Malaya, and the precious metals of south and central Africa. As long as we have access to these, as long as we can realise the assets we have there, as long as we can trade with this part of the world, we [the people of the United Kingdom] will be prosperous. If the communists were to take them over we would lose the lot. Governments like Colonel Nasser's in Egypt are just as dangerous.[24]

When, in the aftermath of the overthrow of the Imamate, events in Yemen threatened to spill over into Federation territory, the moribund

Suez Group transmogrified into the Aden Group. As such, they acted as a powerful quasi-parliamentary body not only to undermine moves towards recognition of the new order in Sana'a, a recognition advocated most forcefully by the Foreign Office, but as events unfolded, lent their political support for the para-diplomacy of both Amery and McLean. It was this para-diplomacy and the emergence as a result of a British-led mercenary organisation that contributed much to Nasser's undoing in the Yemen.

Yemen: The Origins of a Revolution

The revolution in Yemen following the death of Imam Ahmed and the election of his son, Mohammed al-Badr, as the 66th Imam, was a result of the political and economic contradictions that had come to haunt Yemen society. Until the revolution of 26 September 1962, Yemen remained, according to Fred Halliday, 'one of the most isolated and static countries in the world' and 'not changed in fundamental systemic ways from the Yemen of two or even seven centuries earlier'.[25] Aided by a natural geographic isolation, the Imams of the *Mutawakkilite* Kingdom of Yemen actively sought to keep the twentieth century at bay in an effort to preserve their domain from the impact of modernity.

Such was the dominant characteristic of life in the Yemen under the Imamate. Armed with an unyielding belief in the need to safeguard the country from outside threats and maintain an independence that had resisted fiercely the designs of the Ottoman Empire, such isolation was seen as the means to ensure the longevity of an Imamate that wrapped itself in a cloak of religious purity. Among a dynasty that was 'isolationist and xenophobic', exposure to the outside world was shunned to the extent that even regional Arab political movements were treated with disdain.[26] Yemeni nationals were often prevented from leaving the country while those foreigners that were allowed in remained subject to the most draconian controls. Despite joining the Arab League in 1945 and the United Nations (UN) in 1947, foreign diplomatic missions were refused representation in Taiz'z, the diplomatic capital of Yemen. As Halliday observed, '[T]he isolation of [North] Yemen was not a haphazard or aberrant policy of the Imams; it served directly to conserve their position.'[27]

A backward, deeply conservative Islamic society was the result, bereft of modern institutions and intolerant of development. In such a manner, the Yemeni Royal Family, the *Hamid'Ud'Din*, consolidated its power, but also created the conditions for its own downfall. In 1918 the Ottoman Empire, defeated in Europe and no longer able to contain the territorial avarice of the *Hamid'Ud'Din*, recognised its Imams (traditional rulers) as spiritual heads of the *Zeidi* sub-sect of *Shi'a* Islam and temporal rulers. Article 136 of the Yemeni Constitution claimed all laws were based upon *Shari'a*, a claim that in practice served to justify the absolute authority of the Imam in all matters spiritual and temporal. Adherence to the *Zeidi* creed and traditional customs were key legitimising pillars for the dynasty with the Imam elected and supported by the *ulema* or clerics, a powerful group whose public adherence to piety served, in turn, to reinforce the religious credentials of the ruling Imam. The result of this was a stratification of the political order, where social mobility was virtually unknown and the upper elite of the country unchangeable by peaceful means.[28] Politics was the preserve of a tiny minority at the top of a largely closed system, with the only actors able to effect change being members of the ruling oligarchy.

This hierarchical system was also sustained by the mechanisms of social fragmentation and tribalism. Centralising campaigns launched to crush unruly tribes had enabled the *Hamid'Ud'Din* to concentrate power in its own hands. Opponents such as the powerful al-Wazir family who embodied a rival claim to the Imamate were crushed ruthlessly, while unrest among the more troublesome tribal Shaykhs was controlled through bribes, backed by thinly veiled threats to use force if recalcitrance was still encountered. Bribery, a long accepted form of political recompense, was deeply embedded in Yemen's political tradition; its widespread use by all sides in the civil war, in their efforts to secure strategic gains, was but a continuum of cultural mores that had regulated ties between the Imam and his erstwhile subjects for centuries. As a result, the institution of the tribe rather than the state, remained the focus of identity among most Yemenis, thereby allowing the *Hamid'Ud'Din* to manipulate its structures to contain wider social discontent. Where bribery failed, a hostage system, usually involving the abduction of sons of the ruling tribal shaykhs, was used to enforce tribal fidelity. Such measures proved particularly effective in securing the acquiescence to (though rarely acceptance of) the existing *Zeidi* dispensation among the predominantly Sunni *Shaffei* tribes in the south of the country, the cities and along the coastal plain. Equally, it was not unknown for an Imam to allow the *Zeidi* tribes who dominated the mountains of Yemen and who were known to set great store by their martial prowess, to exact tribute from their *Shaffei* counterparts in the most violent manner. For example, in an effort to consolidate his succession as Imam in 1948 following the assassination of his father, the Imam Yahya, Imam Ahmed allowed his *Zeidi* followers to sack the predominantly *Shaffei* districts of Sana'a.[29]

The army itself drew heavily upon the *Zeidi* tribes for its manpower but even here, a division of military labour was apparent in the effort to ensure loyalty to the *Hamid'Ud'Din*. Troops of the Palace Guard drawn from loyal tribes were used to crush tribal rebellion and collect taxes while the regular army remained emasculated, its weapons and ammunition held in secret arsenals. Furthermore, the encouragement of strong tribal loyalties throughout Yemen society served to exacerbate and confirm the condition of underdevelopment, limiting the ability of central government to penetrate that selfsame society without recourse to more draconian measures. The reliance of the Imamate on support from the two great tribal confederations, the *Hashid* and the *Bakil*, support granted in return for local autonomy, ensured that Yemeni society remained static and orientated towards a reactionary traditionalism.

The most open manifestation of this process was the styptic nature of the Yemen economy. With a skeletal administration that could hardly be equated to a functioning civil service, no cabinet or legislative chamber, there was in practice no difference between the Imam's private purse and the state treasury. Such a situation was compounded by Yemen's isolation from the wider regional economy. Little in the way of foreign capital investment flowed into the country; indeed external trade remained a marginal element in the country's economic cycle. Commerce was actively discouraged, with exorbitant taxes placed on both imports and exports. Even foreign companies willing to pay considerable sums for oil exploration rights were rejected. As a result, agricultural practices remained antiquated as modern methods of production were rejected.[30]

Such atavism was more than matched by the levels of health care. In 1962, there were only 15 doctors in the whole of Yemen, all of whom were foreigners given exceptional leave to remain and oversee the country's 600 hospital beds. It was estimated that by the beginning of the 1960s, over 50 percent of the population were estimated to have contracted some form of venereal disease while 80 percent were deemed to be suffering from trachoma. As Halliday notes, there was nothing faintly quaint or romantic about the country the Romans had once referred to as 'Arabia Felix'.[31] Education fared even worse. No public money was invested in pedagogical concerns. Indeed, only five percent of the population attended Koranic schools where learning was limited to the recitation of Islamic texts. If, as M. A. Zabarah maintains, 'revolutions have as their primary objectives the transformation of society', then the venal rule of successive Imams certainly laid the foundations of political and social unrest.[32]

But while contact with the outside world was largely viewed as anathema, the dearth of employment and educational opportunities prompted growing levels of migration to Arab and non-Arab countries alike. This search for the 'good life' inevitably exposed Yemenis to new ideas and political thought. Even where official sanction was given for individuals to study overseas in specific areas – usually associated with military training – this too served to heighten individual awareness regarding the antediluvian nature of Yemen society under its existing dispensation. Military students came to be imbued with radical ideals as well as becoming aware that as representatives of one of the few functioning institutions of state allowed in the *Mutawakkilite* kingdom, they had the potential to wield enormous power. The eventual leader of the Yemeni revolution, Colonel Abduallah as-Sallal, received his education in Baghdad, while many of his co-conspirators – the 'Septembrists' as Dana Adams Schmidt called them – were trained in Egypt throughout the 1950s.[33] Furthermore, émigré students such as the so-called 'Famous Forty' were of note for their informed critiques of the economic, political and social ills under which their country laboured, while concurrently promoting the idea of reform in Yemen and beyond. Drawing their inspiration from the *Ikhwan al-Muslimum* (Muslim Brotherhood), their platform appealed to those Yemenis from the mercantile class – Mohammed Mahmud al-Zubairi being the most apposite example – promoting calls for a Yemeni *nahda* (renaissance – a return to the fundamentals of Sunni Islam and its alternative view of social welfare) as the means to counter the chronic social lassitude that afflicted Yemeni society. Needless to say, their ideas drew the ire of Imam Yahya who initiated a bloody crackdown on their activities in December 1941.[34]

The die was cast however. What Marxist historians would term a 'bourgeoisie' was beginning to emerge in Yemen by the late 1940s, a bourgeoisie that found increasing voice in the form of secular opposition movements. Such opposition was most profound among the Sunni *Shaffei* merchants, who resented the power that the *sayyids,* or Princes, of the *Hamid'Ud'Din* exercised over their daily lives. To be sure, this resentment was fuelled by religious animosity, but also by a feeling that with their attachment to the primitive conditions of life in mountainous tribal societies, the *Zeidi* remained their social, as well as intellectual inferiors. This animus gave birth to the Free Yemeni Movement, founded in Aden in 1944, and with support among expatriate Yemenis in Cairo and Beirut. In essence, the movement arose in opposition to Imam Yahya's control of trade and the failure to provide a climate in which investment could flourish. It sought to reform, rather than overthrow the Imamate, in effect introducing a constitutional monarchy and free trade independent of punitive taxation. The assassination of the Imam on 17 February 1948, however, marked the first time that such opposition was prepared to condone the use of violence to promote change, the bloody removal of the Imam ushering in a brief period of rule by the Abduallah al-Wazir who was duly 'elected' as the new Imam.[35]

Crown Prince Saif al-Islam Ahmed – soon to become Imam Ahmed – moved quickly to restore the *Hamid'Ud'Din*. He appealed to the loyalty of the two predominantly *Zeidi* tribal confederations at the great fortress at Hajja in the north-west of the country and was able to reassert his grip on the Imamate by 25 February. According to Schmidt, who was to cover the Yemen Civil War for the *New York Times*, Imam Ahmed was a tyrant 'in the classic tradition', resorting to the most extreme methods to cultivate a fearsome appearance. As a child, he used to pull a string tightly around his neck until 'his eyes popped out'.[36] The appearance was more than matched by his actions. On consolidating his grip on power, he presided over the public beheading of al-Wazir and thirty of his supporters. He appeared to be cut from the same venal cloth as his father. Indeed, even before his elevation to Imam, he had declared in May 1944 that 'I ask Allah that I do not die until this sword of mine has been coloured by the blood of modernists.'[37]

Amid a tidal wave of Arab nationalism that served to radicalise regional politics, Imam Ahmed initially maintained the vice-like grip on power that had marked the rule of his predecessors, imposing by force a centralisation of power on a fragmented society with no broader sense of identity above the level of the tribe. His use of the hostage system to ensure his rule was expanded to include taking those selfsame hostages with him to Rome in 1959 to receive medical treatment. He summed up his philosophy by proclaiming that '[O]ne must choose between being free and poor and being dependent and rich. I have chosen independence.'[38]

In 1955 however, an uprising by disgruntled army officers that enjoyed the support of his brothers, Abbas and Abduallah ibn Yahya, shook Imam Ahmed from his political turpitude. The proclaimed aim of the plotters was the establishment of a constitutional Imamate, though given that the instigators of such plots found it easier to coalesce around negatives, rather than positives, the ultimate political aims of such political intrigues remained somewhat vague. Even so, the attempted coup convinced Imam Ahmed that defending the *Hamid' Ud 'Din* on the basis of exclusion alone lacked efficacy among the changing regional order. Concessions to modernity, albeit carefully controlled, would have to be introduced. While the executions of his siblings symbolised his determination to crush opposition from which ever quarter it came, Ahmed's concessions allowed the central pillar on which the rule of all Imam's had been legitimised, the maintenance of a *Zeidi* ascendancy, to erode with the infiltration of foreign intellectual trends. As such the concessions introduced, mainly limited to a more progressive foreign policy, were too little too late. To assuage Arab nationalist sentiment for example, Imam Ahmed aligned the *Mutawakkilite* Kingdom with Egypt and Saudi Arabia under the Jeddah military pact of 1956, and in 1958 he allowed Yemen to be confederated with Egypt and Syria to form part of the United Arab Republic (UAR). Such unity of purpose presaged a false dawn. Even so, under the mutual platitudes of brotherhood and fraternity, the Yemeni potentate tolerated, by his terms, a veritable flood of foreign experts and technicians to help establish the rudiments of something equating to a modern infrastructure. Under the Eisenhower Doctrine, Washington despatched technical aid to help construct a road linking Sana'a with the port of Hodeidah. Not to be outdone, Moscow obliged by helping to dredge and expand a deep-water harbour in the same town, while Egyptian, European and Chinese engineers and technicians turned their attention to a multitude of projects in the hinterland.[39] Such measures sharpened rather than ameliorated the contradictions in Yemeni society, while concurrently weakening the aura and fear that shrouded the *Hamid'Ud'Din* among the rest of Yemeni society in general and the *Shaffei* merchants in particular. The political system remained rigid and centred on the Imam as the personification of power; and, as the only figure able to make essential choices and decisions, the Imam was unable to effectively absorb and direct the complex outcomes provoked by exposure, however limited, to this process of modernisation.

This exposure was most keenly felt by the Imam's own son, Crown Prince Mohammed al-Badr. Many harboured doubts over his ability to inherit the mantle of Imam: his own uncle, Prince Hassan bin Yahya, regarded him as singularly unfit to rule; his cousin, Prince Abduallah bin al-Hussein, later to become one of the more proficient Royalist commanders, regarded al-Badr as 'dissolute, incompetent and gullible'.[40] In due course, it was an opinion that came to be shared by McLean and others associated with the Aden group. At the time however, the strong reservations expressed over al-Badr's suitability appeared as much a reaction to his seduction by contact with the outside world. Inspired by time spent in Cairo, Beijing, London and other European capitals, al-Badr became convinced the Yemen's road to social and political rehabilitation could embrace modernity without disrupting the central role occupied by the *Hamid'Ud'Din*. In 1959, and acting in his capacity as Prime Minister, the Crown Prince declared on Sana'a radio – itself a concession to modernity – that Yemen was about to enter a new era. Galvanised by the lure of Nasserism, al-Badr advocated a policy of non-alignment, pan-Arabism and economic development under state management. As he later confessed to McLean, during this period and away from paternal control he was also conniving secretly with Egyptian officials to bring about the early demise of his father's reign.[41]

The objectives sought by Mohammed al-Badr were, however, clearly juxtaposed to the logic of the Imamate system, and on more than one occasion, widespread rioting and disorder in Yemen's urban areas was blamed on his ill-judged comments. Attempts to maintain existing loyalties, such as a 25 percent increase in army salaries and enhanced subsidies to the Shaykhs of the great tribal confederations only upset the delicate balance of terror and tribute that had underpinned the rule of the *Hamid'Ud'Din*. Imam Ahmed's attempts to undo his son's perceived folly included the imprisonment of reform-minded leaders and the execution of Shaykh al-Ahmar of the *Hashid* confederation, whose failure to succumb to the usual blandishments brought about his bloody demise. Even these measures could not reverse the slow unravelling of the *Hamid'Ud'Din* ascendancy. Immediately on the death of his father, al-Badr declared his intent to press ahead with political and social reforms which, ironically, included the introduction of a system of government modelled on Egypt, reform of the taxation and judicial system, but with the monopoly of state power remaining within the gift of the Imamate. Left in isolation to pursue his reforms, al-Badr may have achieved a respite in which to begin the process of nation building. As he himself claimed, 'I thought that if I gave the people what they wanted they would believe in me.'[42] But like the British in Aden, time and timing were not on his side, and the very external actors he once courted as the paragons of progress now conspired to destroy him and the *Hamid'Ud'Din* dynasty.

The Egyptian Intervention

Mohammed al-Badr was proclaimed Imam on the death of his father on 19 September 1962. One week later he was toppled in a coup carried out by Lieutenant Abdul al-Moghny and 15 other officers, all beholden to Sallal. The plan had been to kill the Imam, but the would-be assassin, a palace courtier, botched the attempt while the subsequent shelling of the Royal Palace in Sana'a also failed to bring about the premature demise of the hapless Imam. Instead, al-Badr was able to escape to the *Zeidi* strongholds in the mountains to the north and east of the capital. Resistance soon sprung up among these tribes, with the Princes of the *Hamud'Ud'Din* dispersing among the tribes throughout the Khowlan mountains, al-Jauf plateau and areas close to the Saudi border to organise armed opposition. The Imamate was a powerful symbol among most of the *Zeidi* tribes, and this attachment to the *Hamid'Ud'Din* was expressed in almost eschatological terms. They showed 'a faith in the invincibility of their Imam amounting almost to a belief in his supernatural power', assuming titles such as *al-muta wakil al-Allah* (he who relies on Allah) and 'Commander of the Faithful'.[43] Given the near miraculous manner by which the Imam had escaped death at the hands of apostates, such names reinforced the central belief that the *Hamid'Ud'Din* were the progeny of the Prophet and as such, reinforced the belief in the divine right of the family to rule. Although it was reckoned that the *Zeidi* tribes represented less than half of the population and were deemed by most observers to be less sophisticated than their urban dwelling *Shaffei* compatriots, they certainly held the edge in terms of martial prowess. The success of the September revolution was at best partial. The newly proclaimed Republican government may have controlled the main cities of Yemen, but its writ did not extend beyond much else. In a short period of time, the newly proclaimed Yemen Arab Republic (YAR) was almost entirely dependent on the military munificence of Cairo to ensure its longevity. As Schmidt noted, 'The Imam may have lost his capital, but not his throne'.[44]

Egyptian intervention and support were crucial to the survival of the YAR, and the timely arrival of the Egyptian Expeditionary Force (EEF) undoubtedly prevented its premature denouement at the hands *Zeidi* tribes. Debate has long raged over the extent to which Egyptian intrigue was responsible for the coup. The speed with which Egyptian troops arrived in Yemen suggests, at the very least, a measure of Egyptian connivance, though the timing of the coup itself appeared to be the product of happenstance rather than precise planning. Whatever the truth, such support was required given the narrow base upon which Sallal built his first government. As Halliday notes, 'It included too many unknown faces, too many *Shaffei's* instead of *Zeidis*, too many émigrés from Cairo suspected of being Egyptian nominees, and not enough notables and tribal leaders to impress what was still a deeply conservative and traditional society.[45] The problem was compounded by the fact that despite his military credentials and extolling the ideals of Arab nationalism, his relatively humble background as the son of an artisan deprived Sallal of the requisite respect among the main tribes, a *sine qua non* if their trust was to be gained. Attempts to rectify this by claiming Republican law remained congruent with *Shari'a* failed to undermine the legitimacy of the Imamate among the *Zeidi* Shaykhs. As such, the establishment of a Revolutionary Command Council (RCC) modelled on the UAR, the inclusion of reformers such as Abdurrahman al-Baidani, Moshin al-Aini, Mohammed Ahmed Nomaan and Mohammed al-Zubairi, did little to alter the immediate reality of Yemen as a fragmented polity. Attempts to secure the legitimacy of the regime that at times aped the worst excesses of the Imams Yahya and Ahmed, had little impact. Moreover, the establishment of the YAR never enjoyed the level of support among the more rural Sunni *Shaffei* in the south and west of the country that it had in the cities of Taiz'z, Sana'a and Hodeidah. As Prince Hassan bin Yahya, brother of the late Imam observed, 'They are not fighters. They ask only to be left alone.'[46]

Given such political conditions, the dependence on Egypt to ensure the survival of the YAR became its leitmotif. As the civil war escalated, it became indivisible from Nasser's personal ambition to advance his brand of Arab nationalism, as well as his own national interests, at the expense of the *Hamid'Ud'Din*. Throughout the 1950s, Cairo had certainly done its level best to ingratiate itself with the Royalist court in the years prior to the coup. Aside from Imam al-Badr's flirtation with Nasserism, an Egyptian military mission had been established in Yemen in 1959 which allowed its more radical ideas to influence what little existed of a Yemeni officer corps. Equally, in its reluctant embrace of modernity, Egyptian technicians, advisors, teachers and doctors became a substantial presence in Yemen, particularly in the major towns and cities. But such was Imam Ahmed's suspicion of Egyptian malevolence, that by December 1961, he was publicly attacking Nasser and Arab socialism as ungodly, deriding the Egyptian President's claim that he spoke for all Arabs. By the summer of 1962, Nasser was responding in kind, using the airwaves of Radio Cairo to encourage student protests and urban demonstrations throughout Yemen's main urban centres against the *Hamid'Ud'Din*.[47]

It was hardly surprising therefore that in the aftermath of the Palace coup, Egypt came to dominate the emergent government institutions. Apart from the need to safeguard the Republic, this process was driven by the lack of trained manpower among Yemenis themselves. Equally, this skills deficit among the indigenous labour force allowed Cairo to present its dominance of the newly emerging government structures as an act of benevolence, thereby justifying its presence beyond mere realpolitik. This public face of fraternity soon belied a more sordid reality: Sallal demonstrated little independence from his Egyptian overlords, while at that same time matching the worst excesses of the *ancien régime* in purging those considered to be enemies of the Republic. This included not only supporters of the deposed al-Badr, tribal Shaykhs and other Royal notables, but by 1963, ministers within Sallal's own government. The most notable victim in this regard was al-Zubairi who, until his execution, had occupied the portfolio of Minister of Education. Such actions were backed up by the overwhelming presence of the EEF, its presence in Yemen gaining legitimacy under the Treaty of Mutual Defence signed between Nasser and Sallal on 10 November 1962.

Egyptian intervention was one part of several attempts by Nasser to revive his regional fortunes with the demise of the first, and to date only concerted attempt to place political flesh on the largely rhetorical bones of Arab nationalism: the United Arab Republic. The decision by Syria in 1961 to cede from this union was a bitter blow for the Egyptians. Having championed its creation as the latest step in the dialectic of Arab nationalism, its failure tarnished Nasser's image throughout the Arab world, though not, it must be stated, in Egypt itself.[48] Even so, events in Yemen now took on an added significance. According to Elie Podeh, Nasser was searching '[F]or domestic and foreign compensations. In all likelihood,

Egypt's extensive involvement in the Yemen Civil War . . . was an attempt to somewhat offset the damage of the Syrian succession'.[49]

Others, most notably those associated with the Aden Group, suspected a greater geo-political design being played out. Given the febrile nature of political leadership in Saudi Arabia, Nasser hoped to use the Yemen as a means to subvert the Saudi court, thus making claims on the Kingdom's extensive oil reserves. In the early 1960s, corruption, nepotism and what many Saudis regarded as an abandonment of its strict adherence to the Sunni *Wahhabi* tradition had brought the ruling al-Saud to crisis point. As McLean was to discover, King Saud had lost the confidence of the al-Saud family, and had even courted Nasser in his power struggle with his half-brother, Crown Prince Faisal. For the House of Saud therefore, events in neighbouring Yemen appeared to represent a harbinger of things to come. Seen in this light, Riyadh's vigorous, though for the most part clandestine, support for the restoration of the *Hamid'Ud'Din* was more than just an attempt to thwart the ambitions of the Egyptian President; it was an act of dynastic self-preservation.[50]

For the British government, Cairo's intervention in Yemen appeared more than an attempt by Nasser to appease his own vanity. With his opposition to British imperialism a constant theme of his foreign policy since 1952, the Egyptian President appeared in a powerful position to once more fan the flames of Yemeni irredentism over South Arabia. Successive Imams had based their claim on the fact that Aden and what was known as the Western Protectorate of South Arabia, had, in the seventeenth and eighteenth centuries, been under the suzerainty of the Imamate. This continued claim was deemed by London to be untenable on historical and religious grounds: historically, because the Ottoman authorities who tried to exercise control over Sana'a had defined a notional boundary between Yemen and the Protectorates with the authorities in Aden on the eve of the First World War; religiously because most of the tribal Shaykhs in the Protectorates, having signed treaties with the British as a guarantor of their security and suzerainty, refused to acknowledge the spiritual, let alone temporal authority of the Imamate. London had hoped that the matter had been resolved with the signing of the Treaty of Sana'a in February 1934. While not a formal admission of a defined border between Yemen and the Protectorates it was a public affirmation by London and Sana'a to abide by the terms of the Anglo-Ottoman boundary demarcation for a period of 40 years, during which time it was hoped that a more permanent accord could be brokered.[51]

Hopes that this would assuage the territorial avarice of the *Hamid'Ud'Din* were to be dashed. The exact referent points of the agreed line of demarcation were continuously disputed by both sides, a situation that led London to use air power, and later, locally recruited forces – the

Aden Protectorate Levies – to defend what Aden and London regarded as their rightful boundaries. Even so, the extent to which the Imams could press their claims was limited by the very character of the *Hamid'Ud'Din* and while a unified Yemen was certainly a dream shared by some in Aden, it was not a vision of unity that entertained any role for even a reformed Imamate. This changed, however, with the arrival of Egyptian troops in Yemen. Suddenly, those advocating unity, such as al-Asnaj; were presented with an intoxicating mix of a new order in Sana'a with whom the ATUC could do business, and the ideological foundations on which the dream of unity could be established.

How to deal with Egyptian troops on their Protectorate doorstep now vexed minds in the British Cabinet and provoked intense and acrimonious debate in Whitehall. To recognise the new regime might satiate the rulers in Sana'a but would do little to disabuse the Protectorate rulers of the worst fears of 'perfidious Albion' as London attempted to cohere a more stable Federation to protect its regional and strategic flank. Equally, to not recognise the YAR threatened to exacerbate the age-old claims on unification, claims that now enjoyed growing support among nationalist circles in Aden that threatened the very assets Britain wished to secure. It was the debate over recognition that Britain's future in South Arabia, and the direction and duration of the Yemeni Civil War now hinged.

2
The Legacy of Yemeni Irredentism

The Debate over Recognition of the YAR

In the autumn of 1962, the debate over whether to confer full recognition upon the new Republican Government in Sana'a occupied the minds of the British Cabinet almost as much as parallel events in Cuba. The initial inclination of the Conservative Party leader and Prime Minister, Harold Macmillan, had been to recognise the *de facto* overthrow of the Imamate on condition that the Governor of Aden, Sir Charles Johnston, could persuade the rulers of the Aden and the surrounding Protectorates of South Arabia that this course of action would be in their best interests. While London was quick to identify the scope of the geographic partition of Yemen between Royalist and Republican forces – the former controlling the mountainous terrain mainly to the north and east of the capital, while the Republicans appeared to be in control of the main urban areas, including Sad'ah, Taiz'z and the port of Hodeidah – exactly who exercised control over the bulk of the Yemeni populace remained a contested issue. The evidence available in Whitehall favoured the Republicans. On 31 October 1962, Sir Hugh Stephenson, chairman of the Joint Intelligence Committee (JIC) presented his assessment that the Republican regime in all probability controlled some three-quarters of the total population. Moreover, the military capabilities of the Royalists were confined to sporadic guerrilla operations in the mountainous north and east of the country, actions that were poorly co-ordinated and had little impact on the military superiority of the Republican forces.[1]

The Royalists already appeared to be a busted flush. The Cabinet also noted that Washington, with its policy of courting Nasser, would be most unlikely to take issue with the regime in Sana'a over attacks on Federation territory. Indeed, the Foreign Office argued consistently that failure to recognise the Yemen Arab Republic carried with it the real threat that British diplomatic representation in Taiz'z would be terminated, removing at a stroke 'any chance of influencing the new regime in a direction favourable to our interests in Aden'.[2]

By contrast, Colonial Office officials in Great Smith Street argued that recognition of the Republic would lead to an immediate collapse of morale among pro-British rulers in the protectorate at a time when progress towards establishing the Federation of South Arabia remained finely balanced. Cross-border air raids upon Beihan from aircraft operating from the Yemen had already raised important questions over Britain's political will, as well as military capability to defend the territory of the Protectorates. Although Macmillan concluded that 'recognition of the new regime was sooner or later inevitable', it was decided that the timing of such a move was far from propitious if the plan to merge the Protectorates with Aden Colony was to succeed. Recognition would, however, be considered, though not necessarily conferred, if the new Yemeni government met two conditions: first, that while it was acknowledged that the air attacks on Beihan may have been an unfortunate error due to the ill-defined nature of the border, it should desist from future violations of the border by its aircraft – Britain would in future defend its friends in the region; and second, that Yemen exhort its citizens resident in Aden Colony to desist from political activity detrimental to the internal stability of the Colony.[3]

Some within the government saw recognition as a means to square the diplomatic circle. The Cabinet Secretary, Sir Burke Trend, claimed that recognition of the YAR would not only conflate the interests of Washington and London over ensuring regional stability, but allow pressure to be placed upon Sallal's regime to desist from supporting anti-British activity among the Yemeni community in Aden.[4] At a time of acute superpower tension over events in Cuba, Macmillan remained sensitive to the dangers of Anglo-American discord over the policy towards Yemen. In November 1962, the Prime Minister had a lengthy exchange of letters and telephone calls with President John F. Kennedy, arguing that any open display of Anglo-American disharmony over the Yemen would damage the interests of both London and Washington in the region.

Although cognizant that the issue of non-recognition marked a divergence with the line advocated by Washington, it was clear that the immediate need to cohere a stable Federation from the disparate elements of the Protectorates and Aden Colony determined Britain's immediate priorities and interests. The views of the Colonial Office now proved more influential in determining official British government policy towards the Yemen Civil War, much to the chagrin of the Arabian Department of the Foreign Office. In direct contradiction to the assessment made by the JIC, the government shifted the criteria for recognising the Republic. This would be conferred not only when London was satisfied that Sana'a could claim the allegiance of the majority of its population, but also exercised control over most of its recognised territory. This revision was in no small part due to the influence brought to bear in Cabinet by the reports of one individual whose commitment to the Royalist cause in the Yemen was to remain constant over the next eight years: Lieutenant Colonel Neil 'Billy' McLean, DSO, MP.

It has become fashionable to deride McLean and his associates as little more than right-wing zealots, driven by 'a nostalgia for lost causes' and keen to exact revenge against Nasser for the humiliation of Suez.[5] Christopher Gandy, the British Consul to the Yemeni diplomatic capital of Taiz'z and a man who stood full square behind the cause of recognition referred to them as the 'Aden Group', they 'being survivors of the Suez group which had opposed Eden's agreement with Nasser of 1954 and applauded his attack on Suez in 1956. They viewed Nasser as the Great Satan'.[6] The revanchist nature of the Aden Group was undeniable, but equally it should be recognised that such sentiment was grounded in a sense of patriotic probity which refused to accept a determinism that posited the inevitable triumph of Arab nationalism in general and Nasserism in particular.

In the autumn and winter of 1962–3, the activities of both Gandy, a career diplomat, and McLean came to personify the debate over recognition. Both men provided powerful arguments to back their respective cause. But McLean, while lacking the linguistic skills of his Foreign Office counterpart, enjoyed one great advantage. Unlike Gandy, whose movements remained restricted by the authorities in Sana'a, McLean was able to conduct two extensive tours of the Yemen, visiting Royalist-held areas. His subsequent reports, erudite and for the most part free of the more expressive language usually associated with those promoting a partisan cause carried enough weight for the Cabinet to equivocate over recognition, hesitating to come down on one side or the other while there was a chance that by waiting, longer-term advantage could be garnered from events as they unfolded. As things turned out, events were to take charge of the British.

Recognition: The Early Cabinet Debates

The challenge presented by subversive activity emanating from the Yemen had long exercised concerned minds in Whitehall well before the September 1962 revolution. In pursuit of a territorial irredentism that the authorities in London and Aden regarded as settled under the 1934 Treaty of Sana'a, the Imams of the *Hamid'Ud'Din* continued to sponsor tribal unrest in the Protectorates of South Arabia.[7] More often than not London had replied in kind, sponsoring similar unrest among tribes with grievances against the reigning, Imam and occasionally using air power to silence the more troublesome elements among them.[8] In 1958, with the accession of Yemen to what the Foreign Office referred to as the 'United Arab States', fears grew in Aden that the Machiavellian hand of Cairo was guiding subversion among the tribes of the Aden Protectorates. Such fears, though exaggerated, did have some factual basis. Imam Ahmed's embrace of the United Arab Republic was purely functional, and determined for the most part by the deterrent value it appeared to offer regarding Saudi territorial claims on the Yemen and internal unrest which, irrespective of context, was blamed on the authorities in Aden. By contrast, the idea of Nasserism, with its ill-defined yet compelling vision of Arab socialism, remained anathema to a monarchical order notorious for its antediluvian character. Prior to succeeding his father as Imam however, Mohammed al-Badr had been the most enthusiastic among the *Hamid'Ud'Din* regarding ties with Nasser. It has often been assumed that while he moved quickly to shore up Sallal following the palace coup, Nasser played no role in events leading up to overthrow of the Imamate itself.[9] While the timing of palace coup may have caught the Egyptian leader off guard, evidence exists, albeit subjective, that for some time Nasser had in fact been encouraging subversive activities against the erstwhile feudal order in Yemen.

During the course of an audience with al-Badr in December 1962, McLean made a detailed written record of what he termed the 'Imam's Confession', in effect an éxpose by the newly deposed Imam of his links with Nasser up until the death of his father. These dated back to 1958 when, during a trip to Cairo to negotiate Yemen's accession to the newly formed UAR, Nasser proposed to al-Badr that 'he should carry out a coup d'état in the Yemen against his father'. To expedite this action, Nasser promised al-Badr two cases of pistols, E£25,000 and a further £50,000 sterling. By his own account al-Badr accepted Nasser's offer but 'when the time came, was not able to implement his side of the bargain'. According to al-Badr, the coup was meant to be the first step of a two-stage plan. Once the coup had been completed successfully, 'Yemen would be used as a base by Nasser in alliance with al-Badr for political and subversive operations in Arabia and the Gulf.'[10]

He also detailed further discussions he had with Egyptian officials in Alexandria, including the future Egyptian President Anwar Sadat, and the Egyptian Chief of Staff, Hakim Amr in which the overthrow of King Saud was openly discussed. Nasser, at this point, even offered the services of 'Algerian commandos and saboteurs' who, working under al-Badr, could help ferment unrest throughout Arabia. His father, however, had become suspicious of al-Badr's tryst with Cairo and what he coinsidered the alarming increase in the number of apostate Soviet and Chinese contractors engaged in infrastructure projects inside the Yemen. In a subsequent telegram to Nasser, Imam Ahmed accused the Egyptian President of encouraging his son's dependence on the two great communist powers. Naturally, the Egyptian President denied the charge but according to al-Badr's account, continued in secret to advocate mounting a palace coup.

In the spring of 1962, Egyptian intelligence tried to smuggle a shipment of weapons to al-Badr for this purpose, but the discovery of the arms, disguised as road construction equipment, plus rather premature rumours emanating from Cairo that a coup against the Imam was imminent, undermined the plot. Al-Badr 'confessed all to his father' who, in response, sought to negotiate Yemen's entry into the Ta'if Pact, a defence agreement signed between King Hussein of Jordan and King Saud on 29 August 1962. These diplomatic moves, authorised just three weeks before his death, also saw Imam Ahmed seek to distance the Yemen from reliance upon Soviet and Chinese development aid. According to the 'confession', al-Badr had been instructed in the weeks leading up to his father's death to improve relations with London, seek development loans from Washington and technical assistance from West Germany.[11]

This confession was undoubtedly self-serving, as it was aimed at securing British material support. With its allusion to Moscow's malign involvement under the cloak of Egyptian subterfuge, it portrayed a worse-case scenario should London choose to negate its responsibilities towards the Royalist cause. Equally however, al-Badr's comments had a veracity to them that appeared to be of a piece with suspicions long held by officials in Aden. In May 1962, the Governor of Aden, Sir Charles Johnstone, had warned London that Nasser sought to ferment trouble in the Protectorates by supporting Yemeni territorial claims. Although dismissing any overt military threat to the outlying Protectorates that came to form the territorial bulk of the Federation in January 1963, he concluded that, 'while no doubt Nasser would prefer to play a game of subversion, the possibility must still be born in mind that he could revive military attacks against the frontier, which need to be answered by appropriate measures'.[12] The 'measures' Johnstone proposed included mine laying, hot pursuit operations and what the telegram refers to euphemistically as 'special operations' and 'counter-subversion' on the Yemen side of the border. Clearance for such operations lay firmly with London, but Johnston was making it clear that the time was fast approaching when recourse to such measures, however distasteful to the diplomatic palate, had to be considered as a serious policy option.

Of particular concern to the Colonial Office was the fear that failure to act with resolution against any violation of the 1934 boundary would undermine the viability of the Federation and in particular, the authority of tribal Shaykhs who had allied themselves closely with British policy.

When the Imam escaped to the mountains north of the capital following the coup led by Colonel Abdullah as-Sallal, the issue of border stability was thrust very much to the fore. Meeting on 23 October 1962 to discuss the implications of the revolution for Britain's position in South Arabia, the Cabinet decided in principle to offer recognition provided that Johnstone could persuade the rulers of the Aden Protectorates that such a move was in their best interests. It is doubtful if the Colonial Office were either convinced that such an approach would work, or indeed approved of such an overture. They need not have worried. Meeting three days later to review the situation further, the Cabinet was informed that the Sultanate of Beihan, a Protectorate adjacent to the Yemen had been attacked by Yemeni aircraft. Moreover, intelligence information received subsequently indicated that tribes loyal to the Imam were fighting back and had successfully ambushed a column of Republican troops close to Marib in the east of Yemen.[13]

With hindsight, this Cabinet meeting, chaired by Prime Minister Harold Macmillan, was of great importance. It delayed the issue of recognition until a later date, claiming that recognition amid ongoing attacks on the Protectorates to whom London had defence obligations would appear defeatist. Furthermore, the attack on Marib demonstrated that the Republican regime did not command the loyalty of a substantial portion of the Yemeni population, a prerequisite if Her Majesty's Government was to offer formal recognition.

On 31 October, the Cabinet met once again to discuss the Yemen. Johnston had sent a cable that cast doubt on his ability to persuade the 'Rulers of Aden' that it was in their best interests to accept London's recognition of the new regime in Sana'a. Already, the United States Ambassador in Amman had suggested that recognition could be linked to a withdrawal of Egyptian forces which had already begun to arrive in Yemen in support of Sallal. In a report to London, Johnston suggested that the morale of the Egyptian forces was low, a view that was not supported by the intelligence assessment presented by Sir Hugh Stephenson, a Foreign Office diplomat who chaired the Joint Intelligence Committee. Stephenson, armed with signals intelligence intercepts produced by the General Communications Headquarters (GCHQ) noted that Field Marshal Amr had reported the morale of the troops to be high, with the scale of losses among Egyptian troops clearly exaggerated. Macmillan concluded that recognition was inevitable but that it should be made clear to Sana'a that any further attacks on the Protectorates, or indeed further Yemeni support for political agitation in Aden Colony itself would not be tolerated. Macmillan concluded, 'If the Yemeni authorities responded to this, and the situation in Yemen improved as a result, it would be possible to contemplate recognition with more confidence than was the case now. If they did not respond, there would be greater justification for continuing to withhold recognition.'[14]

Within the Cabinet, Defence Secretary Peter Thorneycroft and Duncan Sandys were the most forthright in opposing recognition of the YAR. In bureaucratic terms, both represented ministries which had invested the most in Aden and the Protectorates. But the opponents of recognition also enjoyed the advantage of more personal, intimate ties, both in government and beyond. As the Minister for Aviation, Julian Amery occupied a portfolio outside of the full cabinet; as Macmillan's son-in-law, however, he had direct access to the inner workings of the Cabinet, a position he used to confront what he regarded as the defensive attitude of a Foreign Office that appeared set on appeasing Nasser. Their defensive attitude was shared, according to the historian and writer Tom Bower, by the head of the Secret Intelligence Service (SIS), Sir Dick White.[15] White is listed as having attended both the October Cabinet meetings. His advice is not recorded directly but, according to Bower, he demonstrated considerable antipathy towards any suggestion from Amery that SIS engage in 'cloak and dagger' operations inside the Yemen. The erstwhile Minister for Aviation was cut from different cloth. His experiences as a member of the Special Operations Executive (SOE) in Albania during the Second World War, where he had served alongside McLean, had instilled in him the belief that covert action and para-diplomacy could be legitimate and effective tools of foreign policy.[16] These tools were now employed not only to undermine the case for recognition in Cabinet, but to try and effect a full British alignment with the Royalist cause. Towards this end, King Hussein of Jordan proved to be a more than willing accomplice.

Undermining Recognition: The Early Attempts

Mutual antipathy marked bilateral relations between Egypt and Jordan at the beginning of the 1960s. Since 1957, Hussein had been forced to implement a series of repressive measures against pro-Nasser elements in the Kingdom following an attempted coup by army officers, orchestrated he believed, by Cairo. These were often desperate times. The overthrow of Jordan's closest regional ally, the Hashemite monarchy in Iraq in the summer of 1958, forced Amman to approach both London and Washington for direct military assistance. The arrival of a brigade of British paratroopers did much to steady the frayed nerves of the Hashemite monarchy, but until the spring of 1959, King Hussein ruled by absolute decree throughout the Kingdom.[17] Even with the restoration of a modicum of parliamentary rule by the end of 1959, the political future of Jordan looked precarious. The monarchy appeared anachronistic when set against the tide of Arab nationalist feeling convulsing the region and was given political expression in the political union between Damascus and Cairo on 1 February 1958. As Zaki Shalom notes:

> In his struggle against the Hashemite Kingdom and King Hussein in particular, President Nasser employed various means, all of them intended to bring about the downfall of the Hashemite regime, or, at least, to destabilise it . . . In his struggle against the Hashemite leadership Nasser employed various tactics (in addition to propaganda warfare). These included assassination attempts on Jordanian personalities known to be loyal to the Hashemite regime, and stirring up civil disturbances and disorder. Egypt's control over Syria greatly improved its ability to carry out insurgency operations within Jordan.[18]

Given such undisguised animus, it came as little surprise that the collapse of the Union between Egypt and Syria on 28 September 1961, following yet another military coup in Damascus, was greeted with euphoria in Amman. Jordan recognised the new government in Syria the following day, an act that was, according to Uriel Dan, 'a bitter humiliation for Abdel Nasser'.[19] Throughout the remainder of 1961 and well into 1962, mutual rancour defined relations between Cairo and Amman. Dan has argued that much of the invective aimed at Cairo was ill-considered, not least because the Jordanian monarch failed to appreciate that Nasser had 'geared his world, ideological and political, to "Arab socialism" rather than "nationalism" with a consequent shift of attention to [Egyptian] domestic affairs'. Instead, King Hussein continued to regard Nasser as an 'unregenerate' and never lost an opportunity to remind the Egyptian President of his diplomatic humiliation.[20] But Hussein, ever aware of the vicissitudes of regional politics now looked to secure the Hashemite dynasty by strengthening strategic ties with Riyadh. The result, the Ta'if pact, with its attendant communiqué declaring 'complete military union' was perceived by Nasser as a calculated snub to Cairo. Before this declaration of intent could be translated into a martial reality however, events in the Yemen intervened.

From the outset, Hussein made it clear his sympathies lay with those seeking the restoration of the Imamate. With Cairo's recognition of the new regime on 29 September 1962, and the subsequent despatch of an expeditionary force to shore up the new Republican regime, the Jordanian monarch looked to promote more proactive measures to defeat what he regarded as little more than the latest example of Egyptian aggrandisement. In the first instance, this involved direct overtures to an ailing King Saud 'to intervene in force in Yemen before it was too late.'[21] While direct military intervention in the Yemen remained beyond the political, let alone military capabilities of Saudi Arabia, the appointment of Crown Prince Faisal as Prime Minister on 17 October 1962 did much to stiffen resolve in a Saudi court that appeared vulnerable to Cairo's intrigues. More immediately however, Hussein turned to London and the key political figure within the Aden Group, Julian Amery.

Amery had remained wary of Foreign Office reports concerning the Yemen, an opinion no doubt reinforced by the fact that Stephenson, a Foreign Office mandarin, chaired the JIC. The spate of air attacks on Beihani territory in October 1962 had elicited urgent calls from Middle East Command in Aden for permission to conduct reconnaissance flights over the Yemen to identify the strength and capability of Egyptian and Yemeni air assets in theatre. These calls had been rebutted by the JIC. In a memorandum of 23 October circulated in Cabinet, it was noted by the JIC that 'they were already in receipt of a great deal of first class intelligence from special sources'. Reconnaissance flights would add little to an understanding of the Egyptian order of battle and might even exacerbate relations at a time when the issue of recognition had not been decided.[22]

Such reasoning cut little ice with the Minister for Aviation. He was looking for information that would confirm his conviction that the Royalist forces not only held large swathes of the Yemen, but also remained a viable fighting force that could lay claim to outside support. On the outbreak of the conflict in Yemen Amery was reputed to have stated, '[I]f I were Hussein, I would do everything to keep Nasser occupied and involved in Yemen – that is where he will have his difficulties'.[23] In the early autumn of 1962 King Hussein met Amery at Claridge's Hotel in London. Amery, through dint of his father Sir Leopold Amery, had long been a close associate of the Hashemite monarchy. It was, in effect, a meeting of minds. The King impressed upon Amery the folly of recognition, noting that Cairo's intervention in support of Sallal was but a first step in the overthrow of the dynastic orders of the Middle East.[24]

At the instigation of Amery, Hussein now agreed to sponsor a trip by Neil McLean to the region to assess first hand the state of the Royalist forces.[25] The Member of Parliament for Inverness was already known to the King, having met him during a brief visit to Amman in the aftermath of the Suez crisis.[26] On 21 October 1962, McLean embarked upon a whirlwind journey that was to take in Jordan, Saudi Arabia, Aden and Yemen in a period of nine days and while the Cabinet was still deliberating the whole issue of recognition.[27] The reports he wrote as a result of his journey proved to be far more detailed and far more influential in Cabinet than anything produced hitherto by the Foreign Office. Having arrived in Amman, McLean remained keen to elicit the views of both Jordanians and European diplomats alike over the situation in the Yemen. Protocol dictated however that his first port of call would be King Hussein. Over luncheon, the Jordanian potentate revealed to McLean that the situation for the Royalists in the Yemen remained 'critical' and that the key to their future lay in securing Saudi support. Nonetheless, Hussein, according to McLean's record of the meeting, believed that 'King Saud had lost his nerve'.[28] Hussein, by contrast, had already begun to translate his convictions into practical support for the Royalist forces. It was later revealed to McLean that in the month of October 1962 alone, Jordan had supplied Imam al-Badr with 10,000 rifles, 1.8 million rounds of small arms ammunition, some anti-aircraft guns and anti-tank weapons.[29]

Later the same day, McLean had a meeting with Sir Roderick Parkes, the British Ambassador to Amman. Parkes expressed sympathy with the position of King Hussein but remained far more judicious in his assessment over the ability of Jordan, let alone anyone else, to alter the course of events in Yemen. The British Embassy reported that Hussein's support for the Imamate ran counter to popular opinion, at least among his Palestinian subjects, who appeared to stand squarely behind the UAR. Christopher Gandy noted that the position of the Jordanian monarch 'will, I imagine, raise his West Bankers against him'.[30] By contrast, the views of the Italian Ambassador to Jordan, Armando Ghia, matched those of King Hussein. He had formerly been Rome's ambassador in Taiz'z and was present in Sana'a when the coup d'état occurred. As such, his assessment carried some weight with McLean, not least because he was well acquainted with the personalities who now comprised the Republican government. In his view, Sallal was 'a useless man' and as such, his ability to retain his grip on power remained dependent on the continued support of the 'Free Yemeni Movement', a Cairo trained cadre of political leaders of whom, in his opinion, Major General Hamud al-Jaifi, Mohammed Mahmud Zubeiri and Abdel Qarim al-Ainsi were the most able and politically astute. Aside from these men, the regime remained weak and with its predominantly *Shaffei* composition, unlikely ever to command the loyalty of the *Zeidi* tribes. The policy commended to McLean was direct and to the point: no recognition of Sallal, withdraw support and boycott Sallal, help the Imam and the opposition.[31]

Such views, however welcome, would remain little more than empty sentiment unless King Saud could be shaken from his lassitude and stirred towards taking more pro-active measures. In November 1956, Saudi Arabia had severed diplomatic ties with London over the Suez affair, though resentment over its expulsion by Britain from the Buraimi Oasis in October 1955 – territory London claimed for the Sultanate of Oman – had long soured bilateral relations. Now King Hussein urged McLean to visit Riyadh. A visit to Saudi Arabia had not been part of the planned itinerary but McLean grasped the opportunity. It proved to be an act of para-diplomacy that helped pave the way for the restoration of diplomatic ties. On 22 October 1962, McLean arrived in Riyadh. While the rest of the world remained gripped by the imminent prospect of a nuclear apocalypse, the Briton remained focused on securing Saudi support to defeat the Egyptian nemesis in Yemen. McLean produced two accounts of his meeting with the Saudi monarch. The first, written in the immediate aftermath of the meeting and cabled to the Colonial Secretary Duncan Sandys on his arrival in Aden on 26 October, was decidedly upbeat. According to the telegram, the King revealed his belief that unless Cairo's territorial malevolence was countered in the Yemen 'there will be an immediate and serious threat to security in the whole of the Arabian peninsula'. The telegram continued, 'H. M. G. should therefore not recognise the rebel government of Sallal but give all possible support to the Imam who is the head of the recognised legal government of the Yemen.'[32]

Those opposing recognition in London could not have hoped for a better response. The icing on the cake was the revelation that the Saudis were anxious to re-establish diplomatic ties with London, the caveat being that some progress be made over the Buraimi dispute, it being deemed 'necessary to safeguard his [King Saud's] prestige among the Saudi people'. Already, the former Saudi Ambassador to the Court of St James, Hafiz Wahba, had proposed a return to the frontiers occupied by both sides prior to 1955, with the Saudis giving their word not to reoccupy the territory. The restoration of ties was not made a sine qua non. 'The King said that with or without diplomatic relations, Saudi Arabia was on Britain's side and he hoped for the closest co-operation on the Yemen question.' On receipt of this telegram, Sandys moved quickly to distribute copies among his Cabinet colleagues. It made a particular impression on Macmillan's Private Secretary, Philip de Zulueta, who argued that the loss of diplomatic ties with Sana'a would be more than offset by the renewal of ties with Saudi Arabia.[33] Macmillan, however, was to prove more cautious in his appraisal.

The telegram was selective in the information it divulged, in particular concerning Saudi resolve. Soon after his return to London on 2 November, McLean produced a more detailed report, whose description of conditions in the Saudi court and the mental and physical condition of King Saud was less than flattering:

King Saud wore dark glasses, talked slowly in a deep voice and moved with heavy and lethargic gestures. His huge yellow hands hung relaxed over the arms of his leopard skin chair but when he was talking they shook strongly like a man in the early stages of Parkinson's disease. By his side was an old wooden box radio set permanently tuned, it is said, to Riyadh Radio, although I privately suspected it was on Radio Israel [*Kol Yisrael* – The voice of Israel] which all in the palace listen to secretly but avidly . . . He also has a nervous gesture of adjusting his head dress when discussing a tricky point, and also keeps taking of his dark glasses to reveal pale watery eyes . . . Strangely enough, he has a strong and deep laugh which contradicts his effete and generally rather sloblike appearance.[34]

Whether McLean was fully aware of the struggle for power between King Saud, with his authoritarian views, and the more reform-minded Crown Prince Faisal is unclear.[35] He was certainly disappointed that a scheduled meeting with the Crown Prince was cancelled without good reason. It was a time of great paranoia in Riyadh – during a meeting with General Habis Mejali, commander of the Jordanian military mission to Saudi Arabia (a body established under the Ta'if pact), McLean learnt of the febrile state of the Saudi armed forces. The air force remained grounded because the al-Saud doubted the political fidelity of its officers, many of whom had been trained in Egypt. Such suspicions also encompassed the Saudi army. Numbering only 20,000, the political leanings of many of the junior officers remained suspect, while whole units based in Kuwait had, according to Mejali, succumbed to the siren-like allure of 'Nasserite propaganda'. Only the *Jaysh al-Abiad* – the White Guard – drawn from the most loyal of the *Wahabbi* tribes – could be counted upon to defend the regime. While similar in strength to the army, they lacked heavy weaponry and the little that was available was, on the whole, poorly maintained. The sum total of Jordanian–Saudi military co-operation appeared to consist of Amman 'unloading inferior military equipment on Saudis and Saudis [sic] unloading even more inferior stuff on Yemenis'.[36] The inactivity of the Jordanian military mission was such that Mejali had recommended their recall to Amman, an act Hussein refused to condone lest it unnerve King Saud still further and undermine efforts to supply the Royalist forces.[37]

It must have been a disconcerted McLean who returned to Amman on 24 October. Atrophy marked the political atmosphere in Riyadh and the suggestion by McLean that he travel directly from Riyadh to the mountains of north Yemen to ascertain the situation for himself was politely but firmly refused by the Saudi monarch on specious grounds. Israeli jets were reported to have shot down six aircraft, tension was high and travel by air down to the border with Yemen was to be discouraged. This concern over McLean's safety did not however extend to lending the Briton use of King Saud's private aircraft to fly back to Amman. Back in Jordan, McLean made immediate arrangements to travel to Aden in an aircraft loaned by the Jordanian monarch. Arriving in Aden on 25 October, McLean launched himself into a round of meetings with officials from Government House, military figures and leaders from the Aden Protectorates.

While McLean was heartened by the more belligerent mood he found in Aden, the verbal reports concerning the state of Royalist resistance were not always encouraging. Sir Charles Johnston noted the lacuna that marked the Royalist leadership. Crown Prince Hassan, the uncle of the Imam, had initially assumed the mantle of Imam on the assumption of the violent demise of his nephew and as such, was perceived as a man of great moral and political authority. The reality paled next to the image. It was an assessment that McLean soon came to share. He had failed to stamp his authority on the Royalist tribes, particularly in the area around Sad'ah. Johnston also detailed the tremendous pressure he had been placed under by the rulers in the Protectorates to retaliate for the Yemeni bombing of the Beihan, a position that London did not fully appreciate. Air Marshal Sir Charles Ellsworthy, Commander in Chief of Middle East Command, believed that the recent air attack that had elicited these protestations had probably been a mistake. Even so, Ellsworthy was outspoken in his belief that recognition of Sallal, which he feared London would 'drift into', should be withheld if the British position in Aden was to be secured.[38]

Such forthright views were shared by Brigadier James Lunt, Officer Commanding the Federal Regular Army (FRA). Lunt made it clear that should Sallal be allowed to consolidate his regime the threat from the Yemen would evolve through three consecutive stages: military incursions into areas surrounding the Protectorate towns of Beihan, Dahla, and Mukeiras; guerilla infiltration into the Allaqi Sultanate and Lower Yafai; and increased disaffection among troops of the FRA, many of who were recruited from the tribes in these areas. This would lead to the collapse of the FRA as an effective military organisation able to ensure the security of the Protectorates and future of the Federation. All British officials made it clear that while the Protectorates had always faced Yemeni-inspired insurrection, Cairo's intervention in support of Sallal now presented them with a threat of an altogether different magnitude. It was an assessment impressed upon McLean most forcefully by Kenneth Trevaskis, Provincial Governor of the West Aden Protectorate and destined to succeed Johnston once the Protectorates had merged with Aden to form the Federation of South Arabia in 1963. It was during these discussions that McLean made the acquaintance of the aide-de-camp of the Governor, Flight Lieutenant Anthony Boyle, who was to play such an active part in furnishing aid to the Royalists from the spring of 1963 onwards.[39]

The meetings with British officials certainly stiffened McLean's resolve but supplied little in terms of hard factual information regarding conditions *inside* the Yemen. This paucity of knowledge was not restricted to the Colonial Office officials in Aden. British intelligence as a whole remained woefully ill-informed regarding the situation inside the Yemen, not only regarding Egyptian military deployment but also concerning the very fabric of Yemeni society: its tribal structures and their corresponding allegiances. In particular, SIS had been found wanting, with only one officer, Hubert O'Bryan Tear, stationed in Aden. His knowledge of the Yemen was slight, a position not helped by the fact that despite Johnston's early concerns over Egyptian-backed subversion, the level of threat was deemed insufficient in Broadway, the headquarters of SIS, to warrant the despatch of an individual 'up country' with all the privations this would entail.[40]

As such, McLean was now more determined than ever to enter Yemen to make his own appraisal of the situation. He was supported in this course of action by Trevaskis as well as Shariff Hussein of Beihan and his son Emir Sallah. On 27 October 1962, having flown by an RAF transport plane to Beihan, McLean crossed the border into the Yemen for the first time. He was accompanied by two Land Rovers provided by the Emir, each carrying an escort and translators to help expedite his passage. His journey took him through the towns of Harib, Marib and the region of al-Jawf close to Sana'a, as well as to the mountains of north Yemen. With hindsight, it was an incredibly bold venture. McLean knew relatively little about the eddies of tribal politics and could never be sure where the loyalties of a particular group actually lay. He arrived in the Saudi border town of Najran on 29 October, the first European to have visited the Royalist forces and assessed independently their strengths and weaknesses. As no direct communication link then existed between Najran and Amman, McLean immediately cabled General Majali in Riyadh with a message to be passed on to King Hussein. He in turn, passed the cable on to Sir Roderick Parkes for onward transmission to London. It read:

> [K]indly notify Aden and my country that I have crossed in all freedom and safety by car, from Beihan through Harib, Ma'areb [sic] and al-Jouf [sic] to Najran, to find all these areas under the control of the Tribes supporting the Imam. All these tribes areas are in the Yemen, and practically all the tribes have joined the Royalists and are fighting very severely the Republicans and Egyptians. I met with many of their leaders and saw many of the tribes moving towards Sana'a.[41]

Among the leaders he saw, the two most important were Ahmed al-Siyaghi, the Deputy Prime Minister and Minister of the Interior of the Royalist government, and Crown Prince Hassan, the Imam's uncle. Based in the recently captured town of Harib, al-Siyaghi left a deep impression upon McLean and embodied the progressive ideals that he hoped the Royalist leadership should aspire to. Siyaghi 'greatly impressed me with his intelligence, toughness and his skill in dealing with the tribes'. He was also unique in being the only commoner to command a position of responsibility in the Royalist hierarchy. He represented a hope that should the Imamate be restored, its power would be devolved to those best able to counter its hitherto antiquated and cruel nature. To this end, his political credentials were impeccable. His opposition to the styptic rule of the late Imam Ahmed had previously forced him into exile in Aden but, 'He believed like many other opponents of the former regime that Sallal and the Egyptians were totally unacceptable to almost all Yemenis'. Al-Siyaghi believed that the Palace coup had deprived Imam al-Badr of the requisite time 'to prove whether or not he was willing and able to put into effect the much needed reforms he had indicated he would undertake.'[42]

By contrast, McLean's impressions of Prince Hassan and the tribes over whom he claimed allegiance were decidedly poor. With his headquarters located in close proximity to Sad'ah in northern Yemen, the Briton expressed surprise that, given the level of resentment openly demonstrated towards Sallal and the Egyptians in the surrounding hills, the town had not succumbed to tribes loyal to the Crown Prince. McLean noted that 'I could not help feeling that Prince Hassan has been very dilatory in his advance towards Sada and with more dynamic leadership on his part he could have captured Sada by now.'[43] The uneven nature of the Royalist leadership was, however, not the most pressing issue, which remained the loyalty of the tribes, and on McLean's reckoning, all the tribes in East Yemen 'had declared for the Imam' while increasing numbers in the mountains of the north were beginning to rally around the Royalist banner. Despite holding the main cities, McLean argued that ultimate political power in Yemen lay with the tribes and not the towns. He concluded:

> Sana is not the key to the Yemen, like Cairo is to Egypt or Damascus is to Syria; for of the Yemen's population of between 4 and 5 million, perhaps not more than 150,000 unarmed people including women and children live in the towns – the remainder being villagers or tribesmen, most of whom are armed and warlike. It is said the tribes can put into the field anything between 100,000 and 200,000 armed men.[44]

McLean strongly believed that the situation was 'more favourable than is thought in Aden or in London', and his reports from the field certainly carried with them the courage of this particular conviction.[45] His circuitous cable arrived in the hands of Duncan Sandys on 31 October just prior to another meeting of the Cabinet convened to discuss the Yemen. The minutes of the meeting contain no direct reference to McLean's report though it is clear that some of the information discussed, most notably the position of the Royalist tribes in the north and east of the country, equates with the information he had provided the Colonial Secretary. Even so, the whip hand appeared to remain with those advocating recognition. The report presented by the chairman of the JIC, Sir Hugh Stephenson, directly contradicted McLean's assessment that most of the population remained outside the writ of the Republican regime. In the view of the JIC, Sana'a, with its control firmly established in the south and east of the country, controlled three-quarters of the total population, more than enough to confer full recognition of the YAR under the government's own criteria.

Macmillan concluded that recognition of the new regime 'was sooner or later inevitable', noting that 'there was no real prospect that Royalist forces would now conquer the country'. But while the momentum appeared to be with those advocating recognition, Macmillan had to assuage the Protectorate rulers that such a course of action remained in their best interests. To this end, Macmillan condoned an approach to Sana'a that linked recognition with two key concessions on the part of the YAR authorities: that it cease attacks on Protectorate territory; and do all in its power to discourage Yemenis living and working in Aden from engaging in subversive activities.[46] Despite the presence of Sandys and Thorneycroft in the Cabinet meeting, both staunch opponents of recognition, it appeared that the establishment of diplomatic ties with the YAR was now just a matter of time. Desperate times required desperate measures and McLean now took a dramatic step.

Foiling Recognition

Just prior to his return to London, McLean had been granted another audience with King Saud in Riyadh. From his typed notes of the meeting, it is clear that McLean was already considering the means by which a guerrilla campaign against the YAR and its Egyptian backers could be waged. While the Royalist forces had clearly enjoyed some success in the field, they lacked co-ordination, proper training and heavy weaponry. He made five key recommendations to the Saudi monarch which included the supply of mortars and anti-tank weapons, the need to cut lines of communication between Sana'a and the main cities of Taiz'z and Hodeidah, and for adequate training for the Royalist insurgents to be provided forthwith. To this end, the Saudi border town of Najran had already been identified as a suitable location.[47]

But McLean realised that attempts to rectify the piecemeal effort of the Royalist campaign would come to nought if London continued on the path of recognition. In his discussions with King Saud, the Briton had highlighted the importance of sound 'Public Relations' in the battle to prevent international recognition of the YAR. While Riyadh could try to exercise some influence over Washington, a coherent propaganda campaign was required that would allow pro-Royalist reports to appear in both the Arabic-language and English press. McLean now acted on his own advice. On 6 November 1962, he published a lengthy article in *The Daily Telegraph*, entitled 'With the Loyalists in the Yemen'. The article was almost a complete reprise of the telegram marked 'Top Secret' that McLean had sent to both Duncan Sandys and Foreign Secretary Alec Douglas-Home on 31 October. Although intended to rouse wider public debate over events in Yemen, the real object of the piece was to mobilise the rank and file of the parliamentary Conservative and Unionist Party. They alone had the power to impress upon their Cabinet colleagues the folly of recognition. Having given details of his trip, including interviews with captured Egyptian paratroopers who had apparently been sent by Nasser to Yemen in the belief that they were to fight the British, the article concluded:

> I believe that the right course for Britain is to refuse to recognise Brig [sic] Sallal, at least until he has proved that he can stand on his own feet without having to rely upon the Egyptian troops and aeroplanes to keep him in power. In conjunction with our allies, we should do what we can to ensure the withdrawal of the Egyptian forces now intervening in the internal affairs of the Yemen, and we should give all the support we can to the Imam, who heads the legal Government and who still controls the greater part of the country. The only alternative is to accept the increasing threat to Aden and the Persian Gulf.[48]

This was the first of many articles that McLean, and later his comrade-in-arms from the SOE, Colonel David Smiley, were to write for the press over the next eight years. Their journalistic endeavours extolled the virtues of Royalist resistance while highlighting the malign intent of Cairo and the atrocities committed by their forces, such as the indiscriminate use of napalm. This foray into Fleet Street appeared to pay some immediate political dividend. Three days after his article appeared, McLean wrote to Crown Prince Faisal that 'I believe that the powers that be here [in the UK] have now had second thoughts about Sallal's regime and the Egyptian intervention in the Yemen.'[49] Events within the Saudi court certainly helped McLean's position. By the end of October 1962, Faisal had effectively usurped the power of King Saud. Holding the portfolios of Prime Minister and Foreign Minister, Faisal now exercised total control over the Council of Ministers, the key decision-making body in the Kingdom. In the aftermath of Suez, Faisal had entertained hopes of a more open policy towards Egypt and Nasser and believed Saudi Arabia could act to 'bridge the gap between the West and Arab Nationalism'.[50] Such hopes came to be dashed by, successively, the crisis over Kuwait in 1961, and Cairo's intervention in support of the YAR. With the zeal of a convert, Faisal's willingness to counter Nasser's designs in the Yemen conflated with the ideas of McLean and found practical expression in his willingness to act upon the recommendations the Briton had made to King Saud on 30 October. Two weeks later, Hafiz Wahba disclosed to McLean the extent of Saudi aid now flowing to the Imam. This included 15,000 rifles, some mortars, bazookas and anti-aircraft guns as well as £200,000 worth of gold sovereigns and the extension of credit worth nearly E£2million for the purchase of Mother Theresa dollars in Aden and Ethiopia. Wahba promised a further 30,000 rifles would be delivered to the Royalist forces by 8 January 1963.[51]

The *Daily Telegraph* report was, unsurprisingly, greeted with enthusiasm in Aden. Copies were circulated among officials with Trevaskis offering McLean fulsome praise for his journalistic endeavours. In a letter to McLean dated 21 November 1962 he restated his belief that London should, at all costs, continue to withhold recognition, noting the parlous state of Egyptian forces. He continued, 'What could save them [the Egyptian army] would be recognition of the Republicans by H. M. G and the United States which would have the effect of doing grave damage to Loyalist morale'.[52] In reality, there was little McLean could do to influence decision-making in Washington but his own party provided a fertile arena in which the seeds of opposition to recognition could take firm root. He had already determined to return to the Yemen at the earliest opportunity. While his first trip had been intensive, it had, until the publication of the *Daily Telegraph* article, remained undisclosed to all but a small coterie of associates. By contrast, McLean ensured that his second trip was known in advance to senior members of his own party who were best placed to stiffen resolve in Cabinet and against those in the Foreign Office who, in the words of Trevaskis were 'searching for reasons to do nothing'.[53] For the Royalist cause to gain support in London, McLean realised that he had to meet Imam al-Badr and demonstrate the efficacy of his leadership among the tribes. With his political course set, McLean arrived back in the Middle East on 1 December 1962.

Amman was his first port of call. King Hussein remained as determined as ever to confront Nasser in the Yemen and the notes taken by McLean of the meeting reveal a convergence of views. Like the Briton, the Hashemite monarch was concerned that the Imam remained conspicuous by his absence. As such, he confirmed McLean in his wider belief that Royalist propaganda had to be placed on a firm footing. But talking a good fight remained somewhat removed from actually engaging in one. The contours of a guerrilla war were already making themselves apparent, but with his experience of irregular warfare in harsh terrain amid a fractured society, McLean understood the value of secure lines of supply, adequate training and proper communication. McLean discussed the potential of suitable personnel from both Jordan and the Protectorates to supervise the training of tribesman in heavy weaponry. The outcome of this discussion was not recorded, though in time some Jordanian officers, operating under cover of the Jordanian Military Mission, did help train Royalist tribesman in the Saudi town of Najran. The idea of approaching the Shah of Iran for military aid was also discussed between the two men for the first time.[54]

After his brief sojourn in Amman, McLean arrived in Riyadh where he

met Crown Prince Faisal. It was clear to the Briton that the Saudi potentate now held the whip hand in matters of national security; where King
Saud had been obscurant over McLean's initial plans to enter the Yemen
through Saudi Arabia, Faisal did all he could to facilitate the journey, even
flying McLean down to Jizan in his own private plane. Here he became
acquainted with the growing logistic set-up to funnel aid to the Royalists
under the command of Crown Prince Mohammed Sudairi. After the al-
Saud, the Sudairis remained the most powerful family in the Kingdom and
had assumed control of the 'Yemen Operation' in both Jizzan and Najran.
Although keen to see the restoration of the Imamate, Prince Mohammed
and his brother Prince Turki, the Governor of Jizzan maintained separate,
though discreet ties with the Yemeni tribes. Ostensibly, this was a logical
step should anything untoward happen to Imam al-Badr but as the civil
war continued, it also allowed Riyadh to manipulate Royalist politics
towards their own designs.[55]

On 4 December McLean, again accompanied by two Land Rovers with
escort, crossed into the Yemen. His journey took him deep into Royalist-
held areas and meetings with the main Royalist commanders, most of
whom were related to the Imam. Politically however, the most important
encounter was with the Imam, Mohammed al-Badr, at a camp located 'a
few miles inside the Yemen and about 30–35 miles west of Sada'.
Conditions here left something to be desired. No attempt had been made
to camouflage the camp and as such, few precautions had been taken
against the ever-present threat of air attack. There existed only one small
slit trench 'which had been dug next to Imam's latrine – and judging by
its smell and appearance – seems to have confused some of the camp
followers as to its proper use'. The rather primitive nature of these ablu-
tions aside, McLean remained nonplussed by the Imam's personal
qualities:

> The Imam himself has an easy, friendly, although perhaps trifle shifty manner; he
> laughs a lot and enjoys a joke; sometimes he even made one about himself. My
> own impression, which was confirmed by what I heard about him from others,
> is that he has physical courage and guts in a time of crisis or war, but lacks ability
> to apply himself seriously to any task other than political plots or intrigues. The
> Imam seemed however, quite determined to fight to the end against Sallal and
> the Egyptians. He was confident that the rest of his family would back him and
> that his family would fully support him in this fight. In this attitude he was at one
> with all the leaders and Princes I met who greatly impressed me with their deter-
> mination, except perhaps for Crown Prince Hassan. I believe that they will fight
> it out to the end against the Egyptians and Republicans.[56]

It was during this visit that McLean recorded the Imam's epiphany over
his *liaison dangereuse* with Cairo. The Imam's real importance lay not in

confessions of his errant political past, however contrite he may have appeared. Rather, it lay in the symbolism of his survival. The fact that he had escaped from Sana'a carried great weight among the tribes, leading to proclamations of loyalty from most of the leaders of the two great Zeidi tribal confederations in Yemen who dominated the mountains north and east of the capital: the *Bakil* and the *Hashid*. Moreover, some *Shaffei* tribes had thrown their lot in with the Imam, including the *Zarinik*, whose tribal lands in and around the port of Hodeidah gave their support a strategic value.

McLean was also heartened by the high levels of morale he found in all Royalist-controlled areas, something that contrasted strongly with the wretched state of the few Egyptian prisoners he spoke to and who were fortunate not to have been killed out of hand. The basic features of the civil war had already become apparent and were to remain unchanged for the next five years. While tribes loyal to the Imam dominated the mountains and high plateaus in the north, north-west and east of Yemen, troops loyal to the YAR and backed by Egypt preferred the relative security of an urban environment, their lack of martial prowess in mountain warfare offset by a superiority in heavy weaponry and most of all, in air power. McLean estimated that the Imam had beween 20–30,000 men in the field, with the potential to 'raise anything between 100,000 to 200,000 if he had the means to supply them with arms, ammunition and money'.[57] He further revealed that attempts were being made to procure 'three or four fighter bombers with volunteer pilots' but such efforts to build a nascent air force came to nought, since the Royalists could not find, let alone secure, a landing strip suitable for such aircraft. Hopes that Saudi Arabia could fulfil this requirement were similarly dashed. The provision of arms, ammunition and supplies to sustain a guerrilla war was one thing. Providing sophisticated weaponry and the use of their own territory at a time when sympathy for Nasser was rife throughout the Kingdom was another matter entirely. Still, it was clear that Royalist forces required heavier weaponry if Republican positions in the towns and cities were to be attacked. Royalist tribes were ill-equipped and even less well trained to conduct such operations, the failure of forces loyal to Crown Prince Hassan to take Sad'ah being the most apposite example. It was mentioned to McLean that an approach had already been made to obtain expert military advice 'possibly from France'. Such steps met with McLean's approbation. Who exactly was behind these approaches remains unknown, but it was the genesis for the emergence of a mercenary organisation which, perhaps more than any other individual, McLean helped to establish.

The subsequent report produced by McLean was the most detailed and thorough exposition of political fortunes in the Yemen to date, but the conclusions reached differed little in conviction or weight of argument from the article in the *Daily Telegraph*. The key difference however, lay in the exposure the report now enjoyed in the Cabinet. McLean's assertion that the Imam could lay claim to the loyalty to at least two-thirds of the Yemeni population conflated neatly with those in the Cabinet whose refusal to countenance recognition was now justified by the very criteria demanded of such protocol by Her Majesty's Government: namely, that a government must command the loyalty of the majority of its subjects.

The exact impact of this second report on Cabinet decision-making remains, nonetheless, difficult to gauge. In his account, Tom Bower claimed the report, delivered personally to Macmillan by McLean on 19 December, was decisive in undermining the case for recognition. A witness to this effect, was, according to Bower, Julian Amery, who claimed, 'It was, one of the few turning points in history which I have witnessed.'[58] While the sentiment expressed may well have been accurate, the written record of this period remains at variance with this account. McLean did not visit Number Ten on 19 December, but rather wrote a letter to the Prime Minister, enclosing a translation of the Imam's confession but not the second report. This was only completed the following month when it was sent to members of the Cabinet. In his letter to Macmillan, McLean declared his intent to 'write a short memorandum' which he would send to the Prime Minister 'when it is completed'.[59] Three days later, McLean received a reply from the Prime Minister's office, thanking him for his correspondence, but informing him that Macmillan was still in the Bahamas.[60] This is not to suggest that Macmillan remained unmoved by McLean's correspondence when he eventually returned to London but it is important to note that the report, in itself, was not the metaphorical straw that broke the back of recognition.

Certainly, those in the Cabinet arguing for recognition placed great value on the despatches sent back to King Charles Street by Christopher Gandy. In October 1962 the Foreign Office had concluded that the forces preoccupied with Yemeni irredentism would be held in abeyance, the new regime being too concerned with shredding the political atavism of its recent past to interfere in the affairs of its neighbours.[61] It was an argument that Gandy repeated forcefully at every given opportunity but his sense of physical isolation in Taiz'z was matched by his sense of political isolation in Aden and Whitehall. His nemesis was Trevaskis, a man Gandy knew from old. He recalled, 'We had been at the same preparatory school, public school and Cambridge college, but, alas, without becoming friends.' It is doubtful if this expression of regret was heartfelt. While schoolboys, it has been alleged that Trevaskis subjected Gandy to a beating for the latter's refusal to participate in team sports.[62] Whatever the legacy juvenile rivalries now exercised on policy debate, Gandy remained in no doubt as to the strength of animus displayed by Colonial Office officials towards both the Yemen and King Charles Street. Soon after his posting to Taiz'z in August 1962 he wrote to his mother, 'The people here look on the Yemen as an implacable enemy with whom they are forced by the FO to make peace on terms which never prove satisfactory.'[63] He continued:

> [M]inisters were afraid that a rejuvenated Yemen would attract the population of Aden and the protectorates away from the idea of a unitary semi-autonomous state. They feared that the new regime would pursue Yemen's claim to Aden with fresh vigour, especially if it enjoyed UAR support. But those in the FO, at least, realised that Britain would have to live with the republic and did not wish to seem hostile to a reformist government. They wanted to apply their normal criteria for recognition (control of most of the territory and support of most of the population), but they had to consider the attitude of the South Arabian ministers, who soon became − or were made by Trevaskis − suspicious of the new regime.[64]

This was an apt summation of the dissonance within Whitehall, but given the agreed criteria for conferring recognition, the reports produced by McLean exposed the weakness of the Foreign Office position. Gandy conceded that the location of the non-Arab diplomats, 'confined to Taiz'z and thus separated from the Arab heads of mission', made it difficult in the extreme to establish alternative sources of information beyond that provided by an American aid mission and some Italian and American medical personnel.[65] No diplomatic channel existed that could confirm or deny that the criteria for recognition had been met. Simply arguing that 'Britain would have to live with the Republic' carried little political conviction when set against reports that detailed a majority of the tribes (and hence the population) owed their allegiance to the Imam.

The momentum towards recognition was, however, far from a spent force. This had less to do with the relative merits of the arguments in favour of recognition than with the implications that non-recognition could have upon Anglo-American relations. Washington's decision to recognise the regime of Abdullah as-Sallal on 19 December 1962 laid the basis for international recognition of the YAR as the legitimate government of Yemen. The following day, the Credentials Committee of the United Nations voted to extend recognition. Of the 101 votes cast by members of the General Assembly, 74 voted in favour, 23 countries abstained, with only Saudi Arabia, Jordan the outgoing Royalist delegation to the UN and somewhat surprisingly, Hungary, voting against. The United Kingdom delegate to the UN Credentials committee, Sir Colin Crowe, voted in favour of the report but added, somewhat ironically, his wish 'to put on record that in voting for the report of the credentials committee, my delegation has done so solely on the grounds that the credentials concerned are, considered as documents, in order. This approval should not necessarily be taken as implying recognition of the authorities by whom the credentials were issued.'[66]

It was pointed out by Crowe that such verbal gymnastics were not new. A similar formula of constructed ambiguity had marked the British response to the Credentials Committee concerning recognition of the People's Republic of China. London therefore could claim consistency in its approach towards states where sovereignty remained a contested issue, while concurrently, citing precedence as justification for refusing to offer *de jure* recognition of the YAR.[67] Despite constant entreaties from Washington, Macmillan resisted pressure to extend formal recognition to the YAR, claiming the continued presence of Egyptian troops was the main obstacle. It was a course of action Macmillan appeared to countenance against his better judgement and certainly drew the ire of those in the Foreign Office who suspected the malign hand of Colonial Office officials.

On 4 January 1963, the British Ambassador to Cairo, Sir Harold Beeley, cabled London, arguing that the policy of withholding recognition was undermining British influence in Egypt and pushing the YAR further into the arms of Nasser. Such a policy could only serve to undermine the very objective that Britain wished to secure: the stability of the new Federal structure and continued use of the Aden base.[68] It was an argument repeated to Macmillan by his Foreign Secretary, Alec Douglas-Home. On 22 January, he wrote to the Prime Minister, rejecting outright the argument that supporting unrest among the tribes inside the Yemen would provide sufficient distraction from Cairo's wider designs in South Arabia. He concluded:

> I do not believe this is so. A campaign of propaganda and subversion could, with Nasser's help, be mounted quickly and I fear that the very large number of Yemenis in Aden would be ready to respond and could gravely complicate the task of the Aden authorities. It is because I believe that there would be no substantial benefit to be gained from further delay and that we have reached the last stage when we can hope to preserve a reasonable relationship with the Republicans that I think we should go ahead now [and recognise the YAR].[69]

Matters were now coming to a head. On 5 February 1963, Gandy, having been recalled to London specifically to address a Cabinet meeting convened to discuss the Yemen, gave an upbeat assessment of the new rulers in Sana'a. While conceding that Sallal himself was not gifted intellectually and lacked charisma, he claimed that his day-to-day dealings with the Republican authorities had proven easier than with the Imamate. He concluded that, 'The Republicans were anxious to maintain and preserve good relations with the UK, but could not be expected to countenance indefinitely our present policy of non-recognition which was equated in their minds with the extension of help or comfort to the Royalists.'[70]

The Cabinet noted the growing involvement of the United Nations in attempting to mediate a cease-fire, but the weight of opinion around the Cabinet table concluded that, 'Our paramount interest was the maintenance of our position in Aden. The Republicans in the Yemen were supported by those in Aden who were hostile to our interests; our recognition of the Republicans could not but encourage our opponents and upset our friends.'[71] The Cabinet also noted that Washington's policy of recognising the Republican regime in the hope of assuaging Nasser had proven to be in vain; the Egyptian President had already begun to increase Egyptian troop numbers. Accordingly, the meeting concluded that 'our recognition of that regime would to this extent be regarded as a victory for Egypt and for the forces of revolutionary Arab nationalism which were everywhere working against us'. The meeting agreed that non-recognition of the Republican regime would remain official British policy unless the United States could persuade Nasser to withdraw his forces. Nonetheless, Macmillan did acknowledge that in the longer term it seemed inevitable that London would recognise the Republicans, noting that it was 'repugnant to political equity and prudence alike' that London continued to align itself with what had been, prior to the revolution, a most despotic regime.

But Sallal had tired of London's 'wait and see' approach on the issue of recognition. On 17 February 1963, the authorities in Sana'a ordered the expulsion of the British consul in Taiz'z, Christopher Gandy.[72] Macmillan acknowledged in his diary that the Foreign Office and the Foreign Secretary, Alec Douglas-Home, were 'upset', a mood that contrasted sharply with the euphoria displayed by Peter Thorneycroft and Duncan Sandys. Macmillan concluded that in the short term at least, the outcome was probably for the best, given the pressing demands of securing the new Federation.[73] It was an assessment that was to be sorely tested in the years to come. For the Foreign Office, non-recognition always remained a flawed policy since it encouraged Sana'a to increase its support for dissident tribal activity, subversion and air attacks on the Federation side of the border in pursuit of long-held territorial claims. Recognition it was claimed, would have forced Sana'a to recognise the British position in South Arabia while concurrently safeguarding the influence of the Federal rulers. For the Colonial Office and Ministry of Defence this was at best pious naivety. Recognition would merely have increased dissident activity, undermining the guarantees Britain had extended to the rulers and thereby threaten the credibility of the Federation and Britain's position in Aden. Violence along the Yemeni–Federation border was therefore viewed not as the cause of London's refusal to offer recognition, but as an ongoing symptom of Yemeni territorial irredentism, an irredentism now backed by Cairo that had, as its goal, a desire to eradicate British influence in South Arabia.

Conclusion

The debate over recognition was shaped by the legacy of Yemeni irredentism, magnified by the persona of Nasser. Given the immediate difficulties in attempting to mould the emergent Federation into a viable polity in January 1963, Macmillan sided with the Colonial Office argument that assuaging the concerns of the Protectorate rulers remained paramount. But equally, with his 'winds of change' speech still fresh in his mind, he remained conscious that the 'tide of history' appeared to favour the Republicans. As such, Macmillan seriously considered offering the Republicans immediate *de facto* recognition, with *de jure* recognition to follow if the terms of any agreement enabled the United Kingdom to safeguard its interests in the Federation. Crucially, the issue of offering *de facto* recognition was to remain contingent upon a positive response from Johnston. From the perspective of the Arabian Department of the Foreign Office, this effectively handed officials in Aden a veto over recognition. Reflecting on his joust with those in Whitehall opposed to recognition, Gandy poured scorn on the malign influence that the Aden Group had over British policy towards the Yemen. He concluded that the decision to withhold recognition was misplaced strategically

> In reality, British opposition to the new regime reinforced, perhaps even created, a determination in Cairo, and its relatively few whole-hearted partisans in Sana'a, to drive Britain out of South Yemen. London, against the advice of the US, and unlike most European and all Arab states except Saudi Arabia and Jordan, obstinately withheld recognition. The Foreign Office itself wanted to maintain contact with the new regime through its man in Taiz'z, a tightrope act which clearly could not last for long.[74]

The delivery of eyewitness reports direct to Number Ten from Neil McLean and others concerning Royalist activities became an established pattern from January 1963 until the demise of the Conservative government following the October 1964 general election. This bypassed any attempt by the Foreign Office to dilute or sanitise these reports before they reached Macmillan and later, Douglas-Home. But the impact of McLean's early reports on the issue of recognition should not be exaggerated. Although they were influential in securing a pause for thought over the sagacity of recognition in Whitehall, and gave succour to those in the

Cabinet and the Conservative Party convinced of Nasser's malign intent towards British interests in South Arabia, the debate over recognition was settled not by the power of McLean's arguments, lucid and persuasive though these were. It was decided by a regime in Sana'a no longer willing to indulge the diplomatic obscurantism displayed by London.

Whether non-recognition did indeed drive Nasser towards a more aggressive policy towards the British remains a moot point. It is worth noting ,however, that even when Macmillan was pondering the viability of offering *de facto* recognition, Yemeni forces had already made several incursions into Federation territory, notably in and around the Sultanate of Beihan. Even if Sir Charles Johnston had been persuaded of the case for recognition, attacks from the Yemen – whether sanctioned in Cairo or not – made his task of persuading the Shaykhs of the Protectorates and later the Federation, to accept such a course of action, all but impossible. One month after the issue of recognition had been decided, Johnston received credible intelligence that originated from a source in Yemen that 'Sallal planned to send a party of deportees from Aden back here [the Federation] accompanied by some trained saboteurs.'[75] The fears expressed by Douglas-Home were, it seemed, coming to pass. For London to retain the confidence of the Federation rulers it would have to be far more pro-active in defending its frontiers. This, in the absence of diplomatic ties, inevitably came to embrace the world of clandestine activity. By contrast, its wings clipped, the Foreign Office now turned to Washington and the United Nations in its attempt to secure the British position in South Arabia through consensus, rather than conflict.

3

Between Whitehall and the White House

Anglo-American Relations

Having lost the argument over recognition, the Foreign Office was obliged to follow a policy it regarded as the triumph of parochial expediency over long-term regional gain. That Washington had seen fit to extend *de jure* recognition to the YAR in December 1962 now threatened a serious rift with London, which continued to place primacy on fulfilling its treaty obligations to the Federation rulers. There remained a strong suspicion among some officials in Aden and London that underpinning American policy was a desire to further usurp British influence in the region. This view was shared by Lieutenant General Carl Von Horn, a Swede whose short tenure as commander of the United Nations Yemen Observation Mission (UNYOM) in 1963 proved to be a sad denouement to an otherwise distinguished career. Recounting his dealings with the United Nations and the US State Department, and their lack of partiality in dealing with both Republican and Royalist forces on an equitable basis, the Swedish officer posed the rhetorical question:

> So here was the United States, apparently acquiescing in steamrollering a small heroic people flat. And why? Because of business interests in the Middle East, a political 'hunch' that Nasser was the next best thing to communism? Or was it through a desire to strike at British oil interests in southern Arabia, allow Nasser enough rein in his drive towards the Gulf to seriously upset the state of Saudi Arabia, bring down King Saud and ensure his replacement with the more sympathetic Prince Faisal?[1]

Certainly, London remained sensitive to American encroachment in an area that Whitehall considered to be an exclusive British domain. The Foreign Office was happy to see the United States upgrade their consular representation in Aden in the autumn of 1964, an act that gave international legitimacy to the new Federation it had hitherto lacked. The mandarins of King Charles Street remained, however, opposed to attempts by the State Department, on a quid pro quo basis to allow for the establishment of a United States Consulate in the Trucial State of Dubai. The State Department claim that such diplomatic representation was required, given the numbers of United States citizens working in the Trucial States was regarded at best as spurious, it being noted that such consular representation had, to date, been dealt with effectively by British officials.[2] British thinking towards the role that Washington could and should play in the Yemen conflict displayed a similar mix of caution and encouragement. While officials in the Arabian Department of the Foreign Office remained circumspect in allowing the United States to increase its influence in and around the Persian Gulf, it was recognised by King Charles Street that entreaties by the White House towards both Sana'a and Cairo remained the only diplomatic means available to protect the British position in South Arabia. It was a position that sat uneasily with officials in the Colonial Office who were only too aware that President Kennedy's 'new frontiers' – the attempt to break away from the restrictions of the Eisenhower Doctrine which viewed Arab nationalist movements as mere vehicles for the expansion of Soviet influence throughout the Middle East – sat uneasily with political reforms designed to cohere the Federation into a viable entity. Unencumbered by the baggage of imperialism, the willingness of the Kennedy administration to accept national movements as legitimate expressions of sovereign will placed clear water between the position of Washington and London. The legacy of antagonism between Cairo and London, coupled with the fact that profits derived from the sale of Gulf oil contributed over £400million to Britain's balance of payments in the early 1960s, determined British policy towards Aden and the Gulf region. As noted by W. Taylor Fain, the United Kingdom 'made no efforts to reach an understanding with the new radical Arab nationalist movement or reconsider its traditional relationships with its conservative client states and dependencies in the region'.[3]

As a collective assessment of British policy-making, Fain's observation carries some weight. But equally Foreign Office officials from the Arabian Department did support proposals by the State Department to involve the United Nations in an attempt to broker a resolution to the Yemen Civil War. It was felt such involvement would bestow international legitimacy upon the Federation and force the authority in Sana'a to forego its claims to Federation territory, a claim successive British governments had always rejected on both historical and religious grounds.[4] This willingness to embrace a UN role found little sympathy within the Colonial Office. Ingrained suspicion of an organisation whose very existence appeared ill-disposed towards colonial rule per se expressed itself in a reluctance among Federation officials, in particular in Aden, to entertain the idea of

UN observers operating along the border between the Yemen and the Federation. This dissonance between the Foreign Office and the Colonial Office undermined coherent decision-making within Whitehall and led to serious disagreements between Washington and London over the means, if not the ends, Britain appeared to employ in safeguarding the viability of the Federation against subversion from the YAR and Nasser. Following the assassination of Kennedy in November 1963, Washington began to take a more benign view of the British position, partly because of the growing distraction of Vietnam, but equally because State Department officials felt that their attempts to use the good offices of the United Nations to broker a disengagement agreement between Cairo and Riyadh had foundered upon the rock of continued Egyptian subterfuge.

Britain and the United States: Recognition and Disengagement

On 19 December 1962 Washington offered *de jure* recognition to YAR. While this act of diplomacy was met with resigned acceptance in London, the reaction of the Imam Mohammed al-Badr was more forthright in expressing indignation. Eleven days previously he had written a personal missive to Kennedy in protest at letters sent by the White House to the governments of Egypt, Saudi Arabia, Jordan, as well as to the new regime in Sana'a without, 'even informing me or my government which is the legitimate Government of the Kingdom of Yemen as recognised by the United States and eighty other nations'. He continued, 'I cannot believe that you, Mr President, and the great freedom loving American people, if they knew the facts, would stand aside or condone, still less assist by diplomatic or other action, this brutal aggression which is only the latest example of Egyptian imperialism in Arab countries.'[5]

The Imam's letter carried little weight in Washington. The United States Ambassador to Riyadh, Parker T. Hart, later disclosed that the venal nature of the Imamate proscribed any immediate sympathy with the Royalist position in the White House. Policy in Washington was driven less by concern with strife in the Yemen, and more by worries over the Egyptian threat to the territorial integrity of Saudi Arabia and the ramifications this could have for continued access to the vast oil reserves of the Kingdom.[6] This position was the direct result of a revision in United States policy towards the Arab world that had already begun in the twilight years of the Eisenhower administration. Events in Iraq, Lebanon and Jordan in 1958 had exposed the ideological limitations of President Dwight D. Eisenhower's self-proclaimed 'doctrine'. Announced before both Houses of Congress in 1957, the Eisenhower Doctrine provided military assistance to Middle East states openly threatened with aggression 'from any nation controlled by international Communism'. In practice, this Doctrine made little attempt to distinguish between types of nationalism on the one hand, and the requirement to contain Soviet influence in the developing world on the other. The perception that United States policy should secure its regional interests *with* Arab nationalist movements, rather than from them, now formed the basis of the 'New Frontiersmen'.[7] Anxious to escape the stigma of open American association with reactionary, feudalistic and often venal regimes in the Arab world, the 'new frontiersmen' of the Kennedy administration sought to break out of the styptic mindset which had hitherto defined American policy towards the Arab world. Even before his election to the White House in 1961, Kennedy's public speeches had taken a benign view of Arab nationalist movements, most notably in Algeria, still in the midst of its struggle against French colonial rule. Such moral altruism aside, hard realist expediency informed Washington's calculations: by wrapping liberation movements and their leaders in the cloak of American munificence – seen in the provision of aid and technical advice – Kennedy was providing an alternative model of development to counter Soviet influence and any attempt to disrupt oil supplies to the West. As John S. Badeau, the United States Ambassador to Cairo noted somewhat wryly, Washington's s policy towards Egypt was less concerned with Egypt per se than Egypt's influence over the wider Middle East.[8]

By means of doing business with Nasser, the Kennedy administration planned to control Moscow's involvement in the Middle East through what might be termed 'containment through kindness'. In 1962, with its own ties with the Kremlin in disarray, Cairo also expressed keen interest in securing better ties with Washington. The previous year, the Egyptian Ambassador to Washington, Mustapha Kamel, voiced the hope that, 'A single three-year food aid commitment would produce greater economic dividends for Egypt and far greater political dividends for the United States'.[9] This proposal was pounced upon by Secretary of State Dean Rusk who argued that the timely provision of substantial aid by the United States would provide Egypt with an alternative to economic dependence upon the Soviet Union. The result was the PL-480 foreign aid package and a commitment by Washington to organise Western assistance through the World Bank for Cairo's five-year development plan. Recognition of the Yemen Arab Republic was therefore an affirmation of a common vision between Washington and Cairo and the public identification by the United States with what the White House perceived as the popular forces of progression throughout the region.

The contours of US policy towards the Yemen Civil War therefore became quickly apparent: to prevent the conflict from spreading beyond the confines of the Yemen while working towards a disengagement agreement between Saudi Arabia and Egypt. This was to be based on the cessation of supplies to Royalist forces by the former, and the incremental withdrawal of its troops by the latter. This plan was first put forward by Washington on 17 November 1962 in the belief that all the main parties to the conflict – Saudi Arabia, Egypt and the newly proclaimed Yemen Arab Republic – had much to gain and everything to lose by not entertaining seriously these nascent proposals. Concurrently, it was made clear to representatives of the Imam, as well as to officials in Riyadh and Amman, that Washington regarded the new regime in Sana'a as constituting the legitimate government in the Yemen. Accordingly, the energies of the Saudi and Jordanian Royal families would be best directed towards domestic reform rather than invested in what White House officials regarded as misplaced foreign adventures. Throughout, Washington continued to press recognition of the Republican government on London, highlighting the benefits to be derived from a disengagement agreement that would, the State Department believed, entail Yemeni recognition of the Federation borders, thereby securing the British position in Aden.[10] It was an argument that found sympathy in King Charles Street but ill-disguised contempt among the Aden Group and their champions in the Cabinet. Washington's diplomatic moves now brought these competing positions in Whitehall to the fore.

The Bunche and Bunker Missions

The Cabinet meeting of 3 February 1963 noted that Washington's decision to recognise the Republican regime had led to an increase rather than a decrease in the numbers of Egyptian troops in Yemen. The United States remained the only actor capable of prevailing upon both Cairo and Riyadh to desist from active intervention in the civil war. Kennedy remained keen to elicit British support for a disengagement agreement, support that Macmillan felt could be given if Washington would 'acknowledge publicly the importance that they attached to the maintenance of our position in Aden'. Such open support, the Cabinet felt, would assuage the concerns of the Federation rulers and allow London to recognise the Republican regime, a course of action that Macmillan believed to be inevitable in the longer term.[11]

As such it was felt that in the short term at least, the British interests in South Arabia would be best served by supporting Washington's efforts to secure a cease-fire. In January 1963, Kennedy suggested to the UN Secretary-General U Thant that he send a special envoy to the Middle East to discuss with the main protagonists the possibilities of securing a cease-fire.[12] The UN was the preferred diplomatic option for the White House, enhancing the impression of impartial mediation untainted by accusations that Cold War considerations continued to determine US policy in the Middle East. Other more seasoned observers of the Yemeni political scene doubted the sagacity of this approach. Dana Schmidt, the American correspondent covering the conflict for the *New York Times*, wrote of this period that in attempting to deal with Nasser, 'Rarely has the American government been so completely deluded.'[13]

Unofficial security assurances given by Kennedy to Crown Prince Faisal in late October 1962 rang hollow in Riyadh. The Saudi town of Najran just across from the Yemeni border was subjected to air attacks by the Egyptian Air Force on 7 January and 13 February 1963, attacks that Cairo argued were designed to disrupt the Saudi supply of arms and ammunition to the Royalist forces. On 16 February, conclusive evidence reached Ambassador Hart that the Egyptians had been hoping to enlist the help of Saudi dissidents to provoke unrest in the Kingdom. Along the length of the Saudi coastline stretching from the Yemen border to the town of Yanbu, the Saudi authorities recovered 119 containers dropped by parachutes carrying arms and ammunition of Belgian, British and American origin. This bungled attempt at a covert operation may have been Nasser's riposte to Riyadh's burgeoning support for the Royalist forces. In November 1962, the Saudi Ambassador to London, Hafiz Wahba, disclosed to McLean the extent of Riyadh's military largesse to the *Hamid'Ud'Din*. He stated that a further 30,000 rifles would be sent to the Yemen by the beginning of January 1963.[14] Nonetheless, Hart believed that a more malevolent purpose lay behind these arms drops. They were, he believed, destined for dissident elements within the Saudi armed forces who intended to mount a coup against the House of Saud, leading members of which were due to attend a *majlis al-shura* in Jeddah on 18 February.[15] On 4 October 1962, during talks with Crown Prince Faisal in Washington, Kennedy had urged the Saudis to embark 'toward the orderly transition from an autocratic monarchy to a more progressive government responsive to the country's socio-economic needs' if the Saudi Royal family wished to avoid the fate of the Imamate.[16] Now, five months later, Riyadh felt that Egyptian attacks were a direct result of Washington's extension of diplomatic recognition of the YAR, a recognition that in the words of Douglas Little gave Nasser 'a hunting licence to go after Saudi Arabia'.[17]

Washington's attempts to steady frayed nerves in Riyadh saw the deployment on 10 July 1963 of six US F100–D fighter-bombers to Saudi Arabia as part of 'Operation Hardsurface'. Even this deployment was not without is problems. While the brainchild of Ambassador Hart, the White House remained wary of over-extending a military commitment of unknown duration and liability. The aircraft should have been in position by the beginning of June, but the styptic debates over where the aircraft were to be based and their rules of engagement near the Saudi–Yemeni border prevented their deployment. This did little to appease the Saudis who continued to suffer from Egyptian air attacks of varying intensity throughout April, May and June. As if to illustrate the impotence of Saudi air defences, Egyptian aircraft flew over the Hejazi coast throughout the spring of 1963.[18]

Although the Kennedy administration considered Egyptian actions to be a disproportionate response to Riyadh's continued support for the Royalists, it reinforced Washington's belief in the value of third-party arbitration. Responding to Kennedy's request, the United Nations Secretary-General U Thant sanctioned the visit of the United Nations Under-secretary for Political Affairs, Ralph Bunche, on a 'fact-finding' mission to the Yemen. It was a visit dogged by controversy from the outset. While the original plan was for Bunche to visit Egypt, Yemen and Saudi Arabia, Crown Prince Faisal denied Bunche permission to visit Riyadh in protest over the refusal by the Under-secretary to visit Royalist-held areas of the Yemen or to meet with the Imam. This position was justified on the grounds that the Imamate was no longer recognised by the United Nations as the legitimate government of the Yemen. Constrained by the position of Saudi Arabia, President Kennedy decided to underpin the efforts of the UN diplomat by sending his own envoy, Ellsworth Bunker, to the region. A man of considerable experience in peace negotiations, Bunker had successfully brokered an agreement between the Netherlands and Indonesia over the future sovereignty of West New Guinea/West Irian and now provided the crucial link between Washington, Riyadh and Cairo. While ostensibly there to promote the mediation efforts of the United Nations, Bunker's first loyalty remained to the White House rather than New York.

The 'Bunche Mission', as it became known, arrived in Taiz'z on 2 March 1963. Its mandate was welcomed by the Foreign Office but greeted with some circumspection by the Colonial Office. Informing the attitude of the mandarins of Great Smith Street was the belief that the institutional bias of the United Nations remained anathema to the very idea of the Federation and the British position in South Arabia. Such tangible differences were not allowed to obscure the official British position which remained one of quiet diplomatic encouragement for both missions. Indeed, despite growing evidence concerning the indiscriminate use of napalm by the Egyptian Air Force against civilian targets – a calculated attempt to depopulate Royalist-held areas in the Yemen – London remained reluctant, despite the prompting of some of the more vociferous backbench MPs to bring the matter before the United

Nations. American efforts at reaching a cease-fire first had to be seen to be exhausted.[19]

Behind Whitehall however, unity of purpose remained a rare commodity. Concern over the exact remit of Bunche mission in particular marked the attitudes of the Colonial Office and its officials in Aden. On 3 March, soon after his arrival in the Yemeni capital, the BBC monitoring service reported comments allegedly made by Bunche to YAR politicians and quoted subsequently on Radio Sana'a that, 'if Britain continues its aggression against the Yemen the United Nations will support you'.[20] On 4 March, Herman Eilts, a diplomat at the US Embassy in London with responsibility for the Middle East, disclosed to the Foreign Office that Bunche's visit to Taiz'z two days previously had left the UN diplomat badly shaken by the reception he had received at the airport. According to a telegram received by Eilts and disclosed to Arthur Walmsley, head of the Arabian Department, 'Dr Bunche's car was impeded by hostile crowds, some of whom were waving banners with Communist, anti-American slogans.'[21] The Foreign Office believed therefore that Bunche's subsequent remarks concerning alleged acts of British aggression appeared to be an attempt to curry favour with his Yemeni interlocutors following his eventful arrival.

Although treating the BBC report with some circumspection, the Foreign Office did seek clarification from the United Nations as to what exactly Bunche had said.[22] Before such clarification was received from UN headquarters in New York, Bunche arrived in Aden on 4 March en route to Cairo. The visit, meant purely as a courtesy call, was extended following mechanical problems with the aircraft taking Bunche to Egypt. The opportunity afforded by this enforced sojourn gave Sir Charles Johnston the opportunity to present the Federation of South Arabia as more than just an artificial creation of British design lacking in regional legitimacy. Johnston arranged for Bunche to meet Federal and Aden ministers for lunch and later, to address a hastily convened press conference. More pressing for London, it allowed the High Commissioner to discover exactly what Bunche had said and whether the United Nations diplomat really was biased against the British position in South Arabia.[23]

The subsequent account of the visit provided by Johnston highlighted all too well the divergent views over policy between British officials in Aden and the United Nations. According to the High Commissioner, Bunche expressed the opinion that, 'The Republican regime was a reasonable one containing a good mixture of service and civilian, young and old. It seemed confident of its future; all the people he talked to, whether Republican leaders, Egyptian officers or Western diplomats assured him the Republic controlled virtually the whole of Yemen.'[24] It was a view that Johnston took immediate umbrage with. In an accompanying telegram to the Colonial Secretary that was circulated throughout Whitehall, he gave vent to his feelings over the UN position. Johnson had tried in vain to impress upon Bunche the weakness of the Republican position in Yemen, a position he had hoped would be reinforced by the luncheon Bunche attended with the Sultan of Lahej, Shaykh Mohammed Farid, as well as two journalists working for the *Daily Express* and *Le Figaro*, both of whom had recent 'first-hand knowledge of Royalist-held territory'. He concluded, however, that his efforts to persuade Bunche to understand let alone accept the British position had fallen on deaf ears. Bunche's intransigence, he felt, was reinforced by the staff accompanying the UN diplomat, who appeared to be cut from an archetypal Republican cloth. Thus he noted:

> Bunche was accompanied by a crew cut Irish colonel of the United Nations whose views on Republicans, Royalists, British etc., could be thought read without undue difficulty. My impression is that Bunche's mind is completely made up and that nothing said to him here made any impression. I am surprised that a man of his experience should have let the Republicans pull the wool over his eyes so successfully. I had also not realised how closely in fact he mirrors the policy of the State Department.[25]

It was an assessment that drew the ire of officials in the Arabian Department of the Foreign Office. In a written note of 8 March, Brian Pridham remarked that Johnson had failed to appreciate that as far as the UN and Washington were concerned, 'the Imam's side does not exist', and that Bunche's efforts at mediation had therefore, by definition, to go through Riyadh. Pridham went on to note that it was probably not lost on Bunche that his fellow guests at the luncheon hosted by Johnston were all Royalist sympathisers, something that Pridham appeared to feel undermined Johnston's own argument.[26] Yet it was the Colonial Office line that continued to dominate government policy. At a Cabinet meeting convened on 6 March to discuss the Yemen – the last to be chaired by Harold Macmillan as Prime Minister, – the Foreign Secretary, Lord Home, concluded that in lieu of a diplomatic breakthrough by either Washington or the United Nations, Nasser appeared set on the continued subversion of Saudi Arabia. The meeting concerned itself primarily with the extent to which retaliatory powers be delegated to the High Commissioner should the YAR and Egyptian attacks continue on Federal territory. It was a debate that was never to be resolved to the satisfaction of Aden. Notable by its absence from the minutes of the meeting was any discussion over recognition, the subject that had dominated previous Cabinet debate over the Yemen.[27] British policy was now clear concerning what it was against. Now it had to decide what it was for.

For the mandarins of the Arabian Department, there now existed only one course of action: London should redouble its support for Washington's continued attempts to mediate a cease-fire and disengagement agreement. The United States Embassy in London kept the Foreign Office fully briefed on these efforts, along with the concern felt in Washington at the continued Egyptian air attacks on Saudi territory. The United States Ambassador to Egypt, Dr John Badeau, estimated that Cairo had 28,000 troops stationed in the Yemen, a tacit admission that recognition of the Republican regime had done little to curb Nasser's apparent ambition.[28] On 7 March, in conversation with the British Ambassador to Cairo, Sir Harold Beeley, Badeau recounted a conversation he had had recently with Nasser. The Egyptian leader stated that his attacks on Saudi towns and airfields were meant only to prevent Saudi supplies and ammunition reaching Royalist-held areas in the Yemen since, 'He could not wait indefinitely while Egyptian troops were being killed with ammunition brought across the [Saudi] frontier'. Nasser agreed to cease such attacks during the course of Bunche's mediation efforts, but Badeau believed that, at most, such a respite would last for only two weeks.[29] Having arrived in Cairo after his somewhat tempestuous reception in Yemen and Aden, Bunche was now pressed by Beeley to clarify his alleged remarks concerning 'British aggression'. Bunche denied having made any such statement but did repeat his opposition to outside intervention in the conflict, including the infiltration of arms across porous and ill-defined frontiers.[30]

There, as far as the Foreign Office was concerned, the matter was allowed to rest. Indeed, Sir Patrick Dean, the British Ambassador to the United Nations, spoke at length to Bunche upon his return to New York about the Yemen. His subsequent cable to the Foreign Office on 9 March clarified the position of the Under-secretary, including the firm belief that the Republican authorities were more firmly entrenched than Johnston believed and that 'In the towns there was genuine support for the Republican regime'. Bunche told Dean that in his view, the Royalists lacked coherence and that the fidelity of the tribes remained a transient commodity, accessible to the highest bidder. Warming to his theme, Bunche also revealed the conditions Sallal believed Britain had to fulfil before Sana'a was willing to give assurances concerning non-interference in the affairs of its neighbours. These included an end to the infiltration of supplies to the Royalists from what was euphemistically labelled the 'outside' and the expulsion of all members of the *Hamid'Ud'Din* from Saudi Arabia. Bunche added that in his view, Sallal would have to come to terms with the tribes in Royalist-controlled areas but that the only way this could happen was 'to cut off the infiltration of arms and money' to the Royalists.[31] Bunche placed the onus upon ending the civil war on Saudi Arabia rather than Egypt. Nasser had given him firm assurances that the attacks on Saudi territory would cease for the duration of his mediation efforts but in what Riyadh regarded as a sin of omission, Bunche failed to impress upon Nasser the need to at least begin the process of withdrawing his troops from Yemen as a gesture of goodwill.

The Saudi refusal to deal with Bunche meant that his mission remained essentially passive, with the UN diplomat reduced to the role of sounding board. Bunker, by contrast, made three extensive trips to the Middle East between March and April 1963, shuttling between Riyadh and Cairo in his efforts to secure a disengagement agreement.[32] Throughout, the Foreign Office was kept fully briefed of his progress. The initial focus of his 'para-diplomacy' was on brokering a meeting between Faisal and Bunche without preconditions. While Crown Prince Faisal remained resolute in his opposition to meeting the UN diplomat, Bunker did obtain acceptance from the Saudi that 'support for the Royalists had to be considered for the purposes of mediation as on a parallel with UAR military operations, and therefore, as something which would have to cease simultaneously with, rather than after, UAR operations.'[33]

In return Washington agreed to increase overt displays of military support for Saudi Arabia. Discussions began on the deployment of United States aircraft to the Kingdom, and these bore fruit with the arrival of F100–D fighter-bombers in July. More immediately, the United States Navy increased the number and duration of its visits to Saudi ports on the Red Sea coast; this was designed to place pressure on Cairo to desist from its attacks on Saudi territory and to engage more fully with the Bunker mission.[34] Encouraged by these developments, the Foreign Office remained keen to explore the remarks made by Sallal to Bunche, which appeared to indicate a softening in the attitude of the YAR towards the Federation. In a confidential memorandum Walmsley suggested that Sir Patrick Dean press Bunche on whether the Yemeni President would move from an assurance over non-interference in the affairs of its neighbours to a formal recognition of the South Arabian Federation.[35] Bunche's response to Dean was guarded. He argued that Sallal could not, under the prevailing circumstances , openly recognise the Federation, but insisted that an assurance of non-interference – an assurance given verbally to Bunche on two separate occasions – held open the promise of future progress should London issue an open declaration of recognition of the YAR.[36] Dean made it clear that it was a position London could not accept.

On 15 March 1963, the State Department briefed the British Ambassador to Washington, Sir David Ormsby-Gore – soon to become Lord Harlech – on the progress made by Bunker. Proposals placed before Faisal on 6 March now formed the basis of a disengagement agreement that was signed between Cairo and Riyadh on 10 April. These proposals codified the linkage between cessation by Riyadh of arms supplies to the

Royalists with the incremental withdrawal of Egyptian troops from the YAR. Given Crown Prince Faisal's initial unease over the Bunker mission, Washington disclosed to the Foreign Office what explained this apparent volte-face on the part of Riyadh. Aside from Washington's guarantees over safeguarding the external security of the Kingdom, the State Department believed that the threat of internal unrest weighed heavily on the mind of Faisal. Ormesby-Gore noted:

> [T]he Americans had noticed a considerable amount of subversive talk in recent weeks, both in the Hejaz and Eastern Province, and even in the Northern tribal area; Saudis were talking increasingly frankly to the Americans about the worthlessness of the Royal family and the need to get rid of them. There might not be an immediate danger of revolution but this was an unhealthy trend which needed to be stopped, and for that purpose it was essential that the Saudi government should cease its intervention in Yemen and concentrate on internal reform.[37]

Such travails were not restricted to Riyadh. Recent political turmoil in Syria and Iraq demanded the attention of Nasser and as such, it appeared he could ill-afford a commitment, both militarily and financial, to a war of unlimited liability. Doubts remained, however, as to Nasser's true commitment to the disengagement plan. It was also noted by the Americans that evidence had come to light of a Saudi approach to France to help in the supply of fighter aircraft and mercenary pilots, an approach Washington had asked Paris and Brussels to reject outright. It remained unclear if this was ever a serious proposition on the part of Riyadh. More likely, it was meant to prompt Washington towards a more expeditious solution concerning the inadequate state of Saudi air defences. Significantly however, the use of 'mercenaries' to secure Saudi interests had become the subject of serious consideration among decision-making circles in Riyadh.[38] Such thinking was prompted by the continued personal diplomacy of Neil McLean. Following a meeting in March 1963 with Crown Prince Faisal, he confided in his notebook, 'There is urgency in the Yemen situation. At present Prince Faisal fights alone. Jordan dropped out and Britain does not help. We should open routes through Beihan. Faisal has resisted US pressure [to stop sending arms to the Imam] and he has put the maximum pressure on the USA'. At the end of this memo, McLean scribbled 'French experts, David Smiley'. It was the written genesis of what became a sustained mercenary involvement in the Yemen Civil War, to be paid for mainly through Saudi largesse.[39]

For the moment however, the Foreign Office remained gratified that the Bunker mission had produced an agreement that undermined the more bellicose stance of the Colonial Office which argued Cairo's regional woes were reason enough to increase the pressure on Nasser in Yemen. Such sophistry was dismissed by senior Foreign Office officials, notably

Ormesby-Gore. Ever mindful of Anglo-American relations, he dismissed suggestions that any skulduggery be entertained as a serious policy option by London. British interests were best served by supporting internal stability in Saudi Arabia, a position inimical to Riyadh's continued material support for the Royalist position. Some officials in the Arabian Department harboured doubts as to whether Riyadh would ever abandon the Imam, a fate preordained should Crown Prince Faisal cease all aid to the Royalists. As one official noted in a handwritten minute, 'It is a cardinal sin in tribal lore to desert someone whom you have taken under your protection.'[40] It proved to be a statement of some prescience.

Britain, Saudi Arabia and UNYOM

On 10 April 1963, Bunker announced that his shuttle diplomacy had secured an agreement between Faisal and Nasser over the principles of disengagement. As conveyed to the Foreign Office, this agreement consisted of seven protocols: (1) That Riyadh cease its support and aid to the Royalists and prohibit the use of its territory by Royalist leaders to continue the struggle in Yemen; (2) simultaneously, Egypt would begin a phased withdrawal of its forces and refrain from taking 'punitive action' against Royalist forces on 'the basis of resistance mounted by Royalists' prior to disengagement; (3) Egypt to cease all attacks on Saudi territory; (4) a demilitarised zone to be established 20 kilometres either side of the Yemen–Saudi border from which military forces and equipment of both sides would be excluded; (5) the stationing of impartial observers on both sides of the border who would certify compliance of the parties with the terms of the agreement; (6) co-operation of Riyadh and Cairo with UN officials on the 'process and verification of disengagement' and (7) Cairo to use its influence with the YAR to prevent 'further inflammatory speeches against neighbouring countries and to reaffirm its desire to live in peace with its neighbours. In response, Nasser agreed to begin the process of disengagement any time after 12 April 1963.[41]

But from the outset mutual suspicion undermined the agreement. The antipathy between Faisal and Nasser produced an agreement that never enjoyed the conviction of purpose that an actual summit between the two men could perhaps have provided. Hart noted that the Egyptian media 'truncated and distorted' the text of the agreement, claiming that the Saudis had agreed to stop all aid to 'aggressive forces', a statement hardly designed to foster the necessary spirit of co-operation.[42] On 1 May, General Carl Von Horn arrived in Cairo to clarify the exact mandate of UNYOM agreed to under article 5 of the agreement. A few days later, the Swedish General held a meeting with Field Marshal Abd el Hakim Amr, overall commander of Egyptian forces in the Yemen, during which Amr openly declared that whatever agreement was reached, Cairo would leave a 'security force' to ensure the survival of the YAR. Amr expressed the hope that as many Egyptian troops would be withdrawn as possible but concluded that this would always remain contingent upon the cessation of Saudi aid to the Royalists. Such entrenched positions led the Swedish General to conclude that neither side had any real intention of upholding the agreement.[43]

Assurances given by Riyadh of its intention to halt arms supplies to the Royalists did not extend to any immediate cessation. One month after Bunker announced the principles of agreement, Saudi arms and supplies continued to reach the Imam's forces. Tony Boyle, a Royal Air Force officer serving as aide-de-camp to Sir Charles Johnston in Aden, disclosed in a letter to Neil McLean details of talks he had held with Shariff Hussein of Beihan in early May 1963. According to Boyle, Faisal informed the Shariff that he intended to 'get all the arms, money and ammunition and equipment inside the Yemen by the time UN observers arrive to patrol the border'.[44] It appeared that Faisal was reluctant to commit, at least for the time being, the cardinal sin of tribal lore. A man of experience in peace-keeping missions ranging from the Congo to the Middle East, Carl Von Horn appeared to be the ideal candidate to head UNYOM. Yet his mission was hamstrung from the outset by bureaucratic squabbles in New York over funding for the mission, its exact remit and the numbers to be deployed. Having pushed hard under the Bunker mission for such a deployment, Washington proved reluctant to commit equipment or personal to UNYOM, a position Washington saw as consistent with its emphasis upon studied neutrality towards the conflict. While the United States had given Riyadh assurances that it would defend the territorial integrity of Saudi Arabia, Secretary of State Dean Rusk had instructed Bunker to tell Faisal that Washington would 'not be dragged into his little war in the Yemen'.[45]

During his talks in Cairo the Egyptians pressed Von Horn to extend the terms of the disengagement agreement and observer mission to include the Federation border and, in particular, the Beihan state. This was not within the remit of the UNYOM mandate, forcing Von Horn to side step the issue by promising to refer the matter to Secretary-General U Thant. Privately, Von Horn knew that this demand would prove unacceptable in London, an assessment based on the belief that such UN involvement on or around Federation territory undermined pledges made to its rulers that Britain alone was responsible for the defence of Federation borders.[46] While reflecting the thinking of ministers such as Duncan Sandys and Peter Thorneycroft, Von Horn's assessment was not accepted by the Foreign Office, who saw two clear gains to made from supporting

UNYOM: First, it provided the means to verify Cairo's compliance with the disengagement plan, thus removing the Egyptian military threat to the Federation; second, by allowing UN monitors to operate on the Yemeni–Federation border, it meant that Cairo and Sana'a recognised de facto that a frontier existed and hence the political legality of the Federation.

As such, the Foreign Office closely followed the progress of Von Horn. The Security Council formally established the United Nations Yemen Observation Mission – UNYOM – on 11 June 1963, but Von Horn had begun the process of cohering his mission at the beginning of May. Early reports reaching the Foreign Office however did not bode well for its future. On 15 May, U Thant disclosed to Sir Patrick Dean that Nasser, in conversation with Bunche, had expressed his intention to keep 'some troops in the Yemen for security and training for some time'.[47] This mirrored the views of Amr, leaving, according to Dean, U Thant concerned over how Riyadh would react to Nasser's intent once it became known. Such truculence on the part of Cairo only added to the woes of a mission yet to take proper shape and form. Having surveyed the extreme terrain and climate of the Yemen Von Horn advised that he would require 1,200 personal, helicopters, two fixed wing aircraft as well as jeeps if the observer mission was to fulfil any meaningful role. Verification of disengagement would take place over a period of three to four months at a cost estimated by the Secretary-General at $800,000. From the beginning, Von Horn felt that this figure was a gross underestimate of the costs involved and pressed hard for the budget to be increased. He was however, the victim of pecuniary circumstance. The UN was in the midst of a funding crisis over peacekeeping operations because of a refusal by France and the Soviet Union to pay their share of costs incurred by UN operations in the Sinai and the Congo. This meant that the viability of UNYOM became dependent upon the financial burden being shouldered equitably by Cairo and Riyadh, something that Egypt, despite verbal assurances to the contrary, often failed to meet.[48]

Both U Thant and the Kennedy Administration were taken aback by the scale of Von Horn's manpower and logistical recommendations. The Foreign Office was informed by Sir Patrick Dean that Washington was 'very anxious that it should not get out that there may be problems' with meeting Von Horn's requirements.[49] The Swede felt strongly however that if the mission was to be credible, the personnel involved had to be given adequate protection in an environment where shifting tribal alliances threatened the security of individual observers. Against this background of financial parsimony, doubts began to surface in Washington over Nasser's sincerity. Under the mistaken belief that Saudi Arabia had suspended all assistance to the Royalist forces, State Department officials informed the British Embassy in Washington that rotation rather than withdrawal had marked the movement of Egyptian troops.[50] But having invested much political capital in the Bunker mission, Washington refrained from threatening any punitive diplomatic measures against Cairo. More in hope than expectation, they looked to UNYOM to curb what they considered to be the recidivist tendencies of Nasser. The Egyptian leader was to be encouraged, rather than cajoled.

The circumstances in which UNYOM finally deployed reflected the fractitious nature of its creation. Washington declared the disengagement agreement to be both operative and binding on Cairo and Riyadh from 7 June 1963, *before* UNYOM had fully deployed. In the event, the total number of UNYOM personal deployed was, in the words of Ambassador Hart, pathetically small. It consisted of 212 persons stationed at Jizan and Najran in Saudi Arabia and Sad'ah, Sana'a, Rawdha and the port of Hodeidah in the Yemen. The small size of the observer mission was not helped by the limited equipment at its disposal. Although provided with fixed wing Caribou and Otter aircraft, these were unsuitable for night time observation. Helicopters could not operate at high altitudes, while only two static observation posts were established in the demilitarised zone that stretched for 650 kilometres along the Saudi–Yemeni frontier.[51]

The paucity in manpower and equipment reflected the styptic nature of the mandate under which UNYOM was expected to operate. In line with both the official position of the UN and the United States, Von Horn was prohibited from establishing contact with forces loyal to the Imam and as such, was not empowered to verify or accept complaints they had over Egyptian violations of the disengagement agreement. Not only did this undermine a sense of impartiality, crucial if the mission was to be seen as effective, it also led to well founded allegations that the UN deliberately ignored reports from the Yemen that Egypt had used napalm and chemical weapons against villages suspected of aiding and abetting the Royalist forces. More immediately, London was becoming increasingly concerned that continued Egyptian air raids in and around the Saudi port of Jizzan had begun to erode support in Riyadh for the disengagement agreement.[52] On 15 June, during the course of a private conversation with Neil McLean, Crown Prince Faisal repeated his view that Nasser would only leave the Yemen as a result of internal pressure from Royalist forces and external pressure from what he termed 'the powers'. McLean, in transit through Jeddah prior to conducting another extensive tour to the Royalist-held areas in the Yemen, noted the desire of the Saudi Prince to establish closer relations with London, unfettered by the legacy of the dispute over the Buraimi oasis.[53]

The Briton knew that Faisal remained crucial to defeating what he perceived to be Cairo's malign regional intent. He alone could provide the necessary arms, ammunition and financial backing required to rally tribes to the Imam's cause. But McLean realised that the demands placed upon Riyadh by the disengagement agreement effectively denied Saudi territory as a staging post for the supply of arms and ammunition to the Royalist forces for the immediate future. Other outlets had to be found for Crown Prince Faisal's financial largesse to be realised in military terms but without incurring Washington's displeasure. McLean provided a solution. He had already approached Colonel David Smiley to conduct an extensive tour of Royalist positions in Yemen, assess their strengths and weaknesses and report back directly to Crown Prince Faisal. Smiley's arrival in Saudi Arabia on 14 June 1963 marked the emergence of a mercenary commitment to the Yemen over the next five years. It was a commitment that proved to be the nemesis of the Egyptian army, an irritant in Anglo-American relations, and, as far as officials in the Foreign Office were concerned, the antithesis of anything remotely associated with protecting British interests in South Arabia.[54]

On 20 June 1963, Sir Colin Crowe, recently appointed as British Ambassador to Jeddah, telegraphed London with assurances he had received from the Saudis that they had stopped all aid to the Imam. He concluded that 'it was a matter of honour for the Saudis that they should observe their word to give him no further support'.[55] In terms of adhering to the wording of the disengagement agreement this was undoubtedly true. But by sponsoring the activities of Smiley and McLean, Crown Prince Faisal was seeking an insurance policy should the disengagement agreement collapse. If Riyadh's embrace of disengagement was lukewarm, Cairo's commitment on both counts was absent. Not only were their troop movements defined by rotation rather than withdrawal, but evidence of Egyptian use of chemical weapons was becoming harder to ignore.

On 4 July 1963, McLean sent Crowe a detailed report of one such attack on the village of Kowma in the north-west of the Yemen. Although he reached the village five weeks after the attack had occurred in mid-May, his eyewitness account made sober reading:

I went to the exact spot in Kowma village where the two bombs had landed. The earth was a slightly different colour to the surrounding area and black in places. Even after an interval of about a month to 5 weeks during which heavy rains fell, and ploughing and planting by the villages took place, I was immediately aware of, from between twenty and thirty yards away, an unusual, unpleasant and pungent smell. It smelt to me rather like a sweet sour musty chloroform mixed with a strong odour of geranium plant. I looked at some of the children who still had scars and some sores which had, I was told, followed upon a rash of black spots . . . I was told that all of the 120 people of the village still have severe coughs; irritation of the skin and of the 22 people injured, many still vomit black blood after severe coughing.[56]

McLean's experience of conditions in Kowma was corroborated by similar reports from David Smiley. Both men took photographs of scarred and wounded inhabitants of the village and collected soil samples and bomb fragments. Smiley passed these on to Crowe, to be sent by diplomatic pouch to London for further analysis as well as to UN representatives in Jeddah. Smiley later disclosed that he also gave bomb fragments to the Israelis. In July, McLean produced further accounts of Egyptian attacks on the villages of al Darb, Jaraishai, Hasan Bini Awair and Asash, all located to the south and south-east of Sad'ah. The injuries of all the victims were similar to those suffered in Kowma. Smiley suspected that the Egyptians were using a form of mustard gas but the results of tests conducted at Porton Down on various bomb fragments cast doubt on this assumption.

In August 1963, Smiley received a letter from the War Office concluding that while positive traces of tear gas had been found in some examples, the metal casing in others was 'most unlikely to have been used to contain a toxic liquid such as mustard gas or other lethal chemical warfare agent'.[57] Smiley remained unconvinced by this technical autopsy. In private correspondence with a Swiss-based news organisation he hoped would give greater exposure to Egyptian use of chemical weapons, Smiley wrote, 'I am convinced that some other type of poison was used. How else can one explain the fact that people died from its effects?' Tear gas alone, Smiley concluded, 'could not explain away the sores caused by contamination; it is therefore my view that this must have been some other poisonous chemical substances in the bomb'.[58]

Nasser maintained that his use of air power fell outside the terms of the agreement since the Royalists had never been party to the accord. Such sophistry failed to disguise the fact that such attacks, either by conventional or non-conventional munitions, were in clear breach of the disengagement agreement. By July, these violations were of such a magnitude that the Foreign Office feared the total collapse of the Bunker agreement. London-based Independent Television News (ITN) had broadcast footage taken in the Yemen of Egyptian aircraft deploying incendiary bombs against a Yemen village, while on his return to the United Kingdom, Smiley had given a number of interviews on national radio and television in an effort to raise public awareness. In the wake of such unwelcome publicity, the Foreign Office believed pressure would build in London for more pro-active measures, diplomatic or otherwise, to be taken against Egypt. The Foreign Office remained sensitive to accusations of passivity in the face of such aggression, with officials concerned that parallels would be drawn in Parliament with similar government inaction during the Spanish Civil War. Afraid that Saudi patience was wearing thin, the Foreign Office cabled Ormesby-Gore, urging him to impress upon the Kennedy Administration the need for the United States to force Cairo to adhere to its obligations under the Bunker agreement.[59]

But Washington's proved reluctant to engage in such diplomatic arm-twisting, preferring to adopt a benign view of Cairo's actions that bordered on the myopic. On 27 July, Washington announced that Nasser had withdrawn 2,000 troops from Yemen, a figure one UN official in Saudi Arabia later admitted was not confirmed and was most likely to have been more than offset by the arrival of new reinforcements.[60] The belief existed in the State Department however that Saudi dependence upon Washington's military munificence would prevent any recrudescence of military support to the Imam. Such casuistry failed to gauge the growing sense of frustration felt in Jeddah towards what was perceived as a UN agenda bent irrevocably on appeasing Cairo. At the end of July, Crowe informed the Foreign Office that it was his belief that Saudi Arabia would soon resume supplies to the Imam.[61]

Protestations from Cairo over suspected Saudi violations of the disengagement agreement aside, Egyptian subterfuge remained the greater cause for concern in London. On 6 August, Crowe cabled London recounting a detailed conversation he had held with Von Horn. The UNYOM commander revealed that Egyptian troops were encamped in the demilitarised zone, only three kilometres from the Saudi border. That such blatant violations could occur with impunity was symptomatic of the wider malaise Von Horn felt afflicted the mission. Notwithstanding the deficit in equipment and manpower, Von Horn regarded his mandate as little more than political inanition, with the injunction that he refrain from any contact with Royalist forces the subject of particular scorn. As Crowe noted, 'He [Von Horn] sees why the Egyptians bomb the Royalists when their troops are ambushed, but equally admits that Royalists are justified in attacking when their villages have been bombed.'[62]

The decision of U Thant at the beginning of August to allow UNYOM personnel limited contact with Royalist forces came too late to prevent the resignation of Von Horn as head of the mission on 20 August 1963. Although a personal friend of David Smiley dating from the time when the Briton had been the United Kingdom military attaché in Stockholm in the 1950s, he had been forbidden from replying to the correspondence he had received from Smiley regarding the failure of UNYOM to investigate the bombing of Yemeni villages. Now, two days after his resignation, he wrote to Smiley, explaining the restrictions which prevented him from responding to his correspondence. He concluded that 'I felt compelled to resign from my post as a last means in my continuous and fruitless efforts to achieve adequate support for this difficult mission which, in spite of its limited size labours under even worse conditions than "The Congo Horror"'.[63]

Von Horn's departure was a body blow to the UNYOM mission from which it never fully recovered. UN Secretary-General U Thant, humiliated by the manner of the Swedish General's departure, quickly moved to replace him, first with an interim commander, Colonel Branko Pavlovic from Yugoslavia, and on 12 September with an Indian commander, Lieutenant General P. S. Gyani. Eventually, overall control of UNYOM was placed in the hands of a senior UN official, Pier Spinelli who was appointed as Special Representative and head of UNYOM on 4 November 1963. Despite his best endeavours, the mission fell into terminal decline. U Thant managed to roll over the UNYOM mandate every two months, but by September 1964 Crown Prince Faisal refused to bankroll a mission which – though now encompassing Royalist-held areas – had failed to monitor Egyptian compliance with the disengagement agreement. When on 4 September 1964 the UNYOM mission was finally terminated, Egypt had over 50,000 troops in the Yemen.[64]

Regaining Liberty of Action

The demise of UNYOM was a particular disappointment for the Foreign Office. It had held out the promise of securing British interests in South Arabia and beyond but without incurring the diplomatic costs they felt would result from the recidivist policies advocated by some Cabinet ministers and the Colonial Office. Despite the best entreaties of the Foreign Office, the Kennedy Administration proved reluctant to take Nasser to task over Cairo's often indiscriminate use of air power. On 15 August 1963, Foreign Secretary Lord Home cabled his American counterpart Dean Rusk a truncated version of a recent conversation he had held with McLean. Home warned Rusk of McLean's bias towards the Royalist cause, but his testimony of protracted aerial attacks upon Royalist-held areas by Soviet-built Ilyushin bombers, was, he argued, making it increasingly difficult for both London and Washington to urge continued restraint on the Saudis.[65] Circumspection that hovered dangerously close to indulgence continued to define the Kennedy Administration approach to Egypt and the Yemen, however. The Assistant Secretary of State, Phillips Talbot, revealed in a letter to one US Senator in July 1963 that the 'United States had never insisted on withdrawal of Egyptian troops after Saudi Arabia had begun to observe the terms of the disengagement agreement, but merely expected the Egyptians " to withdraw in a phased and expeditious fashion"'.[66] Only on 19 October 1963, a month before his fateful trip to Dallas, did Kennedy pen a strong letter to Nasser, raising his concerns that the ball of non-compliance was in the Egyptian court:

> I think it fair to say that the Saudis are carrying out their end of the bargain. Indeed, I gather the United Arab Republic shared the view of our own intelligence that arms supply over the border has been almost if not entirely cut off. We are confident that the United Kingdom Government . . . [is] not aiding the Royalists . . . On the other hand, the United Arab Republic has not made phased withdrawals to a scale consistent with our understanding of the spirit of the agreement . . . we cannot blink at the fact that the United Arab Republic is not carrying out a compact made with the United Nations, and in effect, underwritten by the United States as a friend of both parties.[67]

For the Foreign Office, such strong words were welcome if progress was to be made towards fulfilling the promise of the Bunker agreement. But engagement with the problem of Yemen in the Cabinet had become increasingly conspicuous by its absence in the autumn of 1963. The growing furore over the Profumo affair overshadowed other policy concerns in Whitehall. When on 8 October 1963 Harold Macmillan resigned as Prime Minister, the Cabinet had not met to review policy towards the Yemen for over seven months although it had been raised at the highest level between London and Washington. Four days before Macmillan's departure from Number 10, the Foreign Secretary Lord Home had given assurances to Kennedy in person that Britain had given no aid to the Imam, assurances that Kennedy had gone on to repeat in his letter to Nasser.[68] It seems likely that Kennedy's enquiry had been prompted by reports reaching the White House of European mercenary activity on behalf of Royalist forces.

The State Department regarded such reports, if proven, as a serious impediment to full disengagement, but the assassination of Kennedy on 22 November 1963 removed at a stroke direct concerted involvement by the White House in seeking a resolution to the Yemen Civil War. The new incumbent, Lyndon Baines Johnson, proved, according to Fawaz Gerges, 'less willing to accommodate Third-World nationalist movements and to provide economic aid to states that had friendly relations with the Soviet bloc and that were not receptive to US wishes'.[69] This shift was compounded by increased suspicion in Cairo that while Kennedy may have tried his best to play the 'honest broker' over Yemen, Johnson's more benign attitude toward Israel revealed Washington's true loyalties in the region. Nasser quickly gave voice to such sentiment by accusing Washington of helping Tel Aviv to acquire a nuclear weapons capability.[70]

With the departure of Harold Macmillan, Sir Alec Douglas-Home became Prime Minister, while Richard 'Rab' Butler inherited the Foreign Office portfolio. His initial assessment of the Yemen Civil War conflated with the position of the Arabian Department, including the importance of close policy co-ordination with the United States. On 21 November he sent a memorandum to Home in which he concluded that although Washington had failed to force an Egyptian disengagement, 'Provided we do nothing to make more difficult the task of the United States Government and of the UN in trying to restore peace to the area, or to cause the UAR to take a direct hand in subverting our position in Arabia, this [the civil war] is a situation we can go on living with.'[71]

This memorandum, circulated throughout the Cabinet, brought an instant riposte from Sandys. While acknowledging that the present stalemate in the Yemen best suited the interests of Her Majesty's Government, he argued it was not a situation that could continue forever. Unless aid to the Royalists was forthcoming, he foresaw the triumph of the Republican forces in Yemen with all the attendant risks this held for the British position in Aden and the Federation. Turning his attention to the United States, he concluded that, 'If the real American objective is to secure sooner or later by one means or another a Nasser/Republican victory, we must make it plain we cannot go along with them.'[72]

On 2 December 1963, the Cabinet convened to discuss specifically the situation in the Yemen. The clear strength of opinion that emerged from this meeting concluded that Nasser could not be trusted and as such, hopes of an Egyptian disengagement remained a chimera. Washington's policy of engaging with Nasser, either directly or through the United Nations, had failed and accordingly, 'We should therefore reconsider our present support of the US policy and seek to recover our liberty of action'. This reassessment also extended to the role played by the United Nations. Given the obvious flaws in the UNYOM mission and the belief among Colonial Office officials at least that the UN remained prejudiced against the Federation, the meeting concurred that further UN intervention in the Yemen should be resisted 'since it would be detrimental to our position in Aden if we were forced to side with the Republican party in the Yemen in an attempt by the UN to restore order.' The Cabinet was told that Saudi Arabia had stockpiled considerable quantities of arms and ammunition on the frontier and had resumed the smuggling of weapons to the Royalist forces. While it was agreed that the declared policy of non-intervention in the conflict should be continued, the Cabinet concluded that, 'it might improve our relationship with the rulers in the Aden Federation if we ceased trying to prevent them from supplying arms to the Royalists'.[73]

The decisions reached during this Cabinet meeting effectively sealed the direction of British policy towards the Yemen Civil War for the remaining ten months of the Conservative government. While Macmillan had eschewed recognition of the Republican regime, he had at least kept the diplomatic door ajar for the entry of Washington and the United Nations.

This door was now being closed. The hardening of attitudes towards the YAR and Egypt not only confirmed the ascendancy of the view held in Cabinet, most notably by Duncan Sandys, of Egyptian malevolence, but also reflected the influence that the detailed reports provided by McLean and Smiley had played in swaying opinions, not least those held by the Prime Minister himself. The policy recommendations reached at the end of the Cabinet meeting of 2 December 1963 bore the hallmarks of McLean's thinking previously outlined in the document he circulated to Sandys, Thorneycroft and Home in October 1963. The report was a summary of McLean's impressions of the strength and durability of the Imam's position, based on extensive travels made throughout Royalist-held areas between June and September 1963. In effect a geo-strategic survey, the report, titled 'General Impressions' outlined a 'worst-case scenario' should Nasser emerge triumphant. It argued:

> Once Egyptian power is established in the Yemen, Nasser could even more effectively than before, threaten Saudi Arabia and Aden. America would then again be faced with the choice between Nasser, who they believe to be the main barrier against Communism in the Middle East and their allies, the monarchies of Saudi Arabia and Jordan, and the British in Aden and the Gulf . . . If the Americans were then to try and restrain Nasser, it would be to late for almost certainly he would blackmail them by threatening to join the Russians' camp. They would then be faced with the choice of appeasement or direct intervention.[74]

While the more adventurous recommendations in his report were deemed incongruous with a declared policy of non-intervention by Her Majesty's Government, his cryptic argument that support be given 'to the southern tribes through a number of unattributable channels, some of which already exist', was one clearly taken on board by the Cabinet meeting. David Smiley also enjoyed direct access to the Prime Minister, undoubtedly helped by the fact that his wife was a distant relative of Douglas-Home. On 17 December 1963, having just completed a trip of some 18 days duration to the Yemen, Smiley briefed the Prime Minister in Number 10 on the political and military situation in Royalist-held areas.[75] With the government now willing to explore what other pro-active measures could be instigated to deal with Egyptian-backed subversion from the YAR, Foreign Office officials saw themselves reduced to the role of reluctant tradesmen, trying to sell a diplomatic product in which they themselves had precious little faith.

In the absence of formal recognition of the YAR by London, the Foreign Office had encouraged the efforts of the State Department and the UN to reach a cease-fire. But just as British policy towards the Yemen hardened under Home, so US policy under Johnson became less accommodating towards Nasser, and more sympathetic towards the British view of Egyptian policy bent irrevocably towards regional aggrandisement. By March 1964, officials at the US Embassy in London certainly felt that the State Department, for so long beguiled by Nasser, should be more attuned to British sensitivities throughout the region, including the importance Britain placed on stability in the Federation if the Aden base was to be secured. This was a frank admission that past indifference had characterised State Department policy towards British interests and concerns in South Arabia. Sensing American policy was now more sympathetic to these concerns, officials in London sought to capitalise. Sir Stuart Crawford, Assistant Under-secretary of State at the Foreign Office wrote in a minute that, 'Their [the US Embassy] argument is that a greater knowledge of the problems confronting us in and around Aden will make it easier for the US Government to give its whole hearted support to our position . . . I suggest that we must not neglect to act on this advice from the US Embassy.'[76]

This newfound sympathy for London remained conditional: it did not extend to condoning direct involvement or involvement by proxy in the Yemen. Washington continued to press London to 'state publicly that they were doing everything possible to control activities in the Yemen/Federation border and (in effect) to prevent people in the Federation assisting the Royalists in the Yemen'. Having seen the winds of American policy shift favourably behind the British position in Aden, officials in the Arabian Department felt that such assurances should be forthcoming. The head of the Department, Frank Brenchley, noted that, 'The Americans have been more restrained than we might have expected over the pro-Royalist proclivities of the authorities in the Federation on which they seem well informed'.[77]

On 6 March, Mr Seelye, a State Department official, raised the issue of mercenaries for the first time with the British Embassy in Washington but without pushing for an official explanation. Three days later, U Thant, still struggling to revive the moribund Bunker agreement, repeated assertions to British officials at the UN that arms and ammunition were continuing to reach Royalist forces 'though not necessarily across the northern frontier'. Washington's concerns were of a piece and a cause for some concern in King Charles Street.[78] The whole issue of the Federation was due to be discussed before the UN Committee of 24 which monitored the process of decolonisation. In the spring of 1963, the Committee had received strong representations from those groups in Aden opposed to the creation of the Federation. The PSP and ATUC in particular argued that its very creation was a fiction since self-determination had been denied them. Future support from the United States delegation to the Committee for the British position was deemed crucial if attempts to push forward with constitutional reform within the Federation were to bear fruit.

The Foreign Office was not, however, in any position to give such assurances other than restating to Washington the official policy of non-involvement in the Yemen. This certainly did not wash with the State Department. On 18 March 1964, Ormesby-Gore, (now Lord Harlech) cabled London with details of a meeting held earlier that day with Secretary of State Dean Rusk. 'He [Rusk] was increasingly concerned at reports of activity in the Royalist camp by British Reserve Officers and mercenaries who were facilitating the supply of arms to the Royalists.' Harlech's response was suitably vague, restating that it was government policy to 'discourage' – though not prevent – what he termed this 'private enterprise which was a very amateur operation.' Rusk claimed that Washington had continued to make strong representations in both Cairo and Sana'a in support of the British position in Aden, but such entreaties were undermined when evidence of the involvement of British nationals in the civil war, whether sanctioned or not, carried empirical weight.[79]

The Foreign Office was well aware of the activities of individuals such as Smiley and McLean. It was less well briefed on the extent to which a mercenary organisation, recruited in London and Paris but paid for in the main by Saudi Arabia, had, since the autumn of 1963, been operating in an advisory capacity with Royalist forces. It was clear to the Foreign Office however that their presence could not be explained as serendipitous. Beihan was proving to be a main infiltration route for the mercenaries into the Yemen. Given that Britain remained responsible for the defence of the Federation, the weight of evidence to the informed observer, however circumstantial, pointed to British connivance in their activities. The growing suspicion in the State Department was that the mercenaries were a covert tool sanctioned by London to ensure the restoration of the Imamate.

The gravity of Rusk's concerns was such that they were raised by Butler the following day in a meeting of the Defence and Overseas Policy Committee convened specifically to discuss the increased tension along the Yemeni–Federation border. Butler conceded that retaliatory action along the border in response to Egyptian-backed subversion from the YAR was a necessary evil, if only to stay the frayed nerves of Federation rulers. He argued however that, in particular in the case of Beihan, attacks on Federal territory were themselves a riposte to the pro-Royalist activities of their rulers. Butler referred to a report by the Joint Intelligence Committee which questioned the efficacy of subversive activity as a tool with which to remove the Egyptians from Yemen. Ever conscious of the need to keep Washington on board, Butler then spoke with some conviction, as the minutes of the meeting reveal, over the issue of mercenaries:

> The only way in which we would think that we could make our action more palatable to the Americans would be if ministers will give a clear decision in favour of the Foreign Secretary's proposal, namely that we will not harbour the mercenaries in British territory and will take effective action to discourage the Rulers and Saudis from involving themselves in a civil war from British territory . . . If we could secure this, and could then go to the Americans with clean hands in regard to our non-involvement in the Yemen, we should have a defensible posture with them and the UN. If, on a future occasion, Her Majesty's Government were to authorise a retaliatory air attack, our defence would be a much better one than it could be today when we are, by tolerating mercenaries etc. encouraging the UAR and the Yemeni Republicans to act against us.'[80]

The scope and method of overt retaliatory action dominated the meeting. As much concerned with political necessities as with strict operational requirements, the meeting, in line with the views of Sandys and Thorneycroft, condoned the use of retaliatory air strikes and that 'certain counter-subversion measures be stepped up' in defence of the Federation.[81] By contrast, Butler's proposal failed to gain support. When international opprobrium met Britain's decision to bomb the Republican-held fort of Harib close to the Federation border, in retaliation for an earlier attack on Beihani territory, the Foreign Office once more found itself defending a policy that had few redeeming features to recommend itself to Washington or to the United Nations. On 9 April 1964, the UN passed a resolution condemning the British action at Harib. But for the direct plea by Douglas-Home to President Johnson, the US Ambassador to the United Nations would have voted in favour of the UN resolution. In the event, he was instructed to abstain.[82]

Realising that unilateral action of the kind seen at Harib risked, at the very least, serious discord in Anglo-American relations, the British Ambassador to Washington, Lord Harlech, cabled London with some strong advice. Noting that there was 'resentment in the White House', over the lack of prior consultation regarding the Harib attack he argued that 'If we are to continue to receive American support for our policies in South Arabia as we can reasonably expect to do, it is important that we should continue to keep them closely informed both of our assessment of the situation and our intentions.' In a pithy aside to the position of the Colonial Office, Harlech concluded that Britiain owed no allegiance to Republican or Royalist forces. Whatever the outcome of the war in Yemen, it could never 'slip back to a past of total feudalism under a drug addict', a swipe at those in the Colonial Office and Cabinet whose incantations in favour of the *Hamid'Ud'Din* sought to disguise the dubious character of some of its paladins.[83]

This drew a furious riposte from Sir Kennedy Trevaskis. As the new incumbent of Government House in Aden, he had narrowly survived an assassination attempt in December 1963 at Aden's Khormaksar airport where a close aide had been killed. He regarded the malign intrigues of Nasser as the prime reason for the political turmoil that had begun to grip the Federation. With an eye on the growing unrest in the mountains of Radfan adjacent to the frontier with the Yemen, Trevaskis cabled Sandys and emphasised the need for strong pro-active measures to be taken to prevent a stable Republican government under Cairo's tutelage from emerging. He wrote that, '[I]n my view we should do all in our power to prevent the Y. A. R from acquiring stability and if possible to rid the Yemen of U. A. R and other hostile influences.'[84] This drew an equally tart response from Sir Harold Beeley, who pointed out that the position advocated by the High Commissioner circumvented any meaningful role for the United States at a time when 'we are likely to become increasingly dependent on American support for the preservation of our essential interests in Aden and the Gulf.'[85]

The need to keep Washington informed of British policy in Aden was taken as given. But when Butler met with Rusk in Washington on 27 April, the minutes of the meeting reveal that it was the views of the Colonial Office that held sway. Butler presented Rusk with a document giving details of a sustained campaign of Egyptian backed subversion of the Federation. Sir Stuart Crawford, accompanying Butler on his trip, had already denied to Assistant Under-secretary of State Philips Talbot and other State Department officials that London in any way condoned the activities of the British mercenaries in the Yemen as a means to counter Egyptian subversion.[86] But such subversion, the Foreign Secretary declared, would in turn have to be fought by what he termed counter-subversion. It was the first time that London gave notice to the Americans that it was prepared to engage in clandestine activity, though Butler was keen to emphasise that these measures were defensive in nature. This policy had been decided upon at a meeting of the Defence and Overseas Policy Committee only four days previously.[87] According to the record of the Foreign Secretary's remarks, Butler did not divulge, nor did Rusk enquire, what form these counter-subversion measures would take. Anxious to paint a picture of an obstreperous Egypt, Butler claimed Nasser had the potential to cripple American interests throughout the region. Warming to his theme, he invoked the wider spectre of Cold War competition, noting the recent visit of Sallal to Moscow and Soviet premier Khrushchev's forthcoming visit to Cairo as examples of growing Soviet encroachment throughout the region. Rusk, however, remained unmoved. While the United States continued to favour an Egyptian withdrawal from Yemen, he refused to countenance the use of US aid, despite promptings by Butler, as a lever to exact concessions from Nasser, arguing that such precipitous action would risk 'losing what little influence they

[Washington] had in Cairo.'[88] If the purpose of the meeting was to explain British policy and coax the State Department towards adopting a tougher line with Nasser, it fell some way short.

Matters in this regard were not helped by an ill-tempered meeting at the beginning of June between Duncan Sandys and the United States Under-secretary of State George Ball. Sandys complained that Washington failed to understand the magnitude of subversive operations directed against the Federation and claimed that US aid to Egypt was being passed on by Cairo to help bolster the Republican regime. Ball took issue with this and, according to the minutes of the meeting retorted that 'American relations with Nasser were not for the sake of his [Sandys] blue eyes. If the Americans showed a mark change in their attitude towards the UAR, Nasser might become completely dependent on the Soviets.'[89] The meeting itself was so marked by mutual rancour that, against standard practice, the minutes of the meeting were not circulated among the usual departments. This sin of omission only drew comment when, upon his return to Washington, Ball took issue with the British Embassy over his treatment by Sandys. Noting that the American had been 'somewhat miffed', a British Embassy official, John Killick, wrote with a sense of exasperation, 'Surely Mr Sandys appreciated all this [Washington's ties with Nasser] and realised it was pointless to put pressure on Mr Ball in this way?'[90]

Sandys' behaviour was detrimental to the objective he had set himself. In June 1964, the Colonial Secretary convened a Constitutional Conference in London consisting of members of the Federal and Aden governments to decide upon the mechanism for the transfer of sovereignty to a united Federation. The outcome of the conference, which excluded the avowedly nationalist PSP, agreed to a date of no later than 1968 for Federal independence and the conclusion of a defence agreement under which Britain would continue to maintain a military base in Aden. As Sir Kennedy Trevaskis noted, 'The agreement was not definitive but opened the doors to final solutions of our outstanding problems . . . Outside the conference room there had been agreements, too, that funds would at last be made available for crash development programmes.'[91]

London hoped that Washington could be persuaded to match its aid to Egypt with a package, albeit on a less grandiose scale, to the Federation.[92] This argument found a champion in Parker T. Hart who felt his personal efforts at securing the withdrawal of Egyptian troops from Yemen had been undermined by the personal mendacity of Nasser. Yet his call for closer Anglo-American policy co-ordination in South Arabia continued to run counter, as Sir Colin Crowe noted, 'to a school in the State Department who believe that the UAR presence will prevent Communist penetration'.[93] By the summer of 1964 however, attempts to sway opinion in the

State Department against Nasser played second fiddle to managing the growing crisis throughout the Federation. Increased reports of Egyptian arms caravans entering Federal territory and violence in the Radfan, growing unrest in Aden and continued border tensions in Beihan occupied the immediate concerns of ministers in London.[94] Whatever hopes the Foreign Office entertained of greater policy co-operation with their counterparts in the State Department were never to be realised in a government whose paramount concern remained securing a weak Federation against the endeavours of Egyptian subversion. For the Foreign Office, the position of the Colonial Office was ill-informed and beholden to the often exaggerated reports from the Federation rulers – most notably Shariff Hussein – whose reports of Egyptian malevolence were often a subterfuge plot to enlist the aid of the Federal authorities in pursuit of his own territorial claims. By the summer of 1964, the Foreign Office believed that London could no longer see the Yemeni wood for the Federation trees'.

Conclusion

Until the autumn of 1964, the debates over British policy towards the Yemen were never about the end goal – securing the Federation – but the most expeditious means by which this could achieved. All were agreed on the need to cohere a stable Federation as a requirement for the protection and continued propagation of British interests throughout the Middle East. Concerned that Britain, still struggling to banish the ignominy of Suez, should no longer ignore the reality of Arab nationalism and the popularity of Nasser, Foreign Office officials refused to concede that Cairo's designs in Yemen remained anything but defensive. The encouragement, albeit from the sidelines, of American and UN attempts to broker a regional settlement also bore the unpalatable taste of previous British experience in the region: London no longer had the capacity, even if it so wished, to determine policy against the wishes of the United States.

British policy under the stewardship of Harold Macmillan represented an uneasy amalgam between the competing lines advocated by the Colonial Office and the Foreign Office. Though withholding recognition from the YAR, Macmillan supported the active role of officials in the Kennedy administration and at the UN in brokering a solution to the Yemen Civil War. Certainly, the approach of the 'New Frontiersmen', emboldened with the belief that Arab nationalism represented an ideology compatible with American interests, evoked much sympathy in King Charles Street. Attachment to the 'irrational and antediluvian' meant clinging to the wreckage of discredited regimes as they were swept aside by the tide of historical inevitability.

That this particular dialectic should founder demonstrates all too clearly the role exercised by key individuals. Kennedy's tragic end removed at a stroke the personal interest the White House had taken in the Yemen conflagration. While the State Department continued to advocate a cease-fire and eventual disengagement of all outside parties from the Yemen, President Johnson's footprint on the diplomatic sand was never as firm as his predecessor. With its attention focused firmly on events in south-east Asia, by the summer of 1964 Washington was looking to contain the problem in Yemen rather than resolve it. Anything that threatened this approach was to be resisted, which explains why State Department officials attached particular importance to assurances in London concerning the activities of British mercenaries.

Equally, the political demise of Macmillan signalled a shift in government thinking away from the uneasy balance struck between the competing positions of the mandarins in Whitehall. The Cabinet meeting of 2 December 1963 marked a crucial turning point in this regard, with the Prime Minister, Alec Douglas-Home, overseeing a shift in government thinking towards the use of more robust methods, both overt and covert, to protect the territorial integrity of the Federation. Whether British policy was now hostage to the vicissitudes of tribal politics masquerading under the cloak of Egyptian subversion, as the Foreign Office intimated, remained hard to gauge. It is certainly the case that hostile action in Federal territory, however dependent on Cairo's largesse, remained a potent reminder that Yemen's territorial claims remained inimical to British interests in South Arabia. As such, Nasser's failure to abide by both the spirit and word of the Bunker agreement was mere grist to the mill of those determined not only to maintain the British position in Aden, but to avenge what they saw as its humiliation at the hands of Nasser over Suez. Faced with such a diplomatic impasse, a permissive environment emerged in Whitehall that allowed covert action to increasingly determine British policy towards the Yemen Civil War.

4

A Constrained Response

The Limits of Covert Action

How to counter Egyptian-backed subversion dominated British policy towards the Yemen Civil War from the moment Sana'a severed diplomatic ties with London in February 1963 over the issue of non-recognition.[1] By the late spring of 1964, faced with a rising tide of guerrilla activity in Aden and beyond, Cabinet discussion had moved beyond the scope of diplomacy and moved towards sanctioning clandestine operations, albeit of limited geographical scope, inside the Yemen itself. It was, however, a policy decision forced upon London by need rather than through preferred choice.

The legacy of Suez imposed severe limitations on the extent to which Britain could resort to the overt use of force to protect the Federation borders. The international outcry provoked by the overt use of air power against the Yemeni fort of Harib at the end of March 1964 merely confirmed the prevailing view in London that if armed force was to be used to ensure the stability of the Federation from external threats, it had to be clandestine in nature. This was contrary to the declared government policy of non-intervention and anathema to the mandarins of King Charles Street. The Foreign Office, however, was not only struggling against the policy recommendations of competing departments, but also against the influence of the Aden Group, whose access to key individuals in the Cabinet made them a formidable counterweight to what they regarded as the dilettante views of the Foreign Office. Their influence had already proved decisive, not least in thwarting recognition of the YAR in the winter of 1962. This influence, though not decisive, was again felt in the Cabinet during the summer of 1964 when reports reaching London indicated the low level of morale among Royalist forces and their impending demise.

With the Bunker agreement moribund by spring 1964, clandestine operations were deemed the only option available if Britain was to maintain its strategic interests in South Arabia and blunt Nasser's malign ambitions towards Aden. While clandestine operations were approved at Cabinet level, they never enjoyed wholehearted support throughout Whitehall. Indeed, Alec Douglas-Home placed such restrictions on the size and scope of special operations that they remained, for the most part, defensive and reactive, rather than offensive and proactive. It was only when the Royalist position in the Yemen during the late summer and autumn of 1964 seemed precarious that Home authorised a more aggressive line; but even this was carefully controlled from the centre and directed against a particular target, rather than representing a wholesale shift in policy, or indeed, related directly to aiding and abetting the Royalist war effort. This thwarted the best efforts of McLean, in particular, to link such sanctioned clandestine activity with direct aid to the Imam's forces, but the crisis facing the Royalists in the summer of 1964 was never deemed to be of sufficient magnitude to coax Home beyond agreed policy. Assessments provided by the JIC never equated to the more doom-laden scenarios outlined by McLean and repeated almost verbatim in SIS reports to the Defence and Overseas Policy Committee. Moreover, despite the collapse of the Bunker agreement, London had to remain sensitive to Washington's more lenient, if increasingly less sanguine, view of Nasser. Such conditions on the use and exercise of state power removed, as Sir Percy Craddock noted, 'Britain's capacity for major independent action in the Middle East.'[2] Conditioned by context, clandestine operations sanctioned by London proved less than the sum of their parts: able to wound but reluctant to strike.

Countering Subversion: Overt 'Defensive' Action

It is clear that official British strategy towards countering subversion from the Yemen was often fragmentary, at times half-hearted and subject to continued battles in Whitehall that either diluted or blocked the scope of military action. Nonetheless, officially sanctioned covert action aimed primarily at countering the activities of the Egyptian Intelligence officers along the frontier with Yemen, came to inform Britain's approach towards the civil war in the spring and summer of 1964.

Debate over the efficacy of engaging in clandestine activity in an effort to stem the tide of Egyptian-backed subversion from the Yemen was not new. As early as October 1962 tensions over the type and scale of military assets to be employed against the Egyptian threat had already provoked fierce disagreements in London. The Commander in Chief of Middle East Command (MIDCOM) in Aden had requested permission from London that photo-reconnaissance (PR) flights be conducted over Sana'a to ascertain the strength of Egyptian air assets. (Already, Egyptian aircraft had flown over the border into Federation airspace and attacked a house in Beihan belonging to Shariff Hussein.) The request was denied by the Chairman of the JIC, Sir Hugh Stephenson, on the grounds that there was 'already a great deal of first class intelligence from special sources'.[3] A similar entreaty was made three months later, this time through Johnston, direct to Sandys. It was stressed that continued attacks on the Sultanate of Beihan undermined faith in the British commitment to protect the territorial integrity of the Federation, as well as serving to undermine the morale of Federation troops. The hope was that as Colonial Secretary, Sandys could win cabinet approval for PR flights.[4]

Of particular concern to MIDCOM was the use of frontier villages by Republican forces for launching attacks inside the Protectorate and for organising arms caravans to supply dissident tribesman within the Federation hinterland and in Aden itself. These arms were now finding their way to the National Liberation Front (NLF), a guerrilla movement dedicated to the overthrow of British rule. This was demonstrated most visibly with the attempted assassination of Sir Kennedy Trevaskis at Aden Airport on 10 December 1963. While acknowledging that a threat did exist, the Foreign Office believed that reports of Egyptian backed dissident activity along the border were deliberately exaggerated by people such as Trevaskis, who, it was known, had close contacts with the Aden Group.[5] Responding to a claim by the High Commissioner that 'Egyptian trained Yemeni saboteurs' were engaging in acts of sabotage in the Federation, Sir Stuart Crawford, Under-secretary of State at the Foreign Office, noted tersely that, 'This is an instance of the kind of report which can be used to substantiate the hypothesis of an Egyptian–Yemeni conspiracy against the Federation for which there is as yet no real evidence other than Nasser's speech and the hotting [sic] up of broadcast propaganda.'[6]

Crawford's circumspection notwithstanding, arms caravans and attacks on Federation territory remained a constant headache for MIDCOM. Detailed minutes taken at a meeting of the Chiefs of Staff in June 1964 reveal not only the belief that Nasser wished to oversee the establishment 'in Aden State and the Protectorates of a Cairo orientated Arab nationalist regime', but that they foresaw an increase in Egyptian-sponsored subversive activity among the tribes. The minutes record that:

There have been several reports that the number of Egyptian intelligence officers in the Yemen has increased and that the Egyptians are providing increasing material aid not only for dissidents but also for terrorism and by extremists in the Federation, including Aden State. As activity in the Radfan has recently shown, dissident forces are likely to be increasingly sophisticated in their equipment, training, and discipline.[7]

Reference to the Radfan was of particular note. Though only some 110 kilometres from Aden along a tortuous road, the Radfan was an exceptionally mountainous area of the Federation. The main source of revenue for the dominant tribal grouping of the region, the *Quteibi*, had been subsistence farming and the collection of tolls – 'protection money' for those individuals who wished to travel through the area. The introduction of a South Arabian customs union in 1962 removed this source of revenue, creating genuine resentment at the Federation. This resentment was harnessed by Cairo to sow tribal dissent in the Radfan. Shaykh Seif Muqbil of the *Quteibi* had been exiled by the British. Now under Egyptian tutelage, he stepped up attacks against symbols of the Federation, most notably the border forts manned by Federal Regular Army, the main defence force of the FSA. 'Operation Nutcracker', launched on 4 January 1964, was an attempt to quell this dissident activity and restore faith among the Federal rulers in London's commitment to the stability of the Federation. Operation Nutcracker continued through until August, though the bulk of the fighting was over by June. While deemed a relative success – British and FRA troops fought successfully in some of the harshest conditions imaginable – the minutes of the Chiefs of Staff meeting made it clear that subversive activity would continue. In a letter to the Chief of the Defence Staff, Lord Louis Mountbatten, the Commander in Chief MIDCOM, Lieutenant General Sir Charles Harington, noted that the extreme social and economic deprivation of the region was the single biggest cause of dissent and would always be exploited by the Egyptians unless or until civil aid projects were introduced into the region. Among his recommendations, Harington highlighted the necessity of new irrigation channels, the installation of water pumps and the construction of new roads throughout the Radfan.[8]

The need to engage in a widespread campaign of 'hearts and minds' was clearly recognised in London. In isolation however, it could not provide an immediate panacea to either attacks on Federation territory or the continued pleas by Federation rulers for London to adopt more pro-active measures against both the Republican forces and their Egyptian overlords. From the beginning of 1963, an acrimonious debate had raged through the corridors of Whitehall over the command, control and scope of any overt retaliatory action. Mindful of the wider regional and international repercussions that could result from such action, the Foreign Office lobbied hard for final authority for retaliation to rest with London, and not the High Commissioner in Aden or the CinC MIDCOM. The Foreign Office rightly suspected that some of Federal potentates deliberately allowed their territory to be used for arms supplies to the Royalist forces in the Yemen, a position clearly at odds with the declared policy of Her Majesty's Government on non-intervention. The Foreign Office argued that military action emanating from the Yemen was often a reaction to subversive acts from the FSA, rather than an attempt to undermine the Federation as part of some wider Cairo-inspired plot. With the Colonial Office seemingly unwilling to curb such activities yet determined to uphold British defence guarantees to the Federation rulers, the Foreign Office felt that retaliatory action was unduly influenced by the need to save the rulers from the consequences of their own actions. The recollections of Brigadier David Warren, who served on secondment to the FRA, are instructive in this regard. He claimed that Shariff Hussein was not beyond sending his own tribesman out to shoot at FRA positions in the hope that this would provoke British forces into taking retaliatory action against the imagined YAR aggressor. The end result, it was hoped, would be greater British support for his fiefdom, including his claims on territory in the Yemen.[9]

Accordingly, the Foreign Office had, much to the chagrin of the Trevaskis and MIDCOM, managed to persuade ministers of the need to exert tight control over retaliatory action. While the use of small arms fire, including mortars, was delegated to the commander on the spot, the use of artillery or the use of aircraft in the counter-battery role was heavily circumscribed. Trevaskis, in particular, felt that the time required to obtain authorisation for an effective response to artillery and air attacks on Federation territory, negated the whole exercise as targets were unlikely to remain static. The inability of the United Kingdom to maintain an effective deterrent had long been a bone of contention among the Federation rulers. Shariff Hussein of Beihan had long complained of British double standards. In a letter addressed to Duncan Sandys, dated 15 October 1963, he complained that while the British had encouraged, indeed bolstered, his support for the Royalist cause, they had failed to prevent consistent air attacks upon his territory or to support his claims to territory that fell within the Yemen proper.[10]

The scale of Egyptian air attacks against Beihan, however, did persuade the Cabinet in London to set aside the objections of the Foreign Office and to sanction a punitive air strike. Lists of appropriate targets were provided by MIDCOM and placed into three main categories. Category A targets were deemed to be those of a 'local military significance' within ten miles of the frontier. These included gun emplacements, water distillation plants, barracks, arms dumps, custom posts and forts suspected of being logistical bases for caravans carrying arms and supplies to the NLF. Category B targets were again of parochial concern but situated beyond the ten-mile limit. Category C targets were deemed strategic, and included Egyptian and Yemen military facilities around Sana'a and the deepwater port of Hodeidah. MIDCOM made it clear that while it possessed, in theatre, assets to attack targets listed in the first two categories, it would require four Canberra bombers to be flown from Germany and Cyprus to hit category C targets, requiring a warning time of anywhere between 48 to 72 hours. The cable concluded that 'any retaliatory system based on the use of proposed targets would require *immediate* [my emphasis] reaction to Yemen/UAR air intrusion. If authority is not to be delegated to the High Com[missioner] then a system must be devised whereby Whitehall is in a position to authorise retaliation the same day'.[11]

The response from London was swift. The Cabinet agreed to allow the High Commissioner to sanction an over-flying operation, penetrating not more than 30 miles into Yemeni airspace should UAR aircraft continue to violate Federal airspace. This retaliatory flight was authorised to fly over at least one significant population centre in the Yemen, the declared aim being to 'raise the morale of the tribes in the Federation and depress the morale of the tribes on the Yemeni side of the border.' In the event of an actual air-to-ground attack on a Federation target, a retaliatory attack on a similar scale should be undertaken but only after such measures were sanctioned explicitly by the Prime Minister. It was clear that Her Majesty's Government wished to adhere to at least some form of the Queensbury rules. Confusion over the scope of retaliation remained: Trevaskis wanted the freedom to attack 'opportunity targets' without prior approval should they present themselves as part of a retaliatory operation, as well as permission to inflict human casualties deliberately should they be incurred by the Federation.[12]

It was a situation that reached a dramatic climax in late March 1964. Yemeni aircraft had again engaged in a series of bombing attacks against villages in Beihan. In this respect, the Cabinet decision to authorise a retaliatory strike against the Yemeni fort of Harib directly adjacent to Beihan was determined by the need to be seen to fulfil its treaty obligations to the Federal rulers. It is worth noting that prior to the attack by RAF Hunters on Harib, the Colonial Office received news from Trevaskis that intelligence information in his possession indicated that Harib could fall to the Royalists. This in turn would allow Shariff Hussein to pursue his territorial claim to the Wadi Harib which he regarded as part of his suzerainty.[13] This report was passed on to the Foreign Office where it caused some alarm. On 18 March, Thomas 'Frank' Brenchley, head of the Arabian Department, wrote a detailed appraisal, noting that the capture of Harib was bound to provoke Republican attempts to recapture the fort, leading to a possible confrontation with the FRA should Hussein move simultaneously to enforce his claim. Brenchley made it clear that the duty of the colonial authorities in Aden lay in preventing the Shariff from using Federal territory for active engagement in the Yemeni conflict.[14]

The following day, a full meeting of the Defence and Overseas Policy Committee was convened to specifically discuss the situation in Yemen and the Federation. The Foreign Secretary, Rab Butler, cautioned against any action that would harm London's relationship with the United States and the UN. In particular, he drew attention to increasing reports of mercenary activity in the Yemen, which had already provoked the ire of the United States Secretary of State, Dean Rusk. As a riposte, the Colonial Office highlighted telegrams sent by Trevaskis to Sandys detailing the growing disquiet among the Federation rulers to what they regarded as the marked reluctance on the part of London to counter UAR air attacks on the Federation.[15] The Foreign Office minutes of this meeting were damning of Trevaskis, calling his contribution by telegram 'somewhat hysterical', and noting that in all probability Egyptian air activity was as much a response to the pro-Royalist activities from Beihan as anything else.[16]

In the event, the diplomatic furore over the attack on Harib fort on 28 March 1964 was inversely proportional to the military damage inflicted. London insisted that the RAF give adequate warning to the inhabitants of the fort of the impending attack. Aircraft would drop leaflets to this effect 30 minutes before bombing, a time cut by half on the insistence of the CinC MIDCOM since he believed such a warning would allow air defence preparations to be made, thus endangering the pilots. In the event, ten people were killed and seven wounded. The attack brought international opprobrium upon London at the UN and the Arab League as well as strong condemnation in the British press. The death toll was higher than expected because the leaflets, dropped in bundles from a low-flying RAF Hunter jet fighter, appeared not to have dispersed on impact. Analysis by the Foreign Office immediately after the attack cast doubt on the wisdom of using leaflets as a method of giving advanced warning. Even if the leaflets had dispersed, it was felt that the low levels of literacy among the tribesman would have made it highly improbable that anyone could have raised the alarm.[17] That the attack effectively ended Egyptian air attacks (though not air incursions) on Federation territory for some time afterwards was overlooked amid the immediate diplomatic outcry. On the insistence of the Foreign Secretary, Rab Butler, even the authority to sanction retaliatory over-flights was now removed from MIDCOM and Trevaskis, despite resistance from Thorneycroft.[18] The debate over who had the authority to retaliate and against which targets using which weapons systems was to rumble on well into 1965 and the tenure of a new Labour government. More than any other single event, the international reaction to the Harib attack pushed policy-makers in London towards sanctioning covert operations along the border with Yemen. Such 'deniable' operations led, almost inevitably to closer ties with the Royalist forces.

Covert 'Defensive' Operations

On 14 May 1964, in response to a question put formally to him by Michael Foot MP in the House of Commons regarding allegations of arms supplies to the Royalist forces, Prime Minister Alec Douglas-Home declared: 'Our policy towards the Yemen is one of non-intervention in the affairs of that country. It is not therefore our policy to supply arms to the Royalists in the Yemen and the Yemen government have not requested these in the form of aid.'[19] The statement was not entirely accurate. While London did not supply arms directly to the Royalists, there was no doubt that with eyes wide shut, London and the authorities in Aden allowed arms caravans and mercenary operations to be organised and launched from Federal territory. More immediately however, London sanctioned a policy of covert operations, in particular after the Harib incident, designed to stem the flow of arms from Yemeni territory into the Federation.

This move towards what was in effect 'covert defensive action', marked a shift in the position of Butler, if not on the part of the Foreign Office. In a memo to Douglas-Home soon after assuming office in November 1964, Butler had argued that, 'we should not, as a government, either overtly or covertly, get involved with the Yemeni internal situation . . . we can rely on the Saudis to keep Northern tribes fed with arms and ammunition'.[20] By the following March, Butler's position had begun to shift, conceding that retaliatory action of limited scope should be employed on or near the Federation border with the Yemen but that direct involvement in the conflict be avoided.[21] The Foreign Office remained concerned that any retaliatory action would necessarily exacerbate tensions along the border and, indeed, encourage further Yemeni and Egyptian subversion of the Federation. They poured scorn on the Colonial Office assertions at the beginning of January 1964 that Egyptian army officers were training Yemeni saboteurs to infiltrate into Federation territory and beyond to Aden Colony.[22] Foreign Office circumspection was also a reflection of the deep unease that continued reports of mercenary activity in the Yemen, sustained and supported from Federation territory, were having upon London's relations with Washington.[23] Whether such activity did indeed serve merely to stiffen rather than undermine Egyptian resolve remains the subject of some debate. It is worth noting however that in a conversation with Mohammed Heikal, editor of the Egyptian daily *Al-Ahram* and close confidant of Nasser, the Canadian Ambassador to Moscow, Robert Ford, was told in no uncertain terms that Egyptian support for the NLF was entirely justified given London's continued support for the Imam and the Royalist forces. Moreover, Egyptian forces would remain in the

Yemen for as long as was needed to ensure the stability and longevity of the Republic.[24]

Such views appeared to substantiate a letter that was 'acquired' by Trevaskis and disclosed to Sandys concerning the alleged involvement of a Deputy Minister in the Egyptian government, Hadi Eisa, in organising a campaign of terror inside the Federation. The veracity of this letter notwithstanding – Trevaskis did not disclose its source – such information confirmed an official view in London that increased Yemeni subversive activity in the Federation had begun to emerge during the late spring of 1964. By June, hard evidence emerged that Cairo had established camps at Kataba, Ibb and Rahada for the sole purpose of imparting the skills of sabotage and subversion to their Yemeni pupils. Supplementing the presence of some officers from Egyptian military intelligence were Algerian instructors, keen to impart the lessons of their hard-won experience in guerrilla warfare to their new charges.[25] London now gave Washington notice of its intent to act. During the course of a meeting with US Secretary of State Dean Rusk in the aftermath of the furore over Harib, Butler made it clear that Britain was prepared to undertake covert action just over the border in Yemen in defence of the Federation. He declared:

> We wish to undertake limited local counter-subversion operations in the Yemen designed to discourage or frustrate the UAR and Yemeni effort to subvert the Federation, including the sending in of arms and explosives for use against points which are vulnerable . . . our main aim will be to do this in places and in ways which will not get us involved in the internal Republican–Royalist conflict.[26]

Rusk raised no objections. Already, there had been discussion within the Defence and Overseas Policy Committee over whether to allow British troops to cross the Yemeni border in hot pursuit operations. The Foreign Office raised strong objections to this on the grounds that it was not in keeping with policy in Britain's conflict with Indonesia over Borneo and that such operations would only exacerbate the tensions with Cairo and Sana'a.[27] In the event, the Chiefs of Staff were asked to draw up a paper detailing a range of possible clandestine operations to be discussed at a meeting of the Defence and Overseas Policy Committee on 23 April 1964. The document, marked 'Yemen: Range of Possible Courses of Action Open to us', made the following recommendations (actions approved by the Committee are marked in italics):

I   Retaliatory Actions along the Border with Yemen
(a) *Operation Eggshell – Mine laying;*
(b) *Operation Stirrup – Issuing of arms and ammunition to tribesman in the frontier area;*
(c) *Operation Bangle – Sabotage and subversion in the frontier area.*

2 Actions designed to inhibit UAR/Yemeni authorities subversive activity

(a) *Actions designed to induce Yemeni tribes to neutralise centres of anti-Federation subversion in the Yemen (particularly in Qataba and Baida) to include the supply of arms, ammunition and money;*
(b) The assassination or other action against key personnel directing subversion against the Federation of South Arabia, especially Egyptian intelligence officers;
(c) Support of subversive activity in Sana'a;
(d) *Aid Royalists by allowing them to use wireless stations in Beihan and Nequib;*
(e) *Aid Royalists by allowing arms convoys to be received from Saudi Arabia;*
(f) *Aid Royalists ourselves with the supply of money;*
(b) Aid Royalists with small arms, ammunition, mines, explosives, heavy machine guns and bazookas.[28]

Some of these recommendations were not new. For example, 'Operation Bangle' had already been approved by a ministerial meeting on 19 March, as had the supply of arms and ammunition to the Shariff of Beihan.[29] The most far-reaching proposal, the assassination of Egyptian intelligence officers, in particular those based in Taiz'z, was strongly urged upon the Prime Minister by the Chiefs of Staff. The clear belief was that Taiz'z remained the centre of Egyptian intelligence activity and the removal of key individuals would disrupt and deter future subversive activity in the Federation. Its rejection by the committee was in line with the belief that covert action should remain localised and reactive, rather than far-reaching and pro-active. Of note, however, was the fact that direct aid to the Imam's forces was now on the government agenda and increasingly came to inform discussions over the Yemen throughout the summer of 1964 as reports reaching London suggested an imminent collapse of the Royalist forces.

Such fears certainly lay heavily with Trevaskis. In a strongly-worded telegram to Sandys, the High Commissioner put forward the case for the wholesale subversion of the Republican government and Egyptian influence in the Yemen:

As seen from here, the gravest threat to our [British] position would derive from the emergence of a repeat, a stable government in the Yemen under the influence of the UAR or any other hostile state. Accordingly in my view, we should do all in our power to prevent the Yemen Arab Republic *from acquiring stability* (my emphasis) and if possible to rid the Yemen of the UAR and other hostile influences. In my view, whatever label the Yemen government may carry, the regime is likely to remain antediluvian and irrational for many years to come. What concerns us most is not the nature of the regime but the nature of those who influence it and the extent to which the latter is provided with the means to cause us mischief.[30]

Trevaskis was writing to the converted. In the Defence and Overseas Policy Committee meeting of 19 March, Sandys had argued that London allow Federation rulers to support the Royalists. In effect, this meant arms given to rulers of the Protectorates by the Aden authorities would almost inevitably find their way to Royalist forces, a development Sandys felt would help underpin continued Saudi support of the Imam. It was a view given short shrift by Crawford who noted that the JIC believed that such actions would only serve to entrench, rather than undermine the Egyptian position in Yemen. Of concern to the Foreign Office was that unless clandestine operations were placed on a tight leash and limited to reactive measures, Britain would be dragged into a wider war. As such, continued requests by the Chiefs of Staff to be allowed to conduct PR flights deep inside the Yemen were consistently thwarted by the Foreign Office. These flights were deemed necessary on two counts. First, the construction of a new airfield at Raudha, just north of Sana'a, suggested a deepening strategic commitment on the part of Cairo to the war. The RAF in particular wanted information on the type of air assets that could be located there by examining the length of the runway. Second, the Chiefs of Staff conceded that 'our secret sources for obtaining accurate information are slender and special signals units are unlikely to produce an answer'.[31]

When the request reached cabinet level, Butler stamped on the suggestion. Noting that in the wake of the Harib attack London could not afford further international opprobrium – a view supported by the JIC – he noted that the threat to the Federation was covert subversion and not any overt strategic threat. It was a view supported by Douglas-Home. The reconnaissance flights never left the ground.[32] Yet the request by the Chiefs of Staff revealed a broader concern over intelligence capabilities, namely the 'intelligence deficit' that revealed itself regarding Egyptian intent and capability. As such, British covert activities were limited mainly to reactive, rather than pro-active measures in their attempts to thwart the flow of arms and supplies into the Federation. Throughout June 1964, at a time when operations in the Radfan were being scaled down, reports reached the authorities in Aden that two large arms caravans had crossed into the Western protectorate of Yafa. In addition, it was claimed that the Egyptians were using Beidha, just across from the FRA garrison at Mukairas, as a base from which to launch attacks against 'specific targets'. The report makes no mention of the source of this information but concluded that, 'We are left not in the slightest doubt of the fact that that subversion of the protectorate is being personally directed and conducted by the Egyptians'. The report concluded that the scale of the arms supplies suggested that Egypt was now trying to open 'a second front i.e. other than Radfan'.[33]

Actual detailed intelligence on the size and composition of these caravans remained, nonetheless, a matter of conjecture. The authorities in Aden, while admitting that no British officer had actually seen the reported caravans claimed, however, that the weight of evidence – radio broadcasts from Cairo that urged "revolution against Britain in the south" and two eyewitnesses who travelled with caravans – suggested a sustained Egyptian-backed campaign of subversion was now underway.[34] Thorneycroft asked the Chiefs of Staff to provide a paper outlining possible measures that could be used to thwart these caravans. Their subsequent report was a detailed expose of the limits of applying any effective counter-measures. Given the 'long and ill defined border' between the Federation and Yemen, effective frontier control was all but impossible. Only the use of aircraft could possibly police such vast distances but it would be virtually impossible to distinguish between legal and illegal caravans. The report continued, 'we believe that air action could only be used if early and reliable intelligence on the movement of the caravans was available. We do not have this intelligence at present'.

The report exposed the paucity of accurate intelligence estimates regarding the Yemen. The Chiefs of Staff felt, for example, that the use of ambush techniques could provide an effective panacea to the caravans but again, they remained reliant on real-time operational intelligence that was rarely forthcoming. Given the tribal areas in which troops would have to operate, their presence would undoubtedly be known before an ambush could be sprung. This conclusion was drawn from the bitter experience of a macabre incident that marked the Radfan operation. A patrol from the 22nd Special Air Service Regiment (22 SAS) sent in to secure a landing zone for the arrival of paratroopers had been discovered. After a bloody fight, two members of the patrol had been killed, their heads severed and displayed on pikes for all to see in Taiz'z. The only long-term solution to countering the caravans was the timely accumulation and dissemination of intelligence. As the report noted, 'We believe that every effort should therefore be made to increase the efficiency and scope of our intelligence from the Yemen and in particular, from the areas within the Yemen where the caravans form up'. In this regard, the report recommended that covert operations be directed towards the disruption of those areas, a recommendation that the Chiefs of Staff noted had been made by a meeting of the Defence and Overseas Policy Committee held on 23 April 1964.[35]

Counter-subversion activities were already in progress. 'Operation RANCOUR' was one such operation. Documents released give scant details of Operation RANCOUR, when it began, or if indeed it was meant to be more extensive than the operations already agreed upon to counter Egyptian subversive activity on or near the border. One handwritten note in the corner of an unsigned report on the possibility of delivering aid directly to Royalist forces merely notes 'Code word for current covert operations to exploit dissident tribes up to 20 miles into Yemen to neutralise Egyptian subversive action against Aden'.[36] A memorandum prepared by unnamed officials for a meeting of the Defence and Overseas Policy Committee on 22 July 1964 did, however, elaborate upon the type of covert activity that RANCOUR encompassed. Termed 'defensive action', British officers within the Federation were supplying arms and money to tribes in the border areas in an attempt both to buy their loyalty as well as urge them to attack Egyptian targets. The memorandum noted that some success had been achieved to this end in Baidha but had proved unsuccessful in Qataba further to the west. It went on to state that 'These operations are undertaken as acts of subversion in Yemeni territory against individual targets. They are not done in the name of the Royalists or to promote the secession of towns or areas from the Yemeni Republic to the Royalists.'[37] The problem remained, however, that the scale of counter-subversion appeared only as good as the last arms delivery. The authorities in Aden constantly pressured London to supply the rifles and ammunition on a greater scale to the 'Rulers and state authorities.' The fear of Egyptian-backed dissident activity among the *Fadhli* tribes in Baidha threatened to erode gains already made. Given the need to counter what were termed the unlimited resources of the Egyptians 'for the suborning of our tribes', Aden requested that 'crash action', involving the immediate supply of 5,000 Lee Enfield .303 rifles be delivered by the end of September 1964. Suggesting that covert action was only being implemented half-heartedly, Aden concluded that:

> Without adequate support in the form of arms and ammunition a ruler may have no alternative but to remain passive in the face of dissident activity; or even worse, he way pursue a policy of deliberate non-co-operation with the Federal forces. In the extreme cases, sensing that ultimate victory will go to the other side, he may decide to defect or to withdraw his State from the Federation; however unconstitutional this may be, and declare for the Yemen Arab Republic.[38]

Lacking effective field intelligence, such covert operations could only ever have a limited impact on stemming the flow of arms and ammunition into Federation territory. Attacks on FRA and British troops became an occupational hazard and field intelligence officers attached to the FRA were a prized target. In an attack on Mukairas on 24 July 1964, one such officer barely escaped with his life after a grenade was thrown at his quarters.[39] Where possible, and under the strictest supervision, air attacks on suspected rebel arms dumps within the Federation were authorised. One such operation against an arms dump in caves bordering the Protectorates of Upper and Lower Yafa was approved on condition that the risk to civilian life was minimal and that 'No publicity be given to this operation'.[40]

Given the lack of appropriate intelligence however, it was hard for London to gauge the extent to which arms caravans represented the thin edge of an Egyptian wedge designed to undermine the Federation and the British position in South Arabia, though this was certainly the view of the Colonial Office. To this extent, the activities and reports of those associated with the Aden Group carried a lot of weight in Cabinet discussions throughout the summer and autumn of 1964. Already, the Defence and Overseas Policy Committee meeting of 23 April had sanctioned closer, albeit still circumscribed ties with the Royalists forces. Now, with reports suggesting that Royalist forces were on the verge of imminent collapse, border incursions beyond control and Nasser seemingly ascendant, London now moved closer towards clandestine activities of a more offensive nature.

Covert 'Offensive' Action

From the start of the Yemen Civil War, the Foreign Office, ever anxious to avoid British entanglement in this bitter internecine conflict, argued that Riyadh was more than capable of sustaining the Royalist war effort without any substantive aid from London. In a private memorandum to Douglas-Home dated 21 November 1963, Butler noted that '[T]hey [the Saudis] have shown their ability over the past year to maintain themselves despite the considerable military effort exerted by the Egyptians to crush them'.[41] This view was endorsed by the Cabinet 11 days later, where it was noted that the Saudis had stockpiled considerable quantities of arms and ammunition along their border with the Yemen to be 'covertly' supplied to the Royalist forces. It was argued, however, that it might help London's relations with the Federation if attempts to prevent arms reaching the Royalists from the rulers of the Protectorates were dropped.[42]

This shift in policy was occasioned by the realisation that attempts by UNYOM to broker a cease-fire, which should have included a suspension of Saudi aid to the Royalists in return for Egyptian troop withdrawals, had come to nought. In September 1963, the British Ambassador to Cairo, Sir Harold Beeley, had cabled London that with some 30,000 troops in the Yemen, Nasser was in effect giving as many of his troops as much combat experience as possible, with units rotated every six months. Reports of Egyptian troop withdrawals therefore had to be treated with some scepticism. Beeley, quoting from what he stated to be 'an entirely reliable source', claimed that it would be at least another three years before Nasser would be able to withdraw the bulk of his forces. Cairo would not be withdrawing in the immediate future, even if a threat to the stability of the Republic was no longer deemed to exist.[43]

Aside from official government reports, Douglas-Home was also the recipient of unofficial reports from those associated with the Aden Group, including Colonel David Smiley. Although working for the Saudis as a military advisor, Smiley, through his associates in the Aden Group, was able to report directly to Number 10, thereby circumventing the Foreign Office. In December 1963, he met with Douglas-Home and gave a detailed assessment of the Royalist position. The report was upbeat, including details of a number of tribes that had come over to the Royalists and indications that more 'would come over to the Royalists when the time was right'. He noted that while well stocked with arms, the Royalist forces faced an acute shortage of ammunition. On the broader political environment, he envisaged that no resolution to the conflict was in sight. The Saudis would not agree to a political solution until the Egyptians had withdrawn, while the Republicans would only agree to negotiations so long as the Egyptians remained to back them. Smiley also estimated that Cairo had lost anything between 10–12,000 troops killed and wounded since the start of their intervention.[44] In his own autobiography dealing with his time in Oman and Yemen, Smiley noted that 'the Prime Minister, Sir Alec Douglas-Home, listened carefully to my account, and asked-me to contact him personally whenever I returned from future visits'.[45]

The Foreign Office viewed the role of Smiley and other 'mercenaries' operating in the Yemen with barely concealed disdain. Their main concern remained being dragged into an internecine conflict that could damage Britain's relations with other Middle East states and Washington. The White House had long suspected that the activities of British and other European mercenaries operating from Federation territory was condoned by London – activity that the United States felt undermined their efforts at brokering a cease-fire. While still Foreign Secretary, Douglas-Home had already given explicit assurances to President Kennedy that Britain was not aiding or abetting the Royalist forces in any way. Immediately following this conversation in the Oval Office, Kennedy made his ill-fated journey to Dallas.[46] Fear of alienating the United States continued to inform the Foreign Office approach to the question of direct intervention in the civil war. The United States Secretary of State Dean Rusk made it clear to the British Ambassador in Washington, Lord Harlech, that London should curtail the activities of the mercenaries. In a cable to Butler, the Ambassador noted that State Department officials believed themselves to be the unwitting victims of British subterfuge. Washington now made it clear that 'vigorous action be taken to stop the involvement of British mercenaries and British territory in order to avoid feeding American suspicions of our motives'. Crawford in particular felt that failure to do so only aggravated Britain's position with the United States who, in the absence of diplomatic ties with Sana'a, were representing British interests in the Yemen.[47]

The role of the mercenaries was to have wider international implications. More immediately however, the exigencies facing the Royalist forces in the spring and summer of 1964 prompted a wide-reaching debate on the extent to which London should now actively support Royalist forces. Between May and August 1964, Royalist forces were subjected to a sustained assault of varying intensity but which had at its goal the capture or outright elimination of the Imam and other paladins of the *Hamid'Ud'Din* in their mountain redoubt on Jebel Qara, some 80 miles to the north-west of Sana'a. While Egyptian forces, deploying their technical superiority to the full, were able to take Jebel Qara, the Imam was able to escape, relocating to Jebel Sheda close to the Saudi border. Even so, the Royalists had been badly mauled and while casualty figures remained the subject of bitter debate it was, as the military analyst Edgar O'Ballance noted, 'undoubtedly true that many thousands had been killed and wounded, especially by aerial action.'[48]

Members of the Aden Group were to the fore in agitating for direct aid to be given by London to the Royalist forces. Having made an extensive tour of Royalist positions in the north-west of Yemen in June 1964, McLean produced a detailed report of the strategic and political situation and the likely implications for the British position in Aden. In conversation with officials from the Defence Intelligence Staff at the Ministry of Defence, he noted the low morale among the Royalists, a result of fighting a war of attrition with diminishing resources. Of more immediate concern for McLean, however, was the fear that the main Saudi sponsor of the *Hamid'Ud'Din*, Crown Prince Faisal, was growing weary of shouldering the main burden of support for the Royalist war effort. Already he was estimated to have supplied over 80,000 rifles to the Imam's forces, as well as donating anywhere between £100,000 to £200,000 per month to ensure the continued fidelity of the tribes. Warming to his theme, McLean was quoted as claiming that:

Faisal is not prepared to continue the present scale of assistance on his own, as even with this aid, resistance as a cohesive movement is likely to collapse in the near future. If we do not soon help them to continue the struggle, he will almost certainly decide to come to terms with Nasser before the Royalists collapse. The leaders in the Federation of South Arabia will also be convinced that Nasser is the only effective force and they too will want to jump on the bandwagon. If the Royalists collapse, he (Nasser) will be well on the way to achieving this. He (McLean) also made the point that the Egyptians were using more sophisticated methods to try to win over the tribes of doubtful reliability to the Republican government.[49]

McLean's recommendation was for an immediate clandestine parachute drop to be made to Royalist forces operating in the areas Arhab, Nehin and the mountains of the Khowlan to the north-east of the capital Sana'a. These drops should include 'money, rifles, and ammunition with a token amount of anti-tank guns and mortars'. His appreciation of Nasser's objectives matched an assessment made by the JIC and repeated in a top-secret report prepared by the Chiefs of Staff concerning the situation in Aden and South Arabia at the end of June.[50] The recommendation made by Defence Intelligence Staff was that, on balance, 'covert British assistance should be given to the Royalists'. Direct support for the Royalists was also urged upon the Douglas-Home by a number of backbench MPs. In a private meeting with the Prime Minister at the end of June, they urged that Britain, at the very least, should make credits available to the Royalist forces through Middle East banks which would allow them to purchase fresh stocks of ammunition.[51]

Co-ordinating this intensive lobbying of the Prime Minister and other Cabinet members was Julian Amery. From his office at the Ministry of Aviation, he passed on private correspondence to Cabinet colleagues that he felt could support the argument for direct British aid to the Royalist forces. One such letter he received from Colonel Gerald de Gaurey detailed a meeting that de Gaurey had with Faisal in Riyadh on 6 June 1964. Once again, Faisal's complaint over London's reluctance to supply arms and ammunition to the Imam's forces was aired forcefully. Amery made sure the letter reached the Foreign, Colonial and Defence secretaries as well as the Prime Minister.[52] Amery also used his own personal contacts with the Saudi government to take their representations to the highest level. In a letter dated 7 July 1964, he gave details of a meeting that he had with the Saudi Ambassador to London, Shaykh Hafiz Wahba, to Butler. Noting that the ambassador was an old friend, he provided the Foreign Secretary with a synopsis of the ambassador's concerns. Alongside the now oft-repeated worries over low Royalist morale, the issue of British intervention was forcefully pressed. Given Nasser's openly declared aim of driving the British from South Arabia, London's apparent refusal to engage more fully with the Royalist cause made no sense to the Saudi Crown Prince. Amery emphasised the concern that existed among both Faisal and the Imam that a future Labour government – national elections were scheduled for October – would be 'less well disposed towards the Royalists'. Faisal was now pressing for London to adopt more pro-active measures in the Yemen and help shoulder the burden of supplying the Royalist forces directly. Concluding his summary, Amery wrote, 'I think Shaykh Hafiz must have spoken to me as he did with the deliberate intention that I should give you (Butler) a preview of what he proposed to say to you . . . and that further Saudi Arabian help for the

Royalists may well depend on what is said then to him'. As usual, Amery made sure copies of the letter reached the Prime Minister, the Defence Secretary and the Colonial Secretary.[53]

Saudi frustration at London's apparent reluctance to involve itself directly with the Royalist cause certainly ruffled feathers in King Charles Street. In the wake of the doom-laden reports concerning the Royalist position, the British Ambassador to Jeddah, Sir Colin Crowe, was given explicit instructions by the Foreign Office to discover Faisal's true intentions. The suspicion appeared to be that the Saudis had deliberately exaggerated the predicament of the Royalist forces and had used those associated with the Aden Group to spread alarm throughout Whitehall. In particular, the Arabian Department wanted to know the likelihood of Faisal disengaging from the Royalists and coming to some form of accommodation with Nasser, and if his threats to disengage were prompted by the need to secure his own power base within the House of Saud.[54]

On 19 July Crowe sent two telegrams to the Foreign Office. The first, dealing with a meeting he had had with the Saudi Vice-Minister for Foreign Affairs, Omar Saqqaf, detailed the Saudi view of how the war was progressing in the Yemen. Sketching the precarious position that the Royalists were now facing in the light of a new Egyptian offensive designed to clear Royalist forces from the Khowlan mountains and the al-Jauf plateau, he again pressed for substantial British covert aid. Crowe replied that 'it was one thing for us to do what we could on the borders of the Federation to prevent arms being smuggled against us but it was quite another to intervene in an Arab Civil War'. He went on to note that he did 'not see how aid from Her Majesty's Government could be kept secret, and this would do great harm to the Royalist cause'.[55] While agreeing that the operational security of the Royalist forces left much to be desired – he had learnt of a mercenary parachute drop of arms and explosives while on a trip to Beirut – Saqqaf suggested that Saudi Arabia be used as the supply base for British arms and ammunition, the total cost of which would be in the region of £2 million. Crowe, according to his account, told the Saudi directly that such aid would not resolve the conflict. Of interest however is the answer he solicited from Saqqaf over what he saw as a desirable outcome. 'Saqqaf replied that [the] Saudis hoped that as matters dragged on, Yemenis on both sides would eventually get together; there were moderate Republicans who disliked the Republic and there were Royalists who disliked the Imam. There was probably no future for either Sallal or [the] Imam.'[56] It was to prove a prescient summation.

Crowe had made it clear during the course of this meeting that he believed that the Saudis were demanding a course of action from London that was infinite in its liability. His second cable to London the same day was a detailed summation of how subterfuge was being employed by Faisal in an effort to court British covert aid. In a pithy analysis, Crowe noted:

I understand Royalists have a genuine shortage of small arms ammunition and that Prince Faisal has real internal difficulty in fiddling the accounts to conceal [the] amount being paid to Yemen, but more than this, I suspect that there is some form of woolly belief that we are capable of pulling something out of the bag which will save the Royalists.[57]

The British ambassador suspected that Saqqaf had been playing a double game with him. He believed the Saudi Vice-Minister actually wanted a deal with the UAR, and that with a British refusal to offer direct aid to the Royalists, it would strengthen the hand of those within the ruling circles in Saudi Arabia who, by arguing that Riyadh was isolated diplomatically, could proceed to cut a deal with Nasser. The fact that a summit meeting between Faisal and Nasser in Alexandria to discuss a cease-fire had been scheduled for 5 September 1964 merely added grist to the diplomatic mill. However, Crowe made it clear that Faisal would never curtail Saudi support for the Royalists or recognise the Republic while Egyptian troops remained in the Yemen. Following through on the logic of his argument, Crowe believed that the rash of reports predicting the imminent demise of the Royalists were plainly false. If the last embers of Royalist resistance were indeed starting to fade, Crowe believed that internal pressure within Saudi Arabia would actually force Faisal to come to terms with Nasser. He concluded however that, '[The] Saudis do not seem to have sent aid to north-west Yemen when they should have done so by now if it [the demise of Royalist resistance] is as serious as it has been painted to us'.[58]

Still, the Foreign Office remained anxious that Crowe see Faisal personally and without delay. He was instructed to press upon Faisal that London shared his objective of the removal of all Egyptian forces from the Yemen 'and also the creation of a broadly based political system there which would provide greater political stability'. This was perhaps more in line with Foreign Office thinking than that of the Saudi Crown Prince. The Foreign Office was trying to support a position on the future composition of a government which it felt had backing within the wider Saudi court. Taken to its logical conclusion, it would mean the end of the Imamate, but if such an argument was pushed by London as well, Faisal may have been more accommodating towards a negotiated settlement of the war. Crowe was instructed nonetheless try to impress upon Faisal Her Majesty's Government's good intent. If the Saudi authorities were having difficulty in obtaining certain types of ammunition and small arms, the

Foreign Office would use its undoubted influence to help in the procurement of the requisite export licences from the United Kingdom.[59]

Crowe met with Faisal in Ta'if on 28 July. It was a difficult meeting. Crowe pointed out that it was not the policy of Her Majesty's Government to intervene in the internal struggle of an Arab state. Faisal's response was swift and cutting. If it was a question of non-intervention, then of course, the United Kingdom, Saudi Arabia and Egypt should certainly not do so but this simply ignored the reality of Egypt's presence in the Yemen. It was clear to him that Yemenis were not happy under Egyptian tutelage and were 'crying out for help'. Turning to the position of the United Kingdom, Faisal mocked the apparent weakness of such a 'strong nation' in supporting its position in South Arabia. In Crowe's own dispatch to London, he noted Faisal's attempt to invoke the spectre of a wider geo-political threat. 'Nasser's agents were everywhere undermining the area. The Egyptians were a spearhead for the Russians, who were putting help in secretly. Surely we could likewise help the Royalists?'[60] On the issue of arms export licences Faisal was equally curt, noting that if it wanted, Saudi Arabia could obtain all the arms it required from sources in Europe. Britain was being too timid, not only in its support for the Royalist cause, but also in its exaggerated concerns over international opinion that, as a consequence, denied effective support for the Royalists. Faisal concluded, 'We should hit first and let the United Nations worry'.[61]

Crowe later admitted that 'This was not a very satisfactory interview'. He felt that Faisal's attempts to inflate the threat posed by Nasser had been prompted by the report of one unnamed individual from the Hadrawmaut region of the Federation who had unduly influenced the Crown Prince during the course of his visit to Ta'if. Faisal was equally unimpressed by Britain's offer over arms procurement or the defensive covert action now being taken – the arming of the tribes along the borders of the Federation. Crowe also admitted that perhaps he misinterpreted the original meeting that he had had with Omar Saqqaf, remarking again upon the bullish attitude of Faisal throughout his meeting. Crowe then made an oblique reference to other discussions that were taking place with the Saudi authorities when he noted that, 'If however we are prepared to make some advance in detailed measures which our friends are discussing then I suggest they should be discussed through their channels.' The 'friends', a discreet term applied throughout Whitehall to refer to the SIS, were now part of a wider debate on how best to aid the Royalist forces. Crowe was also concerned that failure to engage with the Saudis over direct aid to the Royalist had the potential to undermine commercial ties with the Kingdom, as well as reopen old wounds left by the dispute with Riyadh over the Buraimi oasis. He concluded, 'Some assistance now may be cheap at the price. Even a token gesture could have a profound effect'.[62]

Ministers in London were, however, already considering more than just a token gesture. At the beginning of July, Thorneycroft prepared a memorandum titled 'Maintaining our Position in South Arabia'. It was a detailed exposition of the main British aim in South Arabia – the retention of the Aden base – and the best means to achieve this. As Thorneycroft himself noted, 'Its existence, however embarrassing at the UNO (United Nations Organisation) remains essential to the objectives of our foreign policy'. To this end, the main threat was identified as Nasser and his support of subversive activity. Either London had to come to an accommodation with Nasser, 'or must oppose him without inhibition'. The former would entail recognition of the Republican regime and whole hearted efforts to prevent assistance reaching the Royalists from Federation territory. Alternatively, Britain had to do its level best to prevent Nasser succeeding in the Yemen. The memorandum made explicit reference to Faisal's discussions with 'unofficial British contacts' – Amery, McLean and SIS and that due to internal constraints, he was finding it increasingly difficult to support the Royalist cause unaided. Now, with the Royalist under pressure, and the defection of a growing number of tribes from the Imam, Thorneycroft argued that 'unless we can offer effective assistance to the Royalists in the next few months, Nasser will have his way in the Yemen by next year '.[63]

Thorneycroft was under no illusions over the ability of the Royalists to secure an outright military victory. Such an optimistic outcome would deny the realities of the type of guerrilla war the Royalists were fighting in the mountains of northern Yemen; rather, he believed that it was in Britain's interests to engage the UAR in a war of attrition that would force Nasser to the negotiating table under conditions more propitious to the stability of the Federation and London's wider objectives. To this end, he recommended that 'we should examine with Crown Prince Faisal, the feasibility of sustaining the Royalists during the coming months and the most effective means for doing so'. He concluded with four main policy recommendations:

(a) A sharp increase in 'deniable' support in terms both of arms and money for Royalist tribes and other tribes capable of interfering with Egyptian plans in Yemen. (b) An immediate effort to ensure that Prince Faisal maintains his efforts to support forces opposed to the Republicans inside the Yemen. (c) Forthright and public protests in Cairo and the UNO against the campaign of subversion waged by Egypt – (i) by radio Cairo (ii) by caravans of arms. (d) Immediate authority for work on road-building and well-digging inside the South Arabian Federation with full publicity for it.[64]

The memorandum was drafted in collusion with officials from the Defence Intelligence Staff and the Ministry of Defence. On reading the original draft, C. Wright, Assistant Under-secretary of State for Defence, noted that direct aid to the Royalists would be a new departure for Her Majesty's Government and would of course be denied, though 'most people probably believe that HMG is behind Colonel McLean and Co. already.' He doubted that any aid given by the United Kingdom could forestall the 'gradual rolling up of the Royalists', but he suggested that a proper clandestine campaign be organised in which Jordanian mercenaries, trained in guerrilla warfare and communications, could act as liaison officers with the Royalist forces. It was clear that officials in the Ministry of Defence viewed the Royalists merely as pawns, however useful, in the wider game with Nasser. As Wright himself noted, 'In general, both the Director General of Intelligence and I feel that we are unlikely to do much more than keep the Royalists going at about their present level of activity which could go on annoying Nasser but would ensure that if we wanted to negotiate with him we could offer to throw them [the Royalists] over.'[65]

The pawns, nonetheless still needed to be sustained. The alarm at the predicament of the Royalist forces was deeply felt in the Colonial Office. Nigel Fisher MP, Parliamentary Under-secretary of State for Commonwealth Relations and the Colonies, wrote a detailed appraisal of the Royalist position for Thorneycroft and Duncan Sandys. Having consulted with 'the Friends' and with McLean, he emphasised the reverses suffered by Royalist forces in the north-west of Yemen, the deterioration in their morale and the shifting allegiance of tribes away from the Imam. The issue of appeasing Faisal through increased aid was again raised, but this time with the added weight that unless such support were forthcoming, the Saudis would cease their aid to the mercenary operation in support of the Royalist forces. The immediate priority for Fisher was for London to come good on the Saudi request, subsequently repeated to Crowe in Jeddah, for £2 million in immediate aid to the Imam. The breakdown of this would be: £1 million cash, £250,000 for arms and ammunition and the rest for the purchase of food and 'maintenance for the tribes' – bribes.[66]

Fisher also made a causal link between aid for the tribes on the Federation border and aid for the Royalists. Two tribes, the *Murad* and the *Qafya*, were demanding rifles for an attack on Harib and in the Khaulan region close to Sana'a, actions that Fisher felt would relieve the pressure upon the Imam's forces. He was, nonetheless, fully aware of Foreign Office opposition to such aid, himself noting in his memorandum that aid to these two tribal groupings would be tantamount to aiding the Royalists directly and therefore in direct contravention of declared government policy. Such inaction he argued, was no longer an option:

> Owing to the fact that we have done nothing for so long, the Shariff of Beihan and other friends of the Royalists in the Federation are already disillusioned, and if we stood by and let the movement collapse we should find other Rulers following the example of the *Fadhli* Sultan and re-insuring with the Egyptians. Sultan Saleh of Audhali is no doubt the key, because of his high reputation and influence in the Yemen. He wants to be loyal but is beginning to be worried about the future. Re-insurance with Nasser by rulers of his stamp and authority would bring about the collapse of all our plans for the Federation and would prejudice our tenure of the base.[67]

The conclusion drawn by Fisher – immediate and direct aid to the Royalist to the tune of £2 million – struck the right chord with Thorneycroft whose own memorandum was due to go before a meeting of the Defence and Overseas Policy Committee on 22 July 1964.[68] Thorneycroft was also heartened by a note he received from Mountbatten, which argued that the domino effect of strategic decline would ensue for Britain's position in the Middle East should the Royalists be subjugated: Saudi Arabia would break up, Britain would be pushed out of Aden and Nasser would then 'have little difficulty in eroding our position in the Persian Gulf'. He concluded that pressure be placed upon the Foreign Office to change what he termed their 'defensive outlook' towards the Yemen to 'a much more positive one'.[69]

Ironically it was Trevaskis who was now in need of a political filip. Following a request from the Colonial Office to give his views on the prospect of an immediate Royalist collapse, he sent a detailed and some-what bitter reply to London, detailing the failure of Her Majesty's Government to give timely support to Federation rulers, some of whom were now throwing in their lot with Nasser. Reminding London of his October 1963 plea for more pro-active measures to be taken to destabilise the YAR, he noted that it was now too late to take effective covert action against the Republicans and their Egyptian backers. Proposals that he had submitted to this effect had been so whittled down that, as far as he was concerned, they had become meaningless. Arguing that Royalist resis-tance was likely to collapse within the year, London was now best advised to cut its losses, come to an accommodation with Nasser which would include recognition of the YAR, the cessation of tacit support for Shariff Hussein and his cross border activities, and recognise the right of the Federation to decide on unification with Yemen after it had been granted full independence from the United Kingdom in 1968. All London could do to maintain its already declining influence among the Federation rulers would be to increase subsidies to the tune of £500,000 and provide them with arms and ammunition for immediate distribution to their tribes solely for the purpose of ensuring their loyalty. While Trevaskis believed that the Royalists could possibly hold on for another year, he ended his telegram by stating that, 'unless we act now on the lines that I have suggested, I fear that, by the end of the year, we shall be heading for certain disaster. In short, this is the last warning I can give'.[70]

Trevaskis's prediction of a collapsing Federation appeared about to be realised. On 19 July 1964 he cabled the Colonial Office details of a conversation with Shariff Hussein. Given the apparent reluctance of London to aid the Royalists, the Shariff informed the High Commissioner that he had little alternative but to come to an arrangement with the Yemeni authorities whereby he would cease aid to the Royalists in return for their recognition of his claim over Abu Tahaif, Nata and Lakhf, which he regarded as Beihan territory. If Britain objected, Trevaskis knew that the Shariff would then invoke Britain's treaty obligations, which made it incumbent upon Britain to support his territorial rights.[71]

How aid to the Federation rulers could be linked to the wider war effort of the Royalist forces was now the subject of detailed planning among the intelligence community in Whitehall. A position paper marked 'Top Secret – Aid to the Royalists', was prepared for ministers to discuss at a meeting of the DOPC scheduled for 22 July. The paper itself has been 'cleaned' of any departmental affiliation, though it bore all the hallmarks of having been compiled in Broadway by SIS staff. It noted the detailed plan submitted by Shariff Hussein, Prince Mohammed bin al-Hussein, commander of the Royalist forces in al-Jauf and Salah al-Misri, the Royalist Minister for Defence, which was received by London in early July. This plan called for the capture of Harib and Juba in the east of Yemen, areas that would then be used to extend Royalist operations south of Sana'a among the predominantly *Shaffei* tribal areas before extending north to cut the main logistical artery for the Yemen Republic, the Hodeidah-Sana'a road. The time scale for achieving this was reckoned to be nine months and would involve a British commitment to supply 11,000 rifles with ammunition, 20 mortars with bombs, 20×0.5inch calibre Browning heavy machine guns for air defence, 20 anti-tank launchers with rockets, 500 anti-tank mines, 57mm and 75mm artillery rounds and £600,000 in cash. The amount of money requested was designed to last initially for three months. Shariff Hussein believed further sums would, nonetheless be forthcoming should the Conservatives return to power in the October 1964 election.[72]

This 'shopping list' was seen as a more detailed version of a similar request submitted by Crown Prince Faisal which also included 2 million rounds of small arms ammunition, 20 Bren light machine guns, 50 Sten sub-machine guns as well as an assortment of grenades, landmines and rockets. The weapons would be deposited by the British in Beihan State. The Shariff was blunt in his appraisal that the scale of such weapons deliveries could not be kept secret for long, but on the other hand, it would bolster support for Her Majesty's Government among the Federation rulers and the Yemeni tribes. The paper also addressed the issue of parachuting some of the weapons requested direct to hard-pressed Royalist forces, which had been requested by the Royalist Foreign Minister, Ahmed al-Shamy. Noting that such operations had been used effectively by the mercenaries using 'specially chartered aircraft', the report highlighted this as an efficient way of delivering arms to where they were needed most, with the added advantage being that it avoided having to pay the heavy tolls imposed by tribes on arms caravans that traversed their particular area.[73]

The paper made clear that 'Aid on this scale cannot in any circumstances be given in an *unattributable* [their emphasis] manner'. It could be delivered to Beihan in trucks from Aden, though 'movement on this scale would however not pass unnoticed'. If ministers were to agree to the aid requested, the most secure form of delivery would be direct flights by RAF transport aircraft to Beihan. It was felt that even if Egyptian intelligence became aware of the increase in air activity, it could be reasonably explained in terms of re-supply operations for FRA troops stationed in Beihan. The optimum mode of delivery would be a combination of such flights and direct parachute drops to Royalist forces, if the ministers would be 'willing to relax the need for deniability to this extent'.[74]

While in line with Thorneycroft's and Fisher's thinking, these proposals were regarded as at best ill-thought out, and at worst, downright dangerous by the Foreign Office. On 18 July, four days before the Defence and Overseas Policy Committee were due to convene, the Cabinet Secretary and former diplomat Oliver Wright sent a strongly-worded note to Douglas-Home, advising him against implementing a 'more forward policy in the Yemen'. Taking the opportunity to take a swipe at the attitude of Sandys, Wright argued:

> Personally, I believe, and always have believed that we made our fundamental mistake when we refused to recognise the new Republican regime . . . Acting on what I consider to be consistently bad advice from Aden, we have since the start of 1963, been in the process of getting ourselves more and more bogged down . . . It is of course more dynamic to go in for gun running and support for the Royalist tribes and decisions to do so give an appearance of resolution. Nevertheless, I think that we should recognise that Nasser has been able to capture the most dynamic and modern forces in the area while we have been left, by our own choice, backing the forces which are not merely reactionary, but shifty, unreliable, and treacherous.[75]

Wright denounced the manner in which advice from the Foreign Office concerning the Yemen had been consistently overruled or simply ignored in the policy-making process. In doing so he was putting forward the

Foreign Office view that, hyperbole aside, Nasser was 'likely to be looking for a way out given the casualties incurred by the UAR forces'. In conclusion, he argued that any aid that was to be offered to the Royalists should be done through Saudi Arabia and limited to the protection of British interests. There could be no 'Great Game' if London wished to secure the Federation and the long-term future of the Aden base.

Wright was accurate in his description of the transient loyalties of the tribes. But equally his appreciation of the Saudi position was based upon the supposition that Faisal would be willing to play the role of willing client. As Sir Colin Crowe discovered, however, it was not a role the Crown Prince was willing to fulfil. Rather than bow to the advice of his Cabinet Secretary, Douglas-Home decided to tackle the malaise at the heart of policy-making in Whitehall towards the Yemen. He made it clear that clandestine operations had their place. In a brief but terse memorandum to Butler just prior to the meeting of the Defence and Overseas Policy Committee he made two key demands: First, that Butler appoint someone of ministerial rank to 'take a grip' of Foreign Office, Colonial Office and Ministry of Defence interests; and second, while keeping options with regard to Nasser open, 'make life intolerable for him with money and (?arms). This should be deniable if possible although if this is impossible, it is no more than we are being already accused of '. The Prime Minister was giving his support for covert operations in the Yemen beyond the immediate environs of the Yemen–Federal border.[76]

Following this edict, a meeting of the DOPC held on 22 July oversaw the establishment of the Joint Action Committee (JAC), chaired by the Secretary to the Cabinet, Sir Burke Trend, with a specific remit to co-ordinate inter-departmental policy throughout Yemen. This included the supply of covert arms to tribal groupings inside the Yemen. Although the JAC agreed in principle to supply arms on the scale demanded by Faisal and Shariff Hussein, the logistical delivery of such a consignment continued to be the subject of much debate. In the interim, requests for arms continued to be assessed by the JAC on a case-by-case basis. At the beginning of September 1964, Shariff Hussein requested the supply of a small quantity of anti-tank weapons and ammunition that would then be forwarded to what was referred to as a 'dissident group' group in Taiz'z. The actual target was not disclosed, though given its known use as a base for Egyptian intelligence officers, this was not hard to surmise. In keeping with the remit of the JAC, the request was circulated to the Colonial, Defence and Foreign Secretaries, as well as the Prime Minister for their ultimate approval. This was duly given. While a small-scale operation, it nonetheless signified a willingness, however reluctantly, by London to now intervene directly where the need dictated in the Yemen Civil War.[77]

Conclusion

Some contemporary observers have argued that, however limited, support for clandestine operations proved to be a double-edged sword for the British. As Anthony Verrier noted, 'The means [covert action] actually chosen, however, were so devious, so costly, and so involved that they not only undermined the security of the Federation but did nothing to contribute to any success in the field which the Royalists sought and which their more partisan British supporters constantly claimed.'[78] Such a judgement is too harsh. If designed to engage the YAR and the Egyptians in a war of attrition and force then to come to terms with the Federation on terms favourable to London, there is some evidence to suggest that this strategy was indeed working by the autumn of 1964. Following his appointment as the new British Ambassador to Cairo in September, Sir George Middleton cabled London, detailing a meeting he had with the Egyptian Foreign Minister Mahmoud Riad. While emphasising that Nasser had no intention of abandoning the Republican regime, Riad expressed a desire to come to some form of accommodation with both the FSA and Saudi Arabia, noting that maintaining UAR forces in the Yemen imposed a heavy burden upon Egypt which, as a developing country, could better use it resources for other purposes. According to Middleton's account, Riad then declared that 'Some people – though he did not necessarily share their opinion – believed that Britain was perhaps maintaining unrest in the area [Yemen] precisely because of the financial embarrassment to the UAR. These are the sort of mistrusts which must be dissipated.'[79]

But the 'heavy burden' being imposed was not just the result, even less a coefficient, of any clandestine activity or special operations condoned by London. The exigencies of context determined that such activity remained under tight scrutiny and was carefully controlled. Official British aid to the Royalist forces, as opposed to the tribes straddling the Federation–Yemeni border, never extended beyond benign neglect over the nefarious activities of the Federation rulers. For Cairo, such deeds remained examples of the nuances of policy and diplomatic protocol played out in the corridors of Whitehall, irrelevant to the wider endgame pursued by London: the removal of all Egyptian forces from the Yemen and the restoration of the Imamate. While clearly a propitious outcome, the constraints placed on London meant that its covert actions were never more than an irritant, rather than a danger to the Egyptian presence in Yemen. Rather, Cairo's real nemesis came to lie elsewhere, most notably in the form of a mercenary operation whose impact upon the shape and course of the Yemen Civil War was out of all proportion to its eventual size and composition.

5

The Mercenary Operations

British Subterfuge and the French Connection

During the course of a visit to London in July 1964, the United States consul in Aden, Harlan Clark, challenged Nigel Fisher MP, Parliamentary Under-secretary of State for Commonwealth Relations and the Colonies, over consistent allegations that Her Majesty's Government was giving tacit support to the activities of British mercenaries operating in the Yemen. Present at the meeting was Sir Stuart Crawford who noted:

> He [Nigel Fisher] told Mr Clark that HMG gave no support to them [the merce-naries] and that the only criticism that could be made of us was that we had not done enough to stop them operating. But there were 'problems' which made this difficult. Mr Fisher went on to say that he had been approached personally by Colonel McLean who had told him that HMG should support the mercenaries because this was good for the HMG's position. Mr Fisher had said that he was quite certain that this was wrong and had made it clear to Colonel McLean that the answer was negative.[1]

The issue of British mercenaries operating in support of the Imam had, since the summer of 1963, been a source of some tension between London and Washington. The Foreign Office in particular remained sensitive to charges that the nationality of these men undermined declared government policy of non-involvement in the Yemen war. As such, the disclaimer offered by Fisher to Clark was in accordance with a strict Foreign Office missive that officials deny any government support of, or involvement with the 'European mercenaries'.[2] However keen the mandarins at the Foreign Office may have been to place clear water between London and what they regarded as the nefarious activities of some of their fellow compatriots, the government of Alec Douglas-Home maintained cautious ties with a mercenary operation which, by dint of political, and in some cases, personal association, enjoyed access to key decision-makers in Whitehall. Given their backgrounds, it is of little surprise to note that collectively and individually the Aden Group also maintained discreet –

though by no means always harmonious – relations with SIS. In part this reflected the vexed relationship that individuals such as Julian Amery and Neil McLean had with 'C', the head of SIS, Sir Dick White. According to his biographer, Tom Bower, White believed those associated with the Aden Group were unduly influenced by a 'nostalgia for lost causes' and as such, beholden to a casuistry whereby political bias undermined any sober analysis of Cairo's true intent in the Yemen.[3]

Yet the age-old intelligence conundrum of intent and capability remained the Achilles heel of SIS. The outbreak of the Yemen Civil War had caught the service off guard, with few assets able to give a coherent picture of the Egyptian–YAR political and military axis or of Royalist resistance. In part this was due to the legacy of the Atlee Doctrine of 1946 which imposed severe restrictions on SIS operating in those areas of a fast-diminishing empire where intelligence remained the preserve of MI5. When the maelstrom of September 1962 enveloped the Yemen, SIS had no assets 'up country' to speak of, and only one officer from P17, the section responsible for South Arabia, in Aden. According to Bower, this officer, Hubert O'Bryan Tear, operating under the cover of Assistant Political Officer to Middle East Command, could add little to the reports filtering back to London from Colonial Office officials that described Egyptian intelligence officers attempting to ferment trouble among the tribes along the Federation border. Even here, an intelligence lacuna existed as O'Bryan Tear had never been tasked by London to produce a detailed guide to tribal groupings or affiliations throughout Yemen.[4]

The fact that members associated with the Aden Group, most notably Neil 'Billy' McLean, could help reduce that intelligence deficit goes some way towards explaining their ability to court political influence at the highest level; SIS was never able to produce the type of detailed reports compiled by McLean and David Smiley. These not only gave details of the material strengths and weaknesses of the various Royalist fronts and the Egyptian order of battle, but were themselves erudite expositions of the political intrigues between Royalist tribes, the Princes and their Saudi benefactors. Equally, the skills required to ferment organised resistance among and between these fronts – weapons training, grounding in basic guerrilla tactics and the establishment of effective communications networks – were no longer part of the SIS repertoire. The dissolution of SOE at the end of the Second World War and the merger of its remnants with SIS represented a bureaucratic triumph for Broadway who had felt that the 'bangs and bullets ethos' that had defined much of SOE activity during the war was ill-suited to the patient collection of secret intelligence. It was precisely these skills, however, that were now required and were to enjoy a renaissance of sorts in the mountains and deserts of the Yemen.

While Smiley and McLean toured the Royalist fronts, keeping detailed inventories of the weapons and supplies required, the training of Royalist forces was dependant in the main upon former French and Belgian soldiers recruited from June 1963 onwards. The intention had been for the mercenary effort to be a French-led operation, but while the quality of individuals recruited in Paris was high, the same could not be said of the accompanying logistics effort. Shortages of heavy weapons, ammunition, communications equipment as well as the currency of choice, Mother Theresa Dollars (MTD), with which to ensure tribal fidelity, did little to evince confidence in Royalist circles over the sincerity of the French effort. By the autumn of 1963, the mercenary operation, while still reliant upon the military advice of the French and Belgian operatives, had become a distinctly British-led affair.

Active Bystanders: SIS and the Yemen Civil War

A distinct paucity of accurate and reliable information over events in the Yemen marked the entrée of British intelligence into the Yemen Civil War. This in part reflected the 'division of labour' within the British intelligence community. The security service, MI5, remained responsible for intelligence and security assessments in Britain's declining, yet still substantial overseas dependencies. Equally however, this intelligence deficit was also a reflection of Sir Dick White's singular aversion to entanglements, particularly of the pro-active type, beyond the arena of Cold War competition in Europe. As Bower noted:

> His [White] imperfect knowledge and indifference to the shifts and eddies of internal affairs in the Third World were a recipe for avoiding mistakes rather than initiating successes. His was the passivity of a counter-intelligence officer, a spy-catcher, rather than a patriotic adventurer fighting communist infiltration into Britain's empire and the Third world.[5]

White's views in this regard were the mirror image to those held by the Arabian Department of the Foreign Office, much to the chagrin of many of his own subordinates. His reluctance to advocate pro-active measures to counter threats to British interests was a reflection of his belief that SIS existed to gather intelligence which could inform sober policy-making. Reflecting on this period, White confided that he did not believe 'SIS could any more set its own agenda.'[6] At the end of October 1962, White attended two Cabinet meetings convened specifically to discuss the Yemen. Although any direct contribution he made would not have been recorded, a resigned acceptance of Republican ascendancy permeates the minutes of the meetings. The assessment of the military situation in the

Yemen by the chairman of the JIC, Sir Hugh Stephenson, confirmed the prevailing view that while Royalist resistance existed in the mountains, it was sporadic, poorly organised and of limited effect. Expounding on this theme, Stephenson discounted reports of low morale among Egyptian forces sent by the Governor of Aden, Sir Charles Johnston and concluded by arguing that while there may be increased tribal resistance to Sallal, this was, 'not enough to alter the assessment that the Republicans would maintain and probably consolidate their present position'.[7]

Given the clear deficit in HUMINT, this assessment relied heavily on intercepts of Egyptian radio traffic by listening stations operated by GCHQ. SIGINT provided the only window on events in Yemen, a process helped by Cairo's continued use of encryption technology based on the German ENIGMA machine. ULTRA – the codename given to intelligence produced from the breaking of the ENIGMA machine by British intelligence in the Second World War – had remained a closely guarded secret in the post-war years. London had encouraged the use of this technology by many newly independent and emerging states, maintaining the fiction that their encoded transmissions using such equipment remained impervious to decryption.[8] By the end of October 1962, GCHQ had not only built up a detailed picture of Egyptian troop deployments, but was also aware of internal friction between Republican ministers in Sana'a and the Chief of Staff of the Egyptian Armed forces, Field Marshal Hakim Amr.[9] The radio net used by Egyptian units in the field hardly met the standards required of an army engaged in active combat operations. According to the recollections of a former British Army signals officer who was later recruited into the British Mercenary Organisation, the Egyptian radio net was so insecure that he used to break their codes 'for a bit of fun'.[10]

Although White's natural caution appeared vindicated by the JIC assessment, it was not a view shared by the Aden Group or many of his own subordinates. According to Bower, Julian Amery acted as a conduit for feeding Saudi intelligence reports to Macmillan, suggesting the JIC had underestimated the coherence, as well as the vehemence of Royalist resistance to the Egyptians. The need to reconcile these contrasting accounts of the actual conduct of the war prompted the first visit by McLean to Saudi Arabia and Yemen. His reports had cast sufficient doubt in the Cabinet for immediate moves by London towards recognition of the YAR to be suspended. This was a triumph for Amery, who now began to use his relatively junior Cabinet position as Minister for Aviation to lobby Cabinet colleagues for covert operations to be sanctioned beyond the immediate borders of the Federation, much to the annoyance of White and the Arabian Department.[11] The reluctance of White to endorse Amery's pro-active stance was not only to be explained by the recrudescence of the contrasting philosophies that had informed the approach of SIS and SOE to intelligence work during the war. Rather, White was aware of the limited capabilities SIS possessed; capabilities that were ill-suited to the type of clandestine activities and special operations advocated by Amery. Richard Aldrich notes that having overseen the effective dismemberment of SOE at the end of the war, SIS was supposed to have maintained a special operations capability. In the words of its then 'C', Sir Stuart Menzies, his officers, located in foreign countries, were best placed to recruit agents and raise resistance networks in as short as time as possible.[12] Yemen demonstrated how far removed from this ideal SIS had become by the beginning of the 1960s. Moreover, even if the requisite talent had been available to SIS, Alec Douglas-Home was informed by White at the end of March 1963 that it would still take a further six months for any meaningful deployment of SIS assets to be made 'up country'.[13]

This problem was a manifestation of both a lack of qualified personnel and political jurisdiction. Surprisingly, given Britain's historical intimacy with the Middle East, there was a dearth of officers proficient in Arabic. Paul Paulson, the SIS station chief in Beirut, was one notable example, his posting having been secured, according to Bower, on the basis of his fluent French.[14] For SIS officers, political context remained all. Unlike the CIA, SIS had not developed into an alternative bastion of foreign policy within Whitehall but remained within the orbit of the Foreign Office. Although the mandarins within King Charles Street had been thwarted over the issue of recognition, the vexed debates in the Cabinet over relations with the United States, the scale and scope of retaliatory action, and the seemingly glacial progress towards securing Cabinet approval for special operations along the Yemeni–Federation border, placed clear operational, as well as political restrictions on SIS. While contacts between SIS and individuals associated with the mercenary operation existed, these only became more frequent in the late spring of 1964 when the parlous position of the Royalist forces had profound implications for the political stability of the Federation.

Prior to this, mutual circumspection marked relations between SIS and the evolving mercenary organisation. David Smiley was to have frequent contact with SIS officers when passing through Saudi Arabia and Aden on his way to and from the Yemen but initially he remained guarded over his contacts with SIS personal operating under the guise of Political Officers in Government House. In a list compiled in the autumn of 1963 of personnel able to facilitate the activities of the mercenaries, Smiley noted of one such officer, Bill Herber-Percy that he was 'sympathetic but don't involve'.[15] Such evidence places some doubt over the claim by Stephen Dorril in his account of British clandestine activity in this period that as '"Minister for Aden", with a remit to covertly organise British support for the Royalists', Amery held the intelligence whip over White concerning special operations in the Yemen.[16] While the Minister for Aviation had certainly held some sway in the Cabinet over the issue of recognition, his influence over how SIS should be used to maintain Britain's position in South Arabia was certainly less than the sum of his many political parts.

The assertion, therefore, that SIS enjoyed close relations with the mercenary operation from the outset needs to be tempered. Yemen did not provide the permissive environment where, free from the lassitude of Foreign Office strictures, SIS officers could implement pro-active measures to undermine the Egyptians. SIS involvement in the war was subservient in character. It was the recipient of various items of Soviet supplied military hardware including radio sets and small arms captured from the Egyptians, but SIS had no recorded role in instigating special operations beyond the immediate environs of the Yemeni-Federation border authorised under operations 'Bangle' and 'Rancour'. Even the equipment that came its way was the result of happenstance rather than through clear tasking. On returning from one of his increasing forays into the Yemen in May 1963, McLean gave a Russian automatic pistol to Flight Lieutenant Tony Boyle, aide-de-camp to Sir Charles Johnston and soon to become a key figure in the logistical planning behind the mercenary operation. In a letter to McLean Boyle noted as a postscript that, 'Your Russian automatic is with the Int [intelligence] boys at present as they want to record the markings on it.'[17] Similarly, John Cooper, perhaps the most effective of the British operatives in the Yemen, recalled how he tried to send a captured Soviet W/T set to SIS officers in Aden. A priceless item of technical intelligence, he was dismayed to discover four months later that it had been returned to him on a Royalist caravan with a note that read, 'Hoping that this will be of great use to you'. It eventually reached its required destination.[18]

Any support offered by SIS to the mercenary operation was discreet and limited to a passive role. This contrasted with the more belligerent views of the CIA, which were juxtaposed onto those held by the State Department. From the perspective of CIA's headquarters in Langley, Nasser's involvement in the Yemen was seen as the entrée for Soviet subversion throughout the region, an argument the Director of the CIA's Middle East Division, James Critchfield, tried to impress upon White. According to Bower, Washington's recognition of the YAR allowed the CIA to post an officer, James Fees, to Taiz'z, where he operated under the cover of a humanitarian relief worker. Through bribery, he was able to provide Langley with a complete Egyptian Order of Battle while decrypts of Egyptian air operations produced by the National Security Agency proved that Soviet pilots were flying TU16s in combat over the Yemen, colouring in the picture of Soviet regional malevolence.[19] Importance was attached to securing fragments or casings of Soviet supplied munitions alleged to have contained chemical agents for analysis back in Washington. In June 1963, travelling under the guise of a Lebanese journalist, another CIA officer, Hatim Khalidi, an Arab-American by birth, located one such exhibit, virtually intact outside Mabta, before transporting it back to Saudi Arabia in the back of truck.[20]

Bower asserts that intelligence gained by Langley was passed on to Amery as part of the standard SIS–CIA exchange of intelligence to 'enhance his own stewardship of the war'. While no doubt the recipient of such information, the extent to which this swayed Cabinet decision-making is debatable. The CIA could contribute little of value to the assessments already being made by the JIC, and until December 1963, debates over retaliatory action and special operations demonstrate a marked sensitivity in London to Washington's attempts at regional mediation. The extent to which the State Department and the CIA held divergent views of the Yemen Civil War was more apparent than real. By June 1964, CIA officers were suspected of attempting to ferment unrest within the Royalist circles at the highest levels. According to McLean, Crown Prince Hassan, the Royalist Foreign Minister, Ahmed al-Shamy, and the Deputy Prime Minister, Ahmed Siyaghi, were the objects of approaches by CIA officers to depose the Imam. Of this triumvirate, Siyaghi was identified as the most pliable. He was known to maintain direct if discreet contacts with Republican officials disenchanted with Cairo and the increasingly venal rule of Sallal. This symbiosis of interest was to find expression from 1965 onwards in the emergence of what McLean termed 'The Third Force', a coterie of those Royalists and Republicans willing to coalesce around a political compromise to the exclusion of their respective political leaderships. Such intrigue certainly conflated with the interests of a State Department still anxious to expedite a solution to the civil war that, while securing its interests in Saudi Arabia, could prevent any recrudescence of the *Hamid'Ud'Din*.[21]

White eventually came to support a more pro-active role for SIS in the summer of 1964, particularly when it appeared that Royalist forces were on the cusp of defeat. But physical involvement by SIS remained beyond the pale of political sensitivities that determined the public face of British policy in South Arabia. Though by no means a linear process, the emergence of the 'mercenary' operation was a reaction to these limitations, both actual and contextual, imposed by Whitehall upon a group of well connected individuals who regarded immediate assistance to forces loyal to the Imam as crucial to securing British interests in South Arabia. The aphorisms 'Musketeers' and 'Buccaneers' have both been used to describe the Aden Group but whatever label is applied a moral certitude informed the actions of men who regarded clandestine operations deep inside the

Yemen as a legitimate tool to secure Britain's rightful position in the Middle East.

Smiley, McLean and the Royalist Fronts

SIS lacked sufficient personnel familiar with the demands of covert action and guerrilla warfare. In this regard, the Aden Group possessed an embarrassment of experience, with Neil McLean, David Smiley, Julian Amery and David Stirling well versed in the demands of special operations and guerrilla warfare. All had 'good wars', with McLean, Smiley and Amery all sharing the dangers and hardships of guerrilla warfare as SOE operatives in the mountains of Albania.[22] Of these, Smiley remained the best attuned to the demands of irregular warfare. Having fought bravely in Albania, he later led an SOE mission into Siam where he was severely burnt when the 'thermite' briefcase he was carrying, designed to incinerate any documents enclosed if the bearer was in immediate danger of capture and/or death, detonated by accident. On recovery, he rejoined his regiment, the Royal Horse Guards, in Germany before being seconded to SIS in 1947. Here, as staff officer in Section I responsible to the Director of War Planning, he was involved in developing proposals for the role played by SOE in the war to be inherited by the SAS, itself in the process of being reformed as a Territorial Army unit having been disbanded, rather presumptuously, at the end of the war.[23] Two years later, Smiley, once more in the employment of SIS, was involved in 'Operation Valuable', a joint operation with the CIA. Using the isolation of a disused fortress on the island of Malta, Smiley was responsible for training a number of Albanian exiles in the skills of clandestine warfare prior to their infiltration back into their homeland. Designed to ferment unrest inside an Albania firmly in the grip of Enver Hoxha, the mission failed, it is alleged, because of the treachery of Kim Philby, though some regard deficient planning and a poor understanding concerning the vagaries of Albanian politics as the more likely culprits.[24]

Following on from a period of service that included commanding his regiment in Germany, and as British military attaché in Stockholm – where he became firm friends with General Carl Von Horn – Smiley accepted secondment as commander of the Sultan of Muscat and Oman's Armed forces. This appointment was impressed upon him by Amery, who, as Under-secretary of State of War, believed Smiley to be ideally suited to the challenge of soldiering in a harsh environment. It was a posting that saw the 'poacher turned gamekeeper' as Smiley confronted an uprising inspired and funded by Saudi Arabia against the Sultan of Oman. With discreet but substantial military support from London, Smiley was able to quell the unrest in a campaign notable for the physical feats of endurance required while fighting in the region of the Jebel Akhdar – the Green Mountain – in northern Oman. Having secured the Sultanate and, by extension, continued British hegemony among the tribal shaykhdoms of the Trucial states, Smiley was offered command of the three SAS regiments on his return to the United Kingdom in April 1961. While keen to accept, he was piqued that the rank of Brigadier did not accompany the post and decided to leave the army.[25]

With a wealth of experience in irregular warfare gained in the tough surroundings of Albania and Oman, coupled with an understanding of the vagaries of tribal politics in Arabia, Smiley was more qualified than most – and certainly more so than anyone in SIS – to offer a detailed appreciation of the Royalist forces in the Yemen. His close ties with Amery and McLean meant that his entrée into formal civilian life was to remain fleeting over the next five years. Smiley was approached by McLean at the end of May 1963 to accompany him on a trip to make a military appreciation of the Yemen.[26] By this time, McLean had already made at least four trips to the region, where he had assiduously courted Saudi and Jordanian support for the Royalist cause. Given the topographical arena in which the fighting took place, it was physically impossible for McLean to compile reports for Crown Prince Faisal detailing the strengths and weaknesses of all the various 'Fronts' and the attendant material and financial requirements while continuing to serve as a member of Parliament. Smiley was first approached by both Amery and McLean about travelling to the Yemen in March 1963 to help compile reports on behalf of the Saudi potentate. Smiley informed SIS about his intentions to travel to the Yemen through O'Bryan Tear. This in turn elicited a response from John Bruce-Lockhart, at the time Director of Middle East operations at SIS. Writing from the comfort of the Reform Club in Pall Mall, he reminded Smiley that 'HMG's policy is to try and avoid as much as possible being involved in the Yemeni war and that any publicity or widespread knowledge of your presence in the Yemen would be counter productive to this policy'.[27]

Unimpressed, Smiley arranged for a journalistic cover to explain his presence in Royalist-held areas of the Yemen. Originally, this was provided by becoming the 'Special Correspondent' for the Household Brigade magazine. These rather flimsy journalistic credentials were stiffened somewhat by the intervention of Julian Amery who arranged for a Press Card to be issued to Smiley accrediting him to the *Daily Telegraph*. It was a convivial arrangement for all concerned, though recounting the event some 40 years later, Smiley noted somewhat wryly that he was never paid for any of the articles he wrote for the London daily.[28] His cover now more plausible, Smiley, accompanied by McLean, departed for Saudi

Arabia and the Yemen on 14 June 1963. McLean hastily returned to London in some haste 48 hours later to take part in a Commons vote over the Profumo Affair. Smiley continued on entering Yemen by truck from Jizzan on 16 June and making his way to the headquarters of the Imam at al-Qara, high in the mountains of north-west Yemen and 150 kilometres from the capital Sana'a. From the eyrie of Imam al-Badr, Smiley conducted an extensive foot reconnaissance of the Royalist 'armies' of the North-West Front before finally returning to Jizzan on 11 July, and five days later, returning to London.

At the behest of Amir Sultan, the Saudi Minister of Defence, Smiley wrote two reports covering his trip. The first was concerned entirely with Egyptian activities in the Yemen and was requested specifically to illustrate the extent of Cairo's violation of the cease-fire agreement that had been brokered under the auspices of Ellsworth Bunker in April 1963. Smiley understood that this report was to be presented by Crown Prince Faisal to Parker T. Hart, the United States Ambassador to Saudi Arabia.[29] The second report dealt solely with the Royalist forces in the Yemen. While remarkable for its percipience, many of the problems identified by Smiley, as well as the means by which they could be addressed, continued to be recurrent themes in subsequent reports.

In July 1963, the Royalist forces were grouped into eight fronts that corresponded either to their geographical location or in the case of the Imam, were named after the individual in overall command. These were: the Imam's Front, based at Qara; the Qaff'l al Udda Front; the West Sad'ah Front, East Sad'ah Front, the Jauf and Barat Front, the Sana'a front, the North Sana'a Front and the Western Front. Each front was either under the command of a Prince belonging to the *Hamid'Ud'Din* or a *Zeidi* tribal leader with close tribal affiliations to the Imam. Each front in turn contained commands of a more parochial nature that existed either to ensure that tribal responsibility brought a concomitant fidelity or simply to give the numerous Princes of the *Hamid'Ud'Din* the required command befitting their social, religious and tribal status. The Imam's front, based at al-Qara, included a rear headquarters at Mabta further to the West under the command of Prince Hassan bin al-Hussan. Equally, the West Sad'ah Front comprised four areas that in essence equated to the location of four distinct tribal groupings under the command of their respective Shaykhs; Sayid Abbas Monsour, Sayid Mohammed al-Mutawakil, Sayid Abduallah Assadi and Sayid Abduallah al-Mahdi. While such command arrangements were necessary for ensuring that sufficient tribes – either through religious affiliation or bribery – would owe allegiance to the Royalist cause, they were hardly conducive to the conduct of a well planned and executed guerrilla campaign that had, at the strategic level, the object of removing Egyptian forces from Yemen.[30]

While noting the high moral of the *Zeidi* tribes allied to the Imam, Smiley used his second report to Amir Sultan to expose key deficiencies in the Royalist forces. Acknowledging that they were well suited to guerrilla warfare, he nonetheless highlighted the growing shortage of ammunition on all fronts as a result of Riyadh's adherence to the terms of the cease-fire agreement. More acute was the lack of anything resembling a secure, coherent radio net linking the Royalist fronts. Command and control was haphazard, with instructions or orders issued by the Imam overly reliant on fleet-footed couriers. Smiley reported, 'This results in the Imam having little control over his commanders, consequently he cannot co-ordinate his plans. From talking to the various commanders I gained the impression that each was fighting his own private war, independently of any commander'. Finally, Smiley derided the tendency of the Royalists to make frontal attacks from their mountain redoubts with the aim of capturing towns and villages. These attacks were, for the most part, wasteful in terms of lives and ammunition among the Royalists. However, 'Where there had been ambushes on roads, the Egyptians had lost many killed and much equipment for little or no Royalist losses; these are the obvious tactics the Royalists should pursue'.[31]

His report confirmed the division of Yemen into distinct geographical–religious areas with the *Zeidi* tribes firmly in control of the mountains in the north and centre of the country, while the Egyptians and Republicans controlled the plains, the coastal area and the southern region of the country bordering the Federation – areas where the predominantly *Shaffei* tribes dominated. In his private notes Smiley was more candid in his criticisms of the Royalists and in particular the Imam. His reliance upon his personal assistant, Yahya al-Hirsi, to deal with administrative matters proved unpopular with the Royal Princes who neither liked nor trusted him. It was an opinion that came to be shared by Smiley who felt that figures given to him by the hapless courtier concerning the strength of Royalist forces were often exaggerated to the point of ridicule. While each front consisted of an 'army' Smiley considered them to be more akin to a militia, with a small core of trained men being supplemented by tribesmen as circumstance dictated. The distribution of weaponry among the fronts was poor, with a lack of heavy weapons, most notably anti-aircraft guns and heavy mortars, compounded by insufficient stocks of ammunition. Even where these were available, a paucity of suitable personnel qualified in their use meant their engagement over distance of Egyptian and Republican targets was ineffective. Compounding these shortages in arms and munitions was a woeful lack of accurate maps and hopelessly inadequate stocks of medical supplies.[32]

Given the deficiencies involved, the fact that a Royalist opposition existed as a fighting force, let alone scored notable triumphs against the

Egyptian Army, was a remarkable feat but also an indictment of the weak tactics, poor leadership and inadequate preparations of the Egyptian High Command. The recommendations made by Smiley were designed to ameliorate Royalist deficiencies while exploiting Egyptian military weaknesses. Along with the urgent need to increase weapon supplies, especially of a heavier calibre, Smiley pressed for Royalist forces to concentrate on attacking Egyptian lines of communication, most notably the main supply routes linking Sana'a with Hodeidah on the coast and Sad'ah to the north. Above all, Smiley urged the need for the establishment of a coherent radio network with a minimum of six Wireless/Transmitters (W/T) along with trained operators that could co-ordinate action between and among the various fronts.

This military prognosis was shared by McLean. Having voted dutifully in the division over the Profumo affair, McLean returned to the Yemen at the end of June, entering from Jizzan in Saudi Arabia on the night of 1–2 July, reaching the border town of Nequb in Federation territory on 31 July. His journey, in terms of geographical area covered, was larger in scope than his compatriot and included travels through Hirshwa and the al-Jauf plateau to the east of Sana'a. McLean was assiduous in keeping an inventory of the requirements of the various fronts through which he travelled; but he was also an astute observer of tribal politics and the personal characteristics of the Princes on whose ability the fortunes of the Royalist cause rested. He found ample evidence of the tribes achieving significant tactical success against Egyptian forces, often using local ingenuity to disable Egyptian armour. While passing through the region of Mabta, he was informed by the sector commander Sayid Ibrahim al-Kibsi, a distant relative of the Imam, that tribesmen of the *Arhab* tribe had been disabling Egyptian tanks by the simple expedient of forcing a mop up the exhaust pipe. When the hapless vehicle tried to accelerate, it would stall, forcing the crew to leave the safety of their armour protection and face the vengeance of the tribes. Few prisoners were ever taken. While this may have appeared offensive to European sensibilities, McLean, having been schooled in the internecine bloodletting of Albania, never allowed moral sentiment or opprobrium to cloud his judgement. He regarded such acts, however distasteful, as reflecting the mores and culture of a predominantly tribal society. Egyptian conscripts, with their deficiencies in training, leadership and morale, expressed their frustrations in behaviour that only served to further alienate them from the *Zeidi* tribes. McLean reported that to the west of Sana'a, the Bini Mathar and the two *Al-Hamaitian* tribes, the *Al-Haima al-Kharajiya* and the *Al-Haima al-Dakhiriya*, had risen against the Egyptians after it was reported that 'Egyptian troops had interfered with some of the tribal women'.[33]

It was hard to discern if such anti-Egyptian activity was, in reality, anything more than just an expression of loathing for a hated occupier. The quixotic nature of tribal politics rarely lent itself to neat classifications and while by the summer of 1963 the Royalist cause appeared to be ascendant among the *Zeidi* tribes, fidelity to the *Hamid'Ud'Din* was often transient and dependent upon the financial profligacy of the Royalist commander *in situ*. This problem was compounded by the poor leadership qualities of the Imam himself. McLean spent the early part of July at the Imam's headquarters at al-Qara. He was distinctly unimpressed by what he witnessed:

> I thought the Imam looked thinner and paler than when I had seen him in March. I was also even less impressed by his powers of leadership than I was previously. During my stay he never once left his bomb proof cave which he shares with Yahya al-Hirsi, the chief of the Royal Diwan. Yahya al-Hirsi is also the Imam's father-in-law, most intimate confidant and former boozing companion. Yahya al-Hirsi is unpopular with the other Yemeni leaders, who are jealous of the influence he exerts over the Imam and they resent his lining his own pockets to excess. Despite the Imam's personal faults, his name carries fantastic prestige among the tribes. He is also lavish with his money which endears him greatly to the tribesman.[34]

McLean provided other vignettes concerning the personal qualities of Royalist leaders. The Imam's uncle and Prime Minister, Crown Prince Hassan, was described as pious, respected but 'not popular with the tribes because he is very mean with his money'. While personally generous to McLean, he was 'harsh and cruel to those who disobey or offend him' while conditions in his camp reflected his state of mind: disorganised and confused.[35] The performance of other Princes, however, met with McLean's distinct approbation. Prince Mohammed bin al-Hussein, for example, commander of a Royalist sector at Alagaba 30 miles north of Marib impressed McLean greatly, not least because his aggression had led to the capture of a considerable amount of weaponry from the Egyptians. All, however, lamented the shortage of ammunition which had led to Royalist defeats in the al-Jauf region in early July. Every Royalist commander demanded increased supplies of ammunition for their heavy calibre weapons, notably the 57mm and 75mm recoilless rifles and bombs for the 81mm and 120 mm mortars. There existed a constant need for small arms ammunition, a logistical headache given that Royalist forces were equipped with a variety of rifles, in addition to a plethora of light and heavy machine guns of varying calibre.[36]

In a report he later circulated to members of the Cabinet as well as officials in Aden and Saudi Arabia, McLean remained upbeat about the chances of a general revolt against the YAR and Egyptian rule among both *Zeidi* and *Shaffei* tribes. The imposition of increased taxes by Sallal to help Egypt pay for the war had begun to alienate the *Shaffei* merchant class who bore the brunt of this pecuniary measure. Matters were not helped in this regard by the precipitous withdrawal from circulation of the standard Mother Theresa dollar (MTD) and its replacement by a new coin, minted in Cairo, which contained considerably less silver. This had pushed many of the urban business elite and merchant classes to directly criticise the Sana'a government and to agitate for Sallal to come to terms with the *Hamid'Ud'Din*. McLean was keen to capitalise on such growing dissent. He wrote:

> The main problem now is to provide the tribes with sufficient ammunition and arms to make a general uprising. The war in the Yemen was already a *jihad* or religious war for the *Zeidis*, but it has now become a National war, supported and approved by the great majority of the Yemeni people, including many of the *Shaffei* tribes of the south. All want the Egyptians to leave their country as soon as possible.[37]

McLean was perhaps guilty of embellishing the strength of the Royalists. More than Smiley, he was all too aware of the transient nature of Royalist politics and the suspect leadership of the Imam. Such short-comings, discussed at length with Smiley and readily confided to his diary, could not be allowed to undermine the public face of a Royalist endeavour that had not only forced the Egyptians into a war of attrition, but, if supported, directed and properly led, would, McLean believed, inflict a humiliating defeat on Nasser.[38]

Both McLean and Smiley worked hard to publicise the Royalist cause on their return to London, making public their views that Egypt had resorted to the use of chemical weapons as well as employing more conventional ordinance against villages suspected of Royalist sympathies. Such activity was not only in clear violation of the Bunker Agreement but in itself constituted a war crime. McLean estimated that one-third of the villages he had travelled through had been subjected to aerial assaults of varying magnitudes from Soviet supplied Iluyshin and TU-16 bombers and Yak fighters.[39] Their efforts were somewhat diluted by what they saw as the supine attitude of the Foreign Office who, when presented with detailed reports and, in the case of Smiley, examples of shell casings from these attacks, failed to press the issue in international forums. McLean had sent a detailed report of his visit to Al-Kowa to Sir Colin Crowe in the hope that the Foreign Office would at least take the matter further and had implored the Foreign Office to send a fact-finding mission to the Yemen 'so that the true facts of this bombing should be ascertained'.[40] Given the inconclusive tests conducted on Smiley's examples, the circum-spection of King Charles Street – a position dictated by the need to avoid an overt clash with Washington – appeared to be fully justified.[41]

With their experience of guerrilla warfare, the Egyptian strategy appeared clear enough to both men; widespread terror bombing, combined with Egyptian ground offensives and the acute shortage of arms and ammunition among the Imam's forces, would eventually break the Royalist forces. In McLean's view, the UN observers were merely tools by which Nasser, under a banner of international legitimacy, could prevent supplies coming in from Saudi Arabia while Nasser completed this task. Smiley estimated that if such conditions continued and Riyadh continued to withhold supplies from the Royalist forces, 'then in a matter of weeks all resistance would cease'.[42]

McLean was in regular contact with Crown Prince Faisal, Emir Sultan, the Defence Minister, Kemal Atham, the head of Saudi intelligence, as well as Prince Mohammed Sudairi, who was responsible for the shipment of arms from Jizzan in Saudi Arabia to Royalist forces in the Yemen. While he impressed upon them the precarious nature of the Imam's position, McLean was well aware that Faisal was under intense pressure from Washington to abide by the Bunker agreement. If the Royalist position was to be sustained militarily, an alternative avenue of supplies and the establishment of an effective W/T net had to be established. In concluding his report, which was sent directly to ministers, McLean set out three recommendations for future British policy: (1) that London should encourage Saudi Arabia not to commit itself to the Bunker agreement, due for renewal and bilateral ratification in November 1963. Instead, London should encourage Riyadh to resume military supplies to the Royalists. (2) Diplomatic support for the Saudi position should be underpinned by British help in providing money, ammunition and 'a few experts if required'. (3) Britain should give help to the southern tribes of Yemen 'through a number of unattributable channels which already exist'.[43]

McLean expounded upon these channels in a draft memorandum, identifying five key areas where a government commitment to clandestine activity could produce the best results. First, the use of Shariff Hussein of Beihan to send money, ammunition and arms to Crown Prince Abduallah bin al-Hussein, Commander of the Royalist front in the Khowlan, as well as to tribes opposite his part of the frontier. This policy should also be extended to Sultan Salleh of Audahli who should be allowed to supply the *Rassas* tribes around Beidha, close to the Federation frontier. Second, the use of unattributable aircraft to drop limited supplies to Royalist commanders in the Nehim and Arhab regions, areas that were largely encircled by Egyptian and YAR forces. Third, a plan to instigate uprisings among tribes in the south of the country, particularly around Taiz'z, Ibb and near the port of Hodeidah. McLean noted that the tribes in these regions were ready to revolt once in receipt of sufficient arms and ammunition. Given that these tribes were predominantly *Shaffei* in their religious affiliation, it confirmed McLean's belief in the emergence of a national struggle against Cairo and the YAR. Fourth, the provision of six W/T sets and between 30 and 50 French volunteers skilled in the use of mortars and heavy weapons, to be attached for training purposes to the Royalist forces. The establishment of a W/T net would be accomplished under 'British auspices and four or five British observers should be present in the Yemen'. Fifth, the acquisition of 'two or three fighter aircraft or light bombers should also be borne in mind'. Based in al-Jauf or the vast desert hinterland of the Rub al Khali, these could be used to make surprise attacks on Egyptian aircraft at the Sana'a and Hodeidah airfields. This final recommendation, made in draft form, was dropped by McLean when his final report and recommendations were circulated to ministers in the autumn of 1963.[44]

The McLean report, which included Smiley's appreciation, was a lesson in the art of studied casuistry, designed to draw London into supporting covert operations way beyond the immediate confines of Federation–Yemeni border. Its impact was felt most keenly at the Cabinet meeting of 2 December 1963. Much to the reluctance of Foreign Secretary, Rab Butler, the government approved in principle an increase in clandestine activity along the Yemen border with the Federation, though such activity was to be subject to strict control in Whitehall. The Cabinet, however, never endorsed the more radical proposals contained in McLean's report. These proposals had, from the summer of 1963, already begun to be realised on the ground in a mercenary operation whose impact was not just felt in the Yemen, but in time, across the wider arena of Middle East politics.

The French Connection

The secondary source literature dealing with the emergence of the mercenary operation in the Yemen is as numerous as it is vague.[45] Most accounts point to a decisive meeting by members of the Aden Group at White's club in London at the end of April 1963 where the decision was taken to recruit French, Belgian and, later, British mercenaries to help train the Royalist forces. According to Dorril, present at the meeting were Amery, McLean, David Stirling, Colonel Brian Franks and Alec Douglas-Home, still occupying the Foreign Office portfolio. Franks had been responsible for the renaissance of the SAS in 1947 and, in conjunction with David Smiley, had lobbied hard for the regiment to take over the role performed during the war by SOE.[46] Although his participation has not been recorded, Smiley also attended the meeting at White's.[47] While significant in laying the groundwork for a mercenary commitment to the Yemen, the meeting did not produce the definitive plan for such involvement; rather, what emerged through the summer and autumn of 1963 was a mercenary commitment whose shape and composition evolved in accordance with immediate exigencies, not as part of an established plan. The meeting at White's was modest in its aims, with the pressing need for a detailed appreciation of the Royalist position in the Yemen coming to be realised in the reports of Smiley and McLean. At this stage, only one other British national, Major Johnny Cooper, an SAS veteran of considerable experience, was recruited by his former wartime commander and comrade-in-arms David Stirling at the end of May 1963 to lead an eight-man team of four Frenchman and three British to the mountains of the Khowlan surrounding Sana'a. By Cooper's own account, this mission, designed to last a month, was tasked with gathering intelligence on the Egyptian order of battle in and around the Yemeni capital; intelligence, it was hoped, that could shed alternative light on the assessments already made by the JIC.[48]

The greatest enigma surrounding the meeting at White's was the presence of Alec Douglas-Home. As Foreign Secretary, he had been scrupulous in avoiding British entanglement in the Yemen and had been among those in Macmillan's Cabinet who – feeling that Macmillan's 'winds of change' were now beginning to blow across the Middle East – had urged recognition of the YAR.[49] The explanation for his presence is simple: he had a change of heart, although as Foreign Secretary and later Prime Minister, Home remained resolute in claiming adherence to a policy of non-intervention.[50] It was only with some reluctance, and despite the best entreaties of McLean and Amery to expand its scope, that he agreed to special operations such as RANCOUR. Even then, they remained confined in geographical scope. Although his earlier enthusiasm for recognition may have dimmed, it is more likely that Home, having got wind through Bruce-Lockheart of what was afoot, requested that he be briefed as a matter of courtesy. Given that his portfolio would inevitably bear the brunt of international and regional opprobrium should the involvement of British nationals with Royalist forces become known, it was the least he could expect given that Amery and McLean were members of his own party.

Home's concerns were somewhat assuaged by the initial composition of the mercenary teams. Sensitive to London's position of non-intervention, McLean had suggested that French mercenaries be recruited following a conversation with Crown Prince Faisal in March 1963.[51] It was an idea that apparently found official favour in Paris following an approach by David Stirling.[52] On 6 June 1963, Cooper was briefed on his mission in the Parisian home of Michelle de Bourbon on the Rue de Fronquenelle. According to his own account, 'We sat around a table into the early hours of the morning with high-ranking officials from both Britain and France.'[53] When Cooper eventually flew to Aden before entering the Yemen from Beihan, he was accompanied by members of the French intelligence service, the Deuxieme Bureau.[54] Their movement through Federation territory was facilitated by the French Consul General in Aden, Paul Carton, who also acted as Ambassador to the 'Royalist Yemen Government'. Towards the end of 1963, Paris cooled its previous ardour towards the Royalist cause, but the contacts Carton had enjoyed with McLean continued, the French diplomat continuing to supply nuggets of intelligence beneficial to the mercenary operation well into the spring and summer of 1964.[55]

Unlike their counterparts in SIS, officials in Paris appeared less concerned if their external intelligence service left footprints in the Yemen. French involvement has often been explained in terms of revenge on Nasser for the support Cairo proffered to the *Front de Libération Nationale* (FLN) in Algeria and alongside Britain, the international ignominy France endured in the aftermath of the Suez debacle. Such score settling aside, Smiley believed that French officials saw an opportunity for commercial gain to be had from the Saudis. In March 1963, Faisal was reported to have considered seriously Paris as a potential source of military equipment, in particular in the much needed area of air defence.[56]

From the outset, the mercenary endeavour rested on two main pillars: money and a secure base. The Saudis supplied the former, using the Royalist Foreign Minister at large, Sayid Ahmed al-Shamy, to dispense their largesse towards the bulk purchase of military supplies and the payment of salaries to those recruited. One notable exception in this regard was Smiley. Technically speaking he was employed as a military advisor to the Saudi government rather than as a mercenary, with a mandate to produce detailed reports on the fluctuating fortunes of the Royalist campaign alongside recommendations for improvements. As such, his salary was paid directly to him by the Saudis. The latter was required because Riyadh's public declaration of adherence to the Bunker cease-fire agreements and the subsequent presence of UN monitors on the Saudi–Yemen border prohibited the use of Saudi territory for supply operations. The only clear alternative was the Federation itself and Beihan state.

This in itself carried its own particular risks. London and the Foreign Office remained opposed to any activity that stood in contradiction to the policy of non-intervention. Both McLean and Stirling had, during the course of separate trips to Aden, been careful to curry favour with key individuals within Government House in a position to facilitate the flow of men and material across the Federation border. The positions of Sir Charles Johnston and his successor, Sir Kennedy Trevaskis, precluded their active involvement in such activity, though in the case of Trevaskis, the circumstantial evidence that he at least knew of McLean's intent is strong.[57] Two other individuals, however, emerged to play pivotal roles in the mercenary operation. The first, Flight Lieutenant Anthony 'Tony' Boyle, a fast jet pilot in the RAF, was serving as ADC to Sir Charles Johnston as part of an obligatory ground tour when he was approached by Stirling in the spring of 1963. He, in turn, recruited Major Peter de la Billiere, an SAS officer on secondment to the Federal Regular Army as a G3 – a junior intelligence officer.[58] McLean was soon in close liaison with Boyle, holding three meetings with the RAF officer in London between 23 April and 2 May. Boyle was already aware that the Shariff of Beihan acted as a conduit for Riyadh's financial and material investment to reach the various Royalist fronts. In a letter to McLean written soon after his return to Aden, Boyle described a meeting with Shariff Hussein and his deputy, Amir Saleh. Saleh acknowledged receipts of an unspecified amount of cash plus 50,000 rounds of .303 ammunition from Saudi Arabia, all of which was being sent to Prince Abdullah bin Hassan at Qara. He then wrote, 'I emphasised that this must not get to the ears of the British authorities, as, if it did, they were unlikely to provide any more assistance.'[59]

Assistance in this case referred to the British commitment to defend Beihan. Public disclosure of Beihan's position as a staging post for launching operations in the Yemen would have been grist to the mill of those in the Foreign Office who had long argued that, far from being a victim of unprovoked aggression, the activities of the Shariff invited retaliation from the YAR and Egypt. For Crown Prince Faisal, Prince Sultan and the head of the Saudi intelligence service, Kemal Atham, brother-in-law of Faisal and considered by many within the Saudi court to have been the *éminence grise* of the Crown Prince, such arrangements allowed for material support for the Royalists to continue, without violating the word of the Bunker agreement.[60]

With Boyle and de la Billiere recruited to establish a 'rat line' – the process whereby arms and equipment were despatched from Aden to Beihan without having to face the unwelcome attentions of customs officials – the recruitment of the required 'soldiers of fortune' gathered momentum. London's reluctance to see British nationals free booting in the Yemen determined the initial recruiting priorities, with Stirling using his connections with the Deuxieme Bureau and former French members of the war-time SAS to approach key individuals. In June 1963, Colonel Roger Falques, a former Legionnaire who had fought in Indo-China and survived incarceration at the hands of the Viet-Minh opened the required employment agency in Paris. Among the first to take the 'Saudi riyal' was Bob Denard, himself a veteran of the wars in Algeria and the Congo, who was chosen to command the French volunteers in the field. As individual soldiers, those recruited were of a high calibre; Smiley regarded them as being of 'a very high class'.[61]

This recruitment process gathered pace exponentially between June and

October 1963. The first batch of French mercenaries, still known only by singular names – Pussy, Michel, Schoen, Lafont, Kim and Phillipe – were ready to depart for the Yemen by the end of June, flying directly to Aden from Paris. By the end of October 1963, their numbers had increased to 25. Of note was the incremental salary structure which reflected the rank held previously by an individual in the French Armed Forces. For the month between 12 August and 12 September, Pussy and Kiki commanded salaries of Fr11,000 and Fr10,000 respectively, while L'Amiral, a former NCO from Brittany, was paid Fr5000. Their attitude towards those to whom they had responsibility for imparting the art of guerrilla warfare was often amusing and patronising. Recounting a meeting with L'Amiral in the Khaulan in February 1965, McLean noted of him:

> He was fundamentally an honest and sincere man, but his suppressed rage against the Yemenis made him abnormal. The slightest accident or imagined insult would put him into a passion when he would insult the Yemenis in atrocious but perfectly understandable Arabic . . . and repeat that all Yemenis were useless, liars, thieves, cowards, crooks and lazy bastards'.[62]

The total cost of the French operation, including salaries, supplies and transportation between 8 July and 16 October was Fr2,756,497. During this time, four separate plane loads of French supplied arms and ammunition were despatched from the French colony of Djibouti to Aden for an onward journey to Beihan. Recounting these arms supplies seven years later, Colonel Jim Johnson, a former commanding officer of 21 SAS who played a key role in the mercenary operation, revealed that a little-known air freight company, Rhodesian Air Services (RAS) owned by Jack Malloch, an old associate of David Stirling, was the company sub-contracted to deliver these arms supplies.[63] On 27 September 1963, according to an inventory kept by McLean, a cargo plane delivered 20×81mm mortars, 200 boxes of 81mm mortar bombs, 30 bazookas, 150 bazooka rockets, 50×MG34 machine guns accompanied by 15,000 rounds of 7.92mm ammunition. The small arms were mainly of German origin, leftovers from the end of the Second World War. From Aden, this cargo was delivered to Beihan in the hold of an RAF Beverley transport aircraft before making its journey to the Yemen.[64] The use of an RAF aircraft for this purpose would have been expressly forbidden by MIDCOM and it can only be supposed that Boyle, using his position as ADC, was able to shield such misuse of government property from the inquisitive gaze of officialdom. Certainly, those dealing with the distribution of weapons in Beihan were not always privy to the wider international consequences of what they were engaged in, though some had a good enough idea. In a letter dated 30 August 1963, a colleague of Boyle's reported the delivery of 'heavy stuff' by Beverley transport in

Beihan while asking, 'we wonder if this French set-up is not just an escape valve for HMG in case anything goes wrong with this lot'.[65]

If the quality of the individual mercenary recruited in Paris was high, the same could not be said for their logistical set-up. In an effort to speed up the delivery of arms and ammunition, the French suggested using an airstrip at Jaw al-Mullah in Beihan itself, circumventing the need to fly via Aden. On the maiden flight, the pilot nearly crashed, after it was discovered, *ipso facto,* that the airstrip was too short for the type of aircraft used. A suggestion by de la Billiere that they use an area of packed gravel some 100 miles to the east was dismissed by a French pilot on closer inspection, leading Boyle to lobby hard for the use of supply drops instead. At a time when Royalist forces were hard pressed to secure their fronts, such delays had strategic consequences. In a letter from Government House, Boyle described the growing irritation of both Shariff Hussein and the Royalist Foreign Minister, Sayid Ahmed Shamy, with the French re-supply effort. They had, Boyle suspected, 'come to the end of [their] patience with the French procrastinatory [sic] activities and, as we are working with them, some of this displeasure is beginning to come our way'.[66]

The problems were not helped by allegations that one of the French officers had been involved in the misappropriation of funds, while a fifth plane, a Constellation transport aircraft registered in Austria and contracted to RAS, was impounded in Djibouti on 11 October carrying 1,500 Mauser 7.92mm rifles and 20 MG34 machine guns.[67] This incident marked a growing shift in Paris away from association with the Royalists, and reflected the desire of President Charles de Gaulle to effect a rapprochement with Arab nationalist movements following the French withdrawal from Algeria in 1962. Responding to a personal letter from the Imam imploring Paris to use its diplomatic influence to mobilise international opinion favourable to the Royalist cause, de Gaulle deftly avoided the issue. In a phrase that could equally have flowed from the pen of a Foreign Office official he noted that 'France will continue therefore, by every possible means, to support any initiative which is directed towards the effective application of the principle of non-intervention.'[68] While French mercenaries were to remain the largest national group working as advisors, and French arms, particularly the 120 mm heavy mortar, remained prized items of weaponry, the structure of the operation had, by the end of 1963, become a British-planned and led operation.

Conclusion

Most explanations for the 'mercenary operation' posit a clear link with the subterfuge of British government policy. Individual contacts were maintained between SIS officers and the likes of Smiley, McLean and Cooper. From November 1963 onwards, Smiley enjoyed the hospitality of a senior SIS officer, John da Silva, when en route through Aden, and that of his counterpart John Christie (followed later by Geoff Douglas) when passing through in Jeddah.[69] But contact does not equate with outright collusion and, wary of broader government policy, any information divulged to SIS was on a strictly need-to-know basis and often the subject of barter. While the reports of Smiley and McLean were more detailed than anything produced by SIS, the perception of bias tempered their impact in the Cabinet. In the final appreciation of Egyptian intentions in the Yemen, the assessments of the JIC continued to hold sway of policy-making.

It is this failure to embolden the government to move beyond the legacy of Suez that underpins the emergence of the 'mercenary operation'. The initial composition of the operatives was a reflection of political constraints imposed by Whitehall, whereas for Paris, it was an opportunity to mix revenge, however limited, with commercial gain. As for Riyadh, the operation represented the ideal: the public commitment to abide by the Bunker agreement while privately, allowing its financial largesse to sustain a viable opposition to Cairo's presence in the Yemen. But with the 'French connection' unable to meet the early expectations, the scene was now set for the emergence of a 'very British affair'.

6

A Very British Affair

The Guerilla Campaign,
October 1963–September 1965

The increasingly haphazard nature of the French contribution forced a fundamental review of the mercenary commitment. While salvaging what it could from the French operation, this review, carried out in the early autumn of 1963, produced a structured plan for a British-led operation to give sustained support and training to the Royalist forces in the Yemen. The establishment of a coherent communications network to link the various fronts remained the top priority, but more creative solutions to the problem of logistics were now sought. For the most part, Royalist forces had been supplied through Beihan and Saudi Arabia by caravans of camels and mules. Often they could take up to three weeks to reach their required destination, far too long in cases where the intended recipients were having to defend themselves against the aggressive attentions of their Egyptian and Republican foes. The slow pace of such caravans, even when travelling under the cover of darkness, made them vulnerable to interdiction. Egyptian military intelligence had quickly identified likely supply routes and, as a consequence, had become profligate with their financial largesse in those tribal areas where they knew the caravans would have to pass through en route to their varied destinations. In June 1963, with Crown Prince Faisal suspending arms shipments – though not payments – to the Imam's forces from Saudi territory, the Royalist position became heavily dependent on what could be transported over the border from Federation territory. The need to overcome the twin obstacles of time and vulnerability led to the most controversial aspect of the mercenary operation in Yemen: the involvement of Israel.

Allusion to the role played by the Jewish State has long been a staple of secondary source literature dealing with the conflict, though precious little in terms of primary source documentation has emerged.[1] The evidence, for the most part, has been circumstantial but has always carried with it a sagacity born from the knowledge that damage inflicted upon Egyptian forces in the Yemen could only have been of benefit to Tel Aviv. This was certainly the view of Mohammed Heikal, Nasser's close confidant and former editor of the Egyptian daily newspaper *Al-Ahram*.[2] Israel retains a thick blanket of security over the extent of its involvement in the Yemen but occasionally officials have allowed a chink of light to illuminate this conjecture. Shabtai Shavit, former director of Israel's foreign intelligence agency, Mossad, and Ariel Sharon, confirmed in separate interviews three decades after the event that the Jewish State had been involved in clandestine activity in the Yemen, though both men remained suitably vague concerning the exact nature and scale of this involvement.[3] What is now clear is that, hamstrung by the vulnerability of land based supply lines, the mercenary operation organised air drops to specific Royalist-held areas in the Yemen. Some, but by no means all of these drops – code named MANGO – were conducted under the auspices of the Israeli Air Force, with aircraft contracted privately to the British mercenary operation either using Israeli air bases or on at least one occasion, Israeli Air Force transport planes themselves making the re-supply drops. In February 1965 such flights were deemed crucial in preserving a Royalist presence in tribal areas where Egyptian pressure was intense.[4]

The government of Douglas-Home was certainly aware by the summer of 1964 – from reports circulating in Whitehall and through contacts between SIS officers and some mercenaries – that air drops had become a logistical feature of the war though it is doubtful that all Cabinet members were fully briefed on the origins of these flights. While the Cabinet had, by the late summer of 1964, approved clandestine operations such as RANCOUR, these remained limited to the immediate jurisdiction of the Yemen–Federation border and were never linked, in a strategic sense, to the activities of the mercenaries. Political propriety of the most pressing kind meant that contact with the Israelis was conducted on a 'private' basis, far removed from any association with Her Majesty's Government should Israel's involvement be exposed. Such circumspection was shared by the mercenaries themselves, all too aware that support in whatever form given by Israel sat uneasily with the political, as well as the religious disposition of their main Saudi benefactor, Crown Prince Faisal. Nonetheless, the impact that the mercenaries had upon the fortunes of the Royalist forces, particularly in their ability to communicate between the various fronts, changed the essential dynamic of the civil war.

The Formation of the British Mercenary Organisation

On 7 September 1963, Tony Boyle, Peter de la Billiere and David Stirling met with the Royalist Foreign Minister, Sayid Ahmed al-Shamy in Aden. The purpose of the meeting, was to establish '[A] new organisation, formed on a military basis . . . to assist the legal Government of the Yemen in every practical way to remove the invaders from their country'. The pressing need for such an organisation was made abundantly clear in the subsequent plan of action that accompanied the meeting:

> Recent efforts to supply the the Yemeni Royalist forces, currently attempting to drive the Egyptians out of the Yemen, have proved unreliable and unproductive. Repeated assurances by French representatives of the imminent arrival of 7.5 tons of stores and equipment, which will no doubt eventually be delivered, have caused dislocation of planning and damage to morale at the fronts. In point of fact, the French have so far only produced 20 unarmed men. We, the few British who put themselves at Sayid Ahmed Ashami's [sic] disposal and who have in attempting to probe the authenticity of the French effort, met with evasiveness and disconcerting indications of inefficiency, intend to do what we can to remedy the situation and hold the French to their current commitment of arms deliveries.[5]

Before the growing doubts over the French effort prompted the Aden meeting, British involvement had been confined to focusing on expediting the flow of men and supplies from Paris to Aden and beyond. The only exceptions to this were the visits of McLean and Smiley in the summer of 1963, and concurrently, the insertion of Cooper with his Anglo-French team into the mountains of the Khaulan surrounding Sana'a. Somewhat surprisingly Smiley remained unaware of Cooper's presence. The British complement of his team was provided by three serving SAS soldiers who, in Cooper's words, 'had been granted one month's leave to join the expedition'.[6] Though on a reconnaissance mission to ascertain the Egyptian order of battle and train the forces attached to Prince Abdullah bin Hassan, Cooper and his team did engage in ambush operations, with one encounter leaving 85 Egyptians dead. The presence of regular British soldiers was, however, the exception rather than the rule. Given the position of London over British involvement in the Yemen, the deployment of three serving special forces soldiers was a risky venture, albeit one prompted by the pressing need to gain detailed intelligence of enemy intent and capability in the Khaulan in the absence of more immediate means. Such a deployment of British regular soldiers was never repeated.

In May 1963, Colonel Brian Franks had been approached by David Stirling to find a suitable person to recruit the requisite personnel for the Yemen. As President of the SAS Regimental Association, Franks had access to privileged information on the activities and whereabouts of former members of the regiment. On his advice, Stirling and McLean invited Colonel Jim Johnson, a former commanding officer of 21 SAS (TA) and a broker with Lloyds of London to co-ordinate the recruitment of ex-servicemen in possession of the particular skills deemed necessary for the

Yemen. The need for soldiers to have a basic grasp of the Arabic language meant that Johnson's initial recruitment efforts were focused on helping Stirling to locate suitable recruits in France, preferably those whose experience of Algeria had allowed them to acquire the basic language skills.[7] But by late August 1963, with investment in the 'French connection' providing few military returns in the Yemen itself, Johnson's efforts were now redirected towards fulfilling the promise of the 7 September meeting. Stirling allowed the recruitment of British operatives to be run from the offices of his media company, Television International Enterprises (TIE), located at 21 Sloane Street, London, though given Stirling's own special forces associations, this attempt at providing cover was somewhat transparent. The structure of the British operation that emerged from the September meeting is outlined in figure 6.1.

This structure expanded over time as more personnel were recruited to what was referred to as the 'Stirling Operation' but its essence remained unchanged over the next three years.[9] Crucial to the viability of the operation was the relationship between Johnson and Boyle. Even before the Aden meeting, Boyle had been sending Johnson reports lamenting the disparate nature of the French operation. On 25 August, he described the purchase of a large quantity of arms and ammunition by the Shariff of Beihan for the Royalist fronts with £28,000 provided directly by Ahmed al-Shami. It was, he concluded, 'excellent news which really, I'm afraid, makes the French look rather silly'.[10]

Ahmed al-Shami was by now receiving considerable sums of money from Crown Prince Faisal with which to bankroll the mercenary operation. At the end of August, Boyle disclosed to Johnson that the Saudi had donated £150,000 as a lump sum to the Royalists, adding, 'money is no object – the important thing is get the supplies to the Royalists'.[11] For Faisal, funding the emergent mercenary operation was a most convenient tool, allowing the fight to be taken to Cairo without incurring the diplomatic opprobrium of officials in Washington still anxious to secure the goodwill of Nasser. The Saudi also urged that arms and equipment be supplied by the most expeditious route, and prevailed upon al-Shami to consider the use of air drops. Such counsel carried the weight of bitter experience. In a letter to Cooper, de la Billiere revealed that on two consecutive nights, 24–25 and 25–26 August, two large caravans, one consisting of over 80 camels, had been intercepted by the Egyptian army on their way to the Jauf, laden with valuable arms and supplies.[12]

The British plan was designed primarily to address the problem of supply and communication, with the recruitment of trained wireless operators and the establishment of an effective radio network a priority. While British mercenaries did help train some Royalist forces and tribesman, this remained, for the most part, the responsibility of the French based at

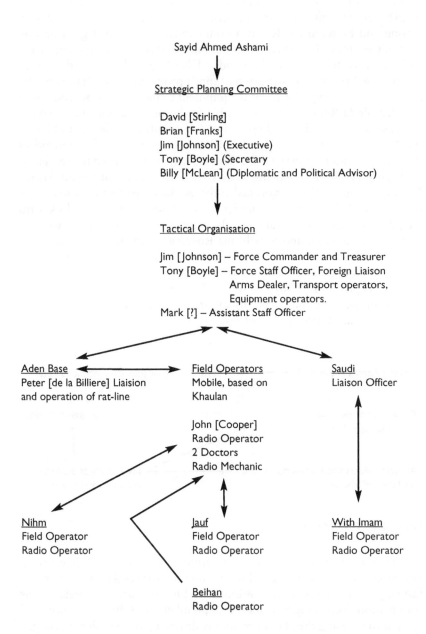

Sayid Ahmed Ashami

Strategic Planning Committee

David [Stirling]
Brian [Franks]
Jim [Johnson] (Executive)
Tony [Boyle] (Secretary
Billy [McLean] (Diplomatic and Political Advisor)

Tactical Organisation

Jim [Johnson] – Force Commander and Treasurer
Tony [Boyle] – Force Staff Officer, Foreign Liaison
     Arms Dealer, Transport operators,
     Equipment operators.
Mark [?] – Assistant Staff Officer

Aden Base
Peter [de la Billiere] Liaision
and operation of rat-line

Field Operators
Mobile, based on
Khaulan

Saudi
Liaison Officer

John [Cooper]
Radio Operator
2 Doctors
Radio Mechanic

Nihm
Field Operator
Radio Operator

Jauf
Field Operator
Radio Operator

With Imam
Field Operator
Radio Operator

Beihan
Radio Operator

Figure 6.1 Structure of British plan of assistance to Royalist government[8]

Khanja on the edge of the Empty Quarter, the Rub al-Khali. The prime British responsibility lay in organising coherent and effective action among and between the Royalist commanders. The 'Strategic Planning Committee' played an executive role, but the day-to-day running of the logistics operation was in the hands of Boyle and Johnson; they were responsible for the administration of funds provided by Al-Shami and the purchase and supply of arms and equipment to the Royalist forces. Based in Aden, de la Billiere was responsible for communications between the organisation in London and operatives 'up country' in Nequb and inside the Yemen, with Cooper, based in Khaulan, given overall command of the British contingent in the field. Cooper, who had returned to the Yemen in August 1963 on an extended leave from the Sultan of Oman Armed Forces, was given three main tasks: the establishment of a communications network between units under his command and a base link with Nequb in Beihan state; to arrange the reception of supply drops to units under his command; and to help the Royalists with skilled advice, most notably in the denial of the Egyptian main supply route between the port of Hodeidah and Sana'a.[13] In short, the British operation looked to play to the strengths of the Royalist forces that had been identified by Smiley and to impose upon the Egyptians a more intensive and refined campaign of attrition that Cairo could not possibly win.

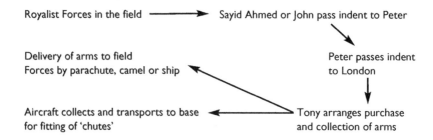

Figure 6.2 Plan of re-supply[15]

Boyle's involvement with the operation now intensified. A growing affliction with severe migraine brought a premature end to his career as a fast jet pilot and rather than continue with his RAF career, he resigned his commission. Returning to Britain in September 1963, he now committed himself to realising the plan of re-supply drawn up in the Aden meeting.[14]

Meanwhile, Johnson's attempts to find suitable recruits were beginning to bear fruit. Priority was placed upon finding wireless operators who could, under Cooper's guidance, be dispatched to the Royalist fronts.

Inevitably, preference lay with those who had some special forces or signals background although this did not necessarily guarantee the qualities of endurance, patience and fortitude required of operations in the Yemen. Among the first to be recruited was Major Rupert France, a wartime officer with the SAS and who had served under Smiley in Oman. On 17 October France arrived in Nequb to help establish an effective link between Aden and the field operatives. With its close proximity to the Yemen border, Nequb quickly emerged as the communications hub of the mercenary operation, and a convenient staging post for operatives both entering and leaving the Yemen. Two other operatives, Mark Milburn (who adopted the *nom de guerre* Jack Millar) and Bill McSweeney, both officers with 21 SAS arrived at this time, the latter being sent directly to the Imam's headquarters at al-Qara. As the operation expanded, new arrivals were sent directly to support the establishment of radio nets and, in keeping with one of the central tenets of special forces operations, dispense medical care to the indigenous population as part of the ongoing process of 'hearts and minds'. These included Sergeant Cyril Weavers, a signals expert with 21 SAS and David Bailey, a former national service officer with the Royal Sussex Regiment whose apparent enthusiasm for the Royalist cause was deemed sufficient to compensate for a lack of suitable experience in special operations. One other radio operative who arrived at this time was David Geary. It appears however that his involvement in the operation was subject to strict control as Smiley noted, on his second visit to the Yemen in November 1963, that he was, 'not in [the] picture'.[16]

In practice, there remained an acute shortage of trained operators. This resulted in mixed Anglo-French teams with McSweeney, for example, operating alongside L'Amiral and communicating with each other in 'pidgin' Arabic, much to the amusement of McLean.[17] As with some of the French contingent, individual British mercenaries found the conditions and attitudes of the Yemen and Yemenis hard to accept. According to Smiley 'Jack Millar' soon became disillusioned with the dirt of his surroundings and the 'persistent unreliability' of the Yemenis. Such complaints cut little ice with Smiley. An entry of his notebook of 20 November 1963 observed, 'Insulted Jack Millar by calling him and the French "adventurers". Could not cite any useful action by the Frogs.' While Smiley's opinion of the French changed over time, his view of the British mercenaries was decidedly mixed. The NCOs he rated highly for their specialist skills but the quality of the officers often left much to be desired. He rated only two, Johnny Cooper, and a late addition to the operation, Major Bernard Mills. Like Cooper, Mills had served in the SAS in Malaya and more recently with the Sultan of Oman Armed Forces. Linguistic ability was all and in Smiley's view, 'British officers who proved their worth were those who understood some Arabic', or had previous exposure to the Arab world.[18]

While ultimately beholden to his Saudi paymasters, Smiley's second trip to the Yemen between 14 November and 8 December 1963 was closely co-ordinated with the British plan of assistance. By dint of his close ties with Riyadh, he emerged as the 'Saudi liaison officer', compiling inventories and assessments for Crown Prince Faisal, Prince Sultan and the head of Saudi intelligence, Kemal Atham, as well as for the mercenary organisation. On arrival in Aden, he was met and briefed by de la Billiere before heading for Nequb and then onto Royalist-held areas east of the Sana'a–Sad'ah road. His cover throughout remained that of a syndicated newspaper journalist.[19]

His report for the Saudis was upbeat, noting that several tribes had defected to the Imam, 'and a greater number have been in contact with the Royalists and expressed their willingness to do so at an opportune time'. A similar vein of optimism ran through his assessment of the progress made in ameliorating the deficiencies in W/T communication and advisors. The French had stations located at Naqub, Khowlan and Bao'a, while seven British W/T operators arrived, sets in tow, when Smiley was in Nequb. Under the tutelage of Colonel Bob Denard and his second in command, Captain Guy Moreaux, the French training camp at Khanja had produced the first crop of troops able to use heavier weaponry available to the Royalist forces, including mortars and 75mm and 57mm recoilless rifles.[20] Privately, Smiley found cause for concern. While the radio and W/T remained in their infancy, he was concerned at the potential overlap between the British and French networks which was deemed not only inefficient but divisive in terms of coherent command and control. Moreover, the sets that had arrived at Nequb were inoperable due to missing parts and could not be distributed to the Royalist fronts. As for conditions at Khanja, the paragon of military efficiency described by Smiley in his report to the Saudis bore little resemblance to the description entered in his notebook. He wrote, 'Set-up at Khanja bad. No attempt whatever at cam[ouflage] – not surprising bomb set off near Amir Moh[amme]d Hussein's cave and nearly 30 cas[ualties] mostly killed. Hygiene appalling. Old food tins, bad food and human excrement everywhere. Flies appalling.'[21]

In fairness to Denard and Moreaux, they had accompanied Smiley in to the Yemen and had yet to stamp their authority upon conditions and training at Khanja. Even so, anxious to impress the Saudis and secure continued funding for the operation, Smiley had engaged in an act of self-censorship of some magnitude. By October 1963, however, a limited W/T link had been established between Johnny Cooper in the Khaulan, Rupert France at Nequb and de la Billere in Aden. The record of traffic that passed through this network in October 1963 gives some idea of the chaotic attempts to put flesh on the bones of the British plan of assistance. Requests for Mother Theresa Dollars to ensure the loyalty of tribesman as well as radio spares dominated signals traffic during this period. Not untypical was the following message sent by Cooper to France on 2 October 1963 which read:

TO RUPERT FROM JOHN INFO ABDULLAH. CRISIS RPT CRISIS. IF ABDULLAH MONEY ARMS CANNOT ARRIVE IN SEVEN DAYS AT [K]SHOLAN 3000 MEN WILL DESERT FROM ROYALIST G. SEND IMMEDIATE INFO ON POSITION MONEY ARMS AND DESPATCH NEXT CARAVAN TO PREVENT DESERTION' [sic].[22]

Some degree of order did, however, begin to emerge by the end of November 1963. Though short of medical supplies, radio parts and trained manpower, Cooper was proving his worth, not only acting as a military advisor to the Imam's cousin Prince Abdullah bin al-Hussein, but leading tribesmen in mining operations that denied free movement to Egyptian military traffic along the main arterial routes leading out from Sana'a. Such operations denied the Egyptians the ability to deploy their armour and heavy artillery to best effect. Many of these operations Cooper described in some detail in a series of letters to Boyle, de la Billiere and Johnson between October and December 1963.[23] In typically direct terms, he exclaimed that such mining operations had 'thrown both the wogs [sic] and Repubs [sic] into complete confusion, they simply have no idea what to do'.[24] It also meant that Egyptian resupply of its more remote garrisons became increasingly dependent upon helicopters, a mode of transport vulnerable to ground fire and incapable of sustaining the necessary levels of logistical support required by the troops 'up country'.

This correspondence also offers an intriguing glimpse into some of the more clandestine aspects of the guerrilla war in Yemen. Besides preparing ambushes, Cooper expended great effort on establishing the exact Egyptian order of battle (EOB). To do this, he was reliant upon the SIASI. The exact acronym remains unclear but at least four tribesmen were recruited by Cooper to infiltrate Republican held areas, including the capital Sana'a, gathering intelligence not just on military dispositions but also on the relationships between the Egyptian High Command and the political leadership of the YAR. They proved highly effective in this regard, running in tandem with 'Keeni Meeni' operations organised by Cooper. The term had entered the lexicon of the SAS in the 1950s following the counter-insurgency campaign against the Mau Mau in Kenya. Swahili in origin, SIASI described the stealthy movement of a snake in long grass while tracking its prey. In time, it became a particularly apt synonym to describe special forces operations where the ability of individuals to merge with their background was crucial to the success of particular missions, including assassinations of key Egyptian and Republican figures.[25] By using his personal intelligence service, Cooper was able to establish that by mid-October the Egyptian and YAR armies had 58 tanks stationed in and around the Sana'a area, a figure that prompted Cooper to demand an urgent increase in supplies of anti-tank and mortar munitions to his 'front'.[26] Beside the military rationale for establishing the EOB sat the political justification. Any evidence that could demonstrate that Egypt was not abiding by the terms of the disengagement agreement could be used by individuals within the Aden group to persuade London and Riyadh that Nasser's appetite for regional gain remained.

This intelligence war was by no means one-sided. While ideological sympathies played some part in swaying loyalties, trust was often only as good as the last payment. Betrayal was a common currency that both sides did their best to encourage. One radio signal reaching Nequb warned that, 'JAWF [radio] OPERATOR IN EGYPTIAN PAY. BRIEFED TO KILL FROGS'. Egyptian ingenuity even extended to the supply of cigarettes to Royalist forces whose threat to the health of the smoker went beyond nicotine. In a message sent on 5 October to de la Billiere, France confirmed 'FAGS BOOBYTRAPPED'. One would-be victim had a narrow escape as, much to his undoubted surprise, his recently lighted cigarette exploded in an ashtray.[27] Under such conditions, maintaining personal security and the security of a mission in tribal societies where the distinction between the public sphere and private space carried little meaning, proved difficult. Cooper remained keen to ensure the integrity of his SIASI network and decided to move his headquarters to a stone house in El Garah where people could be more easily screened. This emphasis on security also encompassed the increasing use of a *nom de guerre* by individual operatives. In November 1963, Cooper insisted in a letter to de la Billiere that he be addressed by his Arabic pseudonym, Abdullah bin Nusr, a practice which soon came to be adopted by other mercenaries.[28] The emphasis on security was most keenly felt with regard to radio codes. Cooper devised a system of encoding his messages to Aden which was all but unbreakable. It was nevertheless, laborious in the extreme. He explains:

I used a simple but effective code based on two French dictionaries. The messages went out with each word encoded as a series of figures. The first digit in a series, either 01 or 02, referred the translator on the other end to one of the dictionaries. Subsequent numbers pointed him to a page, then a column, and finally the word I wanted to send. Thus for example, 0143218 indicated dictionary 01, page 43, column 2, line 18. It was an old and laborious ruse, especially as I had to translate my messages into French, but it worked. If an enemy intercepted the messages and did not know which books were being used, he had virtually no chance of cracking the code.[29]

By extension, the code was also difficult for the British authorities to break. The mercenary operation maintained discreet contacts with SIS which, to the outside observer, smacked of a pro-active collusion. Cooper admits to being debriefed in Naqub after his second sojourn to the Yemen in the spring of 1963 by two SIS officers, Ralph Daly and Bill Herber-Percy.[30] While able to supply intelligence on Egyptian capabilities, as well as useful items of captured equipment, the evidence suggests that the more sensitive areas of the British operation remained off limits to the men from Broadway. Where information was exchanged, it was done on a quid pro quo basis, with intelligence supplied by Cooper rewarded by payments to help finance his 'Keeni Meeni' activities. As early as November 1963, intelligence was being passed on to another officer based in Aden named Radcliffe, but those working at 21 Sloane Street were careful about passing material on to SIS before it had been vetted. On 4 December 1963, Fiona Frazer, daughter of Lord Lovat, and who worked for the mercenary organisation under the cover of TIE, informed McLean that she had received taped material from Peter de la Billiere, but that 'I think it may be unwise to send it to [Terence] O'Brien [sic] [Tear] until we know what is in in [sic]!'.[31]

This circumspection was understandable. While a caucus within SIS had clear sympathies with both the motives and aims of the British Mercenary Organisation, they remained servants of the Crown and subject to the strictures of successive Foreign Secretaries determined to avoid being dragged into the Yemen quagmire. As such, even when SIS was given more latitude, as in the summer and autumn of 1964, its activities remained closely monitored in Whitehall and never moved beyond providing material support for tribes just over the Yemen-Federation border. Yet some evidence exists that officials within the Ministry of Defence did undertake more pro-active measures to monitor first-hand the activities of the mercenaries. In the late autumn of 1963 they circulated an asset whose military background, technical expertise and experience of the Gulf region were ideally suited for the 'Stirling Operation.' Duly recruited into the organisation, this individual closely monitored the activities of the British and French mercenaries for the next three years until his cover was eventually blown. As future events were to show, however, it remains doubtful if any of the information he passed back to London was ever circulated among the hierarchy of the British intelligence community.[32]

Supplying the Royalists

The need to ensure the ready supply of arms and ammunition remained a constant concern for Royalist commanders, all too aware that Saudi munificence remained vulnerable to wider political currents. While Riyadh continued to provide the financial wherewithal to sustain the operation, demand for weapons invariably outstripped supply. This was often less to do with the actual availability of the military paraphernalia required to fight a guerrilla war, and more with the vulnerability of extended supply lines. Until the spring of 1963, Saudi Arabia had been the principal supplier of arms and ammunition to Royalist forces, purchasing surplus military hardware, much of it Second World War vintage on the European market. Adnan Kashoggi, the Saudi arms dealer who came to international prominence in the 1970s, secured his first contract as a result of the Yemen Civil War but Riyadh used other, more circuitous routes to supply the requisite material of war.[33]

Alec Douglas-Home became embroiled in a furious exchange with the Labour MP Richard Marsh, following disclosures in the *People* newspaper that a British arms dealer, Major Robert Turp, had supplied 20,000 Lee Enfield .303 rifles to Shaykh Ibrahim Zahid of Saudi Arabia. The bare facts of the story, sold to the *People* by a disgruntled businessman, Eric Boon, were undoubtedly true. Yet the Prime Minister was justified in responding with some opprobrium to the allegations. Unable to gain an export licence in the United Kingdom, Turp's company Intor (International Ordanance) subcontracted the order to a Briton based in Brussels by the name of Dawson Ellis. The rifles were supplied from surplus Belgian Army stocks, loaded on to Sabena aircraft and flown directly to Saudi Arabia. Given such arrangements, there was little control London could exercise over arms transactions beyond its territorial control.[34]

Whatever the vagaries, political or otherwise, of arms deals on the open market, the time required to supply Royalist forces in such harsh physical conditions remained a constant logistical headache. The problem was compounded by Riyadh's reluctance to breach the Bunker agreement. This resulted in arms caravans having to travel the more lengthy route from Beihan State by camel train or, occasionally, truck, to the various fronts in the mountains of north Yemen. Not only were these journeys laborious – a camel train could take anything up to three weeks to reach its destination – but interdiction by Egyptian-led forces, particularly in and around Marib, a Republican-controlled area, remained a constant threat.

The best method of ensuring a quick despatch of arms and ammunition material was through the use of air transport with supplies either flown into make-shift airfields in Royalist-controlled areas or dropped by parachute along the various fronts as need dictated. This also necessitated the requisitioning of suitable aircraft with trained personnel who were willing to fly missions over a country where air superiority lay in the hands of the Egyptians. Serious consideration was given to establishing an air strip on a plateau in the Jawf region to the east of Sana'a. At the end of November 1963, Smiley, accompanied by a former French Air Force officer, surveyed a site considered suitable for such a strip, 1,100 metres above sea level and some 2 kilometres in length. The strip was considered ideal since the nearby Jebel of Sobra'bin contained caves suitable for storing arms, ammunition and supplies.[35] At a stroke, such a site negated any need to land supplies in Nequb before being despatched on their route by camel. Speed remained of the essence, however, and preference, certainly among the British operators, remained with parachute drops. Even if an air strip inside the Yemen was to become operational, supplies would still have to be distributed by the ubiquitous camels or pack mules to the various fronts. The use of air drops had been a key part of the British plan of assistance and now, with the material demands of war threatening to outstrip supply, the calls for progress to be made in the provision of air drops became more insistent.[36]

None was more vocal in this regard than Johnny Cooper. With his experience of arranging reception committees in France and Malaya, he had begun to identify suitable drop zones in the Khowlan mountains. This included advising on the best routes transport aircraft should take to find his location in the mountains, no easy task when having to fly tactically over rugged terrain to avoid Egyptian radar. One geographical marker he advised pilots to use when approaching from the Red Sea coast was the British-administered island of Kamaran, just off the Yemeni port of Salif which once passed, would allow communication on 'Channel One of our ground to air radio'.[37] Despite such preparations Cooper did not receive his first drop until February 1964, codenamed 'Mango'.[38] By his own admission, the whole operation was shrouded in mystery, not least because the drops were being organised and delivered by what he referred to cryptically as a 'friendly' air force. His description of the event gives some clue as to the origin of these clandestine flights:

To make the drops, they [the friendly air force] had converted a Stratocruiser with a roll off exit at the rear for pushing out the containers . . . On the night of the first drop, the Stratocruiser flew down the Red Sea with Egypt on the right and Saudi Arabia on the left. They had to come in almost at sea level to avoid detection by Egyptian radar, and when they reached the port of Hodeidah, they swung inland towards the mountains, climbing to 10,000 feet. Our friends had muffled the engines and it was very quiet. Then the huge aircraft came in for the

actual drop and as it swept over at about two hundred and fifty feet, sixty parachutes spewed out of the back. It was a beautifully executed professional drop.
Abduallah bin Hassan was delighted. He had the mortars and bombs he needed
together with a plentiful supply of small arms including German Schmeisser sub-
machine guns. The source of these weapons was brilliantly concealed. Every
serial number had been scored out, the parachutes were of Italian origin and
even the wood shavings used in the packing had been imported from Cyprus.
Even the most expert intelligence analyst would have had a job to unravel that
one.[39]

For some time, the circumstantial evidence over the origin of these
covert flights pointed towards Israel, not least because of the flight path
described and make of the aircraft involved. The Jewish State had maintained close military ties with Paris throughout the 1950s and its air force
was mainly equipped with French-built aircraft – Israel was the only state
in the region operating the French-built Stratocruiser. While it is conceiv-
able that Stratocruisers of the French Air Force operated from Djibouti,
de Gaulle's attempts to build bridges with the wider Arab world made
French involvement in such an operation unlikely by the beginning of
1964. Moreover, the Israel Defence Force (IDF) had been equipped in its
early years with a substantial number of small arms and equipment of
German design. By the late 1950s such weaponry was surplus to requirements as the IDF underwent a process of modernisation.[40] Johnson argued
that the rumour of Israeli involvement – freely expressed by British mercenaries to their Royalist charges – was a deliberate ruse designed to obscure
the true source of these re-supply drops.[41] Such an explanation lacks
conviction. Given regional sensitivities about any involvement with the
Jewish State, a cover story that involved other actors, be they state or non-
state, would have been more attuned to political sensitivities. In fact,
Israeli involvement in the covert support of Royalist forces was very real.
It is not hard to discern the strategic gains Israel hoped to accrue by
supporting an operation that could undermine the military capability of
its main nemesis. The exact moment when contact was made with Israeli
officials remains obscure but the documentary evidence suggests that it
was not before the summer of 1963. Between 24 and 25 July, McLean
held a number of talks with Crown Prince Hassan. Point six of the record
of this meeting noted, 'The desirability of an approach to the Israelis for
help, perhaps through Sherif Hussein, or a confidential Israeli Agent or
reliable Jew in Aden, or through the French'.[42] Contrary to the claims of
some authors, no evidence exists that officials in Saudi Arabia knew of,
let alone condoned, such contacts. In notes written after a private audience with Faisal in January 1965, McLean reported the Saudi monarch as
stating that, 'Israel supports Nasser. There is a secret agreement between
Mrs [Golda] Meyer [sic], the Americans and Nasser whereby Nasser

agrees not to attack Israel in exchange for money from America and secret help from Israel'.[43]

Sometime after his return to London – again, the exact date remains undisclosed – McLean contacted the Israeli military attaché, Colonel Dan Hiram. An artillery officer by profession, Hiram had been posted to Britain in 1961.[44] He had used his position to gather intelligence on arms procurement by Arab countries in the United Kingdom, intelligence that proved of immense interest to his counterpart in the French Embassy, Colonel Andre Gille. With the Algerian war still raging, Hiram discovered that arms purchased by the Jordanians from Intor were in fact being diverted to the FLN. Acting on this information, Paris impounded a Jordanian registered ship transporting an arms cargo worth £4.25 million.[45]

Now, in an approach condoned by Crown Prince Hassan and Shariff Hussein, McLean began discussions with Hiram over clandestine support for the Royalists. These resulted in David Smiley, under an assumed name, making the first of four trips to Israel in the autumn of 1963. During the course of the first trip, Smiley was accompanied by Jim Johnson, a logical move given Johnson's areas of responsibility in the hierarchy of the mercenary organisation. Smiley met with the Director General of the Defence Ministry, Shimon Peres, the Commander in Chief of the Israeli Air Force, Ezer Weitzman, Colonel Eitan Avrahami and Lieutenant Colonel Raphael Ephrat from the Agaf Mod'in (Military Intelligence) and Major Ze'ev Liron of the Israeli Air Force.[46] Recounting this *liaison dangereuse* four decades later, Smiley remained struck by the sensitive nature of the Israeli connection. He noted:

The Saudis never knew about the Israeli connection. I think it would have caused a certain amount of trouble if they had known. The Israelis never received payment – it was in their interests to keep the Egyptians tied down in the Yemen. The airdrops were not regular, perhaps two or three, but Jim Johnson may have been doing things behind my back which I never knew anything about.[47]

More recent disclosures give further details of Israel's involvement. In his biography of the Israeli diplomat and rabbinic scholar, Ya'acov Herzog, Michael Bar-Zohar recounts how Herzog, in his position as Director General of the Foreign Ministry, met a representative of the Imam in London on 10 December 1963. This emissary, whom Herzog codenamed the 'Prophet' was most likely Ahmed al-Shamy, the Royalist Foreign Minister. In return for Israel supplying arms, ammunition and providing training for some select Yemeni troops, the Royalist emissary promised recognition of the Jewish State would ensue once victory had been secured. While circumspect in their overall appreciation of the

Royalist position, it was felt that the immediate strategic benefit of bleeding the Egyptian army dry, coupled with the prospect of an entrée in to the dynastic orders of the Arabian peninsula was sufficient to justify the risks involved.[*]

While Bar-Zohar claims that the initial Royalist contact with the Israelis was facilitated by Felice Bellotti, an Italian journalist sympathetic to the Jewish State, the involvement of Herzog and the Israeli head of the Mossad, Meir Amit came only *after* Smiley had made his first trip to Israel. More likely, the involvement of Herzog and Amit was recognition by the Israelis of the extreme political, as well as military sensitivity of the operation and accordingly, the need for tight policy co-ordination with those Britons involved. Therefore, Bar-Zohar's subsequent observation that Julian Amery 'played an active part in proceedings' is of a piece with Smiley's recollection of meeting with Peres at the home of the Minister for Aviation in Eaton Square during this period.[**]

Israeli support was not just restricted to the delivery of arms supplies. Tel Aviv later furnished Smiley's radio operator Jimmy Knox, a former SAS signaller, with an advanced W/T set. It was later returned to the Israelis via the transit hall at Heathrow Airport. In return, Smiley briefed the IDF on the military capabilities of the Egyptian armed forces, as well as supplying them with samples of shrapnel and shell casing which he believed to have contained chemical agents. His knowledge of Egyptian air operations was also harnessed by the Israelis. On one occasion, he was allowed to interrogate an Arab pilot who had defected to Israel in a MiG-21 jet fighter, a type which was deployed widely in the Yemen by the Egyptian Air Force.[48] Like Cooper, Smiley's wartime experience with SOE made him particularly suited to dealing with the reception committees in and around the drop zones. He controlled two such drops from what he termed 'Mangoland' near Amara and Sad'ah, one on the night of 12–13 June 1965, the other following on exactly one month later. The exact number of these night-time operations remains unclear. Tony Boyle accompanied at least two such re-supply missions between 1964 and 1966, communicating with the Royalist reception committees via a 'Eureka VHF' ground-to-air radio set.[49] He shared this experience with Jim Johnson who flew in the aircraft, identified by Smiley on this occasion as a four engine Skymaster, making the July re-supply drop. Recounting this experience, Johnson told Smiley that 'there were so many lights burning below that it looked like they were over a town.' Boyle and

[*]Michael Bar Zohar, *Ya'acov Herzog: A Biography* (London: Halban Publishers, 2005), pp. 237–38.
[**] Email correspondence with Colonel David Smiley, Subject: 'Herzog Book', 31st October 2005; Bar-Zohar, pp. 240–41.

Johnson made sure that home comforts were included in the canisters dropped to the British mercenaries. This not only included personal mail and newspapers, but also the occasional bottle of scotch and cans of beer.[50] Smiley noted that the tribesman receiving the airdrops became 'exultant', boasting happily that 'With all these new weapons we will drive the British out of Aden', hardly the purpose for which they were intended.[51]

The Crisis of 1964

By the end of 1963, the British Mercenary Organisation was already beginning to plan the next two phases of the war, designed to link the Royalist fronts geographically and deny the main supply routes on a permanent basis to the Egyptian forces. This in turn would encourage uprisings among tribes whose territorial domains straddled the main roads linking Hodeidah, Taiz'z, Sad'ah with the capital Sana'a.[52]

The losses incurred by the Egyptians by the beginning of 1964 were heavy, with senior field commanders among the casualties. On 11 February, an ambush at Mafhag on the Hodeidah–Sana'a road proved particularly bloody. Three high-ranking Egyptian commanders, 15 Republican officers and over 1,000 Egyptian and Yemeni troops were killed.[53] McLean estimated that by the end of that month, over 8,000 Egyptian troops alone had been killed, while the cost of the war to the Egyptian treasury was put at $500,000 a day.[54] Whatever the human and financial burden, it was clear that moral among the Egyptian armed forces was low. Despite the danger of hyperbole, reports of suicides among Egyptian officers and of troops bartering arms and ammunition for food indicated an army that had lost its combat efficiency.[55] Such lassitude suggested that the time was ripe for the Royalist forces to implement the next phase of the war, a process McLean hoped would rout the Egyptian forces in Yemen. This he believed had become a matter of urgency but could only be achieved if London was prepared to take more pro-active measures in support of the Royalists. On 3 March, he sent an attached memorandum to the Prime Minister explaining his argument:

> At one time it may have been in HMG's interest that the war in the Yemen should drag on indefinitely absorbing Nasser's energies and imperialist ambitions. Now however, I do not believe this to be so; for recent events in Aden [the attempted assassination of Trevaskis] have shown what we may expect there if Egyptian power remains established even in parts of the Yemen. There is also the danger of increased Russian infiltration into the Yemen as long as the Egyptians are there. Therefore, unless the Egyptians withdraw their troops and the war in Yemen is brought to an end, the defence of Aden will place an ever increasing burden on

HMG in men and money. For these reasons, I believe it is now in HMG's interests to bring the war in Yemen to a satisfactory end.[56]

Whether a causal link existed between the activities of the British
Mercenary Organisation and increased subversion against the
Federation remains a moot point. Ever conscious of pressure from
Washington to circumscribe their activities, the Foreign Office certainly
viewed their activities with opprobrium. McLean's advocacy of more
forceful measures coincided with a plea from the British ambassador to
Washington, Lord Harlech, that 'vigorous action be taken to stop the
involvement of British mercenaries and British territory in the Yemeni
war in order to avoid feeding American suspicions of our motives'.[57] The
Cabinet chose neither course. Instead, the British Mercenary
Organisation continued to operate from Federation territory under what
amounted to 'benign neglect' by the Federal authorities. Measures to
counter subversion from the Yemen remained confined to the immediate
area, though arms and ammunition distributed to the tribes such as the
Murad found their way into Royalist hands. Equally, McLean's direct
appeal to Douglas-Home reveals two interesting facets of the mercenary
operation: First, despite their best endeavours, the logistical challenge of
ensuring consistent and adequate supplies to the Royalist fronts
remained beyond the capabilities of the mercenary organisation; and second, that Cabinet decision-making as being hostage to the Aden Group
was more myth than reality. Douglas-Home certainly failed to deny
Federation territory to the 'Stirling Operation' but equally the urgent
tone of McLean's report underlined the limits of existing government
collusion with an operation from which they hoped to reap the strategic
benefits without incurring any political cost.[58]

Despite invoking the spectre of Soviet encroachment under the guise of
Nasser's opportunism, McLean's call to arms, if not quite falling on deaf
ears, certainly found them distinctly muffled. Cabinet circumspection
over the need to press for a military decision in the Yemen was reinforced
by the assessment of the JIC. As Colonial Secretary, Duncan Sandys
argued consistently for 'support' for the Royalists to be channelled via the
Federation rulers at the behest of Prince Faisal. On 19 March, at a meeting
of the Defence and Overseas Policy Committee, it was disclosed that 'The
JIC do not believe that the Egyptians can be driven out in this way. We
consider the actions of the [Federal] rulers should be confined to repelling
subversion; their involvement in the Yemeni war adds to their difficulties
as well as ours.'[59]

The difficulties were not confined to the limits of special operations that
had been sanctioned in Whitehall. Smiley returned to the Yemen for his
third visit at the beginning of March 1964. The reports he subsequently

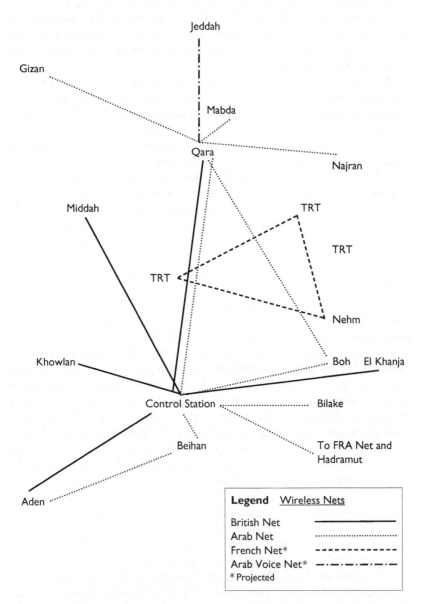

Figure 6.3 **Royalist-operated radio and communications network, April 1964**[60]

wrote for both the Crown Prince Faisal and discussions he had with the Imam were decidedly mixed. Militarily, he found the Royalists to be in better shape, with tribal allegiances, particularly among the *Shaffei*, shifting in favour of the Royalists. Communications, though remaining far from satisfactory, were much improved with coverage extending across most of the Royalist fronts with links established with Nequb, Aden and Saudi Arabia.

He noted, however, that while 'the British operated network is completely secure . . . the Arab network is not and the Egyptians have already broken their codes'.[61] This weakness, an important facet in maintaining operational security, was more than matched by the poor standards of command and control demonstrated by some Royalist commanders in the field. On 18 March, Smiley was present at what should have been a co-ordinated attack against the town of Hajja. It was an important junction, with roads running south-east to Sana'a, north-east to Amran and west to Hodeidah. These routes had been routinely cut by Royalist forces who dominated the surrounding features. The Egyptians, realising its strategic importance, had managed to sustain a company-sized garrison in and around the town. The plan now was to make a co-ordinated, two-pronged assault from the north and south, removing the Egyptian force.

In the event, the assault proved a debacle. Despite overlooking Hajja, Smiley watched with incredulity and growing anger a preliminary bombardment that was wildly inaccurate and inflicted little in the way of appreciable damage upon the Egyptians. Such military incompetence was matched by the actual assault. Objectives in and around the town had been allocated on a tribal basis, and while those on the northern front achieved some success against their designated targets, they had to withdraw once it became apparent that no attack whatsoever had materialised from the south. Smiley had no doubts that the Egyptians were expecting an attack, 'not necessarily from a spy with the Royalists, but because every tribesman within miles of Hajja knew the time and date of the attack for days in advance'.[62] Compounding this military morass was the sin of omission. The roads leading in to Hajja were supposed to have been mined. Later, Smiley watched as a solitary Egyptian truck wound its way up along a *wadi* unhindered into the town.

Putting aside the protocols of court usually required when addressing the Imam, Smiley was blunt in identifying Royalist military deficiencies in the aftermath of Hajja. Planning, supplies, tactics and commanders were all deficient, a situation aggravated still further by what Smiley regarded as weaknesses within the Royalist character: ignorance, inefficiency, indolence and incompetence. There existed, he argued, no commander around Hajja gifted with strategic prescience, an opinion Smiley felt he was justified in holding, given the poor tactics and inadequate supplies attendant to the Hajja operation. He concluded:

> I told the Imam that it was not for me to criticise or try to change the Arab way of life, but unless his men changed their ways, he had little hope of winning the war..Unless a degree of urgency could be impressed on men when time was really a vital factor, then the situation would not improve. Due to apathy and indolence supplies sat for weeks in villages where nobody needed them. Due to ignorance and inefficiency there were continual cases of stores being wrongly split up, and I saw many cases of guns and mortars without sights, mines without fuzes [sic], and explosives without the demolition equipment to detonate the charges . . . On tactics I stated that it must be remembered that the Royalists "soldiers" were not professionals but merely armed tribesmen – in other words a peasant farmer carrying a rifle. They had neither the training nor the discipline to carry out an operation such as the ill-conceived and badly executed set-piece attack on Hajja.[63]

As for some of the Royalist commanders, Smiley felt that the demands of tribal lore, with its 'petty details', consumed too much of their time. 'Wars' he reminded the Amirs, 'cannot be won by writing letters'. Morale among tribes often dropped when a commander left their area to tour another, while 'others I feared imagined themselves generals when they had the minds of a Lance Corporal!' While the Imam took Smiley's harsh appreciation in good spirit, the British advisor felt this had more to do with news of the RAF attack on Harib filtering through to his entourage. In conclusion, Smiley urged that the Royalist forces play to their strengths as guerrillas, attacking Egyptian lines of communication, ambushing convoys and mining roads. Smiley repeated this advice in a letter that accompanied his report to Crown Prince Faisal. It was a subtle, inspired move. While the Imam may have made light of the Briton's advice, he was hardly in a position to do so again if in receipt of a similar entreaty from his main benefactor.[64]

With its emphasis on endurance and perseverance, the campaign of attrition advocated by Smiley did not conflate easily with the need to impose an immediate decision upon Egyptian forces that had been urged by McLean.[65] But the use of martial prowess to harness tribal loyalty remained only one dimension of this war. Smiley had concluded that, unable to sustain its losses in the mountains, Egyptian military intelligence had resorted to 'large scale bribing of the tribes with both money and rifles in order to win their support'. With Royalist forces following suit, tribes were in the happy position of being able to play one side of against the other. The gathering of intelligence became more akin at times to an auction with one tribe in particular, the *Dahm*, proving adept at financially exploiting the changing fortunes of war.[66]

The Egyptian expeditionary force now proved that they were far from a spent force. In the late spring and throughout the summer of 1964, renewed offensives began in the Khowlan, al-Jauf and a pincer movement of Egyptian troops moving north from Hajja and west from Sad'ah, a manoeuvre that aimed to kill or capture the Imam in his redoubt on Jebel Qara – these all placed the Royalist forces on the defensive. Behind the scenes, Egyptian intelligence officers were being equally aggressive in their profligacy among the tribes. At a stroke, any hope that the two-phase strategy outlined in January could move beyond the initial stages was removed. McLean regarded the Royalist position as critical but he was also aware that for all his lobbying of Cabinet colleagues, any covert support the British government was prepared to sanction remained limited in its geographical scope. Taking this as his starting point, he wrote a series of memoranda to Alec Douglas-Home between March and May 1964 requesting that '20,000 rifles, with 200 rounds per rifle, up to a £¼ million in gold and Mother Theresa Dollars and some anti-tank mines be distributed among the tribes of southern Yemen'.[67] This material, McLean argued, could be distributed to the Federation rulers – Shariff Hussein of Beihan, Mohammed Ferid al-Aulagi, Sultan Salleh of Audhli and Sultan Fadhil Bin Ali of Lahej – for distribution to tribes around Taiz'z, Ibb, Rada, Beidha, Marib and Harib. His proposals were deliberately designed to both dovetail with, and expand upon the scope of Operation RANCOUR. By his own admission the 'Member of Parliament for Aden' hoped that the precedent of such arms supplies would whet the appetite of his Cabinet colleagues to increase British involvement way beyond the 20-mile limit authorised under RANCOUR.

Such involvement was given added urgency by McLean's visit to his Middle East domain between 27 May and 14 June. Royalist morale was low, with Prince Abduallah bin al-Hussein, commander of the Royalist front in the Khowlan, exposed to considerable and sustained Egyptian offensives. Pro-Royalist tribes around Arhab and Nehim were isolated and 'had received no supplies for more than a year'. This made them vulnerable to the generous financial inducements offered by the Egyptians, a position compounded by the distinct paucity of both money and military supplies being received from Saudi Arabia. Moreover, the long arm of Egyptian military intelligence had come within an ace of assassinating Crown Prince Hassan. On 23 May 1964, a tribesman from the *Hashid*, paid in the Egyptian shilling, raided Hassan's headquarters at Al-Gahrir, located in the mountains of the Jauf. Simultaneously, members of his own bodyguard mutinied, disgruntled that their pay of three riyals per day was two riyals less than the salary paid by other Princes to their respective paladins. The hapless Prince escaped with his life, but not before losing his hoard of gold.[68] With bribery fast becoming the weapon of choice, McLean urged London to consider sending the equivalent of a million Mother Theresa dollars, preferably in gold sovereigns, to the Royalist commanders. Avarice aside, some tribes were beginning to suffer acute shortages of food in the central highlands of Yemen as the war, well into its second year, disrupted the agricultural cycle. As such, inventories sent by the Royalist commanders began to include requests for substantial quantities of rice and flour. Increasingly, food, as much as the ubiquitous Mother Theresa dollar, was now being used to secure tribal allegiance.[69]

The Royalists continued to receive the occasional parachute drop but given the clandestine nature of these flights, they were no panacea to the deficits in material and money facing all Royalist fronts. By July, securing an effective supply line to the Khowlan had become a matter of urgency. This could only be achieved with the support of tribes such as the *Murad*, the *Gaifa* and *Abida* whose domains encompassed the area stretching from the border of Beihan State to the Khowlan. Frustrated at the piecemeal approach adopted by London, McLean met with Kenneth Strong, Director-General of the Defence Intelligence Staff, soon after his return to Britain. He urged an expansion of all covert operations in the Yemen as a means of not only demonstrating British commitment to the Federation, but as a gesture of support for Crown Prince Faisal.[70] His constant lament at the febrile nature of official British support for the Royalist forces concerned the Aden Group, not least because the British Mercenary Organisation remained dependant upon Saudi largesse to continue its operations. Moreover, Saudi unease at shouldering the financial burden of the Royalist war effort indicated to McLean that those within the Saudi court who advocated a compromise with Nasser – most notably the Saudi Vice-Minister for Foreign Affairs Omar Saqqaf – were beginning to gain the upper hand.[71]

Although the Foreign Office concluded that, irrespective of British policy, Crown Prince Faisal remained as determined as ever to remove Egyptian forces from the Yemen, McLean pressed London to produce more evidence other than meaningless platitudes regarding its commitment to deny Cairo the fruits of its regional ambitions. In July, he pressed ministers sympathetic to the activities of the British Mercenary Organisation to consider, 'SAS commando raids on the ships in Hodeidah and the airfield at Sana'a, attacks he argued that could be 'carried out without undue difficulty'.[72] If such a proposed course of action did not already lie beyond the political pale, then revelations in the *Sunday Times* certainly placed it there for good. On 5 July 1964, its 'Insight' team published five letters addressed to Johnny Cooper, missives which he had never received. The letters, all written in November 1963, were published verbatim on 1 May 1964 in the Egyptian daily paper, *Al-Ahram*. While two of the letters related solely to Cooper's private affairs, the rest, written by Tony Boyle, concerned operational matters associated with the mercenary operation.

On reflection, their revelations could have been worse, given the sensitivities surrounding the air drops. They were undoubtedly a propaganda coup for Cairo, and lent credence to the widely held suspicion that the activities of the mercenaries were officially sanctioned. *Al-Ahram* claimed that a courier, paid to deliver this correspondence, had been intercepted by an Egyptian helicopter near the border with Beihan. This explanation lacks conviction given the time lag between the date the letters were written, November 1963, and their public disclosure six months later. It is more likely that the letters passed through several tribal hands before landing on the desks of first, Egyptian military intelligence and second, the editor of *Al-Ahram*, Mohammed Heikal.[73]

Whatever the truth, the story made the government more wary than ever about extending direct clandestine support to the Royalists. Others in government remained convinced that direct supplies needed to be sent forthwith. Despite his proclamations of righteous indignation over the activities of the mercenaries, designed to soothe ruffled American feathers, Nigel Fisher remained a champion of their cause and of direct covert aid to the Royalists. In a memorandum to Thorneycroft that echoed the sentiments of McLean and Amery, he argued for £2million in aid be given to the Royalists over the course of the next year, 'half in money, ¼ in arms and ammunition and ¼ in food and maintenance for the tribes'. The size of this proposed aid package was far in excess of anything submitted hitherto and originated with Crown Prince Faisal. It was in effect, a litmus test set by the Saudis to judge the extent of British willingness to defend their position in Aden and the Federation. Fisher admitted to Thorneycroft that the 'embarrassing disclosures about Boyle' in the *Sunday Times* and the public support that Britain had given to the Bunker proposals sat uneasily with this proposed course of action. Such support, however, was now essential if Saudi support for the Royalist position was to be sustained.[74]

During the summer of 1964, Fisher became a vital conduit through which McLean passed arms requirements to the Defence and Overseas Policy Committee. On 22 July the Committee met to consider a submission, drafted by Fisher, that called for the following to be supplied forthwith to the Royalist forces: £600,000 in cash, 11,000 rifles, 20 mortars with ammunition, 20×0.5 machine guns with ammunition, 20 bazookas with ammunition, 500 anti-tank mines, 57mm and 75mm ammunition for recoilless rifles. This request closely matched an inventory given to McLean by Prince Mohammed bin al-Hussein which he, McLean, had passed on to Fisher. A further copy of this inventory had been given to SIS officers in Aden by Shariff Hussein. SIS were informed that the weapons, money and supplies would allow for the capture 'of Harib and Juba in east Yemen as a preliminary to extending the Royalist operations to the *Shaffei* south, leading up eventually to the Sana–Hodeidah road and the eventual expulsion of the Egyptians which they [Shariff Hussein of Beihan, Salah al-Hirsi, the Royalist Defence Minister, and Prince Mohammed bin al-Hussein] believe can be achieved in about nine months time.' While regarding the plan as expanding the territorial remit of Operation RANCOUR SIS concluded that the amount of money requested, estimated to be sufficient for only three months, reflected the appreciation among Royalist sympathisers of party political realities in the United Kingdom. 'The Sherif [of Beihan] is aware that we cannot undertake a definite commitment beyond the date of the General Election'.[75]

If McLean was hoping for a decisive outcome from the Defence and Overseas Policy Committee meeting, he was to be disappointed. In lieu of any news, positive or otherwise, he wrote to Fisher on 31 July, once again enclosing Prince Mohammed bin al-Hussein's 'shopping list' and adding, 'I know that you and Duncan [Sandys] have convinced the Government of the need for action but I feel it my duty to tell you that, unless your political decisions are translated adequately into suitable action now, the desired effects in the Yemen and Saudi Arabia will not be achieved.'[76] Five days later, McLean wrote a similar entreaty to Alec Douglas-Home, again imploring the British government to act upon the inventories supplied to the Defence and Overseas Policy Committee meeting. With electoral defeat a distinct possibility for Home's government in the upcoming October general election, McLean asked that 'he [Prince Mohammed bin al-Hussein] get enough supplies to carry on the fight for at least six months'. Unless such measures were implemented at once, 'the Royalist position in the Yemen will collapse suddenly and Prince Faisal would then have to go on his knees to Cairo in September and the Federal Rulers make what terms they can with Nasser.'[77]

On 7 August, Fisher wrote to McLean, detailing the difficulties in discovering exactly what had been agreed upon at the 22 July meeting. His information was based upon conversations with Peter Thorneycroft and Duncan Sandys, who between them disclosed that the meeting had approved between 75 percent and 90 percent of the 'shopping list', including some cash, though Fisher conceded the actual details remained sparse.[78] The letter presaged a false dawn. One week later, Fisher again wrote to McLean. The tone of this missive was decidedly downbeat and ended what hopes McLean may have entertained of conflating an expanded RANCOUR with direct aid to the Royalists. Having now seen the relevant papers and minutes of the Defence and Overseas Policy Committee meeting, Fisher wrote with candour that, 'I am afraid there is no doubt that there has been no authorization for anything on the scale of your "shopping list". Nor frankly do I think that this will be authorised this summer'.[79] It marked the end of any hope that Her Majesty's Government could be induced to offering large-scale assistance to the Royalists on the back of existing but decidedly limited clandestine operations. The British Mercenary Organisation would, for the most part, have to rely on its own efforts to sustain the Royalist cause.

Conclusion

The British Mercenary Organisation, born from expedience rather than design, achieved much in military terms between October 1963 and September 1964. The establishment of a limited communications network and the advisory activities of both British and French mercenaries did much to improve the military efficiency of the guerrilla campaign against Egypt forces. But equally, the transient nature of tribal loyalty meant that operational efficiency in any given area was often only as good as the last arms supply or the comparative size of the financial largesse on offer. The involvement of the Israelis in supplying the Imam's forces, however spectacular in terms of the clandestine nature of these flights, could not by themselves solve the underlying problem of the demands of the Royalist fronts outstripping supply. However poorly trained and led the Egyptian armed forces and their YAR allies may have been, Egyptian military intelligence was on a learning curve. Their ability to offer substantial bribes, coupled with the use of overwhelming air power resulted in severe setbacks for the Imam by the spring of 1964.

The failure of the Aden Group, and in particular McLean, to expand the area and scale of existing British covert operations to dovetail with direct aid to the Royalists was a heavy blow. However dire the predictions of Britain's failure to act may have been, Douglas-Home, despite the best entreaties of those associated with the Aden Group, refused to countenance covert aid of the type and duration urged by McLean. Repeated allegations that policy towards the Yemen had been decided amid the convivial surroundings of White's Club in London, could not disguise the fact that, as Prime Minister, Alec Douglas-Home placed more credence upon the assessments provided by the JIC than the accounts of McLean and Smiley. With a new Labour administration a looming prospect, the British Mercenary Organisation not only had to face their Egyptian enemies in the mountains of Yemen, but equally truculent foes amid the corridors of Whitehall.

7
'Plus ça Change, Plus la Même Chose'

The Labour Government, Aden and the Yemen Civil War

In October 1964, the Labour Party under Harold Wilson won the British general election with a narrow majority. With its widely perceived antipathy towards colonialism, the incoming Labour government carried with it the hope for some, and the fear of others, that policy towards South Arabia and Aden would be radically revised. The most vulnerable following Labour's ascendancy to power were the Aden Group, whose ability to 'win friends and influence people' in Whitehall and beyond came to be increasingly constrained. While many within the Parliamentary Labour Party such as Richard Marsh expressed sympathy for the independence struggle conducted with growing ferocity by the NLF in Aden and the Protectorates, views towards the Arab world in general, and South Arabia and the Yemen in particular, were decidedly mixed.

Some Foreign Office officials felt that the Labour Party, with its intellectual tradition shaped and fostered by the influence of Jewish writers and thinkers, remained too indulgent of pro-Zionist views to improve ties with Cairo or make any progress over the issue of recognition. The new Cabinet included Richard Crossman and Anthony Greenwood, men who, along with Harold Wilson, were open in their admiration of, if not support for Israel.[1] While in opposition Wilson had offered no alternative policies on how best to secure British interests in the Middle East. The sterling crisis of 1966 had yet to force the drastic review of defence commitments and as the Irish historian Robert McNamara has argued, Wilson remained an enthusiastic proponent of Britain's global role, particularly east of Suez. As such, all signs pointed towards retention of base rights in Aden while continuing to work towards bringing the Federation to full independence by 1968.

The Foreign Office had always remained sanguine regarding any major policy shift towards the problem of Yemen. McNamara recorded the views of Peter Laurence, acting head of the North and East African Department of the Foreign Office who, in July 1964, tried to disabuse Washington that any incoming Labour administration would indulge in a major policy shift towards Egypt. Cairo suspected the Labour Party of being influenced by its sympathies towards Tel Aviv and appeared '[A]s committed to defending British interests as is present Tory government, though its methods might vary'.[2]

This was a prescient statement. From October 1964 through to the beginning of 1966 the substance, as opposed to the tone of British policy towards Egypt and the Yemen was marked as much by continuity as by change. While efforts were made by the new Foreign Secretary, Patrick Gordon-Walker, to thaw relations with Cairo, the need to alleviate the security concerns of the Federal rulers meant that special operations such as RANCOUR remained on the menu of policy options. But while relations with Egypt reached their nadir by the end of 1965, the Wilson government refused to indulge the activities of McLean or the British Mercenary Organisation in their hitherto unfettered use of Federal territory as a base for supporting operations inside Yemen. Within one year of the Labour government taking office, most of the logistic effort in support of Royalist forces was being conducted from Saudi Arabia. The move to Saudi territory increased the dependency of the BMO and Royalists upon King Faisal's largesse to a degree that inhibited operational planning. By the end of 1965, the Royalists were increasingly pawns, rather than autonomous players in a game of regional ambition.

This had unforeseen consequences. Wilson's Cabinet remained at best circumspect, at worst outright dismissive, of the reports circulated by McLean and Smiley among the British intelligence community. In retrospect, this attitude blighted rather than informed coherent decision-making. However biased towards the Royalist cause these reports may have been, they remained the best source of detailed intelligence regarding the Imam's fortunes. This was to have profound consequences with regard to the context and timing, rather than the commitment per se towards conferring independence on the Federation, and Britain's decision to leave South Arabia by 1968.

Active Spectators

In the summer of 1964, the JIC concluded that Nasser had three overall aims in South Arabia: First, the survival of the Republican regime in Sana'a; second, the removal of the British from Aden and the collapse of the Federation; and finally, the establishment 'in Aden state and the

Protectorate of a Cairo-orientated Arab nationalist regime'. Based on this assessment the Chiefs of Staff committee, chaired by Air Vice-Marshal J. H. Lapsley argued that 'Although the UAR is likely to want to avoid direct military confrontation with the British, they will welcome and foster tribal revolts against the Federal Rulers and Federal government which would be calculated to deprive these of public confidence and so destroy their authority.'[3] This assessment now shaped the immediate policy options of the Labour Cabinet toward the Federation and Yemen. Most pressing was the best means to counter the growing level of violence directed at British and Federal targets. The Director-General of the Defence Intelligence Staff, Kenneth Strong, left the incoming Defence Secretary, Denis Healey, in no doubt as to where he believed this orchestrated violence was being conducted. In a memo to A. P. Hockaday, Personal Private Secretary to the Defence Minister, he wrote:

> The National Front for the Liberation of the Occupied South is a front organi-
> sation created and financed by the UAR to provide a nationalist cover for the
> UAR's activities directed at South Arabia, and for dissident operations in partic-
> ular. It was intended to provide a rallying point for dissident leaders and defectors
> from Aden State and the Federation. The planning and support for terrorist and
> dissident operations is retained firmly in the hands of the Egyptian intelligence
> service.[4]

Having inherited one of the more demanding government portfolios, Healey quickly ensured that the rules of engagement established under the previous Conservative government would continue to hold sway in South Arabia. While commanders were authorised to return fire against identi-fied targets across the Yemen border, preferably with small-arms, the use of aircraft remained subject to ministerial approval from London.[5] This ruling continued to draw criticism from officials in Aden who regarded such authorisation as meaningless when aircraft operating from bases in Yemen continued to infringe Federation airspace and bomb Federation targets with apparent impunity.[6]

Even the limited authorisation for counter-battery fire vested in Middle East Command (MIDCOM) remained subject to the ebb and flow of regional politics. In November 1964, Republican troops placed two artillery pieces by the customs post at Qat'aba, adjacent to the Federal state of Dahla. The pretext for this move remains unclear, but if it was to test the resolve of officials in Aden in the wake of the Labour victory, the Republicans found it unshaken. It was made clear to the Republican authorities that use of these guns against Federal targets would incur retri-bution, a threat that appeared to cause more alarm among Foreign Office officials than in Sana'a.[7] Such border tensions, seen by Aden as a continuum of Yemeni irredentism, were viewed differently in King

Charles Street. If diplomacy was once more to be given its chance, British relationships with both Egypt and the United States had to be carefully nurtured. The new British Ambassador to Cairo, Sir George Middleton, certainly believed that Nasser was now more amenable to a negotiated settlement. The failure of the Haradh offensive in the autumn of 1964, both in its stated objective of removing Imam al-Badr and the losses incurred by Egyptian forces, had done much to disabuse officials in Cairo of the efficacy of a military solution in the Yemen. In September 1964, Middleton cabled London with details of a conversation he had had with the Egyptian Foreign Minister, Mahmoud Riad. While Riad stated that the UAR had no intention of 'abandoning the Republican regime', he confessed that the presence of Egyptian troops was the cause of mistrust in London and Riyadh. He added, 'that the financial burden [to Egypt] of maintaining UAR forces in the Yemen was a heavy one and an unwelcome burden to a developing country' but that some officials in Cairo believed that 'Britain was maintaining unrest in the area precisely because of the financial embarrassment to the UAR'.[8]

Such comments expressed openly by a senior member of Nasser's government appeared to represent a softening of attitudes in Cairo which the Foreign Office remained keen to explore. Washington's offices were crucial to such overtures. Nasser remained dependent, albeit begrudgingly, on American economic and food aid which the Foreign Office believed gave the White House leverage over Cairo. Washington also continued to represent British interests in Yemen. Accordingly, the Foreign Office strongly felt that, while Washington should be kept fully informed over the threats, real or otherwise, from the YAR, retaliatory acts against Republican targets must be kept to a bare minimum and even then, subject to unambiguous ministerial approval. This was a subtle move on the part of the mandarins. By keeping the Americans, as in the case of Qa'taba, 'fully informed' of the likelihood of violence on the Yemeni–Federation border, the Foreign Office was effectively handing Washington a veto over the scale and type of retaliatory action.[9]

This was an approach fully in accordance with the views of Gordon-Walker, who sought in his brief tenure as Foreign Secretary to break the diplomatic impasse over ties with Nasser. From Cairo's perspective, however, such overtures appeared to be more an improvement in tone rather than substance. In public statements Walker made it clear that London's commitment to the Federation remained undimmed. During the course of a meeting with US Secretary of State Dean Rusk at the end of October 1964, he argued that '[T]here were certain things the Egyptians would have to do for the British before the British would go too far in effecting a rapprochement'.[10] Behind the scenes new brooms were sweeping away individuals deemed to be obstacles to effecting a rapprochement. While reaffirming London's commitment to Aden, Sir Kennedy Trevaskis, a man who had championed the cause of the Federation and had opposed Egyptian designs towards the South Arabia and Yemen with gusto, was removed as High Commissioner by the new Colonial Secretary, Anthony Greenwood.[11] Unlike Duncan Sandys, his Conservative predecessor, Greenwood had little sympathy for the Federal potentates. With their modes of governance rooted in archaic tribal structures, he considered the Federal rulers as the antithesis of political modernity. Intellectually he was more favourably disposed towards nationalist ideals personified by Adeni politicians such as Al-Asnaj, ideals which appeared free of the antediluvian sentiment of the Federal rulers. In place of Trevaskis, Greenwood appointed Sir Richard Turnbull as High Commissioner. A man of considerable colonial experience gained in Kenya where he was noted for his progressive views, Greenwood hoped Turnbull would prove more amenable to implementing the policies of his superior.

The previously benign environment that the British Mercenary Operation had enjoyed in Aden and the Federation was similarly affected. When Labour gained office, State Department officials raised once more the issue of British mercenaries operating in the Yemen with their Foreign Office counterparts. For the State Department, charged with representing British interests in the YAR, their activities made their task more onerous at a time when relations between the Johnson administration and Nasser had begun to sour over the issue of food aid and ties with Israel.[12] On 17 December 1964, Harlan Clark, the State Department official responsible for Yemeni affairs, met with Daniel McCarthy from the Arabian Department of the Foreign Office. Clark had received strong representations from Sana'a concerning the activities of two British operatives in the Khowlan and 'refused to believe HMG was not behind this'.[13]

The American view was of a piece with the mandarins of King Charles Street who had long smarted under the indulgence afforded the likes of Amery and McLean. Five days later Gordon-Walker wrote to Greenwood, arguing that the mercenaries and their political sponsors in London be denied the use of Federation territory to continue with what he regarded as their nefarious activities. He learned of a planned trip by Neil McLean and Julian Amery to Aden and the Federation. These two men, he implored, should be denied the use of RAF transport. He continued:

> I mentioned to you the subject of the mercenaries who have been helping the Royalists there [Yemen]. These mercenaries have been in the habit of going in and out of the Yemen through Aden and have their main centre of wireless communication there. I told you that I thought the time had come when these facilities should be denied to them and that they should be told to move off

British territory. Their presence there is inconsistent with our position that we are not interfering in the internal conflict inside Yemen; it complicates our effort to get on better with the UAR government; and it is liable to encourage the Egyptians inside the Yemen to increase their efforts to make difficulties for us in the Federation.[14]

Concord of a sort had finally been reached between a Foreign Secretary and his Colonial Office counterpart. While mercenaries continued to enter and leave the Yemen via Federal territory (notably Beihan) the indulgence afforded the BMO by officials in Aden under a regime of benign neglect was now a thing of the past. By the spring of 1965, the British Mercenary Operation had, for the most part, relocated to Saudi Arabia. This had two immediate consequences. First, it meant greater dependence upon Saudi political and financial largesse. The latitude for independent action previously enjoyed when operating from Federal territory was now substantially reduced and became increasingly subservient to Riyadh's own regional agenda. Second, the flow of intelligence that the British Mercenary Organisation had traded with the authorities in Aden on a quid pro quo basis began to dry up. This had a profound impact on assessments made in London of the Royalist fortunes. Crawford believed that 'The political and military stalemate there [Yemen] has no effect at all on the capacity of the EIS (Egyptian Intelligence Service) to promote trouble for us and the stimulation of more Royalist activity would do nothing to reduce our problems'.[15] According to McNamara, Crawford's recommendations that London 'hit back across the Yemeni frontier and carry out firm anti-terrorist action', were, in Egyptian eyes, of a piece with aiding the Royalists. In Aden and London, officials failed to appreciate the growing strength of the Royalist forces in the spring of 1965, in particular in the east of the Yemen, or the atrophy that permeated the Egyptian operational planning. The failure of the Haradh offensive in the autumn of 1964 not only damaged the military credibility of the Egyptian forces involved, but represented a severe political setback for Nasser at a time when he was seeking to parley with Crown Prince Faisal from a position of strategic strength.[16]

Egyptian-sponsored subversion remained the preoccupation of the Federal rulers. In November 1964, Greenwood paid his first visit to the Federation. In retrospect, his visit marked the start of a sustained campaign by the NLF, later to be joined by the Front for the Liberation of South Yemen (FLOSY) in a brief but uneasy alliance, to undermine the Federation and remove British influence from South Arabia. Greenwood hoped to used his trip to promote the idea of converting the Federation into a single unitary state, a policy that favoured the Adenis – and by extension, nationalist leaders like Abdullah al-Asnaj – at the expense of the Federal rulers. His intention was honourable, designed to secure British interests and disabuse Sana'a and Cairo of the notion that the Federation was little more than a counterfeit entity. As a means to assuage growing levels of Egyptian-sponsored subversion, it left something to be desired. Throughout his trip, Greenwood was assailed with complaints from the Federal state rulers that moves towards independence were precipitous. On 6 December 1964, during the course of a meeting with the Colonial Secretary, the Amir of Beihan declared that, '[T]hose who were demanding it were playing to the gallery of the Arab world.' Substantial progress towards democratic government and 'rapid economic development' remained prerequisites of independence yet this could never be achieved in the face of 'Egyptian and Yemeni aggression and the sizeable hostile forces on [Beihan] borders, which included mercenaries drawn from the Protectorate'.[17]

Given the freedom the BMO had enjoyed in Beihan territory, there was some irony in the Amir's remarks. But the Federal rulers required assurances that London had retained the political will to rebuff the Egyptian and Yemeni threat and, in the case of Beihan, to remove once and for all military assets that threatened Federal territory. Greenwood, anxious to avoid a repeat of the international furore surrounding the attack on Harib fort, repeated the terms of reference regarding the permissible range of retaliatory actions. Even when the SIS representative at the meeting, Bill Heber-Percy – operating under the cover of a Political Officer attached to Middle East Command (POMEC) – remarked that subversion into Beihan was being organised from the Yemen, Greenwood could only offer the cold comfort that while the British government reserved the right to attack such forces on Federation territory, 'if they then withdrew, the assumption was that they had learned their lesson'.[18]

The need to bolster security along the Federation border with Yemen was more pressing than Greenwood or the Foreign Office realised. By the end of December 1964, the threat of renewed tribal unrest in the Radfan and dissident activity around Dhala and Mukairas had forced MIDCOM to abandon plans to withdraw one infantry battalion from Aden. If both the demands of internal security and the capability to deploy rapidly to Kuwait in the event of the recrudescence of an Iraqi threat were to be met, troop levels not only had to be maintained but possibly increased.[19] This, after all, was the rationale for maintaining the Aden base. To this end, Greenwood now became the unwitting recipient of a stream of cables from officials in Aden requesting authorisation for the use of heavy ordinance against caves suspected of harbouring 'a variety of warlike stores'. On 14 January 1965, Turnbull wrote to his superior asking for permission to use 1,000lb bombs against one such cave complex in Wadis Bana and Yahar, close to the Yemeni border.

Stating that the target had been clearly identified, he added weight to his request by claiming, 'We know that it is the intention of the Egyptians to try and reactivate the Radfan front . . . The trouble in the past has been to pinpoint such targets, and now that we have succeeded in doing so, it is essential that the opportunity for taking effective action should not (repeat not) be missed.'[20]

With memories over Harib still raw in Whitehall minds however, concern was expressed that the use of such heavy ordnance made too much of an 'imperial noise'. Such objections were cast aside in favour of operational exigency. The target was within the jurisdiction of the Federation, the rules of engagement clearly defined and political capital could be accumulated among the Federal leaders.[21] Such actions met with the full approbation of the Shariff of Beihan, who also held the portfolio of Minister of the Interior in the Federal Government. In a paean-like missive to Denis Healey he paid tribute to the assertive action the Labour government was taking, action that 'made me realise that I was mistaken in my ideas about the Leaders of your party prior to your winning the election and am only too pleased I was wrong'.[22] The support given by the British Defence Secretary was not restricted to the aerial bombing of dissident positions. By February 1965, the Labour government of Harold Wilson was engaged in debating the efficacy of special operations across the Yemen border as it sought ways to stem the growing tide of violence in Aden and across Federal territory.

Hesitant Participants

Amid the attempts by the Colonial Secretary, Anthony Greenwood, to push through an agreement between Aden and the Federal states for the establishment of single, unitary state and overtures by the new Foreign Secretary, Michael Stewart, to establish a more cordial relationship with Cairo, subversion across South Arabia continued apace.[23] Blame for the growing scale as well as the audacity of the attacks was directed beyond the heads of the elusive leadership of the NLF to the YAR and Nasser. Taken together, the attacks in Aden and along the Federal border appeared of a piece with a co-ordinated campaign to force the British from South Arabia. Between 15 October 1964 and the 26 March 1965, 11 British and FRA servicemen had been killed and a further 69 wounded while one British civilian had been killed and 16 wounded. The single fatality was the daughter of an RAF medical officer, murdered at a Christmas Eve party after a hand grenade was thrown among the assembled throng through an open window. Given the almost daily occurrence of violence 'up country' it was surprising that the level of fatalities was not higher. The situation report for the week ending 11 January 1965 was not untypical:

> FG (Federal Guard) Forts in DAHLA [sic] area fired at on 13 occasions. Other incidents have involved firing at a border village, British and FRA camps and Political officer's house at Dhala, using mortars, MG (machine guns) and rocket launchers. Quantity of explosives recovered. Attempt to blow up FIO's (Federal Intelligence Officer's) house at MUKAIRAS foiled.[24]

As the attempted assassination of the FIO suggests, a concerted attempt was being made to degrade the human intelligence capability of the FRA and the Aden authorities. This strategy was not new; the FIO in Mukairas having been subject to such treatment in July 1964. But the scale and consistency of the attacks was now of an altogether different magnitude, and bore the hallmarks of having being carefully planned, if not always successfully executed, by those working for the EIS. By February 1965, the attacks on FIOs and political officers (the latter often providing official cover for British intelligence operatives), had become common-place in Audhali, Dhala, Lahej and Beihan, while in Aden Special Branch officers were specifically targeted. Such was the alarm generated by these assassinations that on 5 February, the Chief of the Defence Staff wrote to Healey expressing his concern over the 'shortfall in the numbers and quality of officers being provided for the Special Branches of Sabah, Sarawak, Brunei and Aden'. In point four of his memorandum he argued, 'There is clearly an urgent need to meet the requirements for Special Branch personnel overseas otherwise our large military and financial outlay for countering insurgency and preserving internal security is going to be prejudiced.'[25]

The problem was not restricted to the loss of experienced personnel alone. Recommendations made by the JIC working party in May 1964 on the 'effectiveness of intelligence coverage, assessment and dissemination' in South Arabia and the Federation had never been implemented fully. While the Local Intelligence Committee (LIC-Aden) had assumed respon-sibility for the functions performed previously by a regional subcommittee of the JIC (JIC–Middle East), the Aden Intelligence Centre (AIC), tasked by the LIC to collect, collate and assess intelligence, had proven to be less than the sum of its parts. Veiled criticism had been made in the report of the quality of its staff, notably the Chief Intelligence Officer, but equally, the AIC remained starved of accurate intelligence from the subordinate Federal Intelligence Committee, a problem that appeared to be deliberate impediment rather than bureaucratic inertia. The primary loyalties of individual FIOs lay more with the Federal rulers than with British officials in Aden and the suspicion remained that the intelligence provided by the

Federal Intelligence Committee, despite the cross-representation of some individuals on the AIC, was biased towards demonstrating the continued malevolence of Sana'a and Cairo. Reform of the intelligence structures was also hampered by the change of government in October 1964 and the ensuing problems associated with new ministers and appointees coming to grips with the demands of their respective portfolios. As a result, the suggested reforms of the JIC working party were never implemented in a coherent form; they were introduced piecemeal, without conviction, and with the result being that officials in Aden doubted their efficacy. The bloody removal of experienced personnel and the lack of suitable replacements only served to compound an inchoate intelligence effort where collation and assessment were concerned.[26]

For those charged with securing the Federation against more overt threats, the malign intent of the YAR backed by Egypt was all too visible. Responsibility for ensuring the external security of states in the east of the Federation lay with Brigadier David Warren, serving on secondment with the FRA. With Beihan falling within his parish, Warren recalled the 'semi-war atmosphere' that prevailed at this time, with Egyptian MiG-21 fighters making forays into Federation airspace and flying in a threatening manner. Such behaviour was matched on the ground, with shootings, mortar bombardments and the occasional artillery exchange defining life on the border. The infiltration of Yemeni saboteurs across the border to lay anti-tank mines became almost de rigueur, and with so few metalled roads in the border areas, the toll on the occupants of soft-skinned vehicles of the FRA was high.[27] Healey, having declared in his Defence White Paper, published in January 1965, that it would be 'politically irresponsible and economically wasteful to abandon Aden', now felt that present circumstances justified a return to past precedent to counter the Egyptian-sponsored aggression inside the Federal borders.[28]

In his memoirs, *The Time of My Life*, Healey makes scant reference to the troubles faced along the Yemen–Federation frontier or the measures taken to counter Egyptian- and Yemeni-sponsored insurgents. At the beginning of February 1965 however, Healey sought approval from Cabinet colleagues for RANCOUR operations not only to be continued but extended, a policy that met with the approbation of Prime Minister Harold Wilson and the new Foreign Secretary, Michael Stewart.[29] Stewart proved a keen champion of RANCOUR operations given that Nasser, despite what he perceived as conciliatory gestures made by his own department, appeared unwilling to reign in the campaign of terror in Aden. In a memo that could equally have been written by his more hawkish Conservative predecessors he advised his Cabinet colleagues in March 1965 that:

Nasser had as an objective to eliminate the Western influence in the Middle East based on our positions in the area, with our own as his first target, and that as an immediate aim he wished to expel us from Southern Arabia and thus render untenable our position in the Persian Gulf. His aim in South Arabia is made clear by the campaign of intimidation which is being directed against the South Arabian Federation and against the Colonial Secretary's programme for bringing a new South Arabian state to independence by 1968.[30]

Stewart conceded the need to keep channels of communication open to Cairo, but the attempt to construct a benevolent relationship with Egypt struggled under the weight of mutual distrust. Only Anthony Greenwood expressed reservations over RANCOUR and these were less to do with moral turpitude than with the potential political fallout should backing by a Labour government for such action be publicly revealed.[31] Sir Burke Trend, the Cabinet Secretary, was charged with reprising the dormant role of the JAC, a body established in the final days of Alec Douglas-Home's administration to exercise inter-departmental control over clandestine activity. On 25 March 1965, Trend reported back to the Cabinet that the JAC had produced a paper detailing the scope of future operations. Though the details of these operations, now renamed RANCOUR II remain wrapped in secrecy, their essence appeared unchanged: the exploitation of tribes just inside Yemen to help 'neutralise Egyptian subversive action' against the British position in South Arabia. The following day, Harold Wilson gave his formal approval for RANCOUR II operations to commence, subject to undisclosed qualifications made by the Chairman of the JIC, Sir Bernard Burrows, and Oliver Wright, the Prime Minister's Private Secretary.[32]

A cardinal rule governing the conduct of RANCOUR operations established under the previous Conservative government was that they remained divorced from any association with the Royalist war effort or helped to 'promote the secession of towns or areas from the Yemen Republic to the Royalists.' While unintentional, this is precisely the causal impact that such covert operations now had on the fortunes of war in the Yemen. Having weathered the Egyptian offensives of the summer and autumn of 1964, the Royalist forces had managed to recuperate and replenish their supplies, a process helped by the brief cease-fire negotiated between Royalist and Republican delegations (and overseen by Egyptian and Saudi representatives) in the Sudanese town of Erkwit on 2 November 1964. In particular, the First Royalist Army, under the command of Prince Mohammed bin al-Hussein and located in an extensive area of north-east Yemen that encompassed the Jawf, had been preparing for a thrust that would cut the already tenuous Republican lines of communication between Sana'a, Marib, and beyond to Harib.[33] British and French mercenaries were involved directly in planning this offensive which, if successful, would link the FSA and Saudi Arabia with territory under the control of tribes loyal to the *Hamid'Ud'Din*.

To this end, the forces of Prince Mohammed bin al-Hussein had some precipitous help from the powerful *Murad* and *Abida* tribes whose domains straddled the Federal state of Beihan and the Yemen. On 10 March 1965 Aden Radio reported heavy fighting in the town of Harib, which could clearly be seen with the use of field glasses from inside Federal borders.[34] After two days of fighting, Egyptian and Republican forces in Harib had been routed. This otherwise minor engagement now presented the Labour government with policy dilemmas that had been the bane of coherent decision-making towards Yemen in the past. While the long-term allegiance of the *Murad* to the Royalist cause was open to question, their presence in Harib was bolstered by the timely arrival of 400 Royalist troops from the Royalist First Army. No evidence exists to suggest that this deployment was anything other than the product of Prince Mohammed bin al-Hussein's own strategic initiative. It was a judicious move on his part. Egyptian troops attempted to counter-attack, and while the *Murad* tribesmen fled, the better trained and disciplined Royalist forces stood their ground and repelled the attack. As Dana Adams Schmidt noted, 'It was the first time the Egyptians had been deprived of one of the important towns of the Yemen and had not been able to take it back.'[35]

Such disarray in Egyptian ranks now prompted the Shariff of Beihan to retake territory over which he, with the support of officials in Aden, lay claim. On 12 March, supported by armoured cars of the 10th Royal Hussars and protected by two RAF Hunters circling overhead, FRA troops entered Darb Ahl Ba Thaif, a village which Republican forces had occupied following the fall of Harib to Egyptian forces in the spring of 1963. Alarm bells immediately began ringing along the corridors of Whitehall, the din of which drowned out any voices inside government for London to consider the strategic advantages that could now accrue. With memories of the diplomatic debacle that had followed the bombing of Harib the previous year still fresh, the Foreign Office sought immediate clarification of the role played by British troops in the capture of Darb Ahl Ba Harib. They did not concur with the view expressed by Aden that the village (little more than a hamlet) had, until 1963, been under Beihani suzerainty.[36]

Concerns over the potential for a diplomatic spat with Washington and crises with the United Nations and the Arab League were only part of the equation. While he saw distinct advantages to be gained for the Federation, Sir Richard Turnbull also saw a risk that Britain could be dragged directly into the Yemen conflagration should Egypt and the YAR seek to recoup their position. He cabled the Colonial Office with the news that the pro-Republican *Awadhi* tribe were massing in the nearby town of Abdia with a view to recapturing Harib. With all other routes into Harib firmly in the Royalist grasp, the only alternative approach to Harib was through the Wadi Ablah which traversed Federal territory. Through the offices of the State Department, he urged London to warn Sana'a 'of the consequences of trespassing in Federal territory'.[37] In the meantime, POMEC moved quickly to allay the concerns of King Charles Street that British forces had anyway participated directly in the capture of Darb Ahl Ba Harb or had helped hasten the fall of Harib. The village was abandoned by the Republicans once Harib had fallen and Federal Guards had merely walked in to reclaim it without resistance. As for the RAF Hunter aircraft, their presence overhead during the capitulation of Harib was purely coincidental: They had been patrolling the Federal side of the border on an ad hoc basis in response to air incursions from the Yemen the previous week.[38]

Among his Cabinet colleagues, Greenwood demonstrated the greatest alarm at these developments and suspected foul play by at least some colonial officials. He was in the process of trying to steer the various parties and factions from the Federal states and Aden towards a constitutional conference designed to reach agreement over the political architecture of a single unified state.[39] The unfolding crisis appeared to be undermine these efforts. Greenwood suspected the loyalty of many of the Britons employed in the service of the Federal States, in particular in Beihan. Despite the denials of POMEC – members of which included SIS officers – he could not believe that officials in Aden had not received forewarning of the events that had unfolded in Harib and Darb Ahl Ba Thaif. He raised these suspicions with Turnbull. While the High Commissioner agreed that the motives of some British nationals in the employment of the Federation were suspect, if not 'corrupt' he concluded, 'I am making enquiries to discover at what stage British officers in Baihan [sic] became aware of what was afoot, but my impression is that events moved so rapidly that there was no time for prior consultation. Even the pro-Royalist tribesmen who captured Harib were surprised as anyone to find themselves in the town.'[40]

Turnbull's analysis was correct. No evidence emerged suggesting that information, either from Royalist sources or from FIOs in the field, ever reached Aden only to be quashed while events took their natural course. While both Neil McLean and David Smiley were present in the al-Jauf region, their respective diaries and notes do not record any knowledge of events unfolding around Harib at this time. Like other tribes, the *Murad* were the material beneficiaries of the initial RANCOUR operations, having been furnished with arms, ammunition and money by FIOs. Once such largesse had been dispensed however, the *Murad* were more or less at liberty to decide where, how and when the aims and objectives of Operation RANCOUR were to be met. The fact that Royalist forces arrived in strength to secure Harib and its immediate environs had little to do with any symbiotic planning and everything to do with the strategic acuity of Prince Mohammed. By default, the RANCOUR operations had helped bring about 'the secession of towns and areas from the YAR to the Royalists', the one end they were never meant to achieve.

Two weeks later, the Royalist First Army launched an offensive that drove most of the Egyptian and YAR forces from the al-Jauf and the Khowlan. From a purely strategic standpoint, it represented a high point in Royalist fortunes and offered London, if it had been so inclined, the chance to pursue a military decision in favour of the Royalists, a decision that could have seriously degraded Cairo's sponsorship of the guerrilla campaign by denying the EIS use of training bases in south and east Yemen. But London's grasp of the situation in Yemen and the implications for the British position in South Arabia proved limited. Diplomatic circumspection – not least continued fears of the regional fallout should Britain exploit Royalist successes – determined policy in London. Special operations remained confined to the Yemeni border, occasionally encroaching beyond. The lack of political daring was compounded by the complete absence of any operational or political intelligence reaching London concerning events *inside* [my emphasis] the Yemen. In December 1965, Daniel McCarthy, having been seconded from the Foreign Office to POMEC, wrote a scathing report for the JIC over the lamentable state of the intelligence apparatus in Aden and the Federation. With regards to Yemen he concluded that, 'In the absence of diplomatic relations with the Yemeni Republicans, neither political nor intelligence material from the Yemen of a kind which an Embassy, or its military attachés, would normally provide is forthcoming.'[41]

This was a remarkable statement. While it would be inaccurate to claim British intelligence received a regular stream of intelligence from inside Yemen, they did receive detailed reports, both verbal and written, from British operatives advising Royalist Forces.[42] In the course of his trip to the Yemen in the spring of 1964, and during three subsequent trips made throughout 1965, David Smiley met, at various intervals either entering or leaving Saudi territory, Geoffrey Douglas, Paul Paulson, John Christie and John da Silva, all serving SIS officers, as well as Bill Herber-Percy on one occasion in Beihan. At the start of his involvement with the mercenary operation in the spring of 1963, Smiley had deliberately avoided establishing close contact with SIS officers. Now, with operational security less rigid, Smiley enjoyed more cordial relations with the officials from Broadway, even using Herber-Percy on one occasion to send personal letters back to Moy, his wife. Smiley and other British liaison officers continued to remain circumspect over disclosing more sensitive aspects of their operations since, at least in his case, he answered directly to the Saudis. For example, details of the re-supply drops to Royalist forces in and around Arhab in late January 1965 were supplied to the Foreign Office by the Italian legation in Taiz'z, the origin of the aircraft however 'remaining unknown'.[43] Even so, British intelligence officials were in possession of solid information regarding the disposition and state of Egyptian forces throughout most of the Yemen. Smiley even compiled a detailed report for Douglas concerning intelligence he had gathered during the interrogation of a junior Egyptian engineering officer who had defected to the Royalists.[44] On another occasion he wrote, upon request from the British military attaché in Cairo, Brigadier H. J. Bartholomew a detailed appreciation of the overall impact that involvement in the Yemen Civil War had had upon the combat efficiency of the Egyptian soldier.[45] One can only conclude that either SIS officers did not pass their reports up the chain of command or, given the political predilections in Whitehall, the origin of the reports and by extension, their veracity, were simply not trusted enough to inform JIC assessments. This proved a fatal error for the British. The failure to capitalise on the Egyptian military malaise in Yemen, compounded by growing unrest among the Republicans with Sallal's leadership, only confirmed the belief in Cairo that Britain was responsible for its woes in the mountains and plains of the Yemen. Deemed guilty by association in the eyes of Cairo, Nasser now looked to intensify the pressure upon the British in Aden. The irony remains that in the spring and summer of 1965, the moral and political scruples that shaped policy in London and Aden over support for Royalist suzerainty saved the Egyptian position in Yemen when at its most vulnerable.

Subverting the British

Concern over being dragged into the Yemen Civil War had been the prime determinant of British policy in the crisis over the village of Da Ahli Ba Thaif. On 18 March 1965, Turnbull cabled the Colonial Secretary arguing that now the village was back in Federal hands, 'it is quite unthinkable that I should attempt to prevent the Federal Regular Army going to the assistance of the Federal Guard stationed there'. He added that he believed the Federal rulers had been 'extremely forbearing during the past two years' refraining from demanding that Britain take action to eject YAR troops or tribesman loyal to Sana'a 'despite our treaty obligations'.[46] This view was not shared by the Foreign Office or Greenwood who believed that London had been far too indulgent of Shariff Hussein's territorial avarice. Greenwood, having taken advice from Foreign Office lawyers, questioned whether Da Ahli Ba Thaif was indeed in Federal territory. The 1934 treaty that had demarcated the boundary between the then Protectorates of South Arabia and Yemen remained vague over delineation in a number of areas and, as such, the risk of Federal action sparking a diplomatic furore at the UN was taken as given. In anticipation of the maelstrom to come, the United Kingdom delegation in New York advocated a policy of getting their diplomatic retaliation in first by lodging a complaint with the Security Council over Yemeni aggression. They cabled Greenwood that 'We could briefly say [to the Security Council] that the war in the Yemen has now erupted on the borders of the Federation. We have warned the Yemenis through the protecting power of the dangers of an overspill [sic] into the Federation'.[47]

Outright war had not quite erupted but its rumblings remained all too audible. On 19 March, Turnbull cabled Greenwood with a list of incidents in one 24-hour period that suggested a major intensification of border hostilities. These included over-flights by two MiGs, an aerial assault on a Federal Guard position confirmed by a FIO and an attack on FRA vehicles. Turnbull reported the 'considerable anxiety' of Shariff Hussein and the belief that 'unless hostile attacks are challenged and countered the enemy will be emboldened to launch heavier and more frequent assaults.'[48] Only partially aware of the parlous state of Egypt's position in the Yemen, the increased attacks on the border and in Aden itself were regarded in London as more an expression of Nasser's confidence in the political incoherence of the Federation than an expression of his own military weakness. Requests now began to circulate around Whitehall for a breakdown of casualty figures in South Arabia with particular worries expressed by the chairman of the JIC, Sir Bernard Burrows, over fatalities among Aden Special Branch personnel. With their local knowledge and linguistic superiority over their British counterparts, Arab members were high-value targets of NLF gunmen and even when having escaped the assassin's bullet, the experience was enough to induce some to defect. By the end of March, Colonial Officials conceded the impact of these attacks which, '[W]hen combined with reiterated threats from Radio Sana'a and Radio Cairo have completely demoralised the remaining Arab members in Special Branch, with the result that for the time being it [Special Branch] has had to be staffed entirely by expatriated in the gazetted [sic] ranks.[49]

Arguing that the growing tension on the border undermined his efforts to convene a constitutional conference, Greenwood looked to curb military action by British and Federal forces save for acts of self-defence inside Federal territory, and only then as a last resort. Like Rab Butler before him, Greenwood suspected that the Federal rulers were in large part the authors of their own misfortunes. Thus, when Turnbull requested permission for RAF Hunters to launch air strikes along a 12-mile stretch of the Beihan–Yemeni border and up to six miles inside Yemen itself, action deemed proportionate in Aden for the human and material losses incurred by the Federation, Greenwood stamped on the proposal. He wrote to Harold Wilson that 'we should not embark upon such countermeasures without first having exhausted all possible diplomatic means of securing redress', a position, he was keen to stress that enjoyed the support of officials in the Foreign Office, Ministry of Defence 'and my own office'.[50] This also now extended to RANCOUR II operations. Through the JAC under Sir Burke Trend, such operations had reached the point of 'going critical'. Now, at Greenwood's behest, the extension of clandestine activity inside the Yemen was postponed. At the same time, it was becoming clear to Greenwood that Turnbull was not proving to be the pliant High Commissioner he had hoped for. A clear bifurcation was emerging between policy directives issued from the grand surroundings of Great Smith Street and the reality faced by British officials trying to match the square peg of the Federal states with the round hole of Aden.

By the summer of 1965, the comfortable lifestyle enjoyed previously by the British in Aden was becoming a receding memory. Stephen Harper, a journalist covering South Arabia for the *Daily Express* wrote of this time that 'Cinemas, night clubs and bars became places spiced with undertones of peril. Intelligence reports indicated that about two hundred Adenis had received terrorist training from Egyptian agents in Yemen'.[51] Even allowing for journalistic licence over the actual numbers involved, the claim carried substance. In June 1965, an intelligence estimate produced in Washington placed responsibility for the growing terrorist campaign in Aden firmly at the door of the EIS who were using 'a relatively small group of trained men' and 'who use Yemen as a safe haven'.[52] Such reports were of a piece with continued reports of MiG attacks and Egyptian and YAR troop movements around Harib. On 14 April, the Chief of the Defence Staff wrote to Healey, requesting that approval to engage Egyptian aircraft over Federal territory be delegated to Commander in Chief MIDCOM. Healey wrote in support of the request to Michael Stewart, disclosing that intelligence from an undisclosed source had identified one infantry battalion, a commando unit, tanks and artillery, all supported by Ilyushin bombers and MiG fighters moving on Harib.[53]

The expected attack failed to materialise, and the threat of Greenwood exercising a veto in the Cabinet had fighting spilled over into Federal territory was never put to the test. But the ever-present danger of a border skirmish developing into something more substantial renewed concerns in the Cabinet over policy towards Yemen, not least with the Prime Minister. To protect London's diplomatic flank, Stewart had instructed the British delegation at the UN to keep the Security Council fully informed of developments on the frontier but such was the gravity of the situation that Wilson now began to seriously entertain the idea of making a direct appeal to Nasser in an effort to diffuse tension.[54] While supportive of the situation, Stewart was concerned that the right mix of carrots and sticks be applied in any approach to Cairo, the carrots being reserved for a time when 'we have something positive and constructive to put to him [Nasser] rather than a complaint or a warning'.[55] Representations concerning Republican and Egyptian air incursions were forwarded to the United States legation in Taiz'z for transmission to Sana'a, with the warning that continued infringements on Federal territory invited the prospect of their aircraft being shot down. The threat was more real than apparent. With few air defence assets of note in Beihan, the chances of downing a MiG fighter over Federal territory remained dependent upon providence. Indefinite patrols by RAF Hunters simply could not be sustained on a rolling basis.[56]

Stewart did, however, instruct Sir George Middleton to lodge a complaint with Egyptian Foreign Minister Mahmoud Riad over the continued violation of Federal airspace, attacks on Federal forces and the sharp rise in terrorist incidents in Aden. Riad, according to McNamara's account, 'did not deny that the Egyptians were helping the liberation movement but retorted that the British " had both actively and tacitly given aid to the Royalist forces in the Yemen"'. It was a view repeated directly to Wilson by Mohammed Heikal who, during a visit to London in July 1965 to receive specialist medical treatment, had what is euphemistically refered to as a 'robust exchange of views' with the Prime Minister. In response to Wilson's charge that Cairo was aiding and abetting the violence in Aden and should desist immediately from such provocation, Heikal claimed the violence resulted from the permissive environment fostered by the previous Conservative government that had allowed 'officers on a year's leave and other mercenaries . . . to help the Royalists through Beihan'. Egypt had, according to Heikal, been forced to counter-attack.[57]

Wilson denied that his government or British officials in Aden allowed the use of Beihan state for such activities; indeed, the benevolence once enjoyed by the BMO in the FSA was a thing of the past. But, with the *cause célèbre* surrounding the publication of captured mercenary correspondence to the fore, and with it, the embarrassment this had caused London in Washington and the wider Arab world, Heikal repeated the accusation in *Al-Ahram*. Wilson's public denials on this issue belied private concerns. When, on 3 August 1965, the use of Beihan territory to supply Royalist forces was raised by the YAR delegation to the UN Wilson demanded clarification that Federal territory was emphatically not being used in the ways claimed by Sana'a and Cairo. The accusation was repeated by Heikal ten days later, prompting Peter Le Cheminant, Personal Private Secretary to the Prime Minister, to seek some answers from the MoD. In response, a senior ministry civil servant, John Peduzie, denied that any British officers had been granted leave 'to form guerrilla gangs against the Yemen revolution . . . neither are there now nor have there been serving officers operating covertly in the Yemen.' Peduzie also denied a further accusation levelled by Heikal that British helicopters had been operating covertly inside Yemeni territory from their base at Mukairas.[58]

Cairo gave little credence to such denials. Its support of guerrilla operations and terrorist activities inside the Federation was as much a response to the reversals Cairo had suffered in the Yemen, as ideological affinity with the aims of the NLF. If such a rationale informed Egyptian strategy it soon began to have its desired effect. The increase in British casualties was beginning to sow the seeds of doubt in Whitehall over the efficacy of retaining Aden as a suitable base for defending British interests east of Suez. In May 1965, Wilson had indicated that such a review was being considered when, in conversation with US Secretary of State Dean Rusk, he noted that London 'could not count indefinitely' on retention of a military base in Aden.[59] It was not long before rumours of what was being aired behind the closed doors of Whitehall filtered back to the ears of the Federal government, still struggling to accept the constitutional architecture drafted by Greenwood to secure a unitary state of South Arabia.

These doubts over future British intent now began to have a perceptible impact upon the quality of intelligence co-operation, never convivial at the best of times, between authorities in Aden and the Federal rulers. Believing that London was conceding too much to nationalist politicians in Aden – most notably the avowedly anti-British PSP member Abd al-Makkawi – and increasingly doubtful of British intentions toward the FSA, the Federal government refused permission for British security forces to conduct operations in villages close to Aden state 'where Aden Security Branch know the low grade sabotage and terrorist agents are paid and equipped for activity across the state border into Aden itself '. In a memo to Healey, the Chief of the Defence Staff claimed that not only did such action undermine the morale and resolve of British and FRA troops, but that, 'This is a pity because things are otherwise going rather well in the Federation whereas Nasser is experiencing graver difficulties in the Yemen that at any time since 1962.'[60]

Although never near the intensity or ferocity of the guerrilla campaign being prosecuted in the Yemen, the violence in Aden was such that London could not see the 'Yemen wood' for the 'Adeni trees'. On 5 June 1965, new Emergency Regulations were introduced in Aden State. The NLF was banned as a terrorist organization, and Turnbull given increased powers that included detention without trial and confiscation of the property of those that broke emergency regulations. While the *Times* remarked that the High Commissioner had now, and not before time, started to apply measures gained from his experience fighting the Mau Mau, nationalist politicians in Aden regarded the regulations as little more that 'fascist measures'.[61] The immediate effect of the regulations was felt in the realm of propaganda, with Egypt furnishing the NLF (and later FLOSY) with powerful radio transmitters in Sana'a and Taiz'z that produced a constant stream of nationalist rhetoric to supplement the inflammatory output of Radio Cairo. The British suspected that these broadcasts contained coded messages for operatives and supporters in Aden and the Federation.[62] Such concealed subtleties, if indeed they did exist, appeared almost redundant when Radio Cairo could exhort 'Commandos in Aden and men of the Liberation Army in the South' to 'Kill the occupation forces, and do not worry about the large numbers of British soldiers, their agents and their tails . . . true rebels do not accept compromise . . . We want freedom in the form we intend to have, and not in the form which Colonialism and its tails in the Federation want to give.'[63]

Some officials in Aden felt that emergency regulations had been introduced in haste. Doubts existed over the whether the level of violence had moved beyond the realm of what was acceptable while others expressed doubts as to whether adequate levels of manpower, in particular among the police, existed to actually enforce the regulations. Turnbull remained concerned that heavy handed implementation of draconian measures threatened to make a bad situation worse when the hidden hand of Egypt was the real power pulling the nationalist strings. In a cable to London he argued, 'We are not fighting a local nationalist movement but well-trained and skilfully briefed agents of Egyptian intelligence. [The] Greatest risk we face is being driven to adopt restriction after restriction and thereby antagonising [the] population and jeopardising the harmonious relations that are essential for the future of the [Aden] base.'[64]

Tension in Aden was matched by renewed air incursions into Beihan State by Egyptian MiG fighters. On 29 June 1965, they attacked several targets well inside Federation territory, including a Federal Guard fort at Bulayq, resulting in its destruction. Turnbull, anticipating a flurry of protests from the Federal government, cabled London immediately, warning that the usual diplomatic panacea of referring the matter to the Security Council would carry little weight. He was driven not so much by the expected hyperbole of Shariff Hussein but a broader concern over the adverse impact that such attacks were having upon the morale of the tribes and the Federal forces. Pulling few punches he cabled Greenwood 'That failure to take a resolute line will weaken their allegiance to the central authority' and that accordingly, retaliatory action in kind was justified not only by London's defence obligations to the Federation but by the need to restore confidence in British policy.[65]

In advocating commensurate retaliatory action, Turnbull identified the Republican-held fort of Badiya as a suitable target. Its had long been regarded as a centre of Egyptian-backed subversion against the Federation; its destruction would be a direct blow to the prestige of the Awadhi Shaykh, 'the last tribal figure of any importance in Eastern Yemen supported by the Egyptians.' Turnbull's request enjoyed the full support of MIDCOM who added that, as in the case of Harib the previous year, leaflets would be dropped in the target area prior to RAF Hunters launching their attack.[66] Given that the Federal ministers had argued for an air strike upon Egyptian and YAR positions near Marib, Turnbull felt that his proposal already represented something of a compromise between London and the Federation.

Greenwood remained unmoved. He had worked diligently to coax the Federal Ministers and Aden State representatives to participate in a Constitutional Commission. To this end, he had gained agreement, albeit begrudgingly, from Federal ministers and Adeni politicians for the establishment of a working party to discuss his proposed constitutional reform. The working party was to convene at Lancaster House in London at the beginning of August. As far as Greenwood was concerned, Egyptian air attacks would not be allowed to distract attention from tackling what he considered to be the the crux of the violence: the juxtaposition of the parochial concerns of the Federal ministers with the nationalist agenda of Aden politicians who denied the legitimacy of a British presence in South Arabia. Knowing of the dependence of the Federal states on British military assistance, the Colonial Secretary calculated he could take a more indulgent attitude toward the likes of al-Asnaj and al-Makkawi.

London restricted itself to verbal protests issued in Cairo by Middleton and accompanied by the implicit though increasingly vacuous threat that Her Majesty's Government reserved the right to 'take such measures as we considered to be appropriate'.[67] This distaste for engaging in overt military action beyond the borders of the Federation now extended to taking action on Federal territory itself. On 2 July, Turnbull reported the discovery of a dissident base on Beihan soil, and requested authority from London to authorise an air attack on the camp. While in accordance with the rubric governing the use of air strikes, officials at the Colonial Office argued for a ground incursion to clear the area, it being argued that this would generate less political noise. Even this proposal was tentative, however, as Greenwood, in the midst of a brief visit to Paris, had not been consulted.[68] Before he could interject either way however, Turnbull reported that 140 guerrillas using this base had launched a new attack on the Federal Guard fort at Aatabah before moving to a new encampment close to the Yemeni frontier. The mobile nature of this group, Turnbull argued, negated the use of ground operations which, in any case, would take up to 36 hours to organise. Air strikes had to be authorised and without delay.[69]

Much to his frustration and to the fury of Federal Ministers, Greenwood vetoed the attack, citing the belief that 'Close proximity of rebel positions to the Yemeni-occupied fort at Badiya would, we think, lead Egyptians to claim (and probably genuinely believe) that we were carrying out a reprisal raid for the recent MiG attack'. Greenwood continued that should such an attack be authorised it might undermine attempts to arrange a trip by the Minister of State at the Foreign Office, George Thomson, to Cairo, which Greenwood argued 'could produce a useful détente in Anglo-UAR relations'.[70] Authorisation for the air strike was withheld, although Greenwood added cryptically that the problem of the dissidents could be 'dealt with by other means' which he promised to elaborate upon in a separate telegram.

What exactly these other means entailed remains undisclosed although the DIS was approached to draw up plans, with a Commander Webb tasked with co-ordinating clandestine activity against threats inside the Federation with the help of 'our friends', a known euphemism for SIS.[71] The outcome of the operation, if indeed it ever enjoyed final clearance, remained, politically, an irrelevance. From Aden's perspective, clandestine action of a defensive nature could never accrue political credit with the Federal rulers, which visible, overt action would have bought. As predicted by the High Commissioner, Greenwood was soon in receipt of an emotional letter from the Amir of Beihan, the son of Shariff Hussein. The belief that the 'Amir protests too much' which had for so long informed Foreign Office attitudes towards the fiefdoms of the Federation in general, and Beihan in particular, now influenced Greenwood. The tendency of the Shariff to pursue his own agenda, unfettered by the impact his decisions had on the wider stability of the Federation, meant that not only was he the author of his own misfortunes, but the ghostwriter for those that now dogged British policy in Aden. The Amir's protest, in which he now considered Beihan free of any obligation to abide by treaty agreements, was viewed in Whitehall as little more than the tantrum of an over-indulged child.[72]

On 5 July, Greenwood cabled Aden asking Turnbull to inform the Federal Ministers that diplomacy remained the most efficacious course of action through which to seek redress, that strong protests had been lodged, both in Cairo and with the Security Council in New York, and that some latitude must be given to the view that the MiG attack of 2 July had been made 'on the supposition that the targets were in fact on the Yemeni side of the frontier.'[73] Three days later Turnbull replied to

Greenwood's cable. His missive was shorn of any attempt at diplomatic nicety. He wrote, 'Federal Supreme Council [Federal government] met Tuesday 6 July. I did not however deliver your message since I judged it would have had so harsh a reception as to cause general embarrassment.' Turnbull then listed five points that he knew the Federal Ministers would have reproached him with, which would have caused such discomfort. His cable was written in a style that left little doubt that the third-party views reported also reflected his own. Aside from the failure of Britain to stand by its treaty obligations to defend Federal territory he noted that:

> [I]t is not accepted that the attack [of 2 July] was not intended. Bulaiq [sic] is [a] most distinctive and obvious feature and could not have been confused with any neighbouring target in Yemen. It was attacked in March last year by Egyptian helicopters one day before the Harib operation and must be well known to Egyptian pilots . . . The Federation must be protected; what protection has HMG to offer [other] than Egyptian promises not to do it again; . . . Federal Supreme council was fobbed off with a bromide from the High Commissioner after the air attacks of March and April this year. Now, after [a] more severe attack we get just the same treatment.[74]

If the Colonial Secretary hoped that the cost of alienating the Federal rulers would be offset by progress in the Lancaster House talks he was to be disappointed. The Federation rulers, already distrustful of long-term British policy had their worst fears confirmed when the *Observer* published a front-page article which claimed the MoD was willing to abandon the Aden base as part of a review over defence spending and in light of the internal security situation. As Karl Pieragostini noted, 'The story probably shocked the Federation rulers into considering the prospect that Britain might leave South Arabia completely, and made nationalist leaders more bold in their demands that the base be withdrawn.'[75] Unwilling to accept the inflated demands of al-Makkawi and al-Asnaj that Britain pledge to make an early withdraw from its military base in Aden, the talks collapsed amid chaos on 7 August.

Almost immediately, Al-Asnaj departed for Cairo where, on arrival, he invested his energies in hastening the downfall of the FSA. As for the Federal rulers, they regarded Greenwood as the embodiment of a Labour government whose antipathy towards colonialism undermined any real sympathy with, or understanding of the potentates that successive governments in Whitehall had been more than happy to exploit to secure British interests. It was a view that found sympathy with the Chief of the Defence Staff who wrote to Healey that, '[We] must, at all costs not be manoeuvred into a position where we appear to be supporting the Adenis against the Federation and thus alienating the rulers.'[76] Other historians analysing events at this time went further. J. B. Kelly argued that with further constitutional advance impossible in the face of Nationalist intransigence, '[T]he only logical, if drastic course open to it [the Labour government] was to surrender sovereignty over Aden (other than the base areas) immediately, hand over the colony [Aden] to the Federal Government and leave the latter to impose an Arab solution in a night of the long knives.'[77] It remains doubtful if such a bloody denouement, however logical, would have enjoyed the blessing of a Conservative government, let alone a Labour one. In the event, Greenwood continued to plough a barren furrow in efforts to find a diplomatic solution amid an intensification of the state of emergency and reports that Egypt was now preparing the ground for a renewed military offensive.

The Momentum Towards Withdrawal

Even before the Lancaster House talks had foundered, intelligence assessments by the DIS suggested a major build-up of Egyptian forces was underway. These troop reinforcements, backed by a discernible increase in air activity around the port of Hodeidah caused some consternation among the DIS and JIC. While the intelligence was clear over the capabilities this fresh injection of military blood offered the YAR, the intent remained unclear. On 13 July 1965, the Vice-Chief of the Air Staff wrote to Healey and chairman of the JIC, Sir Bernard Burrows, asking for permission to conduct a photo reconnaissance mission along the Yemen coast between Mocha in the south and Luhayyah in the north. While conceding that the troop reinforcements could be related purely to the Yemen's 'internal security problem', the strategic development of other Yemeni ports, the reported positioning of an anti-aircraft unit near Salif and reports of an increase in fast patrol boat activity along the Yemen coast all suggested something more sinister was afoot. The British-administered island of Kamaran lay only 10 kilometres from the port of Salif and as such, its proximity made it an ideal location for monitoring signals traffic along the Yemen coast. As a physical feature, it had also proved of considerable use as a marker for clandestine flights en route to dropping supplies to the Royalists. Its proximity was also, however, its vulnerability, and the increase in Egyptian naval activity was seen in this light.

Since November 1964, no photographic reconnaissance had been conducted along this stretch of the coast and MIDCOM now pressed the case for such sorties to be flown not just on an ad hoc basis but at regular intervals. The risk that these missions, undertaken by specially equipped Canberra bombers, would be intercepted was regarded as acceptable. The flights would use oblique photography from heights 'between 10,000 and 20,000 feet and 12 miles from the coast', and well inside international airspace.[78] Healey supported the request but when approached, the Foreign Secretary, Michael Stewart, proved less accommodating. Operational requirements had to be balanced against wider political considerations, not least reports that negotiations between Riyadh and Cairo in an effort to convene a meeting between Crown Prince Faisal and Nasser had reached a critical juncture.

In the event, one reconnaissance flight was conducted, the resulting photographs indicating that far from being directed against British possessions, the Egyptian military build-up was part of Nasser's diplomatic strategy to place pressure upon Riyadh to reach a cease-fire agreement in Yemen on Cairo's terms. This assessment, made by the JIC at the beginning of August contained, however, an important caveat. In a memo to Healey, the Director General of Defence Intelligence, Kenneth Strong, added that, 'JIC believe that unless Faisal moves towards Nasser in the negotiations now in progress (about which we know little) Nasser may decide to bomb targets he has recce'd [in Saudi Arabia] . . . If Nasser attacks, it is possible Faisal may appeal to us or the US for help.'[79] Given such a scenario, locating the disposition of Egyptian forces became a high priority. Again, permission was sought for further photographic reconnaissance sorties in an area around the port of Maidi on the Yemen–Saudi frontier. The presence of four Republican MiG-17 interceptor aircraft in Hodeidah was deemed to be of insufficient risk to the RAF Canberra, given their perceived low levels of readiness and limited aerial capabilities.[80]

When the request reached Stewart's desk, he asked for finite postponement of the operation. Not only had the negotiations held in Jeddah between the Egyptian and Saudi leaders reached a delicate stage, but Stewart, in an effort to bridge the ever widening gap between Cairo and London, had been preparing the ground for the Thomson to visit to Egypt. With news emerging that some form of deal had been reached at Jeddah, Stewart advised Wilson that if implemented, an agreement would '[G]ive us a better opportunity of reaching some measure of understanding with the UAR without letting down those to whom we are responsible in Southern Arabia.'[81] The risk of reconnaissance flights being detected or, worse still, shot down, was now deemed too high when, at long last, diplomacy appeared to be building up a head of steam.

Such hopes proved forlorn. Just prior to Thomson's visit at the end of September 1965, the Speaker of the Federal Legislative Council, Sir Arthur Charles, was murdered. As Chief Minister in the Aden State government, al-Makkawi refused to condemn the attack, prompting Turnbull to request his removal, and with permission granted by a dissolute Greenwood, to impose direct rule from Government House over all Aden and the Federation. Nasser refused to meet Thomson when the

Briton arrived in Egypt on 27 September, setting in motion a chain of diplomatic crises that reached their nadir on 17 December 1965 when Cairo broke full diplomatic relations (though not consular ties) with London.[82]

Circumstantial evidence suggests that, freed from the immediate need to defend the YAR against the Royalists, Nasser now turned his attention wholeheartedly towards subverting the Federation. When Crown Prince Faisal had implored London to shoulder greater responsibility for the Royalist war effort a year previously, Britain declined, content in the knowledge that Riyadh's largesse appeared sufficient to curb Nasser's ambition. Now, when continued Saudi support for Royalist operations was perhaps needed most from London's perspective, none was forthcoming. The old aphorism that states never have friends, only interests was an apt summation of the dilemma now facing Wilson's government over South Arabia in the autumn of 1965.

A grim acknowledgement of Nasser's true intent now permeated Cabinet decision-making in Whitehall. A request by Denis Healey to Greenwood that 1,000 1b bombs be used against a 'rebel base and arms dump' inside Federal territory was condoned by the Colonial Secretary without condition, sparing all concerned the tardy exchange of cables between officials and ministers that had hampered effective action in the past and so soured London's relations with Federal ministers.[83] Attention also turned once again to the renaissance of RANCOUR II operations. The initiative came from the Cabinet Secretary, Sir Burke Trend, who, as chair of the JAC, recommended these operations be realised without delay, a view that was endorsed by all Cabinet members and enjoyed the full support of the Prime Minister, Harold Wilson.[84] There is a sense of desperation in this renewed enthusiasm for clandestine action. Given how the political environment had changed since such activity was last placed on Whitehall tables for discussion, RANCOUR II operations offered scant cover for the policy lacuna that was fast emerging in the Cabinet. Even so, no one in the Cabinet was prepared to argue the case for more far reaching measures, which by their very nature meant stepping into Saudi sandals.

It is doubtful, given the lassitude and confusion that marked the intelligence effort in South Arabia, if the limited aims of RANCOUR II could be met by those charged with fermenting unrest along the border. The report produced by Daniel McCarthy for the JIC was an outright attack on the febrile nature of the intelligence machinery throughout the Federation. He declared, 'The British [intelligence] machine, as distinct from Arabised [sic] British is ramshackle and running down and lacks most elements of a basic infrastructure.' His main criticisms were reserved for the bureaucratic friction that undermined the collation, assessment and dissemination of material to the concerned agencies. With regard to the quality of the intelligence reaching Aden from FIOs operating in the more remote parts of the Federation, McCarthy painted a picture of intelligence gathering that was almost medieval in its construct:

> Most of it [intelligence] reaches Protectorate [FI] officers in the field. Many of them live in mud huts, working on trestle tables without secretaries or ciphers, in rooms from which the windows are shot out from time to time. They are harassed by callers and the great effort required to achieve the simplest thing. They have neither the time nor the resources to write everything down, still less in multiple copies of which one could go to a central intelligence point. They tend to report all but the most urgent material orally.[85]

It was under such harsh conditions that many of these men were expected to direct clandestine operations. Moreover, these operations were not about intelligence gathering per se but about subversion, and the suspicion remained that aside from attracting unwarranted Egyptian and Yemeni attention, they produced nothing of value that could be added to the overall intelligence picture. The fear among the Federal rulers that London might abandon the Federation altogether had become so palpable that it now impacted on what little raw intelligence had been forthcoming. McCarthy found that in an atmosphere of political uncertainty the Federal rulers had reached the point where they 'would never, generally speaking, provide their active intelligence product to a British central collating point'. This denial of local intelligence now extended to the British-officered FRA where 'Arab soldiers do not talk when British officers are listening', a mode of behaviour prompted by the all-pervasive feeling that 'Her Majesty's Government puts the Federation second to Aden, and have become the more reserved accordingly.' In sum, by the end of 1965 officials in London and Aden were not just facing a deficit with regard to the gathering of intelligence from the Federation and beyond; it was facing an Arabian black hole.

Against this background, the Foreign Office had begun to turn their attention back to the United Nations, reopening the debate over the efficacy of having UN monitors stationed inside the Federal border, with a special envoy appointed by New York to ascertain where the weight of culpability for the violence in the Federation now lay. Lord Caradon, the British Ambassador to the United Nations, warned London of the pitfalls inherent in this proposal. Support for anti-colonial movements remained strong throughout the UN and any future report produced by New York would be unlikely to look with undue deference upon British policy in South Arabia.[86] However uncomfortable the path through the New York appeared, the need to engage with the UN once more took root among Foreign Office officials. For many, such initiatives had not come a moment too soon. By the end of 1965, the total British and Federal casualties for that year – both military and civilian – stood at 239, of which 35 were fatalities. Faced with such losses the Ministry of Defence had, in September 1965, secretly authorised contingency plans for the evacuation of families and dependants of British servicemen from South Arabia. The mould of future British intentions in South Arabia if not quite cast, was certainly beginning to take shape.[87]

Conclusion

Continuity rather than change marked the policy of the Labour government towards the Yemen from the moment they took office in October 1964. Withholding recognition of the YAR was the most visible feature of this policy but the willingness to sanction RANCOUR operations in an attempt to keep Egyptian subversion on the back foot demonstrated that individuals within Wilson's Cabinet had as much predilection for clandestine activities when required as their Conservative forebears. Where key differences did exist related more to the structure of the Federation itself. Greenwood, with his antipathy towards the archaic potentates of the Federation all too apparent, pressed ahead with the idea of a single unitary independent state of South Arabia, a proposal at odds with the loose Federal structure promoted by Trevaskis. This gave succour to Nationalists who saw in it the seeds of complete dismemberment of British influence in South Arabia, while alienating the Federal rulers who saw their privileged positions being sacrificed on the altar of political expediency.

This was unfortunate for the Labour government since, in the spring and summer of 1965, they had more leverage with all parties in the Federation than they ever realised. The Royalist victories in east Yemen, brought about in no small measure by the assistance proffered by the BMO, opened up an opportunity to place severe pressure on Egyptian bases along the Federal frontier and further afield being used by Cairo to support and sustain its guerrilla campaign throughout the Federation. The policy of the Labour government of no overt involvement in the Yemen and only limited covert activity of a strictly defensive nature – a policy inherited from the Home administration – was calibrated to sustain the status quo in Yemen. But when that equilibrium no longer existed, policy failed to change and with this failure went the one opportunity London had to capitalise on Nasser's discomfort.

Whether the perceived advantages of such action would have been sufficient to justify a more pro-active engagement with Royalist forces must remain a matter of conjecture. The point stands, however, that officials in London and Aden failed to fully appreciate the strategic window of opportunity that had been opened, mainly due to the poor quality of intelligence collation and assessment. SIS officers received detailed reports regarding events in the Yemen from British operatives working with the Royalist armies. Why these reports never came to inform JIC estimates remains something of an enigma. Here, perhaps, is where one of the few differences between the Labour and Conservative governments made itself felt. The benign environment enjoyed by the BMO on Federal territory under Home was denied by his successor. It is more than likely, given McCarthy's lamentation over the lack of credible intelligence from the Yemen, that the reports supplied by the likes of Smiley and others to SIS officers, never made it beyond the proverbial 'in-trays' of officials in Broadway and Whitehall. The Labour government had lost a gilt-edged opportunity to sustain British influence in South Arabia before the looming crisis over sterling came to justify the radical reassessment of Britain's role east of Suez. This is not to suggest Britain should never have withdrawn, but rather to argue that the context in which the decision to leave Aden was eventually taken, could have been shaped on terms far more favourable to London and its influence in the Middle East.

8
From the Jaws of Victory

The Political Defeat of Britain in South Arabia

On 22 February 1966, the Labour government of Harold Wilson published its long-awaited Defence White Paper. It has often been claimed that the sweeping defence cuts it presaged – most notably in equipment procurement and overseas bases east of Suez – were prompted by the fragile state of the British economy. The need to defend sterling required cuts in public expenditure across the board and with the Treasury looking to enforce stringent pecuniary measures, defence spending became the subject of close scrutiny. The given rationale behind the White Paper was the need reduce 'over-stretch' on the armed forces but equally, there had been a growing awareness that £350 million spent annually on maintaining overseas bases was a direct burden on the balance of payments at a time when sterling was under ever increasing pressure in the financial markets. Given the commitment of the Chancellor of the Exchequer, James Callaghan, to invest a greater proportion of national income on social welfare, savings had to be made elsewhere. Accordingly, the Defence White Paper declared that:

> South Arabia is due to become independent by 1968, and we do not think it
> appropriate that we should maintain defence facilities there after that happens.
> We therefore intend to withdraw our forces from Aden base at that time and
> we have so informed the Federal government. We shall be able to fulfil our
> remaining obligations in the Middle East by making a small increase in our forces
> stationed in the Persian Gulf.[1]

Denis Healey remarked that the decision was recognition by London of the diminishing economic return Britain accrued from its last outposts of empire, which, when mixed with the volatile cocktail of local nationalism, served to undermine any strategic argument for retention of the Aden base.[2] The timing of the announcement was not, however, prompted by any immediate sense of dysthymia afflicting Britons over their economic well-being. One month after the publication of the Defence White Paper,

Wilson won a snap General Election, increasing his parliamentary majority from a slim three seats to 97.[3] Rather, what prompted the Labour government to abandon the Aden base and, in so doing, renege on clear commitments to provide for the defence of the FSA given under the Home government, was a loss of political will. Thomas Mockaitis noted that the grounds cited for withdrawal do not, on closer inspection, appear so compelling. He notes that 'As the world's second busiest oil bunkering port, Aden was still a valuable piece of real estate', and that, putting to one side the individual tragedies concealed in the bland columns of casualty figures, the human toll among British forces, their dependants and among members of the FRA and Federal Guard had, since the declarations of the emergency in 1963, been comparatively small, indeed far fewer than comparable combat deaths among British servicemen fighting a parallel counter-insurgency campaign in Borneo. Unlike events in that corner of south-east Asia, however, the drama in South Arabia, and in particular in Aden itself, was unfolding under the glare of the British and international press corps. Mockaitis argues that this media spotlight served to magnify the concern among members of the parliamentary Labour Party who had never been comfortable with London's indulgence of Federal rulers, and which had been bought at the expense of development – both political and economic – of the Federation as a whole and of Aden in particular.[4] Thus Healey could claim in his memoirs that:

> The cost of trying to stay in Aden, with an increasingly hostile population armed and supported by Nasser's agents from neighbouring Yemen was out of all proportion to the gain. The Conservatives had announced in 1962 that they intended to station British troops in Aden 'permanently'; but they agreed in 1964, before Labour took over, to give it independence in 1968. Since the population was hostile to Britain, and deeply riven [sic] by internal divisions, these two promises were obviously incompatible. We found it impossible to make any constitution work and had to impose direct rule in 1965. So we decided to stick to the date for independence but to remove our troops at the same time. All alternatives would have been worse.[5]

The decision to withdraw was greeted with wholesale opprobrium from the Conservative Party, with the epithet 'scuttle' providing an apt summation in their view of the government action. But as the Defence White Paper argued, maintaining the outward appearance of a world military power would remain nothing but a façade if 'it is achieved at the expense of economic health'.[6] Though the economic justification behind the defence review may have been based on sound reasoning, the same could not be said concerning the timing of the review's publication. The agreement reached between Nasser and Crown Prince Faisal at Jeddah at the end of August 1965 set in motion the first tangible withdrawal of Egyptian troops from the Yemen. The Republican government in Sana'a had been in turmoil since the beginning of 1965, Egyptian casualties had continued to mount and the Royalist forces were in the ascendant, particularly in the Khowlan mountains and the al-Jauf region. In April 1965 in what became known as the Humaidat operation, the Royalist First Army under Prince Mohammed bin al-Hussein inflicted a major defeat on Egyptian forces in east Yemen in a co-ordinated offensive that owed much to training, co-ordination, and motivation provided by the British Mercenary Organisation. As Bernard Mills, the British Liaison Officer with the Royalist First Army noted of this time:

> We [the Royalists and BMO] produced a situation where we'd won, where the Egyptians were prepared to pull out completely from the Yemen. They went to see King Faisal in Jeddah and agreed to go and it was at this time that the new British government announced its attention to leave [South] Arabia. So we'd actually won the game, which is why I got so cross, we'd actually won the game and then it was given away politically because the Labour government was committed to a major defence cut.[7]

The Jeddah agreement no doubt convinced some mandarins in Whitehall that, floundering in the Yemeni morass, Cairo had little time or the inclination to continue its nefarious activities in South Arabia. But Nasser was nothing if not an opportunist. The announcement of London's intent to abandon the Aden base saw him not only freeze further troop withdrawals, but sponsor increased levels of violence against British and Federal targets. The casualty figures speak for themselves. In 1965 total casualties among British and Federal forces, European civilians and local nationals totalled 239. The figure for 1966 was 573. If one takes the figures for British service personnel alone the numbers tell a similar tale: in 1965 there were six fatalities with 83 injured. The following year five servicemen were killed with a further 218 wounded. In 1967, when British forces finally withdrew, 44 servicemen had been killed and 325 wounded.[8]

British policy was dictated by an indecent haste that failed to recognise Nasser's ability to break accords and agreements when the constellation of regional forces appeared disposed in his favour. From the spring of 1963, Cairo had breached a series of cease fire agreements when it felt it could gain a unilateral advantage. Now the Labour government repeated the mistake of confusing Nasser's stated intent with practical developments on the ground. Under the Jeddah agreement, Cairo was required to withdraw all its troops from Yemen over a ten-month period. By March 1966, 40,000 had been withdrawn, only for Nasser to then resume the bombing of Royalist positions. The former commander of the FRA, Brigadier James Lunt, attributed this 'volte-face' directly to the publication of the Defence White Paper. The British decision, Lunt wrote, 'confounded all their friends and delighted all their enemies in South Arabia; it was like giving burglars advance notice of one's intention to be away from home. Within months the Egyptian troop strength had been increased once more to 60,000'.[9] If London had delayed publication of its White Paper by four months, Cairo would simply not have had the forces in theatre both to sustain the Republican government and prosecute a guerrilla campaign in Aden and the Federation. The fact that London, according to its own JIC assessments, was making policy decisions over Aden without sufficient intelligence regarding the strength of the Royalist position in the Yemen, meant that appreciation of the context surrounding the withdrawal, and by extension, the timing of Britain's intent to abandon Aden, was fatally flawed.

Increasingly, the key actor in this unfolding drama was King Faisal. His largesse remained crucial to sustaining the Royalist campaign and the support this received from the BMO. Equally however, Riyadh pursued its own agenda which was more anti-Egyptian than pro-Royalist. Much to the chagrin of Neil McLean, the Saudi potentate entertained real hopes that an emergent 'Third Force', an amalgam of leading Republican and Royalist politicians disillusioned with their respective leaderships, would cohere to form an alternative leadership and bring about an end to the war. By the autumn of 1965 such political intrigues had begun to cast growing doubts over the continued viability of the BMO, leading to tensions surfacing among the more senior of its members over the vexed question of future command and control.

A Military Ascendancy of Sorts

The loss of his seat in the General Election of 1964 did nothing to dim the ardour of McLean for the Royalist cause. Freed from his Parliamentary duties, he devoted more time towards promoting and supporting the restoration of the Imamate than ever before. Such an investment he deemed necessary when set against the background of a government whose immediate proclivities seemed ill-disposed towards the Royalist cause. The most immediate evidence to hand were the moves by the Foreign Office, with the full support of the Colonial Secretary, Richard Greenwood, to deny the use of Federal territory to the BMO and their supporters. In this they were only partially successful; British and French mercenaries continued to use Beihan as an entry and exit point into the Yemen but the disruption caused was such that by the spring of 1965, the mercenary operations became increasingly reliant on Najran and Jizzan as gateways.

At the beginning of January 1965, McLean embarked upon his eighth and by far his most extensive trip to Saudi Arabia and the Yemen. Lasting five months, during which time he endured serious privations, the Briton found grounds for encouragement and concern in equal measure. In strategic terms, the Royalist position appeared set on an upwards trajectory. Having weathered the Haradh offensive the previous summer, and survived various thrusts of diminishing intensity to drive them from their redoubts in the Razih mountains close to the Saudi border between December 1964 and February 1965, the Royalist forces now looked to take the offensive.

The most vulnerable point of the Egyptian expeditionary force remained their extended supply routes to their remote garrisons in the north and east of the Yemen. Logistical support for these bases had become a nightmare. The distance from Sana'a to the Egyptian garrison at Marib was 80 miles across the Khowlan mountains but Royalist control of this area meant that re-supply operations had to follow a circuitous route that led out from the capital northwards towards Amran and al-Harf. Here, any convoy had to swing due south towards a place called Farah, before turning south-east along a route that followed the Wadi Humaidat and onwards to Marib and Harib. Given its vulnerability, the plan was to cut this supply artery, forcing an Egyptian collapse throughout north-east Yemen.[10] Such a strategy played to the strengths of the Royalist forces and remained in accordance with the recommendations laid down by both McLean and David Smiley but only ever applied by Royalist forces on an intermittent basis.

By the beginning of 1965, there were six British, 10 French and three Belgian operatives working with the Royalist forces. Of the British, four – Johnny Cooper, Chris Chalma, Bill McSweeney and David Bailey – were located in the Khowlan. Bernard Mills and his radio operator, a former SAS soldier named 'James', were attached to the Royalist First Army under Prince Mohammed bin al-Hussein based around al-Jauf, while Rupert France, responsible for radio communications between London and the operatives in the field, had, in the wake of Greenwood's missives, moved his operational base for the most part from Nequb to the Saudi port of Jeddah. A further addition to the ranks of the 'few British' at this time was Bob Gilbert, another former army officer. For the most part, the French and Belgians concentrated their efforts upon training Royalist forces at Khanja, though some, such as L'Amiral, the former French Warrant officer, preferred to work with British mercenaries due to the fractitious nature of relations with his own compatriots.[11]

However good the quality of the individual operatives, their ability to influence events on the ground remained constrained by the haphazard nature of wireless communication and the capricious nature of some, though by no means all, of the Royalist commanders. On 3 March 1965, David Smiley returned to the Yemen for his fourth visit to appraise the Saudis of the current military status of the Royalist forces. With regard to wireless operations, Smiley noted that 'a drastic reorganisation is necessary' with some 16 radio stations 'using four different types of set – the Collins, the Heath Kit, the NCX and the TRT.' He continued, 'There are different nets, French, British and Arab operators, different codes and frequencies.' The need to establish a coherent and secure net was of a piece with his main recommendation regarding the overall organisation of the Royalist forces:

> This [organisation] is one of the weakest points of the Royalists. Each Amir is fighting his own private war. Each is inclined to keep heavy weapons and European specialists to themselves as status symbols. The 12 Belgian/French and 5 [sic] British para-military specialists are not all being put to best use. Co-ordination is necessary, and this can only be achieved by a commander who is given power to control the heavy weapons, European specialists and the transport. In addition, he must have the right of direct approach to the Amirs, without the usual delays, and the Amir should be urged to listen to, and preferably take, his advice.[12]

It was an assessment that Riyadh took to heart. With the blessing of King Faisal, the Royalist Foreign Minister, Ahmed al-Shamy, and the Saudi Defence Minister, Crown Prince Sultan bin Abdul Aziz, offered Smiley overall command of the mercenaries inside the Yemen. In his published account, Smiley recalls consulting with Jim Johnson, Colonel Roger Falques and his wife, Moy, before agreeing to a contract that included provision for him to take a total of four months leave each year 'to coincide with his children's holidays'.[13] Privately, he also consulted McLean, who advised him to take the position on condition that 'he had complete control himself and did not [McLean's emphasis] depend on the London office and that secondly, there was no question of backing the Third Force'.[14] The fact Prince Sultan was willing to offer such generous terms to Smiley speaks volumes for the high regard in which he was held in the Saudi court. Equally, it is a tribute to his powers of leadership and resolve that he achieved so much in strengthening the Royalist fronts from what, in essence, was a makeshift capacity. Yet the problems outlined by Smiley himself could not be addressed systematically by a commander acting under the terms of his own contract, on a partial basis. Despite his best endeavours, many of the problems associated with the BMO were never resolved, leading to a clash of personalities within the organisation and subsequent friction with their Saudi employers. While remaining supportive of his close friend, McLean's notes reveal growing unease over the direction that Saudi policy was taking towards the Royalist cause and discontent at the manner in which the BMO was being handled by Johnson and Boyle in London.

From the beginning of January 1965, Riyadh had expressed a growing sense of exasperation that its material investment in the Royalist cause had failed to produce any visible strategic return. Kemal Atham, the head of the Saudi Intelligence Services, had assumed overall responsibility for furnishing the Royalists with the financial wherewithal to expand their operations. In November 1964, he had approved delivery of a caravan of 18 camels, loaded with stores and gold sovereigns sufficient to sustain operations in the Khowlan for a period of four months. In addition, it was revealed to McLean that Prince Mohammed bin al-Hussein received a monthly retainer of Saudi Riyals 700,000 (12 Riyals was worth £1) and a further 250–300,000 Riyals per month to dispense as gifts. The total value of Saudi aid to the Royalist cause since October 1962 was revealed to McLean to have reached £25 million.[15]

On the surface at least, Saudi impatience was understandable, the more so if they had been privy to the knowledge that Royalist forces in the Khowlan had been the benefactors of two substantial re-supply drops on 23 January and again on 13 February. The latter was timely, allowing the recipient, Prince Mohammed bin Mohsin, to distribute this 'manna from heaven' among the Arhab tribe whose will to resist the Egyptians in an area of the Khowlan of strategic importance had begun to waver.[16] This incident highlighted the ongoing problems of bending tribal societies with their transient loyalties towards achieving a collective goal, in particular when parochial concerns dominated their immediate political horizons. By the summer of 1965, with the war having disrupted the normal patterns of food production and distribution, famine was becoming a real possibility, particularly to the east of the Khowlan in an area that encompassed Marib and Harib. Food, as well as the lure of gold sovereigns or the Mother Theresa Dollars, increasingly became an important weapon in the battle for the tribal mind.[17] If Riyadh failed to appreciate the constraints imposed by tribal politics on the prosecution of an effective guerrilla campaign, the Royalists, in turn, entertained suspicions of Saudi misanthropy. Such suspicious were not wholly misplaced on either side. As Smiley noted of this period:

> My own view was that the Saudis, for their own reasons, were giving the Royalists just enough help to prolong the war but not enough to win it outright; they also suspected, with some justification, that some of the supplies they sent were misappropriated. I had no doubt that the main factor in winning the war was money, because in the last resort most of the tribal Sheikhs would fight for the side who paid them best; so much so that those of the mercenaries who had served in the SAS would say that their old motto 'Who Dares Wins' should be changed to 'Who Pays Wins'.[18]

The subject of Saudi vitriol was Prince Mohammed bin al-Hussein, the 28–year-old commander of the Royalist First Army in the Khowlan. Of all the Royalists, the First Army most closely approximated a coherent military formation. Prince Mohammed was only too aware of the short-comings of tribal allegiances, and looked therefore to raise a force where discipline and unity of military purpose rose above tribal avarice. He recruited a force of semi-regulars, organised into formal units, or sariya, each containing 45 officers and men. As Dana Adams Schmidt describes them, 'Semi-regulars were supposed to serve for at least a year without returning to their homes. The informal, unrecorded drifting back and forth that was taken for granted in other parts of the Royalist forces was not permitted here.'[19] These semi regulars received regular monthly pay of 15 Mother Theresa Dollars, and in their khaki tunics appeared more like a regular military formation. More importantly, the semi-regulars of the First Army were the beneficiaries of instruction provided by European mercenaries at Khanja, the main mercenary training base located on the edge of the Khowlan. Given the fragmented nature of the Royalist fronts across Yemen, no other 'army' had such ready access to their expertise. As events were now to demonstrate, such training, when married to the martial instincts of tribes prepared to fight, could reap strategic as well as political dividends.

The plan to cut the Egyptian supply route to Marib had first been mooted at the beginning of January but now, under Saudi pressure, Prince Mohammed was informed in no uncertain terms by the triumvirate of David Smiley, Bernard Mills and Jim Johnson, that unless an attack was launched to cut this line of communication, Saudi aid to the Prince would be withdrawn.[20] Despite Smiley recording that Prince Mohammed 'stalled, wriggled, and squirmed' before agreeing to put in such an attack, he later conceded in his report to the Saudis that the Prince was labouring under severe logistical difficulties in ensuring enough men, supplies and ammunition would be in the designated position to ensure the success of the operation. The chosen spot was the Wadi Humaidat which formed a natural choke point along the main Egyptian supply route between the Yemeni capital and Marib. It had been carefully reconnoitred by Mills, who, as the principal liaison officer with the Royalist First Army, imparted a tactical acumen and aggression to his command that set it apart from most other fronts.

Over 300 camels were required to deliver the necessary supplies and equipment to two strategic points, the Jebel Aswad and Jebel Ahmar that overlooked the main route and from where the heavy weaponry – 75mm and 57 mm recoiless rifles, and 81mm mortars – were to be located. The mountains lay in the domain of the *Daham* tribe whose loyalty had, in the past, been given to the highest bidder. Ensuring the fidelity of the dominant tribal grouping added to the time required to mount the operation; the original target date of 4 April was postponed by 11 days. Nonetheless, the military results achieved more than justified the wait. In what was perhaps the most efficient battle fought by the Royalists, 362 soldiers of the Royalist first Army, backed by 1,290 tribesmen from the *Daham* and Barat, and directed by two British and three French mercenaries, cut this main supply route and, despite several days of determined Egyptian counter-attacks, held on to their positions. At the same time, Egyptian positions were subject to attacks at al-Urush north-east of Sana'a, around Sad'ah as well as throughout the Khowlan. The success of the Humaidat operation meant that this supply route was denied to the Egyptian and YAR forces for the rest of the war. The remaining Egyptian garrisons in eastern Yemen, totalling some 5,000 troops, now had to be supplied by air. Before too long, Nasser effectively allowed them to wither on the vine as, faced with such military setbacks and their appalling toll on human lives, he looked to consolidate the Egyptian military presence in a defensive triangle with Sana'a–Hodeidah–Taiz'z forming its points.[21] On 25 July 1965, Marib, the last remaining garrison of any significance in eastern Yemen, finally capitulated to Royalist forces led by Prince Mohammed's brother, Abdullah.

In many ways, the Humaidat operation was the apogee of Royalist military prowess and showed what could be achieved when disciplined forces, free from the parochial concerns of tribal politics, could manipulate those self-same forces towards a strategic end. It proved the value of an integrated radio network as the pivot around which diversionary raids had been co-ordinated and controlled. Finally, while Mills could rightly take considerable credit for the planning of the Humaidat operation, Prince Mohammed bin al-Hussein proved himself to be a commander of some distinction, both in directing his forces and by example of his personal courage. When Egyptian paratroops threatened to retake the strategic heights of Jebel Ahmar, his leadership proved crucial to driving them off the mountain top.[22]

Although the events in Wadi Humaidat represented a strategic triumph for the Royalists, the Wilson government, tied to a policy of non-intervention, failed to grasp its wider political implications for Egyptian hegemony in Yemen. Events around Harib one month previously meant that the whole of east Yemen lay within the Royalist domain, with tribes of the Hashid and Bakil federations – including some who had supported the Republican government – now calling for the withdrawal of Egyptian troops. At a time when public discomfort was growing in Britain over Aden and South Arabia, London was presented with a gilt-edged opportunity to tackle the bases inside the Yemen that lent succour and support to the NLF. This proposal was put to Lieutenant Colonel John

Woodhouse by Prince Abduallah, the brother of Prince Hussein, in the summer of 1965. Having retired as commanding officer of 22 SAS in January 1965, Woodhouse, in the company of what he euphemistically called 'four other British ex-serviceman' toured the Khowlan area between July and October 1965 with the intended purpose of organising more extensive guerrilla operations around Sana'a. Abduallah claimed that with funding from the British government, he could effectively 'secure the area of BAIDHA (opposite MUKEIRAS on the South Arabian frontier) for the Royalists and bring peace to the border.' While Woodhouse told the Prince that it was highly unlikely that British money would be given to him, he argued in his subsequent report that:

[I]f British funds are being used in anyway to disrupt the National Liberation Front in its Yemeni bases, I am convinced that we are likely to achieve more if that money passes through ABDULLAH'S [sic] hands than if it goes from the British to minor Sheikhs. While ABDULLAH will certainly appropriate a part of any money he receives to his own purposes, the part he deducts will be a small fraction of that taken by the always greedy Sheikhs. ABDULLAH is a patriot, unselfish to a fault, and with considerable authority and powers of leadership and persuasion. His knowledge of guerrilla operations and the Egyptians is extensive and based on personal experience.[23]

This was a direct criticism of the limited impact of RANCOUR operations in undermining Egyptian-sponsored clandestine activity. Such proposals, despite their intrinsic logic, carried little weight among either ministers or mandarins in Whitehall. Special operations remained defensive and reactive, rather than aggressive and pro-active. Ignorant of the malaise facing Nasser in Yemen – an ignorance born as much from political preference in the Cabinet as poor intelligence assessments – paying the 'monkeys' rather than dealing with the Royalist organ-grinder remained Whitehall's preferred clandestine option. The opportunity to capitalise on Egyptian misfortunes was never to present itself to London again.

The BMO: The Challenge of Adversity

On his return to London in June 1965, McLean, with his usual attention to detail, wrote an upbeat assessment of the Royalist position in the Yemen. Parsimonious to a fault, his report made three recommendations, all of a piece with maintaining and capitalising on the military success achieved by the Royalist forces in east Yemen. Of the three recommendations, two related directly to the military capabilities of the Royalist forces and the BMO. McLean urged that Royalist forces should now go on the offensive with the aim of cutting all Egyptian lines of communication in north and central Yemen. This renewed offensive would evolve over two phases, the first being the mopping up of the remaining pockets of Egyptian and YAR troops in al-Jauf and the Khowlan mountains, and the cutting of the Sana'a to Sad'ah road, with phase two consisting of an expansion of operations to cut the supply routes between the capital, Hodeidah and Sana'a. An implicit assumption behind the plan was that with a Royalist offensive gaining ground, enough tribes of the two main federations would declare in favour of the Imam to make the Egyptian position untenable. With regard to the BMO, McLean noted that:

> The necessary steps should now be taken to improve Royalist organisation and planning sufficiently to conduct the next phase of the war successfully. This would not be difficult as a senior British liaison officer [Smiley] has now been appointed to advise the Yemenis on how to do this, with special reference to improve their W/T and TRT communications and supply systems. He should have at least five British observers with W/T sets to help in addition to the other foreign observers (French and Persian) already in the Yemen who would be under his operational control. He should also plan and execute the special projects with first priority on the 120mm mortar project.[24]

The appointment of Smiley as the overall commander of all European operatives in the theatre was the most notable development in the BMO but McLean's reference to Iranian participation in the operation meant that it was no longer just the Saudis, or indeed the Israelis, who were anxious to bloody Nasser's nose. The Shah of Iran had, like the Saudis, long feared Egyptian designs throughout Arabia and, it was alleged, had been supplying weapons to the Royalist forces through Beihan since the winter of 1963.[25] Whatever geo-strategic advantage there was to be had was reinforced by the bonds of religion. Constituting a branch of Shi'i Islam, the *Zeidi* tribes who made up the bulk of the Royalist forces had a clear religious affinity with the *Pahlevi* dynasty in Tehran, much to the discomfort of the Saudi authorities.[26] As such, the Shah seconded four officers to the Royalist forces, all having undergone training at a special forces school in the United States. Smiley found them convivial company but felt that despite, or perhaps because of such training, they were ill-prepared for the rigours of life with the Royalist forces. They had entered the Yemen overburdened with personal kit and had spent over £500 on tinned food in Aden, leading Smiley none too impressed by the standards expected of their pupils by US special forces. As he confided to his diary, 'Their [the Iranian officers] standards are far too high for this sort of job'. Even so, Smiley conceded that at least in their company, he always ate well.[27]

The need to rationalise the Royalist communications networks remained crucial to operational efficiency. Like McLean, Smiley had advocated an overhaul of the system, which was now more pressing given his position of field commander. Now that Saudi Arabia served as the main point of entry and exit to and from the Yemen, Jeddah became his main hub of communication with operatives in the field. On 26 May 1965 Smiley arrived back in Jeddah en route to Yemen in his new role as field commander. He was now afforded the luxury of using a Collins radio set located in the office of the Royalist Deputy Prime Minister and uncle of the Imam, Prince Abdurrahman, and later, a radio located in the office of Kemal Atham, the head of Saudi Intelligence, to contact the British operatives in the field.[28] Amara, close to the border with Saudi Arabia, had by now replaced Nequb in Beihan as the main relay station for traffic from the various out stations, though it continued to be staffed by an operative equipped with a Heath Kit radio set. Most of the British operatives were now using the more sophisticated TRT sets, the exception being the Aden station which used an American-built NCX set to communicate with the main office in London. In addition to their Arabic *nom de guerre*, each operative maintaining radio contact with Amara and with Smiley was given a call-sign based on a flower. France operated under 'Crocus', David Bailey and Johnny Cooper, both in the Khowlan were 'Tulip' and 'Snowdrop' respectively, 'Lily' was located in Nehm, Georges, a French operator based at Amara was codenamed 'Rose', while Naqub was known as 'Lilac'. Exceptions to this floral tradition were Mills, codename 'Bravo, Bravo', while 'Coconut' was Smiley's own nomenclature for the radio located in Kemal Atham's office which also linked into the net operated by the Saudi Armed Forces.[29] The main problem remained not so much the different array of communication equipment as the different frequencies used, coupled with the often ad hoc attitude adopted towards radio security by Yemeni operatives operating the Royalist radio net.

By 1965, the Royalists had constructed a fairly effective broadcasting station located among a cave complex at a place called Fida on the Saudi–Yemen border. With the advent of the transistor radio, the ability for propaganda to be disseminated to even the most remote regions of Yemen where levels of literacy remained low was transformed. The initial idea had been for the *Mutawakalite*, or Royalist Broadcast Station, using a 5–kilowatt transmitter to be based in Aden, operating under the auspices of a consortium that included David Stirling's Television International Enterprises. When this proposal was first mooted in February 1964, it was vetoed outright by the Foreign Office, Michael Weir of the Arabian Department noting in a minute that 'I would have thought that this development, if correctly reported, could not fail to have the most damaging effect . . . I should have thought there was also bound to be a dangerous rise in the temperature of the Radio propaganda war in the Middle East.'[30] Aware that Arabia was rife with rumours of British collusion with the Royalists, the Foreign Office wanted to avoid any overt symbol that could undermine London's claims of non-involvement in the conflict. Equally, with the BBC Arabic Service operating relay stations from Aden, nothing could be done that could tarnish its reputation for impartiality throughout the region. In taking this line the Foreign Office had the full backing of the Defence and Overseas Policy Committee. It was made clear to McLean by Lord Carrington, at that time Conservative Minister for State at the Foreign Office, that London remained opposed to the idea of a "'black" Yemeni Royalist broadcasting station being set up on British territory.'[31]

By the spring of 1965, Riyadh had filled the void left by official British recalcitrance and furnished the necessary equipment and finance for the Royalist Broadcast Station. In this battle for the airwaves, the Egyptians attempted, with varying degrees of success, to jam the Royalist signals, much to the annoyance of the main engineer in charge of maintaining this facility, a West German national called Herbert Stoltz. He in turn recommended that Radio Sana'a be jammed, either by a ship in the Red Sea or from one its islands, such as Kamaran, which remained under British control.[32] In his late thirties, Stoltz had originally been in the employ of Imam Ahmed, but had remained on the Royalist payroll following the palace coup of September 1962. Some suspected that, if not quite working for West-German intelligence, he maintained discreet contacts with them (his frequent trips back to Europe to purchase spare parts for his transmitters was deemed by the British mercenaries to be the perfect opportunity for debriefing). While liked as an individual, all operatives treated him with some circumspection which included point-bank refusals form those concerned to divulge the origins of the parachute re-supply drops.[33]

While some semblance of order, at least in terms of frequencies used and patterns of encoding was introduced by the autumn of 1965, the network itself was never fully rationalised or, in terms of the stations controlled by Royalist W/T operatives, ever considered totally secure.[34] Complete radio security was anathema in predominantly tribal societies where disclosure of information was part of a cultural norm. However secure the radio net of the BMO, information still had to be operationalised within a broader context if the tribes were to be directed towards wider strategic goals. As the failed attack on Hajja in the spring of 1964 demonstrated, the 'tribal grape vine' was as much a determinant over the success or failure of operations as signals security. Labouring under such constraints, it is a tribute to the quality of some of the operatives that they achieved as much as they did.

The other main weakness which now needed to be addressed was the lack of heavy weapons in the Royalist armoury. The success of the spring offensives meant that the mountains surrounding the capital and beyond were firmly in the Royalists' grasp. Command of such heights now gave them the opportunity to counter the military advantage enjoyed by Egyptian and YAR forces that, to date, *the* Royalist forces had been unable to counter effectively: air power. The Egyptians, with Soviet help, had constructed a new runway at Arrahaba, some 7 kilometres to the north of Sana'a. With tribes loyal to the Royalist commander, Gassim Monasir, picketing the heights of Jebel Jemima and Jebel Seouda above the Yemeni capital, this strategic target was well within range of Royalist mortars. But while the airfield had been hit, the relatively small calibre of the main Royalist mortar – the 81mm – meant that the bombs were not heavy enough to cause major disruption to this key Egyptian asset.[35]

Since the autumn of 1964, the BMO had been in discussions with the Saudi government on the need to purchase mortars of a much heavier calibre, the 120mm. Riyadh had demonstrated few financial scruples about adding heavier weaponry to the Royalist arsenal if it believed it could be usefully employed. David Smiley's diary entry for 17 March 1965 reads, 'Had a long session with Kemal Atham in the morning and he showed me a new type of French bazooka [anti-tank weapon]. Advised him to order 100 so he ordered 200!'[36] Such profligacy now extended to the purchase of the 120mm mortar built by the French company Hotchkiss-Brandt. The deal itself was brokered officially between Hotchkiss-Brandt and the Saudi Ambassador to Paris, Rachad Pharaon. Given that Colonel Roger Falques, as well as the Royalist Foreign Minister, Ahmed al-Shamy, were also closely involved it seems more than likely that officials at Hotchkiss-Brandt, though not necessarily the Quai d'Orsay, knew their real, as opposed to their apparent destination. In a letter to the Saudi Ambassador, it was made clear that a condition of sale was that the weapons would not be passed on to a third party. The deal negotiated called for the delivery of 12×120mm in three batches, accompanied by a total of 12,000 projectiles of varying capability. The total cost to the Saudi government according to the invoice received by Pharaon was $1,229,000 (FF6,017,200,00), with delivery scheduled to begin once a credit note was deposited with the Banque de L'Indochine in Jeddah. The deal was concluded on 5 June, with Smiley adding his name to the final contract although prompt delivery of the mortars was to be delayed in a financial dispute between Ahmed al-Shamy and Kemal Atham. The latter claimed he had given the required amount for the purchase of the mortars to the former, money the Royalist Foreign Minister denied ever having received.[37]

While the Royalists were eventually to receive the mortars – French mercenaries later used them to bombard the Arrahaba airfield – the dispute over the purchase and delivery of these weapons was symptomatic of the inchoate nature of Royalist logistics. If the Imam's forces were to make a concerted push throughout the Yemen, an efficient supply system, centred upon the proper maintenance and repair of motor transport, had to be established. On his fourth trip to the Yemen, Smiley had identified 'bad driving' and 'mechanical ignorance' as the main culprits, leaving vehicles such as a Toyota jeep, 'barely 10 days old being rendered unserviceable' due to neglect by the driver.' His suggestion that proper mechanical and electrical repair facilities be established in the relatively safe surroundings of Amara had yet to be realised by the start of his fifth trip to Yemen in May 1965. Indeed, even though he toured many of the Royalist positions in the comfort of a Saudi-supplied Land Rover, these lacked a basic maintenance handbook, and while the Middle East was a growing export market for such vehicles, his attempts to get such literature supplied in the Arabic language proved fruitless, leading Boyle to comment that this was 'typical of our [British] export effort.'[38]

The poor state of the logistic infrastructure was brought to the attention of Prince Sultan and Kemal Atham. In an assessment which by inference criticised the poor state of communication of the Imam's forces, McLean wrote:

> One of the main weaknesses in the system of supplies to the Yemen is that requests for supplies come in from individual Princes and Fronts, each ignorant of the requests and needs of the others. This makes it difficult for the Saudis to assess exactly the urgency or priority of these requests. The Yemenis must therefore co-ordinate these requests for supplies. In the East [of Yemen] this could be done by passing all the requests through the HQ at Ammara to Prince Khalid al-Sudairi in Najran. A Prince, probably one of the Hussein brothers could be made responsible for the Yemen. In the west the request could be passed through the Imam at present to Prince Mohammed al-Sudairi in Gizan [sic]. Prince Abdurrahman, the Deputy Prime Minister who is in touch with both the Eastern and Western fronts by W/T could together with the Saudis collate the requests and decide priorities.[39]

Even while acknowledging these operational deficiencies, McLean, convinced that the war was being won, now recommended to the Saudis that his two-phase strategy for securing Nasser's demise in the Yemen be adopted. Behind his confidence over the direction of the war lay a deeper unease over the debates within the Saudi Royal Court over the continued efficacy of supporting the Royalist war effort. His appreciation of the actual strength of the Royalist forces may have been inflated in an effort to forestall moves in Riyadh to end the war on terms that, however humbling for Cairo, fell short of the total humiliation that he believed Nasser now faced in Yemen. But it was Riyadh who paid the 'Royalist' piper and it was King Faisal who was to call the political and diplomatic tune.

Towards the Chimera of Peace

Saudi policy towards the Yemen Civil War had always been driven more by anti-Egyptian sentiment than by any feeling of affinity with the *Hamid'Ud'Din*. This fractitious relationship was rooted in a theological schism that pitted the Sunni Wahhabi tradition of the House of Saud against an Imamate whose *Zeidi* creed remained a branch of Shi'i Islam. Arcane theological disputes apart, more recent events had served to sour the relationship. The founder of modern-day Saudi Arabia, King Abdul Aziz Ibn Saud, had prosecuted a successful war against the late Imam Yahya, leading to a territorial settlement in 1934 that saw Yemen cede the coastal town of Jizzan, and the oasis settlement of Najran some 100 miles further to the east to the Saudi potentate.[40] Even so, given the predominantly ethnic composition of these areas, the Saudis remained suspicious of Yemeni territorial irredentism.

By the summer of 1965, after nearly three years of war, Riyadh now began to seriously entertain the idea of promoting an alternative leadership to the Imamate. Their interest in exploring other political alternatives lay in no small measure in the low esteem with which they held the Imam. While he remained the personification of the Royalist struggle, al-Badr's role in planning and prosecuting the war remained conspicuous by its absence. In January 1965, McLean met the Imam and described in his official report that 'he was as friendly as always and seemed to be in good health'. Privately, he confided to his diary that the Imam and Hassan ibn Hassan, his close confidant, were '[C]hewing qat continuously. Hassan's eyes were rolling around like a toy golliwog: he seemed completely drunk'.[41] However understandable the need to escape the pressures of war, the personal probity of the Imam fell far short of the charismatic leadership required. By the spring of 1965, the Imam's uncle, Crown Prince Hassan, was largely responsible for the political direction of the Royalist campaign, while its military prosecution fell upon the shoulders of Prince Mohammed al-Hussein and his brother, Prince Abduallah.

Little went on among the *Hamud'Ud'Din* which remained unknown to the Saudis. Between Crown Prince Khalid al-Sudairi who directed Saudi operations into the Yemen from Najran; his brother Prince Mohammed, who performed a similar function in Jizzan; and the head of Saudi intelligence, Kemal Atham, King Faisal was able to remain closely informed of the eddies that shaped Royalist politics. Matters were not helped for the Imam when illness forced him to leave the sanctuary of his camp and seek treatment in Jizzan. This was much to the annoyance of the Saudis, who feared that public disclosure of his presence on Saudi soil would both confirm and inflame Cairo's suspicions of Riyadh's continued malevolence.[42]

If Royalist unity was less than the sum of its many potentates, the Republican regime in Sana'a was afflicted by distinct apraxia by the end of 1964. In December, Sallal was faced with the defection to Aden of 60 leading Republicans, all *Shaffeis,* including eight senior army officers. This exodus prompted the resignations of perhaps the three most talented members of the Sallal government: Mohammed al-Zubeiri, Abdul Rahman Iryani and Mohammed Nomaan. Dismayed by what they considered to be Sallal's incompetence, corruption and undue deference to the wishes of Cairo, they proposed a five-member 'Council for Sovereignty' be established as a collective decision-making body. This was followed by a direct appeal by Iryani for Nasser to remove Sallal, a move that met with the erstwhile President declaring a state of emergency on 5 January 1965. With a spate of political arrests among his Republican opponents, Sallal now had to face the growing momentum of a Royalist offensive amid the disintegration of his own government. The Byzantine nature of many of these intrigues did much to shed Cairo of any remaining vestige of the progressive idealism with which it had justified its intervention in Yemen. While dismissing Royalist claims (undoubtedly exaggerated), that it had killed over 6,000 Egyptian and YAR soldiers in fighting on Jebel Rezeh close to the Saudi border, the Egyptian Chief of Staff, Field Marshal Amr, did admit that since 1962, 105 officers and 1,502 other ranks had been killed in action.[43] In fact, total casualties were far in excess of this figure. Records stolen by Yemenis working at the headquarters of the Egyptian expeditionary force revealed that in the period between October 1962 and June 1964 alone, Cairo had lost 15,194 men, an average of 24 fatalities per day over this period. Without even accounting for the number of wounded, the rate of attrition this imposed on an army of some 60,000 men was unsustainable.[44] With his Republican charges in political disarray, his expeditionary force engaged in a war it could not win, and an economy distorted by the demands of funding an unwinnable war, Nasser's position in Yemen had never been weaker.

It was from these dissident Republicans that what became known as the 'Third Force' began to emerge. In an audience with McLean at the beginning of January 1965, King Faisal disclosed to the Briton meetings he had held with those associated with the movement. While they claimed to offer an alternative to Sallal, he informed McLean that they remained suspicious of British intent toward the Yemen.[45] Though recognising that the emergence of the 'Third Force' was a result of circumstances indigenous to the Republican government, McLean came to suspect that Riyadh was paying more than just lip service to its representatives. McLean harboured no illusions about the abilities of the Imam al-Badr, but he remained loyal to the ideal of the *Hamid'Ud'Din* and strongly believed that any support for the 'Third Force' on the part of Saudi Arabia, 'would weaken greatly the war against the Egyptians in the Yemen'. His fears that Faisal was considering abandoning the Royalist ship appeared well founded when he noted in one report that Prince Khaled al-Sudairi would offer his resignation as governor of Jizzan and 'Special Commissioner for the Yemen war' if his government were to transfer their support to the 'Third Force'.[46]

Prominent among the leaders of the 'Third Force' was Ibrahim al-Wazir, whose family had long vied with the Imamate for power in Yemen and who, in 1948, had attempted to usurp the *Hamid'Ud'Din* following the bloody assassination of Imam Yahya. Among the Royalists, McLean suspected that the Ahmed al-Shamy, backed by the Saudi Ambassador to London, Shaykh Hafiz Wahba, the Defence Minister, Prince Sultan and Kemal Atham was prepared to switch allegiance to the 'Third Force' as evidenced by their roles in the drafting of the *Methaq*. In effect a National Charter, the *Methaq* was an attempt to appeal to both *Zeidi* and *Shaffei* confessions by promising freedom of speech and publication within the parameters of Islamic law and where self-determination for the Yemeni people would be underpinned by the Imamate transforming itself into a constitutional monarchy, and real power being transferred to a council of ministers and a consultative assembly.[47] The controversy, however, was in the preamble to the *Methaq* which declared: 'The Yemen people are only working to drive out the Egyptians from the Yemen and are not working to put forward any party or person'. Prince Mohammed al-Sudairi, acting on instructions from Kemal Atham, presented the document at the end of February 1965 for Prince Abdurrahman ibn Yahya, the Royalist Vice-Prime Minister, and the other Princes to sign. If they had done so, it would have meant de facto 'the abdication of the Imam and *Hamid'Ud'Din* family' and 'absolved the Yemeni people from their oath of allegiance to the Imam', while giving the Saudis firm grounds upon which to transfer funding to other groups and parties 'fighting, or pretending to fight the Egyptians.'[48]

Led by Prince Mohammed bin al-Hussein and Crown Prince al-Hassan, the Princes refused point-blank to sign the original draft of the *Methaq*, though a later draft with the preamble removed met with their begrudging acceptance. Unable to obtain Royalist acquiescence, McLean believed that Kemal Atham and Crown Prince Sultan now looked to humiliate the Royalists on the battlefield in their effort to discredit the Imamate and transfer support to al-Wazir. It was for this reason that the Saudis became so insistent that Prince Mohammed bin al-Hussein launch the Humaidat operation. Having forbidden the Royalist from launching any major attacks since the signing of the truce at Erkwit the previous November, the sudden Saudi insistence that Royalist forces renew the offensive – an insistence backed by the threat to withhold future arms supplies if attacks were not forthcoming – was meant to undermine the position of the most able and charismatic of the Royalist field commanders in the belief that the attack would fail. McLean was convinced that Smiley, Mills and Johnson had been used by the Saudis to force action upon Prince Mohammed, unaware of the wider agenda being played out in the Saudi court. Smiley's accounts of the Royalist war effort rarely strayed into the realms of Saudi–Royalist relations, but having been briefed by McLean on the real reasons behind the Humaidat operation, he wrote in his official report for King Faisal:

> It has been my policy to confine myself to military matters. However, as I fear politics may effect the military situation, I consider I must record my view that the support given in SAUDI ARABIA [sic] to the "Third Party" will result in a weakening of the ROYALIST efforts against the Egyptians. This is because I have already seen signs of the ROYALISTS looking over their shoulders and taking their eyes off the target i.e. the EGYPTIANS. During the last war, when I was serving with guerrillas in Albania, the Royalists and Communists at first both fought the Germans. When it was apparent that the Germans were going to lose the war, both stopped fighting the Germans and fought each other. The result was that the Germans were able to make an unopposed withdrawal from the country. I can visualise a similar state of affairs taking place in the Yemen as I know the Royalist Amirs are already very suspicious that the SAUDI and BRITISH governments may support the "Third Party" at the expense of the Royalists.[49]

British support for the 'Third Party' was strongly advocated by John Hidyard, First Secretary at the British Embassy in Jeddah, though it remained unclear if his enthusiasm was shared by the British Ambassador, Morgan Mann. Even so, hopes entertained by some within Royalist and Saudi circles that the 'Third Force' would develop into a political movement able to bridge the *Zeidi–Shaffei* divide while remaining resolute in its opposition to Cairo's presence were soon to be dashed. Mohammed al-Zubairi, a natural ally of the 'Third Force', was assassinated on 1 April 1965. Both Republicans and Royalists, each with reasons of their own to see him removed, blamed each other for his violent demise. Whoever was responsible (and culpability was never fully established) the weight of suspicion fell on Sana'a. Both the main tribal federations, the *Hashid* and the *Bakil*, threatened to march on the Yemeni capital if Mohammed Nomaan was not appointed as Premier. Fearing the loss of the *Shaffei* tribes so crucial to his survival, Sallal, under pressure from Nasser, allowed Nomaan to form a government. It proved to be a brief interlude.

Nomaan, with his distinct Ba'athist sympathies always an irritant for Cairo, did away with the government portfolio of Minister for South Yemen, an indication that he was seeking to improve relations with London and reach an understanding over South Arabia. His attempts to broker an agreement with Royalist tribes and reach an accommodation with Riyadh, moves that implicitly called for the removal of Egyptian troops from Yemeni soil, saw Nasser turn once more to Sallal. On 27 June 1965, backed by Egyptian troops, Sallal removed Nomaan, replacing his cabinet with a Supreme Council of the Armed Forces.[50]

The composition of the 'Third Force' provided a template for the political structure that brought an end to the Yemen Civil War, but in 1965 it lacked sufficient gravity among the *Zeidi* tribes to ever be more than a loose alignment of the discontented. Crucially, it never enjoyed the unequivocal backing of King Faisal who, while arguing that its advocates had a role to play in the wider Arab world by fuelling anti-Egyptian sentiment, regarded the Royalists as the main agency for effecting the removal of the Egyptians.[51] The fact remained however that the Royalists and the BMO remained subservient to the scope and pace of Riyadh's regional agenda and while individuals such as Smiley and McLean had access to the inner working of the Saudi court, they were never in a position to impose policy upon their Saudi benefactors.

McLean's recommendations regarding his two-phase strategy never came to fruition. In a comment to the Briton that appeared to confirm Smiley's observation regarding Riyadh's calibrated approach to the war, King Faisal stated that given Egyptian superiority in the paraphernalia of war, an outright Royalist victory would remain a chimera.[52] Even so, the military initiative clearly lay with the Imam's forces, particularly in east Yemen. The strategic town of Sirwah fell to the Royalists in early June, to be followed by Qaflan, the crucible of the *Hashid* tribal federation. On 16 July 1965, the Egyptian garrison at Marib, deprived of any secure overland route to Sana'a, finally succumbed to forces led by Prince Abduallah bin al-Hussein. With seven armies, each totalling anywhere between 3,000 to 10,000 men, and with the winds of tribal allegiance blowing decidedly in their favour, the Royalists had reached the apogee of their military effectiveness.

By contrast, Nasser now turned to diplomacy, backed by thinly-veiled, though less than credible threats to expand the war into Saudi Arabia should his peace overtures come to nought. Though sufficient to prompt an RAF Canberra reconnaissance flight to ascertain if there had been any movement of Egyptian troops towards the Saudi border, the Egyptian military was in no condition to expand the fighting and Nasser knew it. On 22 August 1965, the Egyptian President flew to Jeddah to seek terms for a cease-fire. While based on the principles of the Erkwit agreement the previous November, the agreement reached at Jeddah was far-reaching. Its main provisions amounted to the terms of an Egyptian surrender in all but name. While Riyadh was required to cease military support 'of all kinds' to the Royalists forces and prevent the use of its territory for clandestine activities in the Yemen, those pertaining to Cairo had far greater political and military implications: Cairo was required to withdraw all its military forces from the Yemen within 10 months from the 23 November 1965. The declared aims of the BMO had always included the removal of the Egyptian forces from the Yemen, while ensuring the restoration of the Imamate. In the late summer of 1965, they could take some comfort that at least one of these aims had now been achieved.

The Woodhouse Reports

With the signing of the Jeddah agreement, the activities of the BMO were now, under Saudi pressure, held in abeyance. Most remained sceptical as to whether Nasser would follow through on the pledges made – troop redeployment under the guise of withdrawal having, in the past, been a favoured strategy of the Egyptian President. Even so, what might be termed the 'phoney peace' allowed time for an assessment of the overall effectiveness of the BMO to take place.

This overview and assessment was conducted by Lieutenant Colonel John Woodhouse, regarded by many, including the founder of the regiment, David Stirling, as the man most responsible for reviving the fortunes of the SAS in the post-war period, with standards of selection and self-discipline second to none. Such standards had already reaped dividends in the jungles of Malaya and Borneo as well as in the mountains of Oman. Denis Healey wrote that 'He was, by common consent among the few who know his record, the greatest guerrilla warrior yet produced by the West – a man to compare with Ho Chi Minh'. Woodhouse was rewarded by the hierarchy of the British Army for establishing the special forces unit *par excellence* by ending his army career commanding NATO rifle ranges on the north German plain.[53]

In January 1965, Woodhouse left the British Army, becoming a part-time consultant to the Foreign Office and Colonial Office on 'counter-coup measures' among the newly independent states of the Commonwealth. However, in line with McLean's phased strategy, he arrived in Yemen in July 1965 with four other Britons to organise, in his own words, 'guerrilla operations around SANA'A with the aims of forcing the Egyptians to abandon the airfields here, and damaging still further their low military prestige.'[54] He was present in the Khowlan mountains when the Jeddah agreement was signed, and with guerrilla operations now suspended, Woodhouse busied himself with writing two reports, one concerning the political and military situation in the Khowlan, the other 'on the organisation and activities of the British mercenaries in the Yemen.' Woodhouse made clear that he was acting in a private capacity, and that his identity as author of the reports should not be disclosed 'except to those in official British positions who need to know'. What he had to say amounted to a bitter pill coated in sugar.

In his first report dealing with the situation in the Khowlan, Woodhouse accentuated the positives. He highlighted the hold the Royalist forces had on the mountains surrounding the capital, a strategic advantage that was helped immeasurably by the poor location of enemy dispositions which were too widely spread and incapable of providing mutual fire support if attacked. The prospects of 'a successful ground raid' on the Arrahaba airfield were good, particularly if any raids were British-led. The delivery of the 120mm mortars with their range of 7.5 kilometres provided an alternative means of attack. He concluded that, 'If the British liaison officers are available and the special items necessary (e.g. tracer, smoke, time pencils, etc.) are supplied the operations envisaged last August (1965) could quickly be executed [if hostilities resumed].'[55] In terms of the Royalist forces, Woodhouse acknowledged the difficulties of conducting a war reliant upon tribes who, in the wake of the cease-fire, had begun to drift back to their homes. While Woodhouse recommended a retainer, amounting to a month's wages be paid to the tribes, the real key to ensuring the continued commitment to the Royalist cause, at least in the mountains of the Khowlan, lay with the tribal Shaykhs. He continued:

> In the KHOWLAN people retain their old loyalty to the Imam, and, more person-ally, to 'their' Emir ABDULLAH bin HASSAN [Hussein] and local Shaykhs. This loyalty has only been strengthened by Egyptian intervention. Though the Imam himself may be expendable, no political solution can secure the support of the KHOWLAN unless the Royal family retains a predominant position in the National Government . . . The local Sheikhs with their uncompromising attitude towards the Republican regime, and their financial interest in a continuation of the war, must be persuaded to support Royalist policies which may and should incorporate some concessions towards a less autocratic monarchy.[56]

An avowedly political observation, Woodhouse nonetheless cautioned against British mercenaries becoming involved in trying to influence the course of events beyond a strict military remit. This was not only to avoid antagonising the Saudis upon whom the edifice of Royalist resistance continued to rest; Woodhouse believed that most of the British liaison officers remained ignorant of the political complexities of the Yemen Civil War and as such, were poorly prepared to deal with the intricacies of tribal politics. Such criticism was not new, Smiley himself having asked questions previously of the calibre of individual recruited to the Yemen operation. In his observations, Woodhouse went further, calling in to question not only the calibre of the operative in the field, but also the qualifications of those running the BMO from London. In the second part of his report, he wrote under the subheading 'Organisation':

> The head of operations concerned himself with liaison and recruiting but took no part in the direction and control of operations in Yemen after allocating men to particular areas. No training or political directives were given to the mercenaries. An assistant, concerned primarily with air supply and administrative details, had no training or experience of guerrilla operations; a fact which inevitably was the cause of friction between those in the field and the headquarters in London.[57]

Under the succeeding subheading 'Achievements' he concluded that, 'In the field the mercenaries did as they pleased. A considerable amount of weapon training was undertaken and both Cooper and Mills organised successful attacks. Others did little apart from providing medical assistance and radio communications and taking air supply drops.'[58] Where criticism was being directed, Woodhouse was careful not to name names, but his description leaves little doubt that he questioned the efficacy of the Johnson–Boyle axis. It should be remembered that most of the British mercenaries recruited had been members of 21 SAS, which though producing tough, motivated soldiers, remained a part-time unit. Both Cooper and Mills had been members of the regular 22 SAS, highly professional soldiers whose experience of guerrilla operations and counter-insurgency gave them a psychological as much as a physical edge over their territorial counterparts. Moreover, given the veiled criticism of Johnson and Boyle implicit in the report it was, as Alan Hoe observed, 'Little wonder that a "them and us" situation' developed between the operatives in the field and those based back in London.[59]

However justified these criticisms may have been, the Woodhouse appraisal was perhaps unduly harsh. His experience of special operations was second to none, but this experience was formed under circumstances where the chain of command (and allegiance) were clear, the objectives – both political and military – defined and where, whatever the practical hardship endured in the field, the resources of the state were readily at hand. The BMO in Yemen enjoyed none of the above and it remains to its credit that it achieved as much as it did, often under the most appalling conditions. Woodhouse maintained that the success achieved was conditional and reminded the reader that 'The poor quality of Egyptian forces should not be forgotten in any lessons to be learned from this operation.' He concluded:

> The mercenary organisation in Yemen played a decisive part in defeating the Egyptian occupation because it sustained Royalist morale. It could have inflicted much more damage on the enemy factions had it been energetically and efficiently directed in the field. Alternatively, if better trained men had been available, its effectiveness would have been greater. Lack of equipment, particularly suitable radios, was a further disadvantage of the amateur status of the organisation, but this weighed more in the minds of the members than it did on the adverse effect on operations.[60]

Given the emphasis that the two old SOE hands – Smiley and McLean – placed on improved radio communications in their reports, the appreciation made by Woodhouse was notable for its variance. Even so, there is some weight to his observation regarding the need for better trained personal and the 'amateur status' of the BMO. Having emerged out of immediate need rather than a planned structure, the BMO acted more as an umbrella organisation than a coherent military unit. While there is a case to be made that more efficient leadership could have led to greater losses being inflicted on the Egyptians, the numbers recruited to the operation remained tiny in proportion to the forces and areas to which they were attached. If official government indulgence of their activities had been more generous, less hesitant and informed by a greater appreciation of the gains to be had in relation to the Federation, then the observation that they could, and perhaps should have achieved more might have carried greater conviction.

Personality clashes both among the BMO hierarchy and the operatives in the field now began to undermine moral. This was in part, brought about by the Jeddah agreement, since, at a stroke, a question mark was placed over the role of the BMO as Smiley went about renegotiating salaries and retainers for the operatives involved. At a more prosaic level, the advent of summer had seen a number of tensions emerge among and between the various national elements of the BMO. At the beginning of July, Johnson wrote to Smiley that one British radio operator was becoming increasingly unpopular with the French, while L'Amiral had become 'persona non-gratta [sic] with JC [Johnny Cooper] and [David] Bayley.' In truth, such tensions among men living cheek by jowl in primitive conditions was to be expected.[61] Of far greater significance were tensions emerging among the hierarchy of the BMO itself.

Under the structure of the BMO established in the autumn of 1963, Neil McLean held the position of diplomatic and political advisor. Given his close ties with Riyadh and Amman, he was the natural choice for such a portfolio and felt, accordingly, that matters of protocol were best dealt with under his counsel. Under the self-same structure, Johnson's responsibilities as the overall task force commander and treasurer included ensuring that the operatives received prompt payment for service rendered in the field. Now, with the Saudis committed to the Jeddah agreement, lines of hierarchy and responsibility conflated to bring about a clash between McLean and Johnson. Johnson felt aggrieved that Riyadh was stalling over the payment of salaries to operatives still in the field. On 19 November 1965, Johnson, along with Smiley and Ahmed al-Shamy, held a meeting with the Saudi Defence Minister, Crown Prince Sultan, to try and resolve the issue. Smiley later confided to his diary, 'The talks lasted over an hour but Jim's approach was very tactless and obviously resented by Amir Sultan, so no result was reached other than being told to write a report.'[62] Smiley found himself in an unfortunate position, with loyalties on all sides. Even so, he felt the wrath of McLean who was aggrieved that not only had Johnson tried to usurp his role, but that in doing so he had offended their Saudi paymasters. Smiley's fault, in McLean's eyes, was his failure to control his errant colleague.

On 1 January 1966, agreement was reached for the renewal of contracts on a four-month basis. Even so, the dissent within the hierarchy of the BMO was never resolved to anyone's satisfaction. McLean remained ill at ease with Johnson's presence, complaining to Smiley that Johnson's plans for future operations smacked of 'opportunism' and that Smiley should 'not be too modest about laying down the law over talking to those who have *not* been there [the Yemen] and do *not* know the form'.[63] By the autumn of 1966, the BMO had become a shell of its former self, and while Smiley, McLean and Johnson continued in their efforts to sustain the Royalist cause, its effectiveness diminished exponentially. By the spring of 1967, disputes over the leadership and direction of the BMO had come to a head, with a clear split emerging between Ahmed Al-Shamy, Neil McLean, David Stirling and Julian Amery on one side, and Jim Johnson and Tony Boyle on the other. The split, ostensibly over command structures and payment was resolved when Johnson and Boyle tendered their resignations, unable to secure either the support or confidence of Crown Prince Sultan or Kemal Atham.[64] From a Royalist perspective, it was an unfitting denouement to an operation that had helped force Nasser back to the negotiating table.

Conclusion

On 24 November 1965, under the provisions of the Jeddah agreement, representatives of both the Republican government and the Royalists attended a meeting at Harad, just inside the Yemen, to discuss the formation of a provisional government and steps to be taken towards holding a national referendum. Both Cairo and Riyadh oversaw proceedings, even going as far to establish a UAR–Saudi peace commission as a sign of bilateral good faith. At a symbolic level, the Harad conference was a triumph for the Imam since it represented de facto recognition of the Royalists existence by Nasser. But such symbolism failed to be translated into any tangible political process. From the outset, mutual acrimony and suspicion marked proceedings: Republicans demanded the exclusion of the *Hamid'Ud'Din* from any provisional government, a position that contradicted the Jeddah agreement which clearly stated that any interim authority be neither Republican nor Royalist. In response, the Royalist delegation insisted on the immediate withdrawal of all Egyptians before a plebiscite could be held; again, a demand that ran counter to the ten-month period granted to Cairo to remove its forces. These points of dispute were never resolved. After one month of barren effort, the conference went into recess without any symbiosis of views having been achieved. The only agreement reached was to reconvene on 20 February 1966.[65]

It appeared that Nasser was abiding by the Jeddah agreement. On 30 September 1965, the Cairo daily newspaper *Al-Ahram* stated that from December onwards, 10,000 troops would be brought back to Egypt every month over seven months. This, as O'Ballance noted, confirmed that the Egyptian Expeditionary Force had numbered at least 70,000 soldiers.[66] In the autumn of 1965, Smiley wrote:

> [I]t is generally thought that there is a genuine desire on Nasser's part to withdraw his troops from the Yemen, though many Yemenis have asked me why it should take ten months to do so. The answer, I believe, lies in the problem of Aden. So long as Nasser has troops in the Yemen, particularly in the south near Taiz [sic] his intelligence officers are able to train and organise the terrorist attacks in Aden. When the Egyptians go these attacks might well cease. It is my view that Nasser is betting on getting the British out of Aden within the next twelve months, while he still has troops in the Yemen. It remains to be seen if he is right.[67]

While his assessment proved accurate, Smiley could not have foreseen that it was to be British policy that saved Nasser. At a stroke, the rationale for removing all his troops from Yemen was gone. Instead, buoyed by London's apparent lack of political will, Nasser felt emboldened enough to concentrate his forces in the Sana'a–Hodeidah–Taiz'z triangle in a strategy that became known as the Long Breath. While he continued to reduce overall troop numbers, there still remained 20,000 Egyptian troops within the triangle by May 1966, and the numbers rose to 60,000 again by November. In support of his volte-face, the Egyptian President expressed disappointment that the Jeddah agreement had not produced the outcomes expected and that accordingly 'he could not abandon the

Yemeni revolution', announcing in the process that he was prepared to commit troops to the defence of Sana'a for another five years. The timing of its release, rather than the actual decision to vacate Aden and the Federation, meant that the British Defence White Paper had saved Nasser from the consequences of his own actions. From May 1966 until the final British departure from Aden, guerrilla attacks and incidents of terrorism remained on an ever upward trajectory.[68] Given the relative success of the Royalist forces throughout 1965, and the contribution made by the BMO, (which despite its deficiencies, contributed greatly to the defeat of Egyptian designs in Yemen), Britain had lost a gilt-edged chance to determine the scope, terms and direction of its eventual departure from South Arabia. Political defeat had truly been snatched from the jaws of military victory.

Conclusions

Political Conviction and the BMO

Emboldened by London's decision to withdraw unconditionally from Aden and abandon its defence commitments to the Federation, Nasser, under the strategy of the Long Breath, looked to consolidate the Egyptian troop presence in the Sana'a–Taiz'z–Hodeidah triangle while free to offer every incentive to the NLF to expedite the departure of the British. Casualty figures between 1966 and 1967 demonstrate the price paid by British servicemen in defending a Federal structure that London had already committed itself to leaving.[1] In a belated attempt to court wider international legitimacy for the FSA, London began to discuss the efficacy of inviting United Nations observers into the Federation in advance of Britain's final departure. It was hoped that their presence would be tantamount to de facto recognition by the UN of the FSA. Attending a meeting of the Chiefs of Staff on 28 September 1966, Sir Bernard Burrows, Chairman of the JIC, argued that '[T]he establishment of a United Nations presence in the Federation in advance of independence would encourage the longer-term acceptance of some responsibility by the United Nations for the protection of the independent state after our departure'.[2] It was also hoped that under the principle of reciprocity, pressure could be brought to bear on Cairo for UN observers to based in and around Taiz'z, still regarded as the epicentre of Egyptian subversive activities against the Federation, though the Chiefs of Staff acknowledged that any UN presence on the border would effectively terminate 'any [British] deniable operations on the frontier'.

By the autumn of 1966, the scale of such operations, alongside continuing contacts with operatives of an ever diminishing BMO, were hardly of a magnitude to negate the perceived advantages to be gained by courting New York. In a position paper regarding the future of what he called the 'European Advisory Group', Jim Johnson wrote of the 'stated indifference to our [British Mercenary Organisation] activities by MI6 (SIS) coupled with the absolute disinterest and lack of use of us at the moment by HRH [Crown Prince] Sultan'. He posited three possible

217

scenarios for the future of the BMO: to effect a total withdrawal of all operatives from the Yemen; for the BMO to become a purely intelligence gathering organisation; and to 'hang on, on the chance that things the other side of the hill are even worse, and that though we have no hope of winning it may be that they [the Egyptians] will loose first'. Johnson admitted, however, that the transformation into an intelligence gathering organisation remained beyond the capabilities of the BMO. Their ethos, and indeed their role in training tribesmen, advising the Royalist commanders and engaging in the occasional ambush or act of sabotage, had always been closer to the ethos that had informed the work of SOE than SIS. Johnson himself wrote:

> If we consider becoming an intelligence gathering and political advice service, we would [be] require[d] to reorganise and to recruit a new type of field operator. These, Arab speaking trained political officers, are not available from any present sources, though their radio operators are, and so we would not be able to continue, and only the Foreign Office [responsible for SIS] could take on this role.[3]

Johnson, citing the Royalist victories of 1965 as the template of success, concluded that '[I]t is in the vital interests of Great Britain and the West, that every clandestine effort should be continued to obtain the withdrawal of the Egyptian Armed forces from the Yemen before we [the British] withdraw finally from Aden and the Gulf'. Johnson continued to believe that only the Saudis could provide the level of support required and raising the spectre of Nasser firmly entrenched in Aden and Sana'a, urged Riyadh once more to dispense its military and financial munificence among the tribes.[4]

Although the rationale for his involvement with the Royalist cause had been removed with the 1966 Defence White Paper Neil McLean remained loyal to the restoration of the Imamate. Aside from the growing personal antipathy between himself and Johnson however, Saudi dealings with the 'Third Party' convinced him that if Riyadh could secure a neutral, independent Yemen, free of Nasser, but also the *Hamid'Ud'Din*, it would cut the requisite deal. As such, while Saudi largesse in all forms would continue to be welcome, McLean now put his energies into securing alternative sources of military support that would allow the Royalists to lessen their military as well as political dependence upon Riyadh.

One month after Johnson wrote his position paper, McLean travelled to Tehran with Prince Mohammed bin al-Hussein to secure a substantial increase in Iranian support. McLean did not meet with the Shah directly, but his subsequent report revealed that in conversation with the Yemeni Prince, the Iranian monarch had 'agreed to give as much as possible of the military supplies requested.' This request was substantial, and included

50,000 rifles, 100×0.5 heavy machine guns, over 130 recoilless rifles of varying calibre, as well as other considerable quantities of military stores. Where deficiencies existed in the material requested, the Shah's Chief of Staff, General Nasseri, promised that Iran would 'purchase that equipment which [we] have not at present got.' Whether the Royalist request was ever met in full is not clear, but they certainly received one substantial delivery from Iran in October 1967.[5] This Iranian commitment to secure the Royalist position also extended to training. Not only was it agreed that 100 Yemenis would be selected for training in Iran, but such training would include induction in the nefarious skills of 'terrorism and sabotage'. In addition, 20 Iranians with the requisite skills would be sent to the Yemen to train Royalist tribesmen, a mission that appeared to rival as much as complement the existing activities of BMO operatives.[6]

Prince Mohammed bin al-Hussein, alongside his brother, Abduallah, had emerged as the most effective of the Royalist Princes. He had always refused to equate gratitude with dependence and as such, remained suspicious of Riyadh's wider agenda. Given that the Royalist armies remained reliant on Saudi subventions, his entreaties to the Iranians were calculated to reassert the hegemony of the *Hamid'Ud'Din*. His striving for greater military as well as political autonomy from the Saudis now drew the ire of his erstwhile benefactors, Ahmed al-Shamy and Prince Hassan bin al-Hassan, both deemed reliable courtiers by Riyadh, who requested via Mclean for the Prince to return post haste to Jeddah for urgent consultations with the Saudis. This the Yemeni refused to do until he had consulted officials in Amman. In fact, King Hussein had suggested that Tehran might be willing to shoulder a greater part of the Royalist war effort and subsequently facilitated the Yemeni potentate's trip to Tehran. The Hashemite monarch had his ardour for the Royalist cause somewhat dampened by American threats to withhold aid, and in 1963 had been pressurised by Washington into formally recognising the YAR. While he conceded that he could not 'un-recognise the Yemen Arab Republic lest this inflame domestic opinion', he agreed to send some instructors back to the Yemen.[7]

Prince Mohammed knew that the Saudis were unlikely to allow the scale of arms he had requested to pass unhindered through Najran and Jizzan, and as such, he looked once more to the overland routes from Beihan State, and where expedient, the use of air drops to supply the tribal areas of the *Hamdan, Bani Matar, al-Haimatain* and *Anis*. Their continuing allegiance was crucial to maintaining the siege around the capital, Sana'a.[8] Who exactly would deliver these supplies and from where remained undisclosed, but the need to circumvent the strictures placed by Riyadh on the flow of arms and supplies to the Royalists – which had hitherto allowed King Faisal to control the scale, if not the scope of the

Royalist endeavour – made airborne re-supply drops an attractive option. There was substance to this accusation. Despite the lavish amounts spent on the French mortar project, Jim Johnson revealed that some of the mortar tubes and base plates were, almost a year later, languishing in Saudi military bases close to the Yemen border. The best that could be said in defence of the Saudi position was that they remained committed to the terms of the Jeddah agreement despite Nasser's volte-face.

Other observers who had spent time with the Royalists conceded that by the autumn of 1966 the flow of arms and money from Saudi Arabia 'was intermittent.' Among the more colourful of these individuals was the explorer and Arabist Wilfred Thesiger. He was known to McLean from their shared association with Abyssinia (now Ethiopia and Eritrea) during the Second World War before going on to serve with the SAS in the Western Desert. In his biography of this great traveller, Michael Asher dismisses the suggestion that Thesiger was engaged in intelligence gathering in the Yemen. However, Thesiger's claim that he was in a war zone to study 'Arabic dialects' lacked conviction, not least because, according to Asher, Thesiger had always shown contempt for 'linguistic dilettantism'. Thesiger proved more than just an interested observer. On his return to London in December 1966 he met with members of the DIS, and highlighted the fragility of the Egyptian lines of communication, concluding that a determined push by the Royalists, whom he regarded as the only alternative to the Republican regime in Sana'a, would bring about its demise. Even so, he was less than generous in his appreciation of the Royalist Princes, noting that there was no outstanding leader among them, while 'The small number of British mercenaries with the Royalists were, on the whole, not very effective. Their greatest value lay in their ability to operate wireless communications which the Arabs did badly'.[9]

Twelve days later, a report prepared by an unnamed member of the Defence Intelligence Staff on the veracity of Thesiger's account was sent to the Secretary of State for Defence, Denis Healey. While in agreement with much of his analysis, the DIS paper believed Thesiger had overestimated the precariousness of the Egyptian position, noting that in any case, the relative size of the EEF was of little importance compared to activities of the Egyptian Intelligence Service based in Taiz'z. It was from here that Cairo's malfeasance towards the Federation had always been organised and which continued to be the epicentre of 'terrorist and dissident operations' aimed against the British, in particular in Aden. The report also challenged Thesiger's claim that the Royalists were the only political alternative, arguing that 'A nucleus of moderate Republicans, some in exile in Saudi Arabia and less extreme Royalists exists which could provide an alternative government.'[10]

If terrorism continued to define the conflict in Aden, however, a form of violence of an altogether different magnitude forced events in Yemen back onto the conscience of the world: the chemical weapons attack on the village of Kitaf, just across the border from Najran. On 5 January 1967 nine Egyptian Illuyshin-28 bombers dropped 27 bombs containing phosgene gas on the village. Although the target was reckoned to be a Royalist cave complex close to the village, most of the casualties were civilian. In his account, the accuracy of which was confirmed six months later by a leaked report from the International Committee of the Red Cross, McLean wrote 'All but 5% of the people within two kilometres downwind of the bombs impact point have died, or in the opinion of the Red Cross representatives are likely to die. Deaths now total over 200'.[11] Many felt that Nasser was using such attacks so close to the Saudi frontier to exert psychological pressure on Riyadh to cease all involvement in the Yemen Civil War. King Faisal, equally keen to claim the moral high ground, requested that the United Nations investigate the tragic events at Kitaf, only to receive the rather lame reply by UN Secretary-General U Thant that 'he was "powerless"' to take the matter further.[12]

Regional events elsewhere, however, finally brought about the withdrawal of the EEF from Yemen. On 5 June 1967, Israel launched a devastating attack on Egypt which destroyed the Egyptian Air Force on the ground and smashed its army in Sinai. Within days of this pre-emptive strike, the IDF was on the banks of the Suez Canal with the Sinai peninsula under its total control. At the time of this military humiliation, which Nasser had done much to bring upon himself by becoming prisoner to his own hubris, Egypt still had over 50,000 troops in the Yemen.[13] In this regard, Israel was perhaps the true beneficiary of the Yemen Civil War, able to secure a military victory that gave it a strategic depth it had hitherto only dreamed of while over one-third of the Egyptian army remained mired in a guerrilla conflict elsewhere. The legacy of that victory continues to shape politics in the Middle East today, not just in terms of Israel's continued occupation of Palestinian land, but in shattering the hope that Arab Nationalism could be anything more than an intellectual dream. The result has been an often uneasy relationship between dominant one-state Nationalism and the exponential rise of various forms of Islamism – ranging from the fundamental yet functional to the radical – that now dominate the political landscape of the Arab world.[14]

The outcome of the June 1967 war not only proved a watershed in the Arab–Israeli conflict, but also proved a catalyst for change in the Yemen Civil War. With his armed forces in ruins, Nasser had little choice but to evacuate the bulk of his army from Yemen, effecting a total withdrawal of all his ground forces by October 1967, one month before the final British withdrawal from Aden. The immediate consequence of the

Egyptian departure was the fall of Sallal. Never a popular figure even among those who supported the idea of a Republic, the removal of Egyptian patronage denied him the means to secure his position. Deposed in a bloodless coup, he went in to exile in Iraq, to be replaced by General Hassan al-Amri, whose main virtue lay not only in his hostility to the *Hamid'Ud'Din* but the deep loathing in which he had held Sallal for his asinine leadership. Al-Amri embodied a political position that had wide appeal: no return of the Imamate but, equally, independence from Cairo.

Still, by December 1967, his grip on power appeared tenuous. Emboldened by the generosity of the Shah and helped, albeit begrudgingly, by the Saudis, Royalist forces under Prince Mohammed bin al-Hussein looked set to take the capital, Sana'a. Ranged against a Royalist army that had, 5000 trained soldiers and could call upon 30,000 tribal warriors, al-Amri only had 7,000 poorly trained troops with low morale. Desperate times produced innovative measures, and the new Republican President managed to raise a 10,000 strong popular militia from its mainly *Shaffei* inhabitants to rally to the capital's defence. At the same time, al-Amri turned to Moscow for help. In January 1968, the arrival of 30 Soviet-piloted aircraft allowed the Republic to dominate the skies above Yemen, bombing and strafing the Royalist positions at will. Having filled the vacuum left by the departure of the British from Aden and crushed the rival claims to power of FLOSY, the NLF also offered its support to al-Amri. In retrospect, reliance on siege warfare rather than a direct assault on the city proved the undoing of the Royalist cause. By the end of January, the tribesmen began to drift back to their villages, bored by the long periods of inactivity, unhappy with the irregular nature of their pay and increasingly demoralised by the constant air attacks. The siege of the city was lifted finally on 8 February 1968 when a strong force of Republican troops with Soviet advisers in tow fought their way up from the port of Hodeidah. Prince Mohammed bin al-Hussein had lost his best chance take the capital, win the war and restore the *Hamid'Ud'Din* dynasty.[15]

Concern in Riyadh at the appearance of Soviet advisors in Yemen was enough to convince King Faisal that an accommodation with the existing rulers in Sana'a be sought as a matter of urgency. In March 1968, Saudi Arabia finally stopped all military and financial aid to the Royalist forces. Without the financial and martial wherewithal to bribe the tribes and sustain their immediate allegiance, the Royalists forces quickly became shadows of their former selves. When in December 1968 the last Royalist stronghold at Hajja fell to the Republicans, a submission achieved more through bribery than martial prowess, the Yemen Civil War was effectively over. By June 1969, the Saudis were engaged in detailed, secretive discussions with both Republicans and Royalists in Jeddah over the formation of a government that would enjoy the political and financial backing of Riyadh on condition that Soviet encroachment was curtailed forthwith. Such diplomacy produced the required outcome. A coalition government emerged that also embraced members of the 'Third Party', and in a move designed to placate fears of retribution in those areas that had demonstrated either pro-Royalist or pro-Republican sympathies, governors of the requisite political hue were appointed. Such magnanimity was not however extended to the members of the *Hamid'Ud Din*. All Princes were excluded from government, with Prince Mohammed bin al-Hussein setting an example by seeking voluntary exile in Saudi Arabia. As for his cousin, Mohammed al-Badr, the last Imam of the *Hamid'Ud'Din* and in whose name the Royalist cause was fought, he too went in to exile, ending his days in the relative obscurity of the English Home Counties.

In Retrospect: Ministers, Mercenaries and Mandarins

The story of British policy towards the Yemen Civil War can be told as a number of 'ifs': *if* Britain had chosen to recognise the YAR in 1962; *if* a Conservative government had bowed to the advice of the Aden Group and engaged wholeheartedly in covert support for Royalist cause; *if* the intelligence collation and assessment more accurately reflected developments in the war itself, in particular in the spring and summer of 1965; *if* a Conservative government had been re-elected in October 1964; *if* the Labour government had delayed announcing its decision to abandon the Aden base by four months. Different decisions, taken at what, in retrospect, were crucial points in the conflict could have produced different results. In the event, only Saudi Arabia achieved anything near its optimal outcome.

What is clear is that British policy towards the Yemen Civil War was never pursued with a unity of purpose or applied with sufficient vigour to safeguard the one asset that until February 1966 all governments, of whatever political persuasion, maintained was crucial to the well-being of Britain: the Aden base. The policy of trying to force the square peg of Aden to fit with the round hole of the Federation can be derided as the great act of colonial self-delusion, but it should not be forgotten that whatever the political animus between the Federal potentates and nationalist leaders, this experiment in state creation almost succeeded. In the past, it has been sufficient to blame its failure on the aforementioned contradictions, but a comprehensive account also has to embrace the impact of the Yemen Civil War on decision-making in Whitehall.

That British policy towards securing the Federation was hamstrung from the start cannot be denied. The legacy of Suez and the need to secure the goodwill of Washington while attempting to cohere the Federation into a viable entity meant that policy in Whitehall was always determined by the lowest common denominator. Recognition of the YAR was the most apposite example. Afraid of Washington's reaction if it withheld *de jure* recognition, but fearful of alienating a Federal political elite of its making if it did, the Macmillan government fudged making a decision until Sallal decided the issue.

Such timidity was also reflected in the manner in which clandestine activity came to determine policy towards the Yemen in the spring and summer of 1964. This was a policy that emerged from the diplomatic lacuna which defined relations with Sana'a and Cairo. The need to assuage increasing unease among the Federal rulers was always tempered by the legacy of Suez. The scale of operations against Egyptian-backed dissidents inside the Federation in the spring of 1964 may have been an attempt to demonstrate London's commitment to their political longevity, but as the relatively minor retaliatory strike on Harib demonstrated, 'imperial noise', however justified, did little to further the cause of the Federation among an already sceptical Arab world or in the wider court of world opinion. In its aftermath, officials in Whitehall felt Britain had few other options but to engage in clandestine activity. Since the 1950s London had engaged in 'special operations' inside the Yemen, mainly linked to fermenting tribal dissent, but by 1964 such special operations were the least preferred method of ensuring stability inside the Federation and were never embraced by London with the enthusiasm required to ensure a measure of longer-term success.

This was most clearly seen in the attempt by McLean in the summer of 1964 to harness RANCOUR operations to aid the beleaguered Royalist armies. In keeping with their own mandate, the government of Alec Douglas-Home refused to entertain the idea. Only one operation that went beyond the confines of RANCOUR was ever sanctioned and this remained limited to one target rather than being linked to the wider Royalist war effort: Egyptian intelligence assets in Taiz'z. In a policy best described as one of benign neglect, London was more than happy to allow responsibility for supporting the Royalist cause to fall on Saudi shoulders. This brings to the fore the question of government collusion with the BMO. On reflection, British government links with this mercenary organisation were not as strong as some observers assumed, but certainly more than they were willing to admit. Cabinet ministers were well aware of the activities of McLean and Smiley and records show that until October 1964, the BMO and its operatives enjoyed unfettered access to Aden and Beihan State, access that should have been denied them if officials in Government House had not paid convenient lip service to the idea of

Federal sovereignty. As such, the policy of 'benign neglect' that emerged suited all those concerned.

The emergence of the BMO was a response to what those associated with the Aden Group regarded as a lack of political will – best seen in the tardy response of the leadership in Broadway – for 'cloak and dagger' initiatives. Although many of the operatives later briefed SIS officers on their way to and from the Yemen, the evidence available suggests that the relationship between senior management in Broadway and the BMO was one of mutual circumspection, hardly what one would expect of an operation that had been officially sanctioned by the government. It should be remembered that David Smiley, a former member of both SOE and SIS, was warned by John Bruce Lochheart that his intention to travel to the Yemen was in direct contradiction of the declared government policy of non-intervention. To this must be added the apparent disregard with which the British intelligence machinery treated the reports handed over by individual operatives to SIS officers stationed in the Federation and Jeddah and presumably passed back to London. There is no evidence in the relevant JIC reports now publicly available that material passed over ever informed a broader assessment or 'estimate' of developments in the Yemen. If the report produced by Daniel McCarthy is an accurate guide, one can only conclude that suspicions of bias prejudiced the impact that such reports might otherwise have had on assessments and policy-making in Whitehall. A greater appreciation of what had been achieved with the help of the BMO in Yemen could have changed the timing, if not the context under which Britain eventually withdrew from South Arabia. This is not to suggest that the rationale behind the decision was flawed, but, when taken alongside Nasser's record of disavowing commitments previously entered in to, it suggests that the government of Harold Wilson was guilty of pious naivety at best and wilful ignorance at worst.

This leads on to the military effectiveness of the BMO. The fact that it was formed at all demonstrates the influence that powerful individuals, notably McLean and Amery, could exercise over foreign governments, who bankrolled its creation. Christopher Gandy may well have been right in his assessment that those responsible for its creation were moved by a 'nostalgia for lost causes'. Even so, between the spring of 1963 and the autumn of 1965 the BMO was driven by a moral certitude that set it apart from the bloody excesses of future mercenary operations. Bernard Mills sums up this 'can do' attitude particularly well:

> If the tribesmen were properly led, which was always terribly difficult, and properly directed then we, as a small force could achieve a great success against a conscript army who didn't want to be there [Yemen] in the first place . . . it was very exciting, it was very exciting because at one stage, we [the BMO] one actually thought, were changing the course of history and one felt we could create

countries in a better image if they were tied to Britain – probably an incredibly arrogant thing to say [then] but we felt we probably could.[16]

The overall military worth of the BMO remains the subject of some debate. The quality of some of the operatives was dubious and both John Woodhouse and Wilfred Thesiger believed it to be less than the sum of its parts. There is some weight to these criticisms but given the relatively small numbers involved (no more than 50 operatives were present in the Yemen at any one time), the primitive conditions under which they operated, the paucity of equipment and supplies, the often haphazard nature of the command structure and the vagaries of tribal politics, their achievements were considerable. It must be remembered that their primary role was not to actually fight, but to train and advise the Royalist forces and their commanders: to impart the necessary skills, supported by a coherent communications network, which allowed a guerrilla campaign to unfold that played to the Royalist strengths. It was an organisation willing to take considerable risks in securing supplies from other sources, such as Israel (and later Iran), despite its overall dependence on Saudi largesse. Given the diplomatic repercussions that would have ensured had Riyadh, let alone Cairo, discovered the clandestine involvement of the Jewish State, it demonstrates the extent to which the BMO considered attainment of the desired end more than justified the risk involved. Johnny Cooper summed up this twilight world when, reflecting on the diplomatic intricacies of the mercenary operation, he noted that it was mounted by governments who approved of its objectives 'but who were not intimately involved in all stages'.[17]

But the organisation was ultimately beholden to Riyadh and as such, the BMO was always a tool, albeit an effective one, serving the broader interests of Saudi foreign policy. Any sentiment for the maintenance of a fellow dynastic regime came a poor second when balanced against the need to ensure the survival of the al-Saud. From the outset, the BMO had three aims: first, the maintenance of the British position in South Arabia; second, the restoration of the *Hamid'Ud'Din*; and third, the defence of Saudi Arabia. If outcomes are the benchmark of success, then the BMO ultimately failed in its endeavours, though in mitigation, the House of Saud was secured while the composition of the new government in Sana'a was more pro-Western. But a sense of failure ultimately pervades. As David Smiley remarked, 'The cause which McLean and I had tried for five years to help was dying; even our reason for helping was scarcely valid any longer, for the Russians were already in Aden at the invitation of the NLF. At least the experience was familiar to us both: the enthusiasm, the excitement, the hardship, the danger – and the final disappointment.'[18]

In the immediate aftermath of Britain's withdrawal from Aden, the military journalist Anthony Verrier wrote:

> It is of course legitimate to argue that since the British government continued to recognise the Royalist regime . . . it was entitled to support them [the Royalists] by whatever means in chose. The means actually chosen however, were so devious, so costly, and so involved that they not only undermined the security of the Federation but did nothing to contribute to any successes in the field which the Royalists sought and which their more partisan British supporters constantly claimed.[19]

The real failure however, was not, as Verrier suggests, the means chosen, but the fact that, having decided upon covert action, such operations rarely carried the courage of Whitehall's political conviction. Operations were unproductive and failed to stem the rising tide of violence in the Federation itself, while eschewing any need to develop HUMINT assets inside the Yemen that could inform policy-making in Whitehall. The reluctance to make better use of the reports produced by BMO operatives remains *the* intelligence failure of the British government in the spring and summer of 1965. The Foreign Office, in particular under the governments of Macmillan and Home, may have felt itself to be the poor relation in Cabinet decision-making, but their diplomatic sensitivities were of sufficient weight to ensure that those clandestine operations that were sanctioned remained reactive and limited in scope. It might not have altered the actual decisions made, but at least the *process* of decision-making would have been better informed.

The dilemmas facing British policy-makers in the early 1960s over the civil war and the context in which policy was decided upon were unique to the conditions in Yemen and Whitehall in the mid-1960s. Even so, the lessons of this war are not without relevance in the contemporary world. The problem of achieving defined ends among societies, such as in Afghanistan, where tribal loyalty suffused with religious piety remains the primary mode of political agency, would be familiar to the those ministers, mercenaries and mandarins who had to deal with the Byzantine politics of Yemen. Equally however, the extent to which PMO/Cs should be included as part of the foreign policy process echoes the dilemmas surrounding how successive British governments in the 1960s should deal with an organisation that legitimised its actions in defence of the realm, maintained contact with the bureaucracies of state, but ultimately operated beyond its sovereign purview. In a world where the privatisation of military force continues to grow exponentially, it remains a dilemma that has yet to be adequately addressed.

Notes

Introduction: Themes and Issues

1 For accounts of the origins Lebanese Civil War see David Gilmour, *The Fractured Country* (London: Sphere Books, 1984); Robert Fisk, *Pity the Nation: Lebanon at War* (Oxford: Oxford University Press, 1991); Hussein Sirriyeh, 'Lebanon: Dimensions of Conflict', *Adelphi Paper* No. 243 (London: Brasseys/IISS, 1989).

2 Donald Snow, *Uncivil Wars* (London: Lynne Rienner, 1997).

3 Stathis N. Kalyvas, 'New and "Old" Civil Wars: A Valid Distinction', *World Politics*, Vol. 54, No. 1 (October 2001), pp. 99–118.

4 For a full discussion of the link between Neo-medievalism and Civil Conflict see Philip Cerny, 'Neo-Medievalism, Civil War, and the New Security Dilemma: Globalisation as Durable Disorder', *Civil Wars*, Vol. 1, No. 2 (1998), pp. 36–64.

5 For an account that is damning of the way in which the UN was used and manipulated over events in a civil war, in this case, the former Yugoslavia see Brendan Simms, *Unfinest Hour: Britain and the Destruction of Bosnia* (London: Allen Lane/Penguin Publishers, 2001).

6 For a trenchant criticism of Washington's self-perceived need to fight casualty free wars, see Michael Ignatieff, *Virtual War* (London: Chatto and Windus, 2000), pp. 161–203.

7 Lieutenant Colonel Tim Spicer, *An Unorthodox Soldier: Peace and War and the Sandline Affair* (Edinburgh: Mainstream Publishing, 1999). For a detailed account of the struggle in Sierra Leone see John L. Hirsch, *Sierra Leone: Diamonds and the Struggle for Democracy* (London: Lynne Rienner, 2001).

8 For an account that was supportive of the role played by PMOs in West Africa in mitigating the worst excesses of violence against civilians see William Shawcross, *Deliver us From Evil: Peacekeepers and Warlords in a World of Endless Conflict* (London: Bloomsbury, 2000).

9 P. W. Singer, 'Corporate Warriors: The Rise of the Privatized Military Industry and its Ramifications for International Security', *International Security*, Vol. 26, No. 3 (Winter 2001/02) pp. 93–198.

10 David Shearer, 'Outsourcing War', *Foreign Policy*, No. 112 (Fall 1998), p. 68.

11 Shearer, 'Outsourcing War', p. 68.
12 Singer, p. 191.
13 For one such informed and objective account of the role performed by merce-
    naries in warfare, see James Larry Taulbee, 'Reflections on the Mercenary
    Option', *Small Wars and Insurgencies*, Vol. 9, No. 2 (Autumn 1998), pp.
    145–63.
14 Ken Silverstein, *Private Warriors* (London: Verso, 2000), pp. 160–1. In truth,
    many PMO/Cs would fall uncomfortably close to this definition, particularly
    those whose origins lie in highly militarised societies. One such company, the
    Israeli based 'Spearhead Limited' established by Colonel Yair Klein, sold its
    undoubted expertise in anti-terrorism to a variety of clients, state and non-
    state alike. These clients were alleged to have included the Colombian drugs
    baron, Gonzalo Rodriguez whose own private militia received instruction in
    the finer points of assassination and bomb-making, as well as the
    Revolutionary United Front, a particularly vicious participant in the Civil
    War in Sierra Leone who specialised in the forced amputation of limbs of
    those, irrespective of age and gender, suspected of siding with the central
    government.
15 Fred Halliday, *Arabia without the Sultans* (Harmondsworth: Penguin Books,
    1975), p. 140.
16 'The Mayfair Set: David Stirling', *BBC2* (UK) Broadcast 19 July 1999.
17 David Smiley (with Peter Kemp), *Arabian Assignment* (London: Leo Cooper,
    1975), p. 155.
18 See Michael Warner, 'Wanted: A definition of "Intelligence"', *Studies in
    Intelligence* (CIA Unclassified), Vol. 46, No. 3 (2002), at
    <www.cia.gov/csi/studies/vol56no3/article02.html>.

I Britain and the Yemen Civil War: Prelude to Intervention

1 DEFE 13/570 77705 Top Secret: Meeting of Chiefs of Staff Committee, Aden
   and the South Arabian Federation, Note by the Secretary to the Chiefs of Staff
   Committee, Air Vice-Marshal J. H. Lapsley, 30 June 1964.
2 See for example, Karl Pieragostini, *Britain, Aden and South Arabia:
   Abandoning Empire* (London: Macmillan, 1991), p. 174.
3 Christopher Gandy, 'A Mission to Yemen: August 1962–January 1963',
   British Journal of Middle East Studies, Vol. 25, No. 2 (1998), p.249.
4 Karl Pieragostini, *Britain, Aden and South Arabia: Abandoning Empire*
   (London: Macmillan, 1991); Joseph Kostiner, *The Struggle for South Yemen*
   (London: Croom Helm, 1986); Robert McNamara, *Britain, Nasser and the
   Balance of Power in the Middle East 1952–1967* (London: Frank Cass,
   2003); Glen Balfour-Paul, *The End of Empire in the Middle East* (Cambridge:
   Cambridge University Press, 1991).
5 Parker T. Hart, *Saudi Arabia and the United States: Birth of a Security
   Partnership* (Bloomington and Indianapolis: Indiana University Press, 1998),
   p. 150.
6 J. B. Kelly, *Arabia, the Gulf and the West* (New York: HarperCollins, 1980),
   p. 46.

7 For example, see Kennedy Trevaskis, *Shades of Amber: A South Arabian Episode* (London: Hutchinson, 1968).

8 Jacob Abadi, 'Britain's Abandonment of South Arabia – A Reassessment', *Journal of Third World Studies*, Vol. XII, No. 1 (1995), p. 155.

9 Abadi, p. 152.

10 Abadi, p. 159.

11 Thomas R. Mockaitis, *British counterinsurgency in the post-imperial era* (Manchester: Manchester University Press, 1995), p. 45.

12 See for example, Joel Migdal, *Strong Societies, Weak States* (Princeton: Princeton University Press, 1988), pp. 142–76.

13 Quoted in Mockaitis, p. 46.

14 DEFE 13/570 77705 Top Secret: Chiefs of Staff Committee, Aden and the South Arabian Federation, 30 June 1964.

15 Spencer Mawby, 'The Clandestine Defence of Empire: British Special Operations in Yemen 1951–64', *Intelligence and National Security*, Vol. 17, No. 3 (Autumn 2002), pp. 110–12.

16 See Kostiner, pp. 38–52.

17 Balfour-Paul, p. 69.

18 Trevaskis, p. 157.

19 Trevaskis, p. 155.

20 Ritchie Ovendale, *Britain, the United States, and the Transfer of Power in the Middle East, 1945–62* (Leicester: Leicester University Press, 1996), pp. 192–4.

21 L. J. Butler, *Britain and Empire: Adjusting to the Post-Imperial World* (London: I. B. Tauris, 2002), p. 144; Ovendale, pp. 216–41.

22 Anthony Nutting, *No End of a Lesson: The Story of Suez* (London: Constable, 1996), p. 22.

23 McLean's maiden speech to the House of Commons made much of the fact that he believed Nasser was little more than the unwitting tool of Soviet expansion throughout the region. For the full text, see Xan Fielding, *One Man in his Time: The Life of Lieutenant-Colonel NLD ('Billy') McLean DSO* (London: Macmillan, 1990), pp. 101–3.

24 Amery's comments, made at the time of the Yemen revolution, were screened as part of the documentary 'The Mayfair Set: David Stirling', *BBC2* (UK), 18 July 1999. In the aftermath of the overthrow of the Hashemite dynasty in Iraq, and attempts to subvert its counterpart in Jordan, Amery argued that 'Britain should retain sufficient forces in the Middle East to fight a limited war with Egypt'. See McNamara, p. 141.

25 Fred Halliday, *Arabia without the Sultans* (Harmondsworth: Penguin Books, 1975), p. 75; R. D. Burrows, *The Yemen Arab Republic: The Politics of Development, 1962–1986* (Boulder, CO: Westview Press, 1987), p. 34.

26 S. M. Badeed, *The Saudi–Egyptian Conflict over North Yemen 1962–1970* (Boulder, CO: Westview Press, 1986), p. 10.

27 Halliday, p. 84.

28 For a definition of an elite in Arab political discourse see Elie Podeh, *The Decline of Arab Unity: The Rise and Fall of the United Arab Republic* (Brighton & Portland: Sussex Academic Press, 1999), pp. 11–18.

29 Halliday, p. 93.
30 Halliday, pp. 90–5.
31 Halliday, p. 93.
32 M. A. Zabarah, 'The Yemeni Revolution seen as Social Revolution', in Brian Pridham (ed.), *Contemporary Yemen: Politics and Historical Background* (London: Croom Helm, 1984), p. 76.
33 Dana Adams Schmidt, *Yemen: The Unknown War* (London: Bodley Head, 1968), p. 24.
34 Leigh Douglas, 'The Free Yemeni Movement 1935–62 ', in Pridham (ed.), p. 38.
35 A. Z. Al-Abdin, 'The Free Yemeni Movement, 1940–48 and its Ideas on Reform', *Middle East Studies*, Vol. 15, No. 1 (January 1979), pp. 36–48.
36 Schmidt, p. 93.
37 Douglas, p. 38.
38 Halliday, p. 84.
39 Schmidt, pp. 25–50.
40 Schmidt, p. 25.
41 IWM-NMP, Box 20. Report on visit to the Yemen, 4–16 December 1962 by Lt. Col. Neil McLean DSO, MP. Part IV, Appendix 1. 'The Imam's Confession'.
42 Schmidt, p. 24.
43 Schmidt, p. 34.
44 Schmidt, p. 20.
45 Halliday, p. 106.
46 Schmidt, p. 122.
47 Schmidt, p. 46.
48 Podeh, p. 192.
49 Podeh, pp. 191–2.
50 IWM-NMP, Box 9. Most Secret. Report on visit to the Yemen 27th–30th October 1962 by Lt. Col Neil McLean DSO, MP. Part II, notes on conversation with King Saud; Nadav Safran, *Saudi Arabia: The Ceaseless Quest for Security* (Cornell: Cornell University Press, 1988), p. 91.
51 CO 1055/11 80075 Confidential: Research Department Memorandum. The Yemeni claim to Aden (LR 6/18), 12 June 1964.

2   The Legacy of Yemeni Irredentism: The Debate over Recognition of the YAR

1   CAB 130/189 Gen 776 The Yemen. Second Meeting, 31 October 1962.
2   CAB 130/198 Gen 776 The Yemen. Second Meeting, 31 October 1962.
3   CAB 130/198 Gen 776 The Yemen. Second Meeting, 31 October 1962.
4   W. Taylor Fain, 'Unfortunate Arabia: The United States, Great Britain and Yemen, 1955–63', *Diplomacy & Statecraft*, Vol. 12, No. 2 (June 2001), p. 141.
5   Tom Bower, *The Perfect English Spy* (New York: St. Martin's Press, 1995), p. 246; Stephen Dorril, *MI6: Fifty Years of Special Operations* (London: Fourth Estate, 2000), p. 679 (fn. 7).
6   Christopher Gandy, 'A Mission to Yemen: August 1962–January 1963', *British Journal of Middle East Studies*, Vol. 25, No. 2 (1998), p. 263.

7 CO 1055/11 Confidential: Research Department Memorandum (LR 6/18) The Yemeni Claim to Aden, 12 June 1964.

8 Spencer Mawby, 'The Clandestine Defence of Empire: British Special Operations in Yemen 1951–64', *Intelligence and National Security*, Vol. 17, No. 3 (Autumn 2002), pp. 105–30.

9 Zaki Shalom, *The Superpowers, Israel and the Future of Jordan 1960–1963: The Perils of the Pro-Nasser Policy* (Brighton & Portland: Sussex Academic Press, 1999), p. 44.

10 IWM-NMP, Box 20, Report on Visit to the Yemen 4–16 December 1962 by Lt. Col. Neil McLean DSO, MP. Part IV, Appendix 1, 'The Imam's Confession'.

11 IWM-NMP, Box 20, Report on Visit to the Yemen, 4–16 December 1962 by Lt. Col. Neil McLean DSO, MP. Part IV, Appendix 1, 'The Imam's Confession'.

12 DEFE 25/128 (File No. 10623/142) Top Secret: From High Commissioner Aden to Secretary of State for the Colonies, 31 May 1962.

13 CAB 130/189 Gen 776: The Yemen: Minutes of Cabinet Meeting, 26 October 1962.

14 CAB 130/189 Gen776: The Yemen: Minutes of Cabinet Meeting, 31 October 1962.

15 Bower, p. 244.

16 Xan Fielding, *One Man and his Time: The Life of Lieutenant-Colonel NLD 'Billy' McLean DSO* (London: Macmillan, 1990).

17 For a full account of British intervention in Jordan in July 1958 see Ritchie Ovendale, *Britain, the United States and the transfer of power in the Middle East, 1945–1962* (Leicester: Leicester University Press, 1996), pp. 198–215.

18 Shalom, p. 41.

19 Uriel Dan, *King Hussein and the Challenge of Arab Radicalism: Jordan 1955–1967* (Oxford: Oxford University Press, 1989), p. 119.

20 Dan, p. 124.

21 Dan, p. 126.

22 DEFE 25/125. Confidential annex to meeting of 23 October 1962. Subject Retaliatory Action against the Yemen – Photo Reconnaissance.

23 DEFE 13/570 77705, Letter from Colonel Michael Webb to Julian Amery, 20 August 1964. The letter recalls Amery's statement.

24 Bower, p. 244.

25 Bower, pp. 244–5.

26 Fielding, p. 107.

27 Bower, p. 244.

28 IWM-NMP, Box 3. Handwritten notes on first trip to Yemen.

29 IWM-NMP, Box 19, Handwritten inventory of Jordanian aid to Royalist forces, October 1962. This inventory was written on a House of Commons compliment slip.

30 Gandy, p. 255.

31 IWM-NMP, Box 19. Amman, Jordan. Notes on conversation with Sir Roderick Parkes, H. M. Ambassador in Amman, Sunday, 21 October 1962; Notes on conversation with Italian Ambassador in Amman, Armando Ghia, 25 October 1962.

32 IWM-NMP, Box 3. Secret Telegram. From the Office of the Governor, Aden to Secretary of State for Colonies, London, 26 October 1962, 934 Priority/Secret.

33 See Robert McNamara, *Britain, Nasser, and the Balance of Power in the Middle East 1952–1967* (London: Frank Cass, 2003), p. 180.

34 IWM-NMP, Box 9. Most Secret. Report on Visit to the Yemen 27–30 October 1962 by Lt. Col. Neil McLean DSO, MP. Part II, Notes on conversation with King Saud.

35 For a detailed discussion of the struggle for power in Saudi Arabia during this times see Sarah Yizraeli, *The Remaking of Saudi Arabia* (Tel Aviv: Dayan Centre Papers 121/Tel Aviv University, 1997), pp. 147–97.

36 IWM-NMP, Box 19. Saudi Arabia: General notes on visit to Riyadh, 22/23 October 1962.

37 IWM-NMP, Box 19. Jordan Military Mission in Riyadh.

38 IWM-NMP, Box 19. Aden, Notes on Conversation with Brigadier Lunt, the Officer commnading the Federal Army, 26 October 1962; Aden: Notes on Conversations 25/27 October 1962.

39 IWM-NMP, Box 19. Aden and Beihan 25/27 October 1962.

40 Bower, p. 243.

41 IWM-NMP, Box 19. Copy: The Royal Palace, Amman, Jordan 30 October 1962. From Maclaine [sic] to Gen. Habes Mejali, Jordanian Delegation, Riyadh.

42 IWM-NMP, Box 9. Most Secret: Report on Visit to the Yemen 27–30 October 1962.

43 IWM-NMP, Box 9. Most Secret: Report on Visit to the Yemen 27– 30 October 1962. In a telegram sent to London on 1 November to Alec Douglas-Home and Duncan Sandys McLean wrote, 'I felt he [Prince Hassan] is perhaps too gentle and humane to lead the tribes in guerrilla war. For example, many [of the tribesman] could not understand his humane treatment of a captured Yemeni captain who is a great friend of Sallal and a sworn enemy of the Royal family. See IWM-NMP, Box 9, Text of Report by Colonel Neil McLean MP on his journey in Yemen between October 27 and 30.

44 IWM-NMP. Box 19. Most Secret: Report on visit to the Yemen, 27–30 October 1962 by Lt. Col. Neil McLean DSO, MP.

45 IWM-NMP. Box 19: The Yemen: General Notes.

46 CAB 130/198 Gen 776 The Yemen: Second Meeting, 31 October 1962.

47 IWM-NMP, Box 19. My remarks to King Saud, 30 October 1962.

48 Neil McLean MP, 'With the Loyalists in the Yemen: A report form the first foreign observer to visit the Imam's forces', *The Daily Telegraph & Morning Post*, 6 November 1962.

49 IWM-NMP, Box 19. Letter form Neil McLean to Crown Prince Faisal, 9 November 1962.

50 Yizraeli, p. 181.

51 IWM-NMP, Box 19. Notes of meeting with Hafiz Wahba, London, 9 November 1962.

52 IWM-NMP, Box 4. Letter from G. K. N. Trevaskis, British Agency, Western Aden Protectorate, Ittihad, to Colonel Neil McLean DSO, MP, 21 November 1962.

53 Kennedy Trevaskis, *Shades of Amber: A South Arabian Episode* (London: Hutchinson, 1968), p. 182. IWM-NMP Box 4. McLean sent letters to the following Conservative MPs and Party members on 30 November 1962: Julian Amery MP, Hugh Fraser MP, The Right Honourable Earl of Dundee, Peter Thorneycroft MP, Nigel Fisher MP, Sir Tufton Beamish MP, John Biggs-Davison MP. Along with the letters he enclosed copies of his first report to the Yemen with instructions that they be circulated to other members of the Conservative Party.

54 IWM-NMP, Box Unnumbered. Notes on Conversation with King Hussein, 1–2 December 1962.

55 IWM-NMP, Box 20. Report on Visit to the Yemen, 4 December–16 December 1962 by Lt. Col. Neil McLean DSO, MP. Section III (1) Visit to the Imam.

56 IWM-NMP, Box 20. Report on Visit to the Yemen, 4 December–16 December 1962 by Lt. Col. Neil McLean DSO, MP. Section III (1) Visit to the Imam.

57 IWM-NMP, Box 20, Report on Visit to the Yemen, 4 December–16th December 1962 by Lt. Col. Neil McLean DSO, MP. Section II(3) Morale and Strength of the Loyalists.

58 Bower, p. 247.

59 IWM-NMP, Box 4. Letter from Neil McLean DSO, MP, to the Prime Minister, The Rt Hon Harold Macmillan MP, the Prime Minister, The Admiralty, Whitehall, SW1, 19 December 1962.

60 IWM-NMP, Box 4. From Admiralty House, Whitehall, SW1 to Neil McLean Esq DSO, MP, 22 December 1962.

61 Gandy, p. 254.

62 Gandy, pp. 249–50; Bower, 246.

63 Gandy, p. 250.

64 Gandy, p. 254.

65 Gandy, p. 252.

66 FO 371/168831 77705, 'United Nations: Seventeenth Session, General Assembly: Provisional Verbatim Record of the Twelve hundred and Second Plenary meeting, New York, Thursday 20 December 1962.

67 FO 371/168831 7705. Confidential: Yemen. From C. T. Crowe to A. R. Walmsley 22 December 1962.

68 Taylor Fain, p. 140.

69 FO 371/168823. Quoted in Gandy, p. 272.

70 CAB 130/198 Gen 776: The Yemen. Third Meeting, 5 February 1963.

71 CAB 130/189 Gen 776: The Yemen. Third Meeting, 5 February 1963.

72 Gandy, pp. 247–74.

73 Taylor Fain, p. 143.

74 Gandy, pp. 263–4.

75 CO 1055/13. Inward Telegram, Secret: From Aden (Sir C. Johnston) to the Secretary of State for the Colonies, 12 March 1963.

3 *Between Whitehall and the White House: Anglo-American Relations*

1 Major-General Carl Von Horn, *Soldiering for Peace* (London: Cassell, 1966), p. 356.

2 FO371/174485 (B 103145/8) Confidential Memo from J. A. Snellgrove to F. D. W. Brown, 15 October 1964.

3 W. Taylor Fain, 'Unfortunate Arabia: The United States, Great Britain and the Yemen, 1955–63', *Diplomacy and Statecraft*, Vol. 12, No. 2 (June 2001), p. 135.

4 CO 105511 80075 (LR 6/18) Confidential. Research Department Memorandum, The Yemeni claim to Aden, 12 June 1964.

5 IWM/NMP, Box 36. 'Full text of letter sent by the Imam of Yemen to President Kennedy, Thursday 6 December 1962'.

6 Parker T. Hart, *Saudi Arabia and the United States: Birth of a Security Partnership* (Bloomington and Indianapolis: Indiana University Press, 1998), pp. 143–4.

7 Michael B. Bishku, 'The Kennedy Administration, the U.N. and the Yemen Civil War', *Middle East Policy*, Vol. 1, No. 4 (1992), p. 118.

8 Bishku, p. 119.

9 Douglas Little, 'President Kennedy and Arab Nationalism', *Journal of American History*, Vol. 75, No. 2 (1988), p. 506.

10 Taylor Fain, pp. 138–9.

11 CAB 130/189 Gen 776: The Yemen, Third Meeting, 5 February 1963.

12 Bishku, p. 122.

13 Dana Adam Schmidt, *Yemen: The Unknown War* (London: Bodley Head, 1968), p. 188.

14 IWM/NMP, Box 19. Record of meeting with Hafiz Wahba, Saudi ambassador to the Court of St James, 15 November 1962.

15 Hart, p. 158. The US Ambassador to Cairo raised the issue of these air drops with Nasser during the course of a meeting on 4 March 1963. According to the British Ambassador in Cairo, Sir Harold Beeley, 'Nasser neither acknowledged nor denied' their existence. FO 371/168831 77705 (BM1071/7) Secret: Cairo to Foreign Office, Telegram No. 165, 7 March 1963.

16 Bishku, p. 119.

17 Little, p. 515.

18 Hart, pp. 205, 210–12.

19 FO 371/168831 77705. Draft reply for Mr Heath of Parliamentary Question by Mr John Biggs-Davison, 26 February 1963. It was also pointed out that Britain had used napalm during the Second World War. To condemn Yemen openly in the forum of the UN of using napalm would, it was felt, have left London open to the charge of hypocrisy.

20 FO 371/168831 77705. From Foreign Office to New York – United Kingdom Mission to the United Nations, Telegram No. 869, 4 March 1963.

21 FO 371/168831 77705: Confidential, Dr Bunche's visit to the Yemen, 4 March 1963.

22 FO 371/168831 77705: Confidential, From Foreign Office To UK Mission New York, Telegram No. 868, 4 March 1963.

23 FO 371/168831 77705: From Aden (Sir C. Johnson) to the Secretary of State for the Colonies, Confidential, Telegram No. 254. Accompanying Bunche was the Yemeni representative to the UN, Moshin al-Aini, who had been deported from Aden in January 1961 following attacks he made in the Aden

press against Imam Ahmed, deemed to be in violation of the 1934 status quo Agreement between Yemen and the United Kingdom. Bunche had allowed al-Aini onto the aircraft as a favour as the Yemeni wished to travel to Cairo. Bunche gave assurances that al-Aini would behave during his enforced transit with discretion. Al-Aini was not placed under any restraint.

24 FO 371/168831 77705 (BM1071/6): Secret. From Sir C. Johnson to the Secretary of State for the Colonies, No. 255, 5 March 1963.

25 FO 371/168831 7705 (BM1071/6): Secret. From C. Johnson to the Secretary of State for the Colonies, No. 256, 5 March 1963.

26 FO 371/168831 77705 (BM1071/6) Subject: Impression of visit to Yemen as conveyed by Dr Bunche (handwritten note – Brian Pridham) 8 March 1963.

27 CAB 130/189 Gen 776: Fourth Meeting 6 March 1963.

28 See for example FO 371/168831 77705: Secret, From Foreign Office to Cairo, Telegram No. 326, 6 March 1963. The telegram detailed reports that that US Ambassador in Cairo, John Badeau, had delivered a 'stiff message to Nasser about these attacks'.

29 FO 371/168831 77705: Secret, From Cairo to Foreign Office, Telegram No. 165, 7 March 1963.

30 FO 371/168831 77705: En Clair, From Cairo to Foreign Office, Telegram No. 167, 7 March 1963.

31 FO 371/168331 77705: Confidential. From New York to Foreign Office, Telegram No. 321, 9 March 1963.

32 For a detailed analysis of Ellsworth Bunker's diplomatic efforts see Hart, pp. 168–90.

33 FO 371/168831 77705: Secret. From Washington to Foreign Office, Telegram No. 753, 11 March 1963.

34 FO 371/168831 77705: Confidential. From Jedda to Foreign Office, Telegram No. 74, 14 March 1963.

35 FO 371/168831 77705 (BM1071/13): Confidential. The Yemen: Discussions with Dr Bunche, 11 March 1963; FO 371/168831 77705: Confidential. From Foreign Office to New York, Telegram No. 933, 12 March 1963.

36 FO 371/168831 77705 (B1071/14): Confidential. From New York to Foreign Office, Telegram No. 333, 13 March 1963.

37 FO 371/168831 77705 (BM1071/16) Secret: From Washington to Foreign Office, Telegram No. 820, 16 March 1963.

38 FO 371/168831 77705 (BM1071/16) Secret: From Washington to Foreign Office, Telegram No. 820, 16 March 1963.

39 IWM/NMP, Box 49. Notes on conversation with Crown Prince Faisal, March 1963. Exact date is omitted from the record.

40 FO 371/168831 7705 (BM1071/16) Subject: Account of Mr Bunker's First Mission to the Saudi Arabia, 19 March 1963.

41 PREM 11 4298 Secret: From Washington to Foreign Office, Telegram No. 1140, 12 April 1963.

42 Hart, p. 190.

43 Von Horn, p. 297–8.

44 IWM/NMP, Box 39. Letter from Tony Boyle, Government House, Aden to Neil McLean, 10 May 1963.

45 Bishku, p. 123; Fawaz A. Gerges, 'The Kennedy Administration and the Egyptian-Saudi conflict in Yemen: Co-opting Arab Nationalism', *Middle East Journal*, Vol. 49, No. 2 (Spring 1995), p. 307.

46 Von Horn, p. 298–9.

47 PREM 11 4928 Confidential: From New York to Foreign Office, Telegram No. 718, 15 May 1963.

48 Karl Th. Birgisson, 'United Nations Yemen Observation Mission', in William J. Durch (ed.), *The Evolution of UN Peacekeeping* (London: Macmillan, 1993), p. 211.

49 PREM 11 4928 Confidential: From New York to Foreign Office, Telegram No. 710, 15 May 1963.

50 PREM 11 4928. Confidential: From Washington to Foreign Office, Telegram No. 1532, 18 May 1963.

51 Birgisson, pp. 213–14.

52 PREM 11 4928 En Clair. From New York to Foreign Office Telegram No. 877, 18 June 1963.

53 IWM/NMP, Box No. 9. Secret: Conversation with Amir Faisal, June 1963.

54 Smiley wrote extensively about his experiences in the Yemen. In total, he made 13 trips to Saudi Arabia and Yemen of varying length over the next five years. See David Smiley, *Arabian Assignment* (London: Leo Cooper, 1975), pp. 103–237.

55 PREM 11 4928 Confidential: From Jedda to Foreign Office, Telegram No. 311, 20 June 1963.

56 IWM/NMP, Box No. 9, Letter to Sir Colin Crowe, 4 July 1963.

57 David Smiley Papers (hereafter DSP) – The Yemen, First Trip: Letter from G. W. Wilson, Private Secretary, Secretary of State for War to Colonel D. de C. Smiley MVO, OBE, MC, 26 August 1963; Interview with Colonel David Smiley, London, 6 August 2002.

58 DSP, The Yemen: The Second Trip. Handwritten letter from David Smiley to Tom Dammann, 10 January 1964; David Smiley, 'Nasser's Air Terror', *The Yorkshire Post*, 5 May 1963.

59 PREM 11 4928 Confidential: From Foreign Office to Washington, Telegram No. 6702, 19 July 1963; DSP – The Yemen, First Trip: Transcript of BBC Light programme, 'Radio Newsreel', broadcast 18 July 1963; Transcript of Border Independent Television programme 'Focus', broadcast 10 September 1963.

60 PREM 11 4928 Confidential: From Jedda to Foreign Office, Telegram No. 457, 28 July 1963.

61 PREM 11 4928 Confidential: From Jedda to Foreign Office, Telegram No. 463, 30 July 1963.

62 PREM 11 4928 Confidential: From Jedda to Foreign Office, Telegram No. 488, 6 August 1963.

63 DSP – The Yemen, First Trip: United Nations – From Carl Von Horn to David Smiley, Sana'a, 23 August 1963.

64 Schmidt, p. 199.

65 PREM 11 4928 Secret: From Foreign Office to Washington, Telegram No. 7957, 15 August 1963.

66 Schmidt, p. 199.
67 Quoted in Bishku, p. 127.
68 PREM 11 4928 Secret: Minutes of conversation between the President of the United States and Lord Home, Washington D.C., 4 October 1963.
69 Gerges, pp. 308–9.
70 Central Intelligence Agency: Intelligence Information Cable: Nasir's reaction to President Johnson's speech at the Weizmann Institute TDCS – 3/572, 910, 9 February 1964. Declassified 13 October 1976. Copy held in Lyndon Baines Johnson Library; Central Intelligence Agency – Intelligence Information Cable: Nasir's Comments on his meeting with Assistant Secretary Talbot TDCS 3/574, 978, 3 March 1964. Declassified 13 October 1976. Copy held in Lyndon Baines Johnson Library.
71 PREM 11 4928 Secret: Memo from Foreign Secretary Rab Butler to the Prime Minister, 21 November 1963.
72 PREM 11 4928 Secret: Memo from Colonial Secretary Duncan Sandys to the Prime Minister, 22 November 1963.
73 CAB 130/189 Gen 776 The Yemen: Fifth Meeting, 2 December 1963. Recorded as present at this meeting were Alec Douglas-Home (Prime Minister), Rab Butler (Foreign Secretary), Duncan Sandys (Colonial Secretary), Nigel Fisher MP (Parliamentary Under-Secretary of State for commonwealth Relations and for the Colonies, Peter Thorneycroft (Secretary of State for Defence), Stuart Crawford, Assistant Under-Secretary of State at the Foreign Office.
74 IWM/NMP, Box 6, 'General Impressions – October 1963'.
75 PREM 11/4928: Note for the record, 18 December 1963. Meeting between the PM and Colonel David Smiley at 10 Downing Street, Thursday 17 December 1963.
76 FO 371/174485 Confidential: Minute by R. S. Crawford – United States Support for the UK position in Aden, 6 March 1964.
77 FO 371/174634 (BM 1041/43) Secret: Yemen/South Arabia – Memorandum for Discussion, Frank Brenchley, 13 March 1964.
78 FO 371/174633 (BM 1041/39) Confidential: Minute by T. F. Brenchley on Fourth Report of the Secretary General on Disengagement in Yemen, 9 March 1964; FO 371/174634 (BM 1041/42) Secret: Draft Memorandum by Sir Stuart Crawford, 13 March 1964.
79 FO 371/174634 (BM 1041/44) Confidential: From Washington to Foreign Office, Telegram No. 1058, 18 March 1964.
80 FO 371 174627 (BM 1022/59G) Secret: Record of Defence and Overseas Policy Committee Meeting, 19 March 1964.
81 FO 371 174628 (BM 1022/154 G) Top Secret: Yemen – The Harib Incident, 14 April 1964.
82 FO 371 174628 (BM 1022/153 G) Confidential: Minutes of Cabinet Meeting on Yemen, 16 April 1964.
83 FO 371 174635 (BM 1041/64) Secret: From Washington to Foreign Office. Subject: UAR/Yemen threat to Federation of South Arabia, Telegram No. 1454, 18 April 1964.
84 FO 371/174635 (BM 1041/64G) Secret: From Aden to the Secretary of State for the Colonies, 23 April 1964.

85 FO 371 174635 (BM 1041/64(B)), Secret: From Cairo to Foreign Office, Telegram No. 308, 24 April 1964.
86 FO 371 174635 (BM 1041/96) Confidential: From Washington to Foreign Office 27 April 1964.
87 DEFE 25/129 Top Secret: Recommendations prepared by the Chief of Staff to the Secretary of State for Defence for the Defence and Overseas Policy Committee meeting, 23 April 1964, 20 April 1964.
88 FO 371 174635 Top Secret: Record of a meeting between the Foreign Secretary, Mr Butler, and the United Secretary of State, Mr Rusk, at the State Department, Washington D.C., 27 April 1964.
89 FO 371 174485 Secret: Record of part of meeting with Mr Ball, Under-Secretary of State at the Foreign Office, 8 June 1964.
90 FO 371 174485 (B 10314/2G) Personal and Secret: From J. E. Killick, British Embassy, Washington to Edward Peck Foreign Office, 15 June 1964.
91 Kennedy Trevaskis, *Shades of Amber: A South Arabian Episode* (London: Hutchinson, 1968), pp. 219–20.
92 DEFE 13/570 77705: Secret: US Aid to the Yemen, 25 June 1964.
93 FO 371/174485 Secret: From Jedda to Foreign Office, Telegram No. 521, 24 August 1964.
94 DEFE 13/570 77705 Secret: From Secretary of State for Defence to the Chief of the Defence Staff, Subject: Caravans of Egyptian Arms, 25 June 1964; DEFE 13/570 77705 Secret: From Aden to the Secretary of State for the Colonies, Subject: Second Front in Dathina, 26 July 1964.

4 A Constrained Response: The Limits of Covert Action

1 For a full account of Foreign Office thinking see Christopher Gandy, 'A Mission to Yemen: August 1962–January 1963', *British Journal of Middle East Studies*, Vol. 25, No. 2 (1998), pp. 247–74. Gandy was the last British representative to Ta'iz, the diplomatic capital of the former Imamate before relations were severed in February 1963.
2 Percy Craddock, *Know Your Enemy: How the Joint Intelligence Committee saw the World* (London: John Murray, 2002), p. 204.
3 DEFE 25/128: Confidential Annex from CinC MIDCOM to Sir Hugh Stephenson: Subject PR over flights, 23 October 1962.
4 DEFE 25/128 From High Commissioner Sir Charles Johnstone to the Colonial Secretary. Subject: PR flights, 18 January 1963.
5 Tom Bower, *The Perfect English Spy* (New York: St. Martin's Press, 1995), p. 248.
6 FO 371 174634 (BM 1041/3/G) From: R. S. Crawford. Subject: Training by Egypt of dissident Tribesman, 2 January 1964.
7 DEFE 13/570 77705, Top Secret – Chief of Staff Committee: Aden and the South Arabian Federation. 30 June 1964.
8 DEFE 13/570 77705 Top Secret: From Lieutenant-General Sir Charles Harington to Admiral of the Fleet, The Earl Mountbatten of Burma. 11 June 1964.
9 Imperial War Museum Sound Recording 13041/3: Brigadier David John Warren. Warren was attached to the FRA from 1964 to 1966.

10 CO 1055/11 80075. Secret: From Sir Kennedy Trevaskis to Christoper Eastwood, Colonial Office. Letter from Sharif Hussein bin Ahmad al-Habili, 2 December 1963.

11 CO 1055/29: Top Secret – From Sir Kennedy Trevaskis to Secretary of State for the Colonies, 19 March 1964; C0 1055/29 Top Secret: From CinC MIDEAST to MOD London 27 March 1964.

12 CO 1055/29 Top Secret: From MOD London to CinC MIDEAST – Operational Immediate, 27 March 1964.

13 CO 1055/11 80075: Secret and Personal: From Sir Kennedy Trevaskis to Secretary of State for the Colonies, 12 March 1964.

14 CO 1055/11 80075. Secret: From Brenchley to R. C. A Shegog, Colonial Office, 18 March 1964.

15 CO155/29, Top Secret: From Sir Kennedy Trevaskis to Secretary of State for the Colonies, 20 March 1964.

16 FO 371 174627 (BM1022/59 G) Foreign Office Minutes of DOPC Meeting held on 20 March 1964, by R. S. Crawford, 24 March 1964.

17 CO/1055 29: Confidential – From D. J. McCarthy, Foreign Office to Colonial Office and Ministry of Defence, 30 March 1964.

18 CO 1055/29 (FS/64/36): Top Secret – the Yemen. From R. A. Butler to Secretary of State for Defence, 6 April 1964.

19 FO 371/174639 BM/1051/10 Subject: Parliamentary question by Mr Michael Foot MP for Ebbw Vale.

20 PREM 11/4928, Situation in the Yemen: Memo from Foreign Secretary Butler to the Prime Minister 21 November 1963.

21 FO 371/174648 BM 1022/59G, 24 March 1964. Minute by R. S. Crawford concerning comments of Foreign Secretary Butler in a meeting of the Defence and Overseas Policy Committee, 19 March 1964.

22 FO 371/174634 BM 1041/3G Subject: Training of Dissident Tribesmen, 2 January 1964.

23 FO 371/174627 BM 1022/61 Subject: Memo to the Prime Minister (PM/64/38) from R. A. Butler, 1 April 1964.

24 FO 371 174636 BM1041/130 Subject: Record of conversation between Ambassador Robert Ford and Mohammed Heikal. Cable forwarded by Canada House to the Foreign Office, 12 May 1964.

25 IWM/NMP, Box 6. Notes on conversation with Paul Carton, 1–2 June 1964.

26 DEFE 13/569 Top Secret Minute from Foreign Secretary Butler to the Prime Minister. Subject: Record of conversation with Secretary of State Dean Rusk. 20 April 1964.

27 FO 371 174627 BM/1022/59 G The Yemen: Record of DOPC meeting, 19 March 1964.

28 DEFE 25/129 From J. H. Lapsley, Air Vice Marshal and Secretary to the Chief of Staff to the Secretary of State for Defence. Subject: Recommendations prepared by the Chiefs of the Defence Staff for the Defence and Overseas Policy Committee meeting, 23 April 1964: Date 20 April 1964; DEFE 25/129 Marked Top Secret: From acting Chief of the Defence Staff to the Prime Minister. Subject: Elimination of sources of subversion, 22 April 1964.

29 FO 371 174627 BM/1022 /59 G The Yemen: Record of DOPC meeting, 19 March 1964.

30 FO 371 174635 BM/1041/64 From: Sir Kennedy Trevaskis to Secretary of State for the Colonies, Duncan Sandys, 23 April 1964.

31 DEFE 25/129 From: Chiefs of Staff Committee to the Chief of the Defence Staff. Subject: Special Flights over the Yemen, 2 April 1964.

32 DEFE 13/569 Top Secret: From Foreign Secretary Rab Butler to the Prime Minister, 10 April 1964.

33 DEFE 13/570 77705 Secret: From Aden (Acting High Commissioner) to the Secretary of State for the Colonies: Subject: Caravan of Egyptian Arms, 24 June 1964.

34 DEFE 13/570 7705, From Aden (Acting High Commissioner) to Secretary of State for the Colonies, Subject: Caravans, 30 June 1964.

35 DEFE 13/570 77705: Top Secret. From the Chief of the Defence Staff to the Secretary of State for Defence. Subject: Infiltration of Egyptian Arms into the Western Aden Protectorate, 3 July 1964.

36 DEFE 13/570 77705 Top Secret: Aid to Royalists, 19 July 1964.

37 DEFE 13/570 7705 Top Secret: Yemen – Memorandum for Consideration by Ministers at DOPC on 22 July 1964, dated 21 July 1964.

38 DEFE 13/570 77705 Top Secret: From Aden (Acting High Commissioner to the Secretary of State for the Colonies), Subject: Supply of Arms, 12 August 1964.

39 DEFE 13/570 77705 Secret: From Aden (Acting High Commissioner) to the Secretary of state for the Colonies, Subject: Dissident Activity 24th/25th July 1964, 27 July 1964.

40 DEFE 13/570 77705 Top Secret: From CINC MIDEAST to MOD UK, 9 July 1964; DEFE 13/570 77705 Secret: From MOD UK to CINC MIDEAST 10 July 1964.

41 PREM 11/ 4938: Subject: The Yemen. Memo from Foreign Secretary Butler to Prime Minister Alec Douglas Home, 21 November 1963.

42 CAB 130/189 GEN 776: The situation in the Yemen, 2 December 1963.

43 PREM 11/4928: Secret. From Cairo (Sir Harold Beeley) to Foreign Office (No. 702), 12 September 1963.

44 PREM 11/4928: Note for the Record, 18 December 1963. Meeting between the PM and Colonel David Smiley at 10 Downing Street, Thursday 17 December 1963. The Foreign Office was informed of the gist of the meeting *after* it had occurred.

45 David Smiley (with Peter Kemp), *Arabian Assignment* (London: Leo Cooper, 1975), p. 166.

46 PREM 11/4928 Secret: Text of conversation between President of the United States and the Lord Home, 4 October 1963.

47 FO 371 174627 BM 1022/59G. Memorandum by Stuart Crawford on meeting of the Defence and Overseas Policy Committee, 19 March 1964: Subject: Yemen and the South Arabian Federation, 24 March 1964.

48 Edgar O'Ballance, *The War in the Yemen* (London: Faber, 1971), p. 128.

49 DEFE 13/570 77705. Note of Discussion with Colonel McLean, on 20 June 1964, 2 July 1964.

50 DEFE 13/570 77705 Top Secret: Chiefs of Staff Committee, Aden and the South Arabian Federation, 30 June 1964.

51 PREM 11/4980 Note for the Record: Meeting between the Prime Minister and Sir Peter Agnes, Mr Neil McAllen, Mr Paul Williams, Mr Michael Clark-Hutchinson, Mr Anthony Fell, Mr F. W. Bennett, 30 June 1964.
52 DEFE 13/570 77705. Covering Letter form Julian Amery to R. A. Butler, 25 June 1964. Letter form Colonel Gerald de Gaurey to Julian Amery, 20 June 1964.
53 DEFE 13/570 77705, Top Secret. From Julian Amery to Rt Hon. R. A. Butler, 7 July 1964.
54 DEFE 13/570 77705 Secret: From Foreign Office to Jedda: Subject, The Yemen, 18 July 1964.
55 DEFE 13/570 7705 Top Secret: From Jedda to Foreign Office: Subject, The Yemen, 19 July 1964.
56 DEFE 13/570 7705 Top Secret: Telegram No. 460: From Jedda to Foreign Office: Subject The Yemen, 19 July 1964.
57 DEFE 13/570 77705 Top Secret: Telegram No. 461: From Jedda to Foreign Office: Subject The Yemen, 19 July 1964.
58 DEFE 13/570 77705 Top Secret: Telegram No. 461: From Jedda to Foreign Office: Subject The Yemen, 19 July 1964.
59 DEFE 13/570 77705: Top Secret, Telegram No. 718: From Foreign Office to Jedda, 24 July 1964.
60 DEFE 13/570 77705: Top Secret: Telegram No. 472: From Jedda to Foreign Office, 29 July 1964.
61 DEFE 13/570 77705: Top Secret: Telegram No. 473: From Jedda to Foreign Office, 29 July 1964.
62 DEFE 13/570 77705: Top Secret: Telegram No. 473: From Jedda to Foreign Office, 29 July 1964.
63 DEFE 13/570 77705: Top Secret: Maintaining our position in South Arabia: Memorandum by the Secretary of State for Defence, 13 July 1964.
64 DEFE 13/570 77705: Top Secret: Maintaining our position in South Arabia: Memorandum by the Secretary of State for Defence, 13 July 1964.
65 DEFE 13/570 77705 Top Secret: To Private Secretary, Secretary of State for Defence: Subject – Aden and the Yemen, 13 July 1964.
66 DEFE 13/570 77705: Top Secret. From Nigel Fisher to Secretary of State for Defence: Aid to Royalists, 14 July 1964; Covering Letter 'Aid to Royalists', 15 July 1964.
67 DEFE 13/570 77705: Top Secret. From Nigel Fisher to Secretary of State for Defence: Aid to Royalists, 14 July 1964; Covering letter 'Aid to Royalists', 15 July 1964.
68 DEFE 13/570 77705: Top Secret: From Secretary of State for Defence Peter Thorneycroft to Nigel Fisher MP, 17 July 1964.
69 DEFE 13/570 77705 Top Secret: From the Chief of the Defence Staff to the Secretary of state for Defence, 16 July 1964.
70 DEFE 13/570 77705: Top Secret, Personal No. 493. From the Secretary of State for the Colonies to Aden (Sir Kennedy Trevaskis) 18 July 1964; DEFE 13/570 77705 Top Secret, Personal No. 585. From Aden (Sir Kennedy Trevaskis) to the Secretary of State for the Colonies, 18 July 1964.
71 DEFE 13/570 77705 Top Secret: Personal No. 590. From Aden (Sir Kennedy

Trevaskis) to the Secretary of State for the Colonies, 19 July 1964.

72 DEFE 25/129 Top Secret: Yemen: Memorandum for Consideration by Ministers, 21 July 1964; DEFE 13/570 77705 Top Secret: Aid to the Royalists, 19 July 1964.

73 DEFE 13/570 77705 Top Secret: Aid to the Royalists, 19 July 1964.

74 DEFE 13/570 77705 Top Secret: Aid to the Royalists, 19 July 1964.

75 PREM 11/4929 Secret: The Yemen: From J. O. Wright to Alec Douglas-Home, 18 July 1964.

76 DEFE 13/570 77705 Top Secret: South Arabia and the Yemen: From the Prime Minister, Alec Douglas-Home to Secretary of State (Foreign Office), 20 July 1964.

77 DEFE 13/570 7705 Top Secret PM/64/103. From R. A. Butler to the Prime Minister: Subject. Supply of Arms to Dissident Group in Taiz, 11 September 1964.

78 Anthony Verrier, 'British Military Policy on Arabia: Some Lessons for the Future', *Journal of the Royal United Services Institute*, Vol. CXII, No. 648 (November 1967), p. 351.

79 FO 371/174482 B1022/12 Confidential: From George Middleton to R. S. Scrivener Foreign Office, 18 September 1964.

5   The Mercenary Operations: British Subterfuge and the French Connection

1 FO 371 174637 (BM 1041/225) Secret: Mercenaries in the Yemen – Record of conversation between Mr Harlan Clark and Mr Nigel Fisher, 15 July 1964.

2 FO 371 174637 (BM 1041/224) Confidential: From D. J. McCarthy, Foreign Office to C. S. Roberts Colonial Office, Notes for Guidance, 10 July 1964.

3 Tom Bower, *The Perfect English Spy* (New York: St. Martin's Press, 1995), pp. 217–53.

4 Bower, p. 243.

5 Bower, p. 219.

6 Bower, p. 231.

7 CAB 130/189 GEN 776: Secret, The Yemen – Second Meeting, 31 October 1962.

8 Richard J. Aldrich, *The Hidden Hand: Britain, America and Cold War Secret Intelligence* (London: John Murray, 2001), p. 243; Bower, p. 250.

9 CAB 130/189 GEN 776: Secret, The Yemen – Second Meeting, 31 October 1963; Bower, p. 250.

10 Private Interview, 29 November 2002. Name withheld on request.

11 Bower, p. 247.

12 Aldrich, p. 80. On the disbanding of SOE and its ingestion into SIS see also Mark Seaman, 'A Fourth Arm – Some Aspects of the British Experience of Special Forces and Irregular Warfare during and after the Second World War', *The Second World War in the XXth Century History* (St Just La Pendue: Brochage, 2000), pp. 115–26.

13 Stephen Dorril, *MI6: Fifty Years of Special Operations* (London: Fourth Estate, 2000), p. 684.

14 Bower, pp. 232–3.

15 DSP, The Yemen – Second Trip. Handwritten note of personal in Aden and the Federation, undated.
16 Dorril, p. 684.
17 IWM-NMP, Box 39. Letter from Anthony Boyle, Government House, Aden to Neil McLean, 10 May 1963.
18 Johnny Cooper with Peter Kemp, *One of the Originals: The Story of a founder Member of the SAS* (London: Pan/Macmillan, 1992), p. 171.
19 Bower, pp. 250–1.
20 IWM-NMP, Box 49, Report on visit to the Yemen by Lt. Col. Neil McLean DSO, MP, June–September 1963.
21 IWM-NMP, Box 36, Personal Narrative of Journey (to the Yemen) 27 May–14 June 1964.
22 For an account of this time see David Smiley, *Albanian Assignment* (London: Chatto & Windus, 1984).
23 Interview with Colonel David Smiley, London, 16 September 2002.
24 Aldrich, pp. 160–4. Aldrich casts convincing doubt on the Philby explanation. For an alternative, though less convincing explanation see Peter Harclerode, *Fighting Dirty: the Inside Story of Covert Operations from Ho Chi Minh to Osama Bin Laden* (London: Cassell, 2002), pp. 46–58.
25 David Smiley, *Arabian Assignment* (London: Leo Cooper, 1975), p. 103.
26 Smiley, p. 104.
27 IWM Sound Archive 10340/7 Colonel David Smiley; IWM-NMP, Box 49, Notes on conversation with Crown Prince Faisal, March 1963.
28 Interview with Colonel David Smiley, London, 16 September 2002.
29 DSP: The Yemen, First Trip. Diary entry for 13 July 1963.
30 IWM-NMP, Box 41. Rough Estimate of Royalist Forces, July 1963.
31 DSP: The Yemen, First Trip, Military Memorandum on a Visit to the Yemen by Colonel D. de C. Smiley, 14 July 1963.
32 DSP: The Yemen, First Trip, Report on a Visit to Royalist areas of the Yemen by Colonel David Smiley MVO, OBE, MC (handwritten), 14 July 1963; Personal Notebook.
33 IWM-NMP, Box 41, Diary of Journey in the Yemen in July 1963.
34 IWM-NMP, Box 41, Report on Visits to the Yemen by Lt. Col. Neil McLean DSO, MP, June–September 1963.
35 IWM- NMP, Box 41, Report on Visits to the Yemen by Lt. Col. Neil McLean DSO, MP, June–September 1963.
36 IWM-NMP, Box 41 Requirements of Royalist forces. The main rifles used by the Royalists were the British bolt action Lee Enfield .303 rifle Mks III and IV, the American M1 (Garand).30 semi-automatic rifle and the German bolt action Mauser 7.92mm rifle. Light machine guns included the British .303 Bren light machine gun and the Browning .5 heavy machine gun. The latter was a valued weapon in the anti-aircraft role.
37 IWM-NMP, Box 41, Report on Visits to the Yemen by Lt. Col. Neil McLean DSO, MP, June–September 1963.
38 IWM-NMP, Unmarked Box. Notes from conversation with Colonel David Smiley, Marsta, 11 July 1963.
39 Smiley appeared on several radio and television programmes to repeat his

claim of Egyptian use of Chemical weapons in the Yemen. DSP, First Trip to the Yemen, Transcript BBC Light Programme 'Radio Newsreel, "Gas Bomb Attack in the Yemen"', 18 July 1963.

40 IWM-NMP, Box 4. General Note, August 1963.

41 IWM-NMP, Box 39, Secret: Letter to Sir Colin Crowe, 4 July 1963. Box 4, General Note, August 1963.

42 IWM-NMP, Box 10., The Yemen: First Trip, Military Memorandum on a visit to the Yemen by Colonel D. de C. Smiley MVO, OBE, MC, June–July 1963.

43 IWM-NMP, Box 41, Reports on Visit to the Yemen by Lt. Col. Neil McLean DSO, MP, June–September 1963.

44 IWM-NMP, Box 41, Reports on Visit to the Yemen by Lt. Col. Neil McLean DSO, MP, June–September 1963. See the attached memorandum, 'Unattributable Channels', dated September 1963.

45 See for example Tony Geraghty, *Who Dares Wins: The Story of the SAS since 1945* (London: abc Books, 1982), pp. 89–92; Anthony Kemp, *SAS: Savage Wars of Peace* (London: John Murray, 1994), pp. 81–8; Jonathan Bloch and Patrick Fitzgerald, *British Intelligence and Covert Action: Africa, Middle East and Europe since 1945* (Dingle, Ireland: Brandon Books, 1983), pp. 127–31; Alan Hoe, *David Stirling: A Biography* (London: Warner Books, 1996), pp. 354–413.

46 Dorril, p. 684. This account is heavily reliant upon Alan Hoe's work. See Hoe, pp. 356–7. The meeting was also described briefly in the BBC documentary, 'The Mayfair Set: David Stirling', BBC 2, broadcast 18 July 1999.

47 Interview with Colonel David Smiley, London, 16 September 2002.

48 Johnny Cooper with Peter Kemp, *One of the Originals: The Story of a Founder Member of the SAS* (London: Pan/Macmillan, 1991), pp. 158–9.

49 Bower, pp. 244–5.

50 FO 371/174639 (BM1051/10) Parliamentary Question – Mr Michael foot (Ebbw Vale), 14 May 1964. In response to a question from Michael Foot MP concerning allegations of British aid to the Royalists, Home replied, 'Our policy towards the Yemen is one of non-intervention in the affairs of that country. It is not therefore our policy to supply arms to the Royalists in the Yemen.'

51 IWM-NMP, Box 49. Notes on conversation with Crown Prince Faisal, March 1963.

52 Alan Hoe, *David Stirling: The Authorised Biography of the Creator of the SAS* (London: Warner Books, 1992), p. 360.

53 Cooper, p. 158. While Cooper mentions no names, it is likely that the senior British Government official present was Julian Amery; Hoe, p. 60.

54 Cooper, p. 171.

55 IWM-NMP, Box 6. Notes on conversation with Paul Carton, 1–2 June 1964.

56 Interview with Colonel David Smiley, London 16 September 2002; FO 371/168831 77705 (BM1071/16) Secret: From Washington to Foreign Office, Telegram No. 820 16 March 1963.

57 IWM-NMP, Box 39. According to McLean's diary entry for the 2 May 1963 he met Trevaskis, along with Flight Lieutenant Tony Boyle and Bill Allen and the following day with Trevaskis and and Julian Amery. Bower for one also

claims that Trevaskis was more deeply involved in covert support of the Royalist cause. See Bower, p. 248.

58 Peter de la Billere achieved the rank of Lieutenant General, exercising overall command of British Forces in the Kuwait Theatre of Operations in the 1990/91 Gulf War. He gave a self-censored account of his recruitment by Boyle in his autobiography. See Peter de la Billiere, *Looking for Trouble* (London: HarperCollins, 1994), pp. 204–5.

59 IWM-NMP, Box 39. Letter from Tony Boyle, Government House, Aden to Neil McLean, 10 May 1963.

60 Smiley, pp. 181–2.

61 Hoe, pp. 360–1, Dorril, pp. 685–6. IWM Sound Archive 10340/7 David Smiley.

62 IWM-NMP, Box 19, Inventory of salaries and equipment; Box 36, Personal diary of visit to the Yemen, January–May 1965 by Lt. Col. Neil McLean.

63 Ian Colvin, 'Rhodesia plane flew Iron Curtain arms to Yemen Royalists', *The Daily Telegraph*, 5 February 1970.

64 IWM-NMP, Box 19, Inventory of salaries and equipment; Box Unmarked, letter dated 30 August 1963.

65 French aircraft delivered supplies on 11 August, 10 September, 27 September and 4 October 1963.

66 IWM-NMP, Box Unmarked, Letter dated 30 August 1963. This letter was addressed to Colonel Jim Johnson though the signature of the writer remains unclear.

67 IWM-NMP, Box Unmarked. Letter from Tony Boyle to Colonel Jim Johnson, Government House, Aden 25 August 1963.

68 IWM-NMP, Box Unmarked. Letter from Tony Boyle to John Cooper, 29 November 1963. This letter never reached Cooper. The courier carrying it from Beihan into the Yemen was captured by Egyptian troops. Its contents were published in the Egyptian newspaper *Al Ahram* and broadcast on Egyptian radio, on 1 May 1964.

69 IWM-NMP, Box 9. Translation of letter from General de Gaulle to the Imam, December 1963.

70 DSP, Second Trip to the Yemen, 14 November–8 December 1963. Diary of Events.

6 'A Very British Affair': The Guerilla Campain, October 1963–September 1964

1 See for example Andrew and Leslie Cockburn, *Dangerous Liasions: The Inside Story of the US–Israeli Covert Relationship* (London: Bodley Head, 1992), pp. 127–30.

2 Mohammed Heikal, *Secret Channels: The Inside Story of Arab–Israeli Peace Negotiations* (London: HarperCollins, 1996), pp. 123–5.

3 Yossi Melman, 'Former Mossad Director admits: Israel was involved in the war in Yemen', *Ha'aretz* (in Hebrew), 21 February 2001; Aahron Barnea and Yaron London, 'Thirty Years Ago we had daring, now we are a Protectorate – An interview with Ariel Sharon', *Yediot Aharonot* (in Hebrew), 3 May 1997. I am grateful to Professor Joseph Nevo and Dr Zach Levey of the University of Haifa for pointing out and translating these articles for me.

4 IWM-NMP, Box 36. Personal Diary of visit to the Yemen, January–May 1965, by Lt. Col. Neil McLean DSO. The weapons were dropped to Royalist forces in and around Neh'm in the Khowlan.

5 IWM-NMP, Box 9. British Plan of Assistance to Royalist Government, Aden, 6 September 1963. This was a draft prepared in advance for interested parties.

6 These were Sergeant Geordie Dorman, a Corporal Chigley and a Trooper Richardson. Cooper, p. 159.

7 Hoe, pp. 359–61; Cooper, p. 166; Smiley, p. 115.

8 IWM-NMP, Box 9. British Plan of Assistance to Royalist Government, Aden 6 September 1963.

9 Private interview, 29 November 2002. Name withheld on request.

10 The quantities purchased were truly impressive and included 230,000 rounds of .303 ammunition, 25 boxes of 75mm shells, 32 boxes of 57mm shells as well as landmines, anti-personal mines, bazooka rockets, and medical supplies. IWM-NMP, Box 39. Letter from Tony Boyle to Colonel Jim Johnson, Government house, Aden 25 August 1963.

11 IWM-NMP, Box 39. Second letter form Tony Boyle to Colonel Jim Johnson, 25 August 1963.

12 IWM-NMP, Box 39. Letter from Peter de la Billiere to John Cooper, 30 August 1963.

13 IWM-NMP, Box 39. British Plan of Assistance to Royalist Government, Aden, 6 September 1963.

14 There remains some doubt, howeve,r as to the precise reasons and exact timing of his departure from the RAF. In his autobiography, de la Billiere cites the medical reason for the premature end of his service career and places his departure sometime in September. Documents in the McLean archive suggest, however, that Boyle had planned to commit himself earlier to the mercenary operation. In a letter to Johnny Cooper, dated 30 August 1963, de la Billere remarks 'T [Tony Boyle] sends his best wishes and is counting the days to when he is on the job full time'. See de la Billere, p. 207; IWM-NWP, Box 39. Letter from Peter de la Billere to John Cooper, 30 August 1963.

15 IWM-NMP, Box 39, British Plan of Assistance to Royalist Government, Aden 6 September 1963.

16 IWM-NMP, Box 39, 'Traffic Passed since Opening the Line at Negub [sic]; DSP – Yemen, The Second Trip. Handwritten Note Listing Personal; Interview with Colonel David Smiley, London, 16 September 2002; Cooper, p. 174.

17 IWM-NMP, Box 36. Personal Diary of Visit to the Yemen January–May 1965 by Lt. Col. Neil McLean.

18 DSP – Yemen, The Second Trip. Notebook Entry of 20 November; Smiley, pp. 156–57, 162, 187.

19 DSP –Yemen, the Second Trip. 'Second Trip to the Yemen. 14 November–8 December 1963. Diary of Events'. Smiley did publish an account of his journey for wider public consumption. David Smiley, 'More Support for Royalists', The Scotsman, 21 December 1963.

20 DSP, Second Visit to the Yemen. Report on Second Visit to the Yemen by Colonel David Smiley.

21 DSP, Second visit to the Yemen. Note book entry 25 November 1963.

22 IWM-NMP, Box 39. 'Traffic Passed since Opening the Line at Nequb'.

23 IWM-MMP, Box 39. Letter from Johnny Cooper to Peter de la Billiere, El Garah [sic] Khowlan, 6 October 1963.

24 IWM-NMP, Box Unmarked. Letter from Johnny Cooper to Jim Johnson, Same Place [sic] 19 October 1963.

25 The number of SIASI agents was probably small. In a letter sent sometime in October 1963 to de la Billiere, Cooper requested he send 4 watches costing 3 apiece as presents for his 'SIASI boys'. On SIASI see IWM-NMP, Box 39. Letter from Johnny Cooper to Peter de la Billiere, 10 October 1963; Letter from Johnny Cooper to Peter de la Billiere, Base, 11 October 1963; Letter from Johnny Cooper to Peter de la Billiere, 12 October 1963; Letter from Johnny Cooper to Peter de la Billiere, 21 October 1963; Letter from Johnny Cooper to Peter de la Billiere, undated.

26 IWM-NMP, Box 39. Letter from Johnny Cooper to Jim Johnson, Same Place [sic] 19 October 1963.

27 Subsequent radio messages make to mention of the fate of the would be assassin. IWM-NMP, Box 39. Traffic passed since Opening the Line at Nequb.

28 IWM-NWP, Box 39. Letter from Johnny Cooper to Peter de la Billiere, Harush, 26 October 1963. For example, Bill McSweeney was 'Gassim' and David Bailey 'Ahmed'.

29 Cooper, p. 178. This system was also used by Cooper to communicate with other outstations in the Yemen. See IWM-NMP, Box 39. Traffic passed since opening the line at Nequb.

30 Cooper, p. 178.

31 IWM-NMP, Box 39. Letter from Fiona Frazer to Neil McLean, 4 December 1963; Box 6, Transcript of message from Peter de la Billiere to Johnny Cooper, 4 January 1963.

32 Private interview, 29 November 2002. The name of this individual has been withheld on request.

33 Kashoggi's involvement in the supply of arms was revealed by the Palestinian journalist and writer Said Aburish during the course of a BBC television documentary. See 'The Mayfair Set: David Stirling', BBC Television, broadcast 18 July 1999.

34 DEFE 7/1304. Details of House of Commons furore over allegations of Government backing of arms supplies to the Royalists.

35 DSP, Second visit to the Yemen. Report on Second visit to the Yemen.

36 IWM-NMP, Box 39. Traffic passed since opening the line at Nequb. See for example the radio traffic from Johnny Cooper dated 26 October 1963, 15:03 hrs.

37 IWM-NMP, Box 39. Letter from Johnny Cooper to Peter de la Billiere, Harush 26 October 1963.

38 The codename 'Mango' was chosen because according to Johnson 'it was the only Egyptian fruit I knew that dropped when ripe'. See Ian Colvin, 'Rhodesia plane flew arms to Yemen Royalists', *The Daily Telegraph*, 5 February 1970.

39 Cooper, pp. 177–8.

40 See the entry for Israel in *The Military Balance 1964–65* (London: International Institute for Strategic Studies, 1965), p. 32. The Israeli Air force was equipped with French Noratlas and Stratocruiser transport aircraft.
41 Ian Colvin, 'Rhodesia plane flew Iron Curtain Arms to Yemen Royalists', *The Daily Telegraph*, 5 February 1970.
42 IWM-NMP, Box 41. Diary of Journey in the Yemen in July 1963. Points discussed with Crown Prince Hassan, 24/25 July.
43 IWM-NMP, Box Unmarked. Notes on conversation with King Faisal – Jan 1965. The allegation of Saudi–Israeli collusion is made by Stephen Dorril. See Dorril, p. 680.
    One other author claims that the former deputy director of SIS, George Young, was approached by Mossad 'to find an Englishman acceptable to the Saudis'. According to this account, Young actually introduced McLean to Hiram. 'The Israelis promised to supply weapons, funds and instructors who could pass themselves off as Arabs, and the Saudis eagerly grasped the idea.' Given, however, Faisal's known loathing of Israel, some doubt must be cast on the veracity of this account. See Anthony Cavendish, *Inside Intelligence: The Revelations of an MI6 Officer* (London: HarperCollins, 1997), p. 194.
44 'Aluf Megan Hiram Nespach be'London vemakos Givli (Colonel Hiram posted to London to replace Givli', *Yediot Aharanot,* 21 April 1961.
45 DEFE 7/1304 77705 The story of this arms shipment was revealed in an *affidavit* given by Eric Boon to *The People* newspaper, 30 January 1964.
46 Peres went on to occupy the highest government portfolios in Israeli politics, including Foreign Minister, Defence Minister and Prime Minister. Weizman became Defence Minister and Foreign Minister and later the State President. DSP, Second visit to the Yemen. Handwritten note of Israeli officials and officers.
47 Interview with Colonel David Smiley, London, 16 September 2002.
48 Interviews with Colonel David Smiley, London, 6 August 2002, 16 September 2002.
49 Interview with Colonel David Smiley, 16 September 2002; Cooper, p. 178. Boyle described accompanying one such re-supply flight on 30 March 1964, turning in across the Red Sea coast with the lights of Hodeida shinning 40 miles to starboard. See *The Daily Telegraph*, 5 February 1970.
50 DSP, Fifth visit to the Yemen 25 May–19 July 1965; Special Consignment No. 9, Special Consignment No. 10. Consignment No 9 for example consisted of 16 card boxes that contained 60,000 rounds of .303 ammunition, 200 Lee Enfield .303 rifles, 12 Bren light machine guns, 100 anti-tank mines, 10 Sten sub-machine guns, 5000 rounds of 9mm ammunition, 6 bottles of whiskey, 2 cases of beer, 2 cases of beef, 2 cases of peas, 1 case each of tinned carrots, pineapple and apricots, 5 gas masks and 100 detonators for anti-tank mines.
51 Smiley, p. 199.
52 IWM-NMP, Box 36, Note on Next Phase in the War.
53 IWM-NMP, Box 6, Yemen News.
54 IWM-NMP, Box 6. Introduction to Memorandum on the Yemen by Lt. Col. Neil McLean DSO, MP.

55 IWM-NMP, Box 6. Notes on conversation with Prince Hassan bin al Hassan, 27 February 1964.
56 IWM-NMP, Box 6.Introduction on Memorandum on the Yemen, 3 March 1963.
57 FO 371 174627 (BM 1022/59). Minutes of the DOPC meeting – The Yemen, 19 March 1964. Harlech's views were presented before a meeting of the DOPC.
58 Bower, p. 249.
59 FO 371 174627 (BM 1022/59). Minutes of the DOPC meeting – The Yemen, 19 March 1964.
60 DSP, Third Trip to the Yemen, 7 March–1 April 1964. Diagram of wireless nets established.
61 DSP. Third Trip to the Yemen. Report on a visit to the Yemen, 7 March–3 April 1964, by Colonel David Smiley.
62 DSP. Third Trip to the Yemen. Report on a visit to the Yemen, 7 March 1964–3 April 1964, by Colonel David Smiley. Appendix "B", The Attack on Hajja.
63 DSP, Third Trip to the Yemen. Report on a visit to the Yemen, 7 March–3 April 1964, by Colonel David Smiley. Appendix "C". Summary of what I told the Imam.
64 DSP. Third Trip to the Yemen. Letter from Colonel David Smiley to His Royal Highness, the Crown Prince Faisal of Saudi Arabia, 8 April 1964.
65 DSP, Third Trip to the Yemen. The Battle for Hajja, 18 March 1964.
66 Interview with Colonel David Smiley, London, 6 August 2002.
67 IWM-NMP, Box 6. Memorandum on Aid to the Royalist forces in the Yemen.
68 IWM-NMP, Box 6. Personal Narrative of Journey, 27 May–14 June 1964.
69 Private Interview, 29 November 2002. Name withheld on request.
70 DEFE 13/570 77705 Confidential: Note of discussion with Colonel McLean, 20th June 1964.
71 DEFE 13/570 77705 Top Secret. From Julian Amery to Rt. Hon. R. A. Butler, 7 July 1964.
72 IWM-NMP, Box 6. Rough Notes on Possible Operations in the Yemen, July 1964.
73 'The story behind these five captured letters', The Sunday Times, 5 July 1964; BBC-SWB, ME/1544/A-8–11, 4 May 1964; Cooper, pp. 179–80.
74 DEFE 13/570 77705: Top Secret: To the Secretary of State for Defence: Aid to the Royalists, 15 July 1964.
75 DEFE 13/570 77705 Top Secret: Aid to the Royalist, 19 July 1964; DEFE 13/570 77705 Top Secret: Yemen – Memorandum for consideration by Ministers at DOPC on July 22; IWM-NMP, Box Unmarked, List from Prince Mohammed bin al-Hussein.
76 IWM-NMP, Box Unmarked. Letter from Neil McLean MP to Nigel Fisher, MC, MP, 31 July 1964.
77 IWM-NMP, Box Unmarked. Letter from Neil McLean DSO, MP, to The Rt Hon Sir Alec Douglas-Home KT, MP, 10 Downing Street, London SW1, 5 August 1964.

78 IWM-NMP, Box Unmarked. Letter from Nigel Fisher MC, MP to Neil McLean 7 August 1964.
79 IWM-NMP, Box Unmarked. Personal and Confidential. Handwritten Letter from Nigel Fisher MC, MP to Neil McLean DSO, MP.

7 'Plus ça change, plus la même chose': The Labour Government, Aden, and the Yemen Civil War

1 Robert McNamara, *Britain, Nasser and the Balance of Power in the Middle East 1952–1967* (London: Frank Cass, 2003), pp. 208–9.
2 McNamara, pp. 207–8.
3 DEFE 13/710 77705. Top Secret: Chiefs of Staff Committee, Aden and the South Arabian Federation, 30 June 1964.
4 DEFE 13/710 77705: Secret. From K. W. D. Strong (DGI/MoD) to Private Secretary, Secretary of State for Defence, 29 October 1964.
5 CO 1055/29 Top Secret: From Secretary of State for Defence, Denis Healey to the Prime Minister, 28 October 1964.
6 CO 1055/11 80075 Secret: South Arabia – Secretary of State's Visit: Brief No. D2: The South Arabia/Yemen Frontier: The Yemeni Claim and the Delegated authorities for Defence of the Frontier, Aden Department, November 1964.
7 CO 1055/29: Top Secret. From Aden (Acting high Commissioner) to Secretary of State for the Colonies. Telegram No. 956. Threat of Frontier Incident at Dahla, 26 November 1964.
8 FO 371/174482 (B1022/12), Confidential: From Sir George Middleton, British Embassy Cairo to Ronald Scrivener, North and East African Department, Foreign Office, 18 September 1964.
9 CO 1055/29. Secret: From Washington (Lord Harlech) to Foreign Office, No. 3918, 26 November 1964. Yemen.
10 Quoted in McNamara, p. 209.
11 Kennedy Trevaskis, *Shades of Amber: A South Arabian Episode* (London: Hutchinson, 1968), p. 225.
12 McNamara, p. 212.
13 FO 371 179863 (BM1071/11). Confidential: From D. J. McCarthy (Aden) to T. F. Brenchley. Subject. Record of Talks between Harlan Clark and Acting High Commissioner, 22 December 1964.
14 FO 371/174638 BM 1041/369G): Secret (FS/64/133) From Patrick Gordon Walker to Secretary of State for the Colonies: Subject: hopes that Mr Julian Amery and Colonel Neil McLean can be refused RAF transport during their visit to Aden and that the mercenaries in Aden should be told to vacate British territory, 22 December 1964.
15 Quoted in McNamara, p. 213.
16 Dana Adams Schmidt, *Yemen: The Unknown War* (London: Bodley Head, 1968), p. 182.
17 CO 1055/29: Secret. Record of Private discussion between Secretary of State and the Amir of Beihan, Sunday, 6 December 1964.
18 CO 1055/29: Secret. Record of Private discussion between Secretary of State and the Amir of Beihan, Sunday 6 December 1964.
19 DEFE 13/710 77705 Top Secret: From CinC Mideast to MOD UK, 22

December 1964; DEFE 13/710 77705 Top Secret. From CinC Mideast to MOD UK, 2 January 1965; DEFE 13/710 77705 Secret: To the Secretary of State for Defence from the Chief of the Defence Staff, 6 January 1965.

20 DEFE 13/710 77705 Secret: From Aden (Acting High Commissioner) to the Secretary of State for the Colonies, 14 January 1965.

21 DEFE 13/710 77705 Secret: From F. H. Burlace (Head D.S.11) MoD to Permanent Secretary/Secretary of State MoD, 15 January 1965.

22 DEFE 13/710 77705: Letter from Shariff of Beihan, Minister of the Interior, Federation of South Arabia to the honourable Mr Denis Healey, British Minister of Defence, 13 January 1965.

23 Glen Balfour-Paul, *The End of Empire in the Middle East: Britain's relinquishment of power in her last three Arab dependencies* (Cambridge: Cambridge University Press, 1994), pp. 82–4; McNamara, pp. 214–16.

24 DEFE 13/710 77705. Restricted. Summary of Incidents in South Arabia, 15 October 1964–26 March 1965.

25 DEFE 13/710 77705. Secret: To the Secretary of State for Defence from the Chief of the Defence Staff, 5 February 1965.

26 CAB 182/49 Top Secret: Cabinet – Joint Intelligence Committee Intelligence Organisation (Middle East) Working Party. Recommendations of the Working Party. Note by the Chairman, P. A. Wilkinson, 26 May 1964. Peter Wilkinson had been a senior member of SOE, and was therefore well versed in the bureaucratic inertia that could impact adversely upon the production of timely intelligence assessments.

27 IWM Sound Recording 13041/3. Interview with Brigadier David John Warren; DEFE 13/710 77705. Restricted. Summary of Incidents in South Arabia, 15 October 1964–26 March 1965.

28 Quoted in Balfour-Paul, p. 84.

29 DEFE 13/710 77705 Top Secret. Copy of Minute by the Prime Minister, Reference: Foreign Secretary's minute to the Prime Minister, 8 February 1965, "RANCOUR Operations", 9 February 1965.

30 CAB 129/120, Pt 2. Memo by Secretary of State for Foreign Affairs, 'UK Relations with the UAR', C65, 24 March 1965, quoted in McNamara, p. 215.

31 DEFE 13/710 77705: Top Secret. From Secretary of State for Defence, Denis Healey to the Prime Minister, Rancour Operations, 9 February 1965.

32 DEFE 13/710 77705 Top Secret (PM/65/55): From Michael Stewart to the Prime Minister, RANCOUR II Operations, 26 March 1965; DEFE 13/710 7705, Top Secret: Letter from Oliver Wright to WI McIndoe, Colonial Office, Subject RANCOUR II Operations, 26 March 1965; DEFE 13/710 77705, Top Secret, From WI McIndoe Colonial Office to Sir Bernard Burrows KCMG, Subject RANCOUR II, 26 March 1965.

33 Schmidt, pp. 214–15.

34 CO 1055/11 80075 Copy: Reuters Report of Fighting on Aden Radio, 10 March, 15 March 1965.

35 Schmidt, p. 215.

36 DEFE 13/710 77705 Confidential, Telegram No. 257 From Foreign Office to the Political Office Middle East Command (Aden) Subject: Darb Abu

Tuhaif, 13 March 1965; CO 1055/11 80075 Confidential, Telegram No. 258 (Emergency) From Foreign Office to Political Office Middle East command (Aden), 13 March 1965.

37 CO 1055/11 80075 Secret: From Aden (Sir R.Turnbull) to the Secretary of State for the Colonies, Secret sand Personal No. 241, Subject Baihan/Yemen Frontier, 13 March 1965.

38 DEFE 13/710 77705. Top Secret. From POMEC (Political Office Middle East Command) to Foreign Office, 13 March 1965.

39 DEFE 13/710 77705 Secret: From the Secretary of state for the Colonies to the Prime Minister, subject: South Arabia, April 1965. Greenwood's proposals included election, rather than appointment of ministers of State representatives to the Federal Council, the reform of Trade Union law and the encouragement of Federal rulers to create conditions conducive to the emergence of independent political parties.

40 CO 1055/11 80075 Confidential: From Aden (Sir R. Turnbull) to the Secretary of State for the Colonies, Telegram No. 251, Subject: Darb Ahl Ba Tuhaif, 15 March 1965.

41 CAB 182/54 Top Secret: JIC (IAF)(63)3 Cabinet: Joint Intelligence Committee: Intelligence Organisation in Aden and the Federation working Party/Intelligence Organisation in Aden, 17 December 1965.

42 In the late summer of 2003, the author showed this JIC report to a former British mercenary intimately involved with the Yemen operation. Recalling how he personally had briefed British officials in Jeddah on the 'state of play' he remarked that the JIC assessment concerning intelligence in the Yemen was 'bullshit'. Name and place of discussion withheld on request.

43 FO 371 179863 (BM 1071/44/G) Secret: Memo From R. N. Posnett, Subject: Reports from Italian legation, Taiz'z, 8 March 1965.

44 DSP, Fifth Trip to the Yemen, 25 May–19 July 1965. Smiley compiled the report on 14 June 1965.

45 DSP, Fifth trip to the Yemen, 25 May–19 July 1965. Letter from Brigadier H. J. Bartholomew OBE (British Embassy, Cairo) to Colonel D. de C. Smiley CVO, OBE, MC, 29 April 1965. The letter was delivered to Smiley care of the Foreign Office.

46 CO 1055/11 80075 Secret: From Aden (Sir R. Turnbull) to the Secretary of State for the Colonies, Subject: Wadi Harib, 18 March 1965.

47 DEFE 13/710 77705 Secret: From the United Kingdom Mission to United Nations New York to the Secretary of State for the Colonies, Subject: Wadi Ablah 20/21 March 1965.

48 DEFE 13/710 77705 Secret: From Aden (Sir R. Turnbull) to the Secretary of State for the Colonies, subject: Beihan/Yemen Frontier, 19 March 1965.

49 DEFE 13/570 77705 Top Secret: ISD 65/2/01 – Letter from J. W. Stacpoole (Colonial Office) to W. I. McIndoe, 29 March 1965.

50 DEFE 13/710 77705 Secret: From Aden (Sir R. Turnbull) to Secretary of State for the Colonies, Telegram No. 345, 6 April 1965; DEFE 13/710 77705 Secret. From A. W. J. Greenwood to the Prime Minister, 12 April 1965.

51 Stephen Harper, *Last Sunset: What Happened in Aden* (London: William Collins, 1978), p. 55.

52 McNamara, p. 217.
53 DEFE 13/710 77705 Top Secret: From Chief of the Defence Staff to Secretary of State for Defence, 14 April 1965; Top Secret: From Secretary of State for Defence to Foreign Secretary/Colonial Secretary 14 April 1965.
54 DEFE 13/710 Secret. From J. O. Wright to N. M. Fenn, Minute from the Prime Minister, 22 April 1965.
55 DEFE 13/710 77705 Secret: From the Foreign Secretary Michael Stewart to the Prime Minister (PM/65/65) Message to Nasser, 4 May 1965.
56 This argument was put forcefully by Turnbull in a cable to the Colonial Secretary. Explaining why air defence of Beihan was so problematic he wrote, 'Provision of anti-aircraft network would take considerable time [to construct] and would be of token value only. Landing ground [in Beihan] too small for Hunters and the necessary extension woulf, according to RAF authorities, take 18 months to complete. Continuous patrolling by Hunters is impracticable on account of the numbers of aircraft that would be needed.' DEFE 13/710 77705 Secret: From Aden (Sir. R. Turnbull) to Secretary of State for the Colonies, Telegram No. 345, 6 April 1965.
57 McNamara, pp. 217–18.
58 PREM 13/1923 Confidential: From Cairo (Sir G. Middleton) to Foreign Office, Telegram No. 652, 13 August 1965; PREM 13/1923 Top Secret (MOD Ref 796/65) From John Peduzie to Peter Le Cheminant, 31 August 1965.
59 Quoted in McNamara, p. 218.
60 DEFE 13/710 77705 Secret: From the Chief of the Defence Staff to Secretary of State for Defence, Subject: Situation in the Federation of South Arabia, 11 June 1965.
61 Karl Pieragostini, *Britian, Aden, and South Arabia: Abandoning Empire* (Basingstoke: Macmillan, 1991), p. 120.
62 See Julian Paget, *Last Post: Aden 1964–67* (London: Faber, 1968), p. 117.
63 DEFE 13/710 77705 Secret: From CinC Middle East to Vice Chief of the Defence Staff, Subject: Extract from the Monitoring of Radio Cairo, 20 September 1965.
64 DEFE 13/710 77705 Secret: From Aden (Sir R. Turnbull) to Secretary of State's Office, 21 June 1965.
65 DEFE 13/710 77705 Top Secret: From Aden (Sir R. Turnbull) to Secretary of State for the Colonies, Telegram No. 700, Subject Beihan/Yemen Border, 29 June 1965.
66 DEFE 13/710 77705 Top Secret: From CinC Mideast to MOD UK, Operational Immediate, 29 June 1965.
67 DEFE 13/710 77705: Secret: From the Secretary of State for the Colonies to Aden (Sir R. Turnball) Telegram No. 572, 30 June 1965.
68 DEFE 13/710 77705 Secret: From Aden (Sir R. Turnbull) to the Secretary of State for the Colonies, Telegram No. 709 Subject: Dissident base in Beihan, 2 July 1965; DEFE 13/710 77705 Secret: From Colonial Office to Aden (Sir R. Turnbull) Telegram No. 581 Subject Dissident Base in Beihan, 2 July 1965.
69 DEFE 13/710 77705 Secret: From Aden (Sir R. Turnbull) to Secretary of Sate for the Colonies, Telgram No. 712, Subject: Dissident Base in Beihan, 4 July 1965.

70   DEFE 13/710 77705 Secret: From Secretary of State for the Colonies to Aden (Sir R. Turnbull) Telegram No. 584, subject: Dissident Base in Beihan 4 July 1965.
71   DEFE 13/710 77705: Top Secret: Memo to the Secretary of State for Defence from John Peduzie, Subject: Dissident Base in Beihan, 8 July 1965.
72   DEFE 13/710 77705 Secret: Letter from the Hashemite Habali Amirate, Baihan to His Excellency the Rt. Hon. Mr Greenwood, Secretary of State for the Colonies 3 July 1965 (translated from the Arabic).
73   DEFE 13/710 77705 Secret: From the Secretary of State for the Colonies to Aden (Sir R. Turnbull) Telegram No. 589, Subject M.I.G Attack, 5 July 1965.
74   DEFE 13/710 7705 From Aden (Sir R. Turnbull) to the Secretary of State for the Colonies, Telegram No. 724, 8 July 1965.
75   Pieragostini, p. 124.
76   DEFE 13/710 77705 Top Secret: Memo form the Chief of the Defence Staff to the Secretary of State for Defence, 6 August 1965.
77   A. J. Kelly, *Arabia the Gulf and the West* (New York: Basic Books/Harper Collins, 1980), p. 25.
78   DEFE 13/406 101680 Top Secret. From the Vice Chief of the Air Staff to the Secretary of State for Defence, Ref: VCAS-3808, Subject: Photographic Reconnaissance of Yemeni Coast, 13 July 1965.
79   DEFE 13/710 77705: Secret. From K. W. D. Strong (DGI) to Secretary of State for Defence, Subject: Saudi/Egyptian Relations, 4 August 1965.
80   DEFE 13/406 101680 Top Secret: From the Minister of State for the Armed Forces (RAF) to the Foreign Secretary, Subject: Photographic Reconnaissance of the Yemeni Coast, 20 August 1965.
81   Quoted in McNamara, p. 219.
82   McNamara, pp. 221–3.
83   DEFE 13/710 77705 Secret: From Denis Healey to the Colonial Secretary, Subject: Use of 10001b bombs against a rebel base and arms dump in South Arabian Federation, 29 October 1965.
84   DEFE 13/710 77705 Top Secret: Minute from From J. A. Peduzie (MoD) to W. K. Reid (Cabinet Office) Subject, Rancour Operation, 12 October 1965; DEFE 13/710 77705 Top Secret: Minute from Prime Minister to Sir Burke Trend, 12 October 1965; DEFE 13/710 77705 Top Secret: Memo from A. H. Poynton (Colonial Office) to Sir Burke Trend, Subject RANCOUR II, 15 October 1965.
85   CAB 182/54 Top Secret: Cabinet, Joint Intelligence Committee. Subject: Intelligence Organisation in Aden and the Federation Working Party – Report by Mr McCarthey [sic], 17 December 1965.
86   DEFE 13/710 77705 Secret: From New York (Lord Caradon) to Foreign Office, Telegram No. 2329, Subject: Aden, 1 October 1965.
87   DEFE 13/710 77705 Top Secret: Memo from the Chief of the Defence Staff, Field Marshall Sir Richard Hull to the Secretary of State for Defence, Subject: The Situation in Aden, 25 September 1965. For the breakdown of casualty figures see Paget, p. 264 (Annex D).

8 'From the Jaws of Victory': The Political Defeat of Britain in South Arabia

1 *Statement on the Defence Estimates 1966 Part 1*, 'The Defence Review', HMSO February 1966, Cmnd 2901.

2 Denis Healey, *The Time of My Life* (New York: W.H. Norton, 1990), pp. 280–4.

3 Jeffrey Pickering, *Britain's Withdrawal From East of Suez: The Politics of Retrenchment* (Basingstoke: Macmillan/Institute of Contemporary British History, 1998), p. 151.

4 Thomas Mockaitis, *British Counterinsurgency in the Post-Imperial Era* (Manchester: Manchester University Press, 1995), pp. 63–4.

5 Healey, p. 284.

6 *Statement on Defence Estimates 1966 Part 1*, 'The Defence Review', HMSO February 1966 Cmnd 2901.

7 Mills made this statement on camera for the documentary 'The Mayfair Set: David Stirling', BBC2 (UK), 18 July 1999.

8 For a full breakdown of these figures see Julian Paget, *Last Post: Aden 1964–67* (London: Faber, 1969), p. 264.

9 James Lunt, 'The Imam's War: Royalist and Republican in the Yemen', *War in Peace*, p. 759.

10 Dana Adams Schmidt, *Yemen: the Unknown War* (London: Bodley Head, 1968), pp. 221–2.

11 IWM-NMP Box 36. Personal Diary of visit to the Yemen, January–May 1965 by Lt. Col. Neil McLean; DSP, Fourth Trip to the Yemen, 3 March–9 April 1965. In his list, titled 'Friends', Smiley omits McSweeney's name. His list is as follows: British, John Cooper (Khowlan), Chris [Sharma] (Khowlan) David Bailey (Khowlan), Bernard Mills (Jauf) James (Jauf), Rupert France (Jeddah). For the French and Belgians Smiley gives no surnames. Roger [Falques] (French Colonel, senior Frenchman, Paris–London–Yemen), François (French Colonel), Louis (French Major – Khanja), Philippe (Belgian Corporal – Khanja), Freddie (French Sergeant – Khanja), Rene (French – Khanja), Georges (French Lieutenant – Amara), Daniel (French Lieutenant – Kitaf), Edward (French operator – injured by a mine and evacuated to Paris), Gabriel (French medical orderly – Khanja) Marcelle (Belgian Sergeant – Radio Station at Fidah), Charles (Belgian – Radio station at Fidah) L'Amiral (French Warrant Officer Nehem).

12 DSP, Fourth Trip to the Yemen: Secret – Report by Colonel David Smiley on 4th Visits to the Yemen March 10–April r 1965.

13 David Smiley, *Arabian Assignment* (London: Leo Cooper, 1975), p. 191.

14 IWM-NMP Box 36. Personal Diary of Visit to the Yemen: January–May 1965 by Lt. Col. Neil McLean DSO. Diary entry for 1 April 1965.

15 IWM-NMP Box 6. 'Notes on conversation with Sayid Ahmed al-Shamy: Subject – Aid from Saudi Arabia; Box 36. Personal Diary of Visit to the Yemen: January–May 1965 by Lt. Col. Neil McLean DSO. Diary entry for 28 February 1965.

16 The customer for the first parachute drop was Johnny Cooper. He received, according to McLean's account, 400 Lee Enfield .303 rifles, 100,000 rounds

of ammunition, 4×.5inch Browning heavy machine guns, 20,000 rounds of.5 inch ammunition, and 200 anti-tank mines. Two planes of unspecified make made the drop. The second drop included 200 Lee Enfield .303 rifles, 50,000 rounds of .303 ammunition, 150 anti-tank mines, petrol, batteries, and 4 Bren .303 Light Machine Guns. IWM-NMP, Box 36. Personal Diary of Lt. Col. Neil McLean DSO. Diary entry for 28 February 1965.

17 Interview with British Liaison Officer, 29 November 2002. Name withheld on request.
18 Smiley, p. 192.
19 Schmidt, p. 216.
20 Smiley, pp. 187–8; DSP, Fourth Trip to the Yemen. Diary 3 March to 9 April 1965, diary entry for 29 March 1965.
21 DSP, Fourth Trip to the Yemen. Secret: Report by Colonel David Smiley on 4th Visit to the Yemen, March 10–April 5 1965, Appendix "D", Schmidt, pp. 221–3.
22 Smiley, p. 190.
23 IWM-NMP, Box 36. Report on Yemen – July to October 1965. Woodhouse did not identify himself as the author of the report.
24 IWM-NMP Box 36. Report on Visit to the Yemen (Jan–May 1965) by Lt. Col. Neil McLean, Parts 12–13, London, June 1965.
25 Schmidt, p. 162.
26 Edgar O'Ballance, *The War in the Yemen* (London: Faber, 1971), p. 138.
27 DSP, Fifth Trip to the Yemen. Diary entry for 9 June 1965. See also Smiley, p. 193. Interview with Colonel David Smiley, London, 6 August 2002.
28 Interview with Colonel David Smiley, London, 16 September 2002.
29 DSP, Fifth Visit to the Yemen, 25 May–19 July 1965. The various networks and equipment used sketched out in a notebook. See also IWM-NMP, Box 36: Personal Diary of visit to the Yemen, January to May 1965 by Lt. Col. Neil McLean, Diary entry for 4–6 March 1965.
30 FO 371 174634 (BM 1041/33/G) Secret: Minute from M. S. Weir, Subject: Radio Assistance for the Yemeni Royalists – Proposal by International Television Enterprises to set up transmitter to counter Republican propaganda, 14 February 1964.
31 FO 371 174627 (BM 1022/59G) Secret: Minute of meeting of the Defence and Overseas Policy Committee of 19 March 1964, Part 4(ii), 24 March 1964.
32 DSP, Fourth Trip to the Yemen, 3 March–9 April 1965: Secret: Report by Colonel David Smiley on 4th Visit to the Yemen, 10 March–5 April 1965, point 19.
33 DSP, Fifth Trip to the Yemen, 25th May–19th July 1965. Diary entry for 10 June 1965. See also Smiley, pp. 192–3.
34 DSP, Fifth Trip to the Yemen, 25 May–19 July 1965. Diary entry for 5 July 1965. Rupert France was reportedly 'horrified' at the state of the wireless security throughout the Royalist net and in particular that of Prince Abdullah Hussein.
35 IWM-NMP, Box 36, Report on visit to the Yemen (Jan–May 1965) by Lt. Col. Neil McLean, London June 1965.
36 DSP, Fourth Trip to the Yemen, 3 March–9 April 1965. Diary entry for 17 March 1965.

37 DSP, Fifth Trip to Yemen, 25 May–19 July 1965: Invoice and Correspondence (No. 2594/5) from Hotchkiss-Brandt to His Excellency, Dr Rachad Pharon, (in French) Ambassador for the Royal Kingdom of Saudi Arabia, Paris, 20 May 1965; Diary entry for 5 June 1965. The outline of the dispute and its effect on the completion of the 120mm project is contained in a letter sent by Jim Johnson (Jay) to Smiley, 3 June 1965 and from Tony Boyle to Smiley, handwritten letter dated 11 June 1965. In a playful pun on his name, both Johnson and Boyle address Smiley as 'Grin' in their correspondence.

38 DSP, Fifth Trip to the Yemen, 25 May–19 July 1965. Letter from Tony Boyle to 'Grin', 3 June 1965.

39 IWM-NMP, Box 36, Report on visit to the Yemen (January–May 1965) by Lt. Col. Neil McLean, London June 1965, Part II, Note 14, 'system of supplies'. McLean recommended the Saudis supply as a matter of course the following arms and supplies to Royalist forces: money, ammunition for heavy weapons (75mm, 57mm recoilless rifles, 81mm, 82mm, 60mm mortars with up to 200–250 rounds per weapon, 5" machine guns, rifle ammunition, spare parts for all the above, rifles and ammunition for distribution to the tribes, A/T mines and explosives, 120mm mortars and ammunition, W/T equipment, hand grenades, medical supplies, food, more motor transport.

40 Schmidt, p. 34.

41 IWM-NMP, Box 36. Personal Diary of Visit to the Yemen, January–May 1965 by Lt. Col. Neil McLean; Report on visit to the Yemen (Jan.–May 1965) by Lt. Col. Neil McLean, p. 4.

42 Smiley, p. 182.

43 O'Ballance, p. 141.

44 Schmidt, pp. 234–5. The Egyptian casualty figures were passed over to a Western intelligence agency but Schmidt does not disclose which one.

45 IWM-NMP, Box 9. Notes on Conversation with King Faisal – Jan 1965.

46 IWM-NMP, Box 36, 'The Third Force', April 1965.

47 O'Ballance, pp. 137–8.

48 NMP-IWM, Box 36, The Third Force', April 1965.

49 DSP, Fourth Trip to the Yemen, 3 March–9 April 1965: Secret, Report by Colonel David Smiley on Visits to the Yemen March 10–April 5 1965, point 22.

50 For a more detailed analysis of the Byzantine nature of Republican politics at this time see Schmidt, pp. 224–32; O'Ballance, pp. 142–7 and Fred Halliday, *Arabia without the Sultans* (Harmondsworth: Pelican, 1975), pp. 112–13.

51 IWM-NMP, Box 36: Notes on conversation with King Faisal, 19 May 1965.

52 IWM-NMP, Box 36: notes on conversation with King Faisal, 19 May 1965.

53 Healey, p. 230.

54 IWM-NMP, Box 36. Report on YEMEN – July to October 1965.

55 IWM-NMP, Box 36, Report on YEMEN – July to October 1965, 'Future operations' part 4(b).

56 IWM-NMP, Box 36, Report on YEMEN – July to October 1965, 'Political' part 5(a).

57 For an authoritative appraisal of the second part of the Woodhouse Report see Alan Hoe, *David Stirling* (London: Warner Books, 1996), pp. 374–5.

58 Hoe, p. 374.

59 Hoe, p. 364.

60 Hoe, p. 375.

61 DSP, Fifth Trip to the Yemen, 25 May–19 July 1965. Letter from Jim Johnson to David Smiley (handwritten) London, 1 July 1965.

62 DSP, Sixth Trip to the Yemen 13 October–10 December 1965, Trip to Saudi Arabia and Yemen, Diary entry for 18 November 1965; Interview with Colonel David Smiley, London, 6 August 2002.

63 DSP, Seventh visit to the Yemen, 12 March–21 April 1966, Letter from Neil Mclean to David Smiley, 1 May 1966.

64 DSP, Eighth Trip to the Yemen, 17 –27 April 1967. Letter form David Smiley form Jedda Palace Hotel, 13 April 1967.

65 DSP, Sixth Trip to the Yemen, 13 October–10 December 1965. Diary entries for 23 November–1 December 1965. Smiley attended the conference using his cover as a journalist with the *Daily Telegraph*. Journalists were in fact kept well away from the conference proceeding, relying on briefings that were long on rhetoric and short on content from Saudi officials. In the event, Smiley was forced into a hurried departure from Harad when Prince Abduallah Sudairi revealed that the Egyptians now knew about his activities with the mercenaries. See Smiley, p. 202. For an overview of the Harad conference see Schmidt, pp. 238–44; O'Ballance, pp. 153–56.

66 O'Ballance, p. 155.

67 DSP, Sixth Trip to the Yemen, 13 October–10 December 1965, 'The War in the Yemen by Colonel David Smiley'. Draft of article for the *Kenya Weekly News*.

68 For the monthly casualty figures in this period see Julian Paget, *Last Post: Aden 1965–67* (London: Faber, 1969), p. 264 (Annex D).

Conclusion: Political Conviction and the BMO

1 Between 1966 and the final withdrawal of British forces from South Arabia in November 1967, 49 servicemen were killed and 543 wounded. See Julian Paget, *Last Post: Aden 1964–67* (London: Faber, 1969), p. 264.

2 DEFE 32/10 101680, Top Secret: Minutes of a Chief of Staff (Informal) Meeting, 28 September 1966.

3 IWM-NMP, Box Unmarked. 'Report on the Yemen War', by H. J. J. (Jim Johnson) 1 October 1966.

4 A truncated account of the report prepared by Johnson and his own version of the demise of the mercenary organisation was given in an interview to the British daily newspaper *The Daily Telegraph*. See Ian Colvin, 'Nasser sent gold to Yemen Tribal Leaders', *The Daily Telegraph*, 6 February 1970.

5 DSP, Twelfth Visit to the Yemen, 6 October–23 October 1967. Diary entries for the 6–7 October 1967.

6 IWM-NMP, Box Unmarked, 'Yemen: Notes on Conversation with Prince Mohammed ibn al-Hussein', Tehran, 3 November 1966; Yemen: Notes on conversation with Prince Mohammed ibn al-Hussein, Tehran, 7 November 1966.

7 IWM-NMP, Box Unmarked, 'Yemen: Notes on Conversation with Prince Mohammed ibn al-Hussein', Tehran, 7 November 1966.

8 IWM-NMP, Box Unmarked, 'Prince Mohammed ibn al-Hussein's List for Parachuting', November 1966.

9 DEFE 13/571. Confidential: Minute of talk with Mr Wilfred Thesiger, 9 December 1966.

10 DEFE 13/571. Secret: To the Secretary of State for Defence, Subject Yemen, 21 December 1966.

11 IWM-NMP, Unmarked. Gas Activity in the Yemen, 24 January 1967; Notes on Gas Bombs in the Yemen (undated).

12 Dana Adams Schmidt, *Yemen: The Unknown War* (London: Bodley Head, 1968), p. 263.

13 For accounts to the background of the June 1967 'Six Days War', see Avi Shlaim, *The Iron Wall* (London: Allen Lane/Penguin Publishers, 2000), pp. 218–82; Benny Morris, *Righteous Victims* (London: John Murray, 2000), pp. 302–46.

14 For explanations regarding the denouement of Arab Nationalism and the rise of Islamic Fundamentalism and Radicalism see James Piscatori, *Islam in a World of Nation States* (Cambridge: Cambridge University Press, 1986); Ibrahim Karawan, 'The Islamist Impasse', *Adelphi Paper* No. 314 (London: Oxford University Press/IISS, 1997).

15 For a more detailed exposition of the siege of the Yemeni capital on which this account is based see Edgar O'Ballance, *The War in the Yemen* (London: Faber, 1971), pp. 189–202.

16 Bernard Mills comments were made during the course of 'The Mayfair Set: David Stirling', BBC2 (UK), 18 July 1999.

17 Johnny Cooper made this comment during the course of 'The Mayfair Set: David Stirling', BBC2 (UK), 18 July 1999.

18 David Smiley (with Peter Kemp), *Arabian Assignment* (London: Leo Cooper, 1975), p. 237.

19 Anthony Verrier, 'British Military Policy on Arabia: Some lessons for the Future', *Royal United Service Institute Journal*, Vol. CXII, No. 648 (November 1967), p. 351.

Bibliography

Primary Sources

National Archives (formerly the Public Record Office)

Foreign Office: Series FO 371/164094; 164156;168816; 168831–44; 174482; 1746633–39.
Colonial Office: Series CO 1015; 1055/2/3/4/5/6/7/10/11/13/29/216.
Ministry of Defence: Series DEFE 7/1304; 13/406; 13/569; 13/570; 13/571; 13/710; 25/128; 25/129; 32/10.
War Office:WO 181/354.
Cabinet Office: CAB 130/189; 182/49; 182/54.
Prime Minister's Office: PREM 11/4928, 4980, 4929; 13/1923, 2688.

Imperial War Museum

Papers of Lieutenant Colonel Neil 'Billy' McLean, Boxes 3, 4, 6, 9, 10, 19, 20, 36, 39, 41.
Sound Recordings 10340/7 (Colonel David Smiley); 11454/4 (Edward Shackleton); 13041/3 (Brigadier David Warren).

Churchill College Cambridge

Sandys Papers.

Private Archive

Papers of Colonel David Smiley, Files for the Yemen 1963–1966.

Published Government Documents

Statement on the Defence Estimates 1966 Part I 'The Defence Review', HMSO, February 1966, Cmnd 2901.
Statement on the Defence Estimates 1966 Part II 'Defence Estimates 1966–67', HMSO, February 1966, Cmnd 2902.

Interviews

Colonel David Smiley, 6 August 2002, 16 September 2002.
British Liaison Officer (Name withheld on Request) 19 November 2002.

Bibliography

Microfilm

CIA Research Reports – Middle East 1946–1976 (Bethesda, Maryland: University of America Publications, 1983). Reel 1 (0214); Reel 2 (0039, 0058, 0064, 0068).

Secondary Sources

Books

Aldrich, Richard J. *The Hidden Hand: Britain, America and Cold War Secret Intelligence* (London: John Murray, 2001).

Arnold, Guy. *Mercenaries: The Scourge of the Third World* (Basingstoke: Macmillan, 1999).

Asher, Michael. *Thesiger* (London: Penguin Books, 1995).

Badeau, John S. *The American Approach to the Arab World* (New York: Council on Foreign Relations, 1968).

Badeeb, Saeed M. *The Saudi–Egyptian Conflict over North Yemen 1962–1970* (Boulder, CO: Westview Press, 1986).

Balfour-Paul, Glen. *The End of Empire in the Middle East* (Cambridge: Cambridge University Press, 1994).

Barthrop, Michael. *Crater to the Creggan: The History of the Royal Anglian Regiment 1964 –1974* (London: Leo Cooper, 1976).

Bloch, Jonathan and Patrick Fitzgerald. *British Intelligence and Covert Action* (Dingle, Co. Derry: Brandon Book Publishers, 1983).

Bower, Tom. *The Perfect English Spy* (New York: St. Martin's Press, 1995).

Bulletin du Comité international d'histoire de la Deuxième Guerre Mondiale, *The Second World War in the XXth Century History – Oslo August 11–12, 2000* (St-Just-La-Pendue, France: Brochage, 2000).

Burrows, Bernard. *Footnotes in the Sand: The Gulf in Transition 1953–1958* (Salisbury: Michael Russell, 1990).

Burrows, R. D. *The Yemen Arab Republic: The Politics of Development, 1962–1986* (Boulder, CO: Westview Press, 1987).

Cable, James. *Intervention at Abadan: Plan Buccaneer* (Basingstoke: Macmillan, 1991).

Cavendish, Anthony. *Inside Intelligence: The Revelations of an MI6 Officer* (London: HarperCollins, 1997).

Clayton, Peter. *Two Alpha Lima* (London: Janus Publishing, 1994).

Cockburn, Andrew and Leslie Cockburn: *Dangerous Liaison: The Inside Story of the US–Israeli Covert Relationship* (London: Bodley Head, 1992).

Cooper, Johnny (with Peter Kemp). *One of the Originals* (London: Pan/Macmillan, 1991).

Craddock, Percy. *Know Your Enemy: How the Joint Intelligence Committee saw the World* (London: John Murray, 2002).

Dann, Uriel. *King Hussein and the Challenge of Arab Radicalism* (Oxford: Oxford University Press, 1989).

De la Billiere, Peter. *Looking for Trouble* (London: HarperCollins, 1994).

Dorril, Stephen. *MI6: Fifty Years of Special Operations* (London: Fourth Estate, 2000).

Bibliography

Dresch, Paul. *A History of Modern Yemen* (Cambridge: Cambridge University Press, 2000).

Durch, William J. (ed.). *The Evolution of UN Peacekeeping* (Basingstoke: Macmillan, 1993).

Fielding, Xan. *One Man in His Time: The Life of Lieutenant-Colonel NLD ('Billy') McLean DSO* (London: Macmillan, 1990).

Fiennes, Ranulph. *Where Soldiers Fear to Tread* (London: The Travel Book Club, 1976).

Fisk, Robert. *Pity the Nation: Lebanon at War* (Oxford: Oxford University Press, 1991).

Geraghty, Tony. *Who Dares Wins: The Story of the Special Air Service* (London: Book Club Associates, 1980).

Gilmour, David. *The Fractured Country* (London: Sphere Books, 1984).

Halliday, Fred. *Arabia without the Sultans* (Harmondsworth: Penguin Books, 1975).

———. *Revolution and Foreign Policy: The Case of South Yemen 1967–1987* (Cambridge: Cambridge University Press, 1990).

Harclerode, Peter. *Fighting Dirty: The Inside Story of Covert Operations from Ho Chi Minh to Osama Bin Laden* (London: Cassell, 2002).

Harper, Stephen. *Last Sunset: What Happened in Aden* (London: Collins, 1978).

Hart, Parker T. *Saudi Arabia and the United States: Birth of a Security Partnership* (Indianapolis: Indiana University Press, 1998).

Higgins, Rosalyn. *United Nations Peace Keeping: Documents and Commentary* (London: Oxford University Press/Royal Institute for International Affairs, 1969).

Healey, Denis. *The Time of My Life* (New York: Norton, 1990).

Heikal, Mohammed. *Secret Channels: The Inside Story of Arab–Israeli Peace Negotiations* (London: HarperCollins, 1996).

Hirsch, John L. *Sierra Leone: Diamonds and the Struggle for Democracy* (London: Lynne Rienner, 2001).

Hoe, Alan. *David Stirling* (London: Warner Books, 1996).

Ignatieff, Michael. *Virtual War* (London: Chatto and Windus, 2000).

Jackson, William. *Withdrawal from Empire: A Military View* (London: BT Batsford, 1986).

Kelly, J. B. *Arabia, the Gulf and the West* (New York: Basic Books, 1980).

Kemp, Peter. *The SAS: Savage Wars of Peace* (London: John Murray, 1994).

Kerr, Malcolm, *The Arab Cold War 1958–1964: A Study of Ideology in Politics* (Oxford: Oxford University Press, 1965).

Kostiner, Joseph. *The Struggle for South Yemen* (London: Croom Helm, 1984).

Kyle, Keith. *Suez* (London: Weidenfeld and Nicolson, 1991).

Mann, Michael. *The Trucial Oman Scouts: The Story of a Bedouin Force* (Norwich: Michael Russell, 1994).

McNamara, Robert. *Britain, Nasser and the Balance of Power in the Middle East, 1952–1967* (London: Frank Cass, 2003).

Mockler, Anthony. *The New Mercenaries: From the Congo to the Seychelles* (London: Sidgwick and Jackson, 1985).

Mockaitis, Thomas R. *British Counterinsurgency in the Post-imperial Era* (Manchester: Manchester University Press, 1995).

Morgan, Michael. *A Very Private War: High Jinks in the Desert!* (London: Minerva Press, 1998).

Morris, Benny. *Righteous Victims: A History of the Zionist–Arab Conflict 1881–1999* (London: John Murray, 2000).

Nutting, Anthony. *No End of a Lesson: The Story of Suez* (London: Constable, 1996).

O'Ballance, Edgar. *The War in the Yemen* (London: Faber, 1971).

Ovendale, Ritchie (ed.). *British Defence Policy since 1945* (Manchester: Manchester University Press, 1994).

———. *Britain, the United States and the transfer of power in the Middle East, 1945–1962* (Leicester: Leicester University Press, 1996).

———. *The Origins of the Arab-Israeli Wars* (2nd edn.) (Harlow: Longman, 1992).

Paget, Julian. *Last Post: Aden 1964–67* (London: Faber, 1969).

Phythian, Mark. *The Politics of British Arms Sales since 1964* (Manchester: Manchester University Press, 2000).

Pickering, Jeffrey. *Britain's Withdrawal East of Suez* (Basingstoke: Macmillan, 1998).

Pieragostini, Karl. *Britain, Aden and South Arabia: Abandoning Empire* (Basingstoke: Macmillan, 1991).

Piscatori, James P. *Islam in a World of Nation States* (Cambridge: Cambridge University Press, 1986).

Podeh, Elie. *The Decline of Arab Unity: The Rise and Fall of the United Arab Republic, 1958–1961* (Brighton & Portland: Sussex Academic Press, 1999).

Pridham, Brian (ed.). *Contemporary Yemen: Politics and historical Background* (London: Croom Helm/Centre for Arab Gulf Studies, University of Exeter, 1984).

Safran, Nadav. *Saudi Arabia: The Ceaseless Quest for Security* (Ithaca: Cornell University Press, 1988).

Schmidt, Dana Adams. *Yemen: The Unknown War* (London: Bodley Head, 1968).

Shalom, Zaki. *The Superpowers, Israel and the Future of Jordan 1960–1963* (Brighton & Portland: Sussex Academic Press, 1999).

Shawcross, William. *Deliver Us From Evil: Peacekeepers and Warlords in a World of Endless Conflict* (London: Bloomsbury, 2000).

Shlaim, Avi. *The Iron Wall: Israel and the Arab World* (London: Allan Lane/Penguin Publishers, 2000).

Simms. Brendan. *Unfinest Hour: Britain and the Destruction of Bosnia* (London: Allan Lane/Penguin, 2001).

Silverstein, Ken. *Private Warriors* (London: Verson, 2000).

Smiley, David. *Arabian Assignment* (London: Leo Cooper, 1975).

———. *Albanian Assignment* (London: Chatto & Windus, 1984).

———. *Irregular Regular* (Norwich: Michael Russell, 1994).

Stephens, Roger. *Nasser* (Harmondsworth: Penguin Books, 1978).

Stookey, Robert W. *Yemen: The Politics of the Yemen Arab Republic* (Boulder, Colorado: Westview Press, 1978).

Bibliography

Tickler, Peter. *The Modern Mercenary: Dog of War or Soldier of Honour?* (Wellingborough: Patrick Stephens, 1987).

Thompson, Julian (ed.). *The Imperial War Museum Book of Modern Warfare* (London: Sidgwick & Jackson/Macmillan, 2002).

Thompson, Robert. *Defeating Communist Insurgency* (London: Chatto & Windus, 1966).

Thwaites, Peter. *Muscat Command* (London: Leo Cooper/Pen & Sword, 1995).

Trevaskis, Kennedy. *Shades of Amber: A South Arabian Episode* (London: Hutchinson, 1968).

Von Horn, Carl. *Soldiering for Peace* (London: Cassell, 1966).

Wint, Guy and Peter Calvocoressi. *Middle East Crisis* (Harmondsworth: Penguin Books, 1957).

Yizraeli, Sarah. *The Remaking of Saudi Arabia* (Tel Aviv: Tel Aviv University/Moshe Dayan Center for Middle Eastern and African Studies, 1997).

Articles

Al-Albin, A. Z. 'The Free Yemeni Movement and its Ideas on Reform', *Middle East Studies*, Vol. 15, No. 1 (January 1979), pp. 36–48.

Abadi, Jacob. 'Britain's Abandonment of South Arabia – A Reassessment', *Journal of Third Studies*, Vol. 12, No. 1 (1995), pp. 152–80.

Bishku, Michael B. 'The Kennedy Administration, the U.N. and the Yemen Civil War', *Middle East Policy*, Vol. 1, No. 4 (1992), pp. 116–28.

Cerny, Philip. 'Neo-Medievalism, Civil War, and the New Security Dilemma: Globalisation as Durable Disorder', *Civil Wars*, Vol. 1, No. 2 (1998), pp. 36–64.

Fain, W Taylor. 'Unfortunate Arabia: The United States, Great Britain and Yemen, 1955–63', *Diplomacy and Statecraft*, Vol. 12, No. 2 (June 2001), pp. 125–52.

Gandy, Christopher. 'A Mission to Yemen: August 1962–January 1963', *British Journal of Middle East Studies*, Vol. 25, No. 2 (1998), pp. 247–74.

Gerges, Fawaz A. 'The Kennedy Administration and the Egyptian–Saudi Conflict in Yemen: Co-opting Arab Nationalism', *Middle East Journal*, Vol. 49, No. 2 (Spring 1995), pp. 292–311.

Jones, Clive and John Stone. 'Britain and the Arabian Gulf: New Perspectives on Strategic Influence', *International Relations*, Vol. 13, No. 4 (April 1997), pp. 1–24.

Jones, Clive. 'Among Ministers, Mavericks and Mandarins: Britain, Covert Action and the Yemen Civil War 1962–64', *Middle East Studies*, Vol. 40, No. 1 (January 2004), pp. 99–126.

Kalyvas, Stathis N. 'New and "Old" Wars: A Valid Distinction?', *World Politics*, Vol. 54, No. 1 (October 2001), pp. 99–118.

Karawan, Ibrahim. 'The Islamist Impasse', *Adelphi Paper*, No. 314 (London: Oxford University Press/IISS, 1997).

Kostiner, Joseph. 'Arab Radical Politics: Al-Qawmiyyun al-Arab and the Marxists in the Turmoil of South Yemen, 1963–1967', *Middle East Studies*, Vol. 17, No. 4 (1981), pp. 454–76.

Lunt, James. 'The Imam's War: Royalist and Republican in the Yemen', *War in Peace* (1983), pp. 756–59.

Mawby, Spencer. 'The Clandestine Defence of Empire: British Special Operations in Yemen 1951–1964', *Intelligence and National Security*, Vol. 17, No. 3 (Autumn 2002), pp. 105–30.

Shearer, David. 'Private Military Force and Challenges for the Future', *Cambridge Review of International Affairs*, Vol. XIII, No. 1 (Autumn–Winter 1999).

——. 'Outsourcing War', *Foreign Policy*, No. 112 (Fall 1998), pp. 68–81.

Singer, P. W. 'Corporate Warriors: The Rise of the Privatized Military Industry and its Ramifications for International Security', *International Security*, Vol. 26, No. 3 (Winter 2001/02), pp. 186–220.

Sirriyeh, Hussein. 'Lebanon: Dimensions of Conflict', *Adephi Paper*, No. 243 (London: Brasseys/IISS, 1989).

Smith, Simon C. 'Rulers and Residents. British Relations in the Aden Protectorate 1937–59', *Middle East Studies*, Vol. 31, No. 3 (July 1995), pp. 509–23.

Taulbee, James Larry. 'Reflections on the Mercenary Option', *Small Wars and Insurgencies*, Vol. 9, No. 2 (Autumn 1998), pp. 145–63.

Verrier, Anthony. 'British Military Policy on Arabia', *Royal United Services Institute Journal*, Vol. CXII, No. 648 (November 1967), pp. 349–55.

Warner, Michael. 'Wanted: a Definition of "Intelligence"', *Studies in Intelligence* (CIA Unclassified), Vol. 46, No. 3 (2002), at <www.cia.gov/csi/studies/vol46no3/article02html>.

Newspapers

BBC Summary of World Broadcasts
Le Monde
The Daily Telegraph
The Guardian
The Scotsman
The Times
The Sunday Times
The Yorkshire Post
Ha'aretz (Israel)
Yediot Aharonoth (Israel)

Broadcast Programmes

'End of Empire: Aden', *Channel 4* (UK), Broadcast 10 June 1985.
'The Mayfair Set: David Stirling', *BBC 2* (UK), Broadcast 18 July 1999.

Index

Index

Printed and bound by CPI Group (UK) Ltd, Croydon, CR0 4YY

09/06/2025

14685958-0001